PROSECUTORS AND DEMOCRACY

Focusing on the relationship between prosecutors and democracy, this volume throws light on key questions about prosecutors and the role they should play in liberal self-government. Internationally distinguished scholars discuss how prosecutors can strengthen democracy, how they sometimes undermine it, and why it has proven so challenging to hold prosecutors accountable while insulating them from politics. The contributors explore the different ways legal systems have addressed that challenge in the United States, the United Kingdom, and continental Europe. Contrasting those strategies allows an assessment of their relative strengths – and a richer understanding of the contested connections between law and democratic politics. Chapters are in explicit conversation with each other, facilitating comparison and deepening the analysis. This is an important new resource for legal scholars and reformers, political philosophers, and social scientists.

Máximo Langer is Professor of Law and Director of the Transnational Program on Criminal Justice at UCLA School of Law. He is an expert in comparative and international criminal justice. His work has been translated into several languages and has received awards from multiple professional associations, including the American Society of Comparative Law.

David Alan Sklansky is Stanley Morrison Professor of Law at Stanford Law School and Faculty Co-director of the Stanford Criminal Justice Center. A former federal prosecutor, he is the author of *Democracy and the Police* (2008).

ASCL Studies in Comparative Law

ASCL Studies in Comparative Law is designed to broaden theoretical and practical knowledge of the world's many legal systems. With more than sixty years' experience, the American Society of Comparative Law have been leaders in the study and analysis of comparative law. By promoting the investigation of legal problems in a comparative light, whether theoretical or empirical, as essential to the advancement of legal science, they provide an essential service to legal practitioners and those seeking reform of the law. This book series will extend these aims to the publication of monographs and comparative studies of specific legal problems.

The series has two general editors. Mortimer Sellers is Regents Professor of the University System of Maryland and Director of the Baltimore Center for International and Comparative Law. He is an Associate Member of the International Academy of Comparative Law. Vivian Curran is Distinguished Professor of Law at the University of Pittsburgh School of Law.

Prosecutors and Democracy

A CROSS-NATIONAL STUDY

Edited by

MÁXIMO LANGER

UCLA

DAVID ALAN SKLANSKY

Stanford University

CAMBRIDGE
UNIVERSITY PRESS

CAMBRIDGE
UNIVERSITY PRESS

University Printing House, Cambridge CB2 8BS, United Kingdom

One Liberty Plaza, 20th Floor, New York, NY 10006, USA

477 Williamstown Road, Port Melbourne, VIC 3207, Australia

4843/24, 2nd Floor, Ansari Road, Daryaganj, Delhi – 110002, India

79 Anson Road, #06–04/06, Singapore 079906

Cambridge University Press is part of the University of Cambridge.

It furthers the University's mission by disseminating knowledge in the pursuit of education, learning, and research at the highest international levels of excellence.

www.cambridge.org
Information on this title: www.cambridge.org/9781107187559
DOI: 10.1017/9781316941461

First published 2017

Printed in the United States of America by Sheridan Books, Inc.

A *catalogue record for this publication is available from the British Library.*

Library of Congress Cataloging-in-Publication Data
NAMES: Langer, Máximo, editor. | Sklansky, David A., 1959– editor.
TITLE: Prosecutors and democracy : a cross-national study / edited by Maximo Langer, David Alan Sklansky.
DESCRIPTION: Cambridge [UK] ; New York : Cambridge University Press, 2017. | Series: ASCL studies in comparative law | Includes bibliographical references and index.
IDENTIFIERS: LCCN 2017026224 | ISBN 9781107187559 (hardback)
SUBJECTS: LCSH: Prosecution – Political aspects. | Prosecution – Decision making – Comparative studies. | Public prosecutors – Comparative studies. | Criminal procedure – Political asepcts. | Judicial discretion. | Democracy. | BISAC: LAW / Comparative.
CLASSIFICATION: LCC K5425 .P773 2017 | DDC 345/.01262–dc23
LC record available at https://lccn.loc.gov/2017026224

ISBN 978-1-107-18755-9 Hardback

Contents

Contributors

Shawn Boyne is Professor of Law and Mosaic Faculty Fellow at Robert H. McKinney School of Law at Indiana University.

Mathilde Cohen is Associate Professor of Law and Robert D. Glass Scholar at the University of Connecticut School of Law.

Angela J. Davis is Professor of Law at Washington College of Law at American University.

Antony Duff is Emeritus Professor of Philosophy at the University of Stirling.

Ingrid V. Eagly is Professor of Law and Faculty Director of the David J. Epstein Program in Public Interest Law and Policy at UCLA School of Law.

Jacqueline S. Hodgson is Professor of Law and Director of the Criminal Justice Centre at the University of Warwick School of Law.

Máximo Langer is Professor of Law at UCLA School of Law and Director of the UCLA Transnational Program on Criminal Justice.

Daniel C. Richman is Paul J. Kellner Professor of Law at Columbia Law School.

Jonathan Simon is Adrian A. Kragen Professor of Law and Director of the Center for the Study of Law and Society at the University of California, Berkeley, School of Law.

William H. Simon is Arthur Levitt Professor of Law at Columbia Law School.

David Alan Sklansky is Stanley Morrison Professor of Law at Stanford Law School and Faculty Co-director of the Stanford Criminal Justice Center.

Introduction

Máximo Langer and David Alan Sklansky

There have been times and places in which the central protagonists of criminal justice, the officials most responsible for the fairness and effectiveness of penal administration, have been judges. At other times and in other places, police officers have seemed to play that role. Today, the pivotal figures in criminal justice systems throughout much of the world appear, more and more, to be prosecutors. This is notably true in the United States, where scholars and reformers increasingly focus on prosecutors as the key to how the criminal justice system is administered, and increasingly blame prosecutors for the system's failures. It is true, as well, in the United Kingdom and in continental Europe, where prosecutors seem – as in the United States – to be accreting more and more authority. It is true in Japan and in Taiwan, as well as throughout much of Latin America.

Prosecutors do not play precisely the same role in all of these countries, and in many cases, the differences in their powers and functions are substantial. Still, there is a strikingly broad trend around the globe toward vesting greater discretion and greater responsibility in prosecutors, accusatory officials situated between the police and the courts. Despite their growing importance, prosecutors remain much more poorly understood than either the police or the judiciary. Not only is information about the day-to-day work of prosecutors far more limited than is the case for police officers or judges, but the expectations on prosecutors, and the criteria for evaluating them, are murky and often inconsistent.

The relationship between prosecutors and democracy is particularly unclear. What is the proper role of prosecutors in a democracy? What implications does a commitment to democratic government have for the powers and responsibilities of prosecutors, for the organization of prosecutorial offices, and for the amount and the kinds of discretion vested in prosecutors? What role, if any, should democratic processes play in the selection and oversight of prosecutors? What should or can prosecutors do to strengthen democracy? How, if at all, should democratic values affect how prosecutors approach their jobs? None of these questions have clear answers. Nor is it clear whether and how the answers should vary from one democratic country to another.

This book is a collective effort to begin untangling the connections – actual and aspirational – between prosecutors and democracy, and to examine the ways in which those connections vary with, on the one hand, the functions and powers of prosecutors, and, on the other hand, different modes and conceptions of democracy. The effort is, by design, cross-national and interdisciplinary. The authors are legal scholars, political philosophers, and social scientists. They carry out their work in the United States, in the United Kingdom, and in continental Europe. (We had hoped to include, as well, authors who work in Asia and Latin America, but the scholars we invited from those areas were unable to take part.) The authors draw on conceptions of democracy that include representative democracy, participatory democracy, and deliberative democracy. Some of them focus on the work that prosecutors do in negotiating guilty pleas; for others, the heart of the prosecutor's job takes place at trial. Some of the authors foreground concerns about equality; others emphasize fair process or, in one form or another, accountability. Some of the authors are guardedly sympathetic to the peculiar American practice of electing head prosecutors; others find that practice very hard to defend.

Despite these differences in focus and approach, this book is also, by design, a conversation, not a series of soliloquies. Initial drafts of the chapters were presented in January 2016 at a roundtable workshop hosted by the Transnational Program on Criminal Justice at UCLA School of Law, bringing together the authors and a select group of distinguished discussants. That workshop was collaborative and interactive, and it has resulted in chapters that engage with each other, rather than speaking past each other. It has also resulted, we think, in a set of essays that think in hard and productive ways about the relationship between prosecutors and democracy.

Antony Duff's chapter, which begins the collection, exemplifies these strengths. He poses the question of what the proper role is for a prosecutor in a democratic polity, and how the prosecutor should carry out that role. Democracy for Duff means participatory, deliberative democracy, and the role of criminal law in such a democracy is first and foremost, he argues, to allow citizens to call each other to account. The central mechanism for that is the criminal trial. It follows for Duff that the primary job of prosecutors is to act and speak for the polity in calling wrongdoers to account, and in deciding whether to do so in the first place. From this conception of the prosecutor's role, Duff then derives a rich and nuanced set of principles for the appropriate kinds of discretion prosecutors should enjoy, and for how that discretion should be exercised. He argues, for example, that prosecutors cannot take it as their job to prosecute all apparent violations of the criminal law; they must sometimes consider whether a particular violation implicated the interests the prohibition aims to protect, as well as whether other social interests outweigh the demands of penal justice, and whether social injustices have deprived the polity of "standing" to call the defendant to account.

Duff's chapter is very much in conversation with later chapters in this book. Duff responds, in particular, to concerns about equality and systemic discrimination raised in the chapters by Mathilde Cohen, Angela Davis, and Ingrid Eagly, and to some of the suggestions in Daniel Richman's chapter about how prosecutors can strengthen democracy.

Richman, like Duff, focuses on the role of prosecutors in calling others to account; Richman, in fact, leans in part of Duff's arguments for placing this function of prosecutors at the forefront. But Richman places less weight than Duff on the criminal trial as the central mechanism for calling to account. Richman highlights the web of professional and institutional arrangements within which prosecutors are situated. He stresses the role of prosecutors not just in calling criminal offenders to account, but also in calling police officers to account, and he explores the various avenues for holding prosecutors themselves to account. Richman insightfully draws out the many ways in which these forms of accountability – including, in the United States, the ballot box – combine and interact, sometimes working synergistically and other times at cross-purposes. The general theme of account giving is employed by Richman to arrive at concrete suggestions for the kinds of cases prosecutors should prioritize, and also for criteria that can be used to evaluate how best to hold prosecutors accountable for the way they exercise their vast power and discretion.

Like Richman, Jacqueline Hodgson focuses in her chapter on the institutional arrangements within which prosecutors find themselves situated; she points out the ways in which those arrangements both reflect and can help to shape how the work of prosecutors is conceived. Hodgson compares prosecutors in two different legal systems: England and Wales, on the one hand, and France, on the other. France is more statist than England and Wales; England and Wales put a greater emphasis on divided government, with the judiciary acting as a check on the executive. Hodgson shows how this ideological difference is reflected in different expectations not only about the judiciary, but also about prosecutors, particularly with regard to the critical issue of how best to balance the accountability of prosecutors with their political independence. That balance is set, Hodgson points out, not just by the relationships between prosecutors and elected officials, and between prosecutors and the courts, but also by the relationship between prosecutors and the police. Prosecutors work more closely with the police in France than in England and Wales, and Hodgson notes the ways that those close working ties can wind up making French prosecutors dependent on the police.

The authority of individual prosecutors in the jurisdictions Hodgson studies is also shaped by the internal operation of their agencies. In England, prosecutorial discretion is openly acknowledged and explicitly regulated; the Crown Prosecution Service has promulgated and published guidelines for exercising charging discretion in particular controversial areas. There is no parallel to this in France. Hodgson argues that individual prosecutors in France are therefore less constrained by policy than their counterparts in England and Wales, although nominally they are subject to greater hierarchical oversight.

French prosecutors are also the focus of Mathilde Cohen's chapter. Cohen assesses the democratic legitimacy of French prosecutors in four respects: the mechanisms through which they are selected and promoted; the degree to which they operate in a manner consistent with separation of powers; the extent to which they are required to justify or to defend their decisions; and their demographic diversity – i.e., the degree to which they constitute a "representative bureaucracy." Cohen gives her subjects low marks along all four of these dimensions. Like Richman and Hodgson, though, Cohen stresses the ways in which the accountability and independence of prosecutors are configured to a large extent by the internal structures of the organization in which they work, by their sense of professionalism, and by their relationships with other professionals. In the French case, Cohen argues, a key fact is that prosecutors are members of the judicial branch. Although they are overseen by the executive branch, French prosecutors have the same training and occupational status as judges, they typically share offices with judges, and they conceive of themselves, in many ways, as part of the same work team. Perhaps paradoxically, Cohen suggests that this identification with the judiciary serves both as a check on prosecutorial discretion and as a basis for prosecutorial independence. She makes a similar point about decentralization and specialization within the French prosecutorial service, suggesting that these processes have served to insulate line prosecutors from hierarchical control – something that has also been promoted, she suggests, by unionization.

Cohen's chapter, like Hodgson's, thus serves as a reminder that democracy can be understood to impose a wide variety of demands on prosecutors, and that many of these demands are intertwined with the tension between independence and accountability – a tension that, as Richman notes, has long been at the center of scholarship on European prosecutors. The tension between independence and accountability is a major theme of Shawn Boyne's chapter on German prosecutors. Boyne describes the manner in which the German system has tried to strike a balance between the independence and accountability of prosecutors, and she notes that, despite some recent high-profile controversies, the German prosecutorial service has not received nearly the volume of criticism as, say, prosecutors in the United States, and the criticism they have received largely has to do with cases they have not brought, rather than cases they are thought to have prosecuted too energetically.

Boyne ties the perceived legitimacy of the German prosecutorial system – and also some of its challenges – to fundamental structural and ideological features, in particular German federalism, the structure and traditions of its governmental bureaucracies, and, perhaps most importantly, the concept of *Rechtsstaat*, which Boyne argues is related to but distinguishable from the Anglo-American ideal of the "rule of law," particularly with regard to its implications for the prosecutor's role. She thus shows how the transnational concern of balancing the independence and accountability of prosecutors is addressed in a specific national and sociopolitical context.

One important part of that context, Boyne argues, is a strong norm of collegial decision-making among German prosecutors, which Boyne suggests is often more significant than hierarchical oversight in shaping their exercise of prosecutorial discretion. Her argument thus provides some support for William Simon's suggestion, in his chapter, that prosecutors should embrace what he calls "post-bureaucratic" modes of organization, in part but not exclusively for their democracy-reinforcing qualities. Post-bureaucratic organizations, Simon explains, are characterized by rules that are explicit, but only presumptive and by heavy use of root-cause analysis, peer review, and performance measurement. Simon argues that the existence of these forms of organization means that it is a mistake to imagine that the only alternative to individual, professional judgment is top-down bureaucracy. He also says that the rigorous and repeated collegial discussions that characterize post-bureaucratic forms of organization, together with the commitment of those organizations to explicit but presumptive rules, creates new openings for making prosecutors' offices democratic, along two different dimensions. First, he suggests, democratic accountability can be enhanced by the greater transparency of post-bureaucratic organizations. Second, Simon argues that "stakeholder democracy" can be fostered by the forms of local participation to which post-bureaucratic organizations lend themselves; he suggest that experiments with "community prosecution" are a promising example of this.

Angela Davis focuses in her chapter on a particularly important challenge for any set of ideas about prosecutors and democracy in the United States: what they have to say about the persistent and notorious racial imbalances in American criminal justice. Davis's starting point is the opening given to racism – conscious or unintentional – by the vast discretion that American prosecutors enjoy in selecting charges and negotiating plea agreements. The principal check on state prosecutors in the United States, the ballot box, has proved deficient in the past in reducing racial disparities in charging and plea bargaining, and Davis explores the reasons why. She also notes, though, that recent events provide some grounds for hope that elections are becoming better tools in this regard, in part because the politics of criminal justice in the United States may be changing, at least at the local level. And Davis suggests that there is much that can be accomplished by an elected prosecutor committed to reducing racial disparities in the criminal justice system. She illustrates the point by reviewing steps taken in this regard by John Chisholm, the District Attorney for Milwaukee County, Wisconsin.

Ingrid Eagly provides another test case for the democratic legitimacy of prosecutors in the United States: the treatment of noncitizens. She asks whether the ways in which noncitizens are prosecuted for crimes in the United States are consistent with a commitment to core democratic values of equality, transparency, and accountability, and answers that question in the negative. The blending of criminal law and immigration enforcement in the United States has allowed and even encouraged prosecutors to use deportation as a tool of crime control and imprisonment as a deterrent to illegal entry, and the result is the widespread, systematic deployment of pretextual prosecutions and what might be called pretextual immigration enforcement. Moreover, the blended system of "crimmigration" is administered largely out of public view, and it is marked by low levels of protection for noncitizens accused of crime. The result, Eagly argues, is an unacceptable concentration of power in the hands of prosecutors, and unequal, excessively draconian treatment of non-citizens. Remedying these conditions, she argues, is essential if the American system of prosecution is to be consistent with a meaningful commitment to democracy.

Like the chapters by Davis and Eagly, the final two chapters of the book also focus on prosecutors in the United States. Jonathan Simon's chapter picks up on the suggestion in Davis's chapter that recent trends suggest prosecutorial elections can be used to achieve better prosecutorial policies. Simon suggests that the politics of prosecution in the United States are in flux. He identifies two different routes of departure from traditional "tough on crime" politics. The first, "smart on crime," emphasizes cost savings and recidivism rates. As Simon explains, this is an agenda and a rhetoric embraced by a growing number of prosecutors in the United States. While conceding that "smart on crime" is an improvement on "tough on crime," Simon also identifies a second, more dramatic and – he argues – more hopeful route of departure from traditional prosecutorial politics. This more radical route of departure is what Simon characterizes as a "prosecutorial politics of dignity"; he suggests it is consistent with a broad but still emerging trend toward the embrace of dignity as a core legal value. Simon sees manifestations of the prosecutorial politics of dignity in the actions and rhetoric of prosecutors who humanize criminal defendants and take responsibility for the excesses of the carceral state; he suggests that the politics of dignity is also consistent with an emphasis on procedural justice that prosecutors should find congenial. Still, Simon emphasizes the contingency and possible fragility of the prosecutorial politics of dignity – a lesson that seems all the more important in the wake of Donald Trump's successful campaign for president as the "law and order candidate." If Americans value the development of a politics of dignity, they must take care to encourage and sustain it.

David Alan Sklansky's chapter is focused not on the substantive politics of prosecution in the United States, but on the nature of the connection between prosecutors and democracy in the United States – on what it means for American prosecutors to be "democratic." The chapter argues that the answer depends both on what one means by "democracy" and on one's conception of the prosecutor's role. Both of these latter questions are contested, the chapter suggests. There are at least two different, influential accounts of American democracy: democratic pluralism and participatory democracy. And our expectations for prosecutors are various and conflicting; above all, in fact, the prosecutor's role is defined by intermediation and boundary blurring. This makes it difficult to arrive at a consensus set of desiderata for democratic prosecution. Nonetheless, despite – and to some extent because of – these layers of complication, Sklansky argues that a commitment to democracy in the United States implies certain imperatives for reforming prosecutors' offices. One of those imperatives is to increase the demographic diversity of prosecutors; another is to reconsider the emphasis our legal culture increasingly places on flexibility and boundary-blurring; and still another is to give communities better tools for understanding and evaluating the day-to-day work of prosecutors' offices.

We defer until the epilogue an extended discussion of themes and lessons we extract from the wide-ranging chapters of this book. For now, we will offer just three observations. First, the book's chapters underscore the difficulty of saying, as a general matter, exactly what implications democracy should have for prosecutors, or whether it should have any strong implications at all. This is the result not only of the diverse approaches taken by the authors, and the varied national contexts they address, but also of the multiple meanings of, and conceptions about, "prosecutors" and "democracy." Our goal in this book is not to advance a particular account of what is or should be the relationship between prosecutors and democracy. Rather, we hope to identify different ways of thinking about this relationship and then to put these different approaches in a conversation with each other. We hope this exercise will help future researchers deepen their own conceptions about what is or should be the relationship between prosecutors and democracy; we also hope it will help researchers with different conceptions avoid talking past each other.

Second, precisely because of this difficulty, and precisely because of the substantial variations in the way democracy and the prosecutorial role are defined in different political and legal systems, there is great value in cross-national work on prosecutors and democracy; it throws light on what is constant and what is contingent. The point of this book is not to conduct a rigorous empirical study of prosecutors and democracy along various dimensions, but rather to use comparative law as a tool for identifying different meanings and conceptions about prosecutors and democracy and their relationship, and for gaining perspective on our own legal systems.

Third and finally, despite its ambiguity, democracy is an essential concept – if not *the* essential concept – in modern political thought, and that makes it a useful, if not essential, lens through which to understand how the prosecutorial role is configured and defended, and how it might be reconceived, at least within those political systems that define themselves as democratic or aspire to be democratic.

This book is the work of many hands, and not just those of the authors. We owe thanks, in particular, to Norman Abrams, Devon Carbado, Shih-Chun Chien, Beth Colgan, Ernesto Matías Díaz, Sharon Dolovich, Sandra Marshall, Richard Re, Sherod Thaxton, and Loïc Wacquant for their valuable and insightful contributions to the workshop discussions at UCLA in January 2016. We hope the book ignites debates as vibrant, enlightening, and productive as those we enjoyed around that conference table.

1

Discretion and Accountability in a Democratic Criminal Law

Antony Duff*

INTRODUCTION

What kind of practice of prosecution is appropriate to a democratic polity's criminal law? What should the role of prosecutor be in such a system of criminal law?

Such questions beg important prior questions: they assume that democratic polities would not only maintain distinctive systems of criminal law, but would so structure the criminal law as to have a recognisable role of 'prosecutor'. To justify such assumptions, we would need an account of democracy, of the kind of criminal law that would be appropriate to a democratic polity, and of the institutional structure of such a criminal law, but the most I will be able to do here is gesture towards the shape such an account should take.

Another preliminary problem is that of parochialism. This is a pervasive danger for legal theorising: it is too easy to offer an account of what 'criminal law' is, or ought to be, as if this holds good universally for all times in all places – when what one is actually doing is offering a local account of criminal law in a particular kind of polity at a particular time in its history.[1] That danger becomes more acute the more specific the account becomes as to the criminal law's institutional structures and roles; why should we expect just one kind of institutional structure, and just one set of roles, to be suitable for every kind of polity? One can talk of 'prosecutors' in a range of systems, but the

* I'm grateful to the editors of this volume, to participants in the workshop on *Prosecutors and Democracy* at UCLA, and especially to Mathilde Cohen (my commentator at that workshop) for helpful comments on an earlier version of this chapter.

[1] See, e.g., Nicola Lacey, 'In Search of the Responsible Subject: History, Philosophy and Criminal Law Theory', *Modern Law Review* 64 (2001): 350; Lindsay Farmer, *Making the Modern Criminal Law: Criminalization and Civil Order* (Oxford: Oxford University Press, 2016).

label refers to quite different specific roles in different systems – not just as between 'adversarial' and 'inquisitorial' systems, but within each type of system.[2]

I hope to bypass some of these problems of parochialism by focusing on what must be a central prosecutorial function in any system: for whatever else a 'prosecutor' might do (for instance, in investigating crime, in gathering evidence, in sentencing), it must at least be her job to prosecute – to present the case against the accused person. In adversarial systems, this is paradigmatically done in court at a criminal trial, and it is on that kind of 'prosecution' that I will focus in what follows. It is of course true that, even in notionally adversarial systems, very few criminal cases are decided by a contested trial: the vast majority of cases that go to court are settled by guilty pleas (often on the basis of plea bargains), with little or no formal presentation of the case, and prosecutors can dispose of many cases without going to court at all, for instance by imposing a 'prosecutor fine'.[3] In more inquisitorial systems, the criminal trial also plays a less distinctive role within the criminal process. However, I will argue later that central to a democracy's criminal law should be a process through which those accused of criminal offences are called to answer the accusation; that process need not always involve a formal trial, but it is exemplified most clearly by the criminal trial. Although my discussion will focus on adversarial criminal trials, I therefore hope that the values and goals to which I will appeal also find a home in more inquisitorial systems, and in other ways of dealing with criminal cases, even if their precise institutional manifestations and operations are different.[4]

---

[2] See Michael Tonry (ed.), *Prosecutors and Politics: A Comparative Perspective Crime and Justice: A Review of Research*, vol. 41; Chicago: University of Chicago Press, 2012); Máximo Langer, 'Strength, Weakness or Both? On the Endurance of the Adversarial-Inquisitorial Systems in Comparative Criminal Procedure', in *Research Handbook on Comparative Criminal Procedure*, ed. J Ross and S Thaman (Northampton, MA: Edward Elgar, 2016); also the papers in this volume by Shawn Boyne, Mathilde Cohen, Angela Davis, and Jacqueline Hodgson. As an illustration of the very different understandings of prosecutorial roles in different systems, prosecutors in Germany are standardly described as 'second judges' (see Boyne in this volume, 141), and it is natural for Americans to talk of a prosecutor's 'constituents' (see Davis in this volume, 207): such ways of talking about prosecutors will strike English ears as very odd – even improper.

[3] See Peter Duff, 'The Prosecutor Fine', *Oxford Journal of Legal Studies* 14 (1994): 565; also, more generally, Andrew J Ashworth and Mike Redmayne, *The Criminal Process*, 4th ed. (Oxford: Oxford University Press, 2010), ch. 6.

[4] I would add that, though I cannot discuss the problems of plea bargaining here, it is also important that the case against the defendant is formally presented in court even when a plea bargain has averted the need for a contested trial: see, e.g., Darryl Brown, 'Reforming the Judge's Role in Plea Bargaining', in *The Future of Criminal Law?*. ed. M Dempsey et al. (Minneapolis: Robina Institute of Criminal Law and Criminal Justice, 2014), 75.

In what follows, I will (in s. 1) sketch a conception of the kind of criminal law that could be appropriate to a democratic polity – to a republic of equal citizens; that account will give the criminal trial a central role. I will then, in s. 2, discuss the prosecutorial function of the prosecutor in such a system – a role that centrally involves deciding whether, and with what, to charge the person who is accused of committing a crime, and (if the decision is to charge) presenting the case against the accused. In ss. 3–4, I will turn to a central question about that prosecutorial function, concerning the kind of discretion that a prosecutor should (or cannot but) have in making such decisions, and how it should be exercised. Finally, in s. 5, I will discuss the ways in which that discretion can be made appropriately accountable – and the particular issues about accountability that arise in polities that are marred by serious social injustice.

1 A CRIMINAL LAW FOR CITIZENS[5]

There is no space here to spell out a detailed account of a democratic republic; I can say that the conception on which I rely is of a participatory, deliberative democracy that takes an inclusionary attitude towards its members (although the account I will offer of a prosecutor's role should also be congenial to other conceptions of democracy), but that is just to mention a set of slogans, each of which requires unpacking. However, I can highlight some presently relevant features by commenting briefly on two slogans: 'equal concern and respect', and 'the eyeball test'.

Equal concern and respect are central to Dworkin's account of liberalism. His concern is with what governments owe their citizens – a government must 'treat all those in its charge as equals, that is, as entitled to its equal concern and respect';[6] but that is also what citizens owe each other. In our private lives – as members of families, as friends – we do not owe the same concern and respect to all: what I owe my children or my friends is different from and typically more than what I owe others. In our mutual dealings as citizens, however, we owe each other equal concern and respect. This is what should guide our conduct in the public, civic realm, in which we interact not as friends or family members, but as citizens. The content and scope of that civic realm is a matter for democratic deliberation, and different polities will develop different conceptions. It is the realm in which we live with each other as citizens; it includes

---

[5] In what follows, I draw on work that Sandra Marshall and I have been doing on civic roles and the criminal law: see especially 'Civic Punishment', in *Democratic Theory and Mass Incarceration*, ed. A Dzur, I Loader, R Sparks (Oxford: Oxford University Press, 2016) 33.

[6] Ronald Dworkin, *A Matter of Principle* (Oxford: Oxford University Press, 1986), 190.

public goods, spaces and services, and public or civic activities, notably those that constitute our 'public discourse', in which citizens discuss the terms of their shared civic life. Concern is a matter of welfare, although polities will take different views about what sorts of welfare should be provided publicly by the polity, or privately by individuals. Respect concerns such values as dignity, autonomy, and privacy; it is exemplified by the way in which citizens engage in public debate – their willingness to listen to each other as equal participants in the enterprise of self-governance, and in the limits set on the ways in which citizens, and the government, intrude into individuals' lives. That concern and respect is equal, because citizens should recognise each other as equal participants in the civic enterprise. In their private lives, they may be partial to friends, family, or other intimates, but when acting in the public realm as citizens, they must see and treat each other as equals.

This leads us to the 'eyeball test' as a test of civic recognition. As Pettit explains it, it is a one-way test of republican freedom as non-domination: free citizens 'can look others in the eye without reason for the fear or deference that a power of interference might inspire'.[7] But it should be a two-way test: republican citizens must be willing, as well as able, to look each other in the eye – to recognise each other as participants in the civic enterprise. That is one way in which we display equal concern and respect for each other: in our willingness to look each other in the eye, with a look not of threat or fear, but of recognition of fellowship.

It might be objected that it is a mistake thus to emphasise citizenship, since so many of those who suffer the law's coercive attentions are not citizens: that we should instead follow Ingrid Eagly in arguing that 'democratic principles should be applied to all defendants, according to universal membership rules that do not delineate between citizens and noncitizens'.[8] All I can say here is, first, that an account of criminal law must answer the question of whose law it is – and that in a democracy, the answer must be that it is the law of the citizens of that polity. Second, however, a decent republic will be welcoming to would-be citizens rather than treating them with exclusionary distrust; and non-citizens within a polity's jurisdiction should be treated as guests, a distinctive normative position that requires concern, respect, and recognition – and equal treatment by the criminal justice system.[9]

---

[7] Philip Pettit, *On the People's Terms* (Cambridge: Cambridge University Press, 2012), 84.

[8] In this volume, 248–9; see also Lucia Zedner, 'Is the Criminal Law only for Citizens?', in *The Borders of Punishment*, ed. K F Aas and M Bosworth (Oxford: Oxford University Press, 2013), 40.

[9] See Antony Duff, 'Relational Reasons and the Criminal Law', *Oxford Studies in Legal Philosophy* 2 (2013), 175, at 189–91, 207–8.

Another objection is that such slogans as 'equal concern and respect' and 'looking each other in the eye' do not mark out a truly democratic conception of equal citizenship. 'Equal concern and respect' are typically afforded, not to every member of the polity, but only to the members of favoured, socially advantaged groups. The eyeball test reflects a particular, and culturally biased, conception of how equal recognition is expressed.[10] As far as equal concern and respect are concerned, the objection is misdirected. The slogan expresses an aspiration – one of which the actual social and political structures of contemporary democracies fall well short: but the failure to accord equal concern and respect to *all* members of the polity (which is a failure to treat them as full members of the polity) marks a failure not of that democratic slogan, but of the polities that fail to live up to it. Such failures, as we will see in s. 5, have significant implications for criminal justice and the criminal process, which cannot simply ignore them in the attempt to do equal (criminal) justice to all; but at this stage, our concern is with the slogan as partly defining what a democratic polity should aspire to be(come). As for the eyeball test, what matters is that members of the polity be ready to recognise each other as equals and as fellows. The social and material forms through which such recognition can be expressed will vary between different cultures. In those in which it can be displayed in a willingness to look each other in the eye (and denied by a refusal to do so), the eyeball test is a useful democratic slogan. If, in other cultures, that is not a way of expressing a recognition of others as one's equal fellows, other slogans will be appropriate.

Democratic citizens owe each other equal concern and respect, and equal recognition as fellow members of the polity. Now prosecutors, like other officials, are also citizens: 'citizens in uniform'.[11] That is to say, although they hold a distinctive official role, which gives them a specified type of authority over other citizens (as well as specified duties towards them), they are also still citizens, subject to the same demands and duties of democratic citizenship as all their fellows. We must therefore ask whether, and how, they can satisfy such requirements of democratic citizenship in their work. How can they treat those with whom they have to deal, in particular those accused of crimes, with the equal concern and respect due to all citizens? Can they, as they prosecute a defendant, look him in the eye, and enable him to look them

---

[10] Thanks to Mathilde Cohen for pressing this kind of objection.
[11] See John Gardner, 'Criminals in Uniform', in *The Constitution of the Criminal Law*, ed. R A Duff et al. (Oxford: Oxford University Press, 2013), 97; applying Albert V Dicey, *An Introduction to the Study of the Law of the Constitution*, 6th ed. (London; Macmillan, 1902), 189–90.

in the eye, as an equal member of the polity? Can their treatment of him display a recognition of his status as a fellow citizen?

There are actually two sets of questions here. One set concerns the role of prosecutors in a tolerably just polity, in which those with whom a prosecutor deals are generally treated with the appropriate concern and respect by their fellows and by officials. The other set concerns the role of prosecutors in polities more like our own, in which these requirements are not met in relation to many suspects or defendants. I'll focus initially on the first set, since it is useful to ground normative theorising in an account of criminal law in a just polity; but I will say something about the second set in s. 5. (I will also, in s. 4, comment on some more ambitious questions that might be asked about the relationship between prosecutors and democracy.)

The role that prosecutors could play in a democratic republic depends on the role that the criminal law should play in such a polity. Again, I can here only sketch a conception of a democratic criminal law – a law for citizens.[12] An initial gesture towards that conception is found in the idea of criminal law as common law:[13] not common law as opposed to statutory law, but law that is common in the sense that it is our shared law, not one imposed on us by a separate sovereign. But what would make a law a genuinely common law? We can begin to answer that question by sketching two central functions of criminal law as thus understood.

First, in its substantive mode, the criminal law defines a set of public wrongs (and also the conditions under which people will be held liable for committing such wrongs). Criminal law is concerned with wrongs: with kinds of conduct that are not merely harmful or undesirable, but that merit censure as wrongs. It is not, however, concerned with every kind of wrong,[14] but only with wrongs that are properly described as 'public'. What makes a wrong 'public' is not that it directly harms or otherwise impacts on 'the public', as distinct from an individual victim, but that it properly concerns 'the public', i.e. members of the polity, in virtue of their citizenship; it is a wrong that is our collective business, since it falls within the 'public' realm that constitutes our civic life.[15] If we ask why we should have legal institution

---

[12]   This is *not* to apply Jakobs' notorious distinction between 'citizen' and 'enemy' criminal law (see Günther Jakobs, 'Kriminalisierung im Vorfeld einer Rechtsgutsverletzung', *Zeitschrift für die gesamte Strafrechtswissenschaft* 97 (1985), 751).

[13]   See Roger Cotterrell, *Law's Community* (Oxford: Oxford University Press, 1995), ch. 11.

[14]   Contrast Michael Moore, *Placing Blame* (Oxford: Oxford University Press, 1997), ch. 1.

[15]   See Sandra Marshall and Antony Duff, 'Criminalization and Sharing Wrongs', *Canadian Journal of Law and Jurisprudence* 11 (1998), 7; Antony Duff, 'Towards a Modest Legal Moralism', *Criminal Law and Philosophy* 7 (2014), 217.

that focuses in this way on wrongs, rather than, for instance, focusing our collective concern on individual or social harms,[16] the simple answer is that this is part of what is involved in taking seriously the values by which a polity defines itself, and taking each other seriously as responsible agents who are bound by those values: we take such formal notice of violations of them.

For, second, in its procedural and penal modes, criminal law provides for an appropriate response to such wrongs. Theorists of criminal law often focus on punishment as central to the criminal law's response to crime (understandably, in societies as punitive as our own). However, in a democracy that treats its citizens as responsible members of the polity, the criminal trial is an important part of the response to (alleged) crime. If we ask how a polity's members would appropriately respond to wrongs that they commit, the answer is not just that they would seek to prevent further such wrongs, or to inflict retributive burdens on those who commit them, by imposing punishment, but that they would seek to call those who commit them to public account. In doing so, they do justice to the victims of such wrongs: we show a recognition of the wrong that another has suffered by seeking to call to account the person who committed the wrong.[17] They also do justice to those who have committed such wrongs: calling another to account for his wrongdoing is one way in which we display our recognition of him as a responsible fellow member of a normative community.

That is why the criminal trial is central to the criminal law of a democratic republic, not just as an instrumental link between crime and punishment, but as the formal process through which a polity paradigmatically calls alleged wrongdoers to public account, to answer to their fellow citizens. A defendant is called, initially, to answer *to* a charge of criminal wrongdoing, which he does (in adversarial trials) by pleading 'Guilty' or 'Not Guilty'. If the prosecution proves, or if he admits, that he committed the crime charged, he is called to answer *for* that crime: he can do this either by admitting his guilt, and accepting the censure expressed in a conviction; or by offering a defence that admits responsibility for the crime, but then seeks to block the usual inference from responsibility to liability.[18] (To say that the defendant is called to answer is to say that in a tolerably just polity, he has a *civic* duty to answer – to answer to the charge, and for his criminal conduct if it is proved; he owes

---

[16] As is advocated by 'social harm' theorists (Paddy Hillyard et al., *Criminal Obsessions: Why Harm Matters More Than Crime* (London: Crime and Society Foundation, 2005); see Nils Christie, 'Conflicts as Property', *British Journal of Criminology* 17 (1977), 1.

[17] Which is not of course to say that this is *all* that we owe the victims of crime.

[18] See further Antony Duff, Lindsay Farmer, Sandra Marshall, and Victor Tadros, *The Trial on Trial (3): Towards a Normative Theory of the Criminal Trial* (Oxford: Hart, 2007); Antony Duff, *Answering for Crime* (Oxford: Hart, 2007).

this to his fellow citizens, as a member of the polity whose law is supposed to be his law. That is not to say, however, that he has or should have a *legal* duty thus to answer: there are very good reasons, to do with the need to protect accused persons from the oppressive power of the legal system, and to allow dissenters to express their dissent by refusing to take part in their trial, by leaving defendants the legal freedom to remain silent in court.)

Two points should be noted about this conception of criminal law. First, it captures both the traditional '*mala in se*' (crimes consisting in conduct whose wrongfulness is independent of the law), and the so-called '*mala prohibita*' that constitute the majority of contemporary offences – crimes consisting in conduct that is wrongful only because it is a violation of a legal regulation. The latter count as public wrongs if and when they violate a regulation that the perpetrator had a civic obligation to obey. Second, the question of what should count as a public wrong – what should count as a public concern, and what kinds of 'public' conduct should be counted as wrongs – is a matter for democratic deliberation. In criminalizing a type of conduct, the legislature declares it to be a public wrong: citizens (and theorists) might of course disagree with that declaration, and a crucial challenge for any democracy is to work out ways of dealing justly with such disagreement.

2 THE PROSECUTOR'S ROLE

On the view of the criminal law and the criminal trial sketched above, a prosecutor plays an important democratic role. Her role is not simply that of a state functionary administering the law; it is to act and speak for the polity in calling to account those accused of committing public wrongs. More precisely, her role is to decide whether to call suspected wrongdoers to such public account, and to call them if they should be called. Whatever else 'prosecutors' may do, this is central to their civic role.[19] The most salient way in which they discharge that civic role is in deciding whether to charge a suspected person, and (if they charge him) in bringing him to a criminal trial, in which he is a defendant formally and publicly accused of a specified crime: either an uncontested trial in which he enters an honest and voluntary plea of 'Guilty',[20] or a contested trial, in which they must attempt to prove his guilt. (As I noted earlier,

[19] A further question that I cannot discuss here is whether only those formally employed as criminal prosecutors should prosecute; or should others (police; officials of various kinds of inspectorate; even private individuals) have the power to bring prosecutions?

[20] The proper aims of the trial are served by a 'Guilty' plea only if that plea is voluntary and honest; one problem with our current systems of plea bargaining is that they lead to pleas that are neither voluntary nor honest.

prosecutors can also often dispose of (minor) cases in which a suspected person admits his guilt without going to trial, for instance by imposing a 'prosecutor fine', or by authorising a 'conditional caution':[21] in such cases, we can say that the prosecutor is still calling the defendant to public account, in the sense that he is held accountable by a public officer of the law, acting in our collective name – an officer who must herself also be publicly accountable.)

The labelling of criminal cases in adversarial systems is thus symbolically significant. In polities that retain traces of their non-democratic history, the case might be listed as '*Regina v. D*': the defendant is called to answer by and to his sovereign. More apposite, for democratic republics, is '*People v. D*', or '*Commonwealth v. D*', which make it explicit that the prosecutor speaks and acts in the name of the polity and its members. ('*State v. D*' is less appropriate: it encourages a view of criminal law not as our law, but as a law imposed on us by 'the state'. That is too often how the law is, reasonably, perceived by those on whom it is imposed, but it marks a serious failing in the preconditions of the law's legitimacy.)

How then should prosecutors discharge this central prosecutorial function of deciding who should be formally accused of what, and presenting the case against the accused person in court?

One further background principle of a democratic republic must be mentioned here – the presumption of innocence (PoI). In its most familiar form, the PoI bears directly only on the criminal trial: the court must convict a defendant only given proof of his guilt. This might seem to bear indirectly on the prosecutor's role: a prudent prosecutor will not take a case to court unless she thinks she has a good chance of being able to prove it – why waste resources on cases that are doomed to fail? This would be right if the prosecutor's role was to secure convictions, so that an acquittal marked a *failure*. That is how the role is often understood, by prosecutors and by others – which is at odds with the idea that the prosecutor should be a 'minister of justice';[22] but it is not how the role should be understood in a democratic polity. A prosecutor who sees the criminal trial as I have suggested it should be seen, as a process of calling to account, and who sees those with whom she deals as fellow citizens to whom she owes equal concern and respect (rather than as criminals who have lost their civic standing),[23] will not see her role simply as that of securing convictions within whatever side-constraints the demands of

---

[21] See n. 3 above; Ashworth and Redmayne, *The Criminal Process*, 168, 178–80.
[22] See Richard Young and Andrew Sanders, 'The Ethics of Prosecution Lawyers', *Legal Ethics* 7 (2004) 190, at 195–6; Ashworth and Redmayne, *The Criminal Process*, p. 65.
[23] Compare Ashworth and Redmayne, *The Criminal Process*, p. 77, on the 'toe-rag theory'.

justice might set. Her task is to call to account for alleged criminal wrongs those whom the polity has good reason thus to call: but what could constitute such a 'good reason'?

The good reason will have to do with the likelihood that this person committed a criminal wrong, but a broader version of the PoI requires that likelihood to be a high one. This broader version applies to our civic dealings with each other as citizens and to officials' dealings with their fellow citizens. It reflects a conception of 'civic trust' as an essential feature of a viable polity: the idea that we should, in our civic dealings, regard and treat each other as innocent (of past criminal wrongdoing or of intended future wrongdoing) until the other gives us good reason to treat him as non-innocent.[24] What counts as good reason, for what kinds of different treatment (what can defeat the presumption, to what effect), will vary from context to context; we must focus here on the prosecutor, and her decisions about whether (and on what charge) to prosecute. She must begin by treating those with whom she has to deal as innocents, and should pursue a criminal charge only if that presumption is defeated: but what can defeat it? We cannot say, as we can say of the PoI within the trial, that only proof (beyond reasonable doubt) of his guilt can defeat it: it is for the court, not the prosecutor, to determine whether guilt has been proved to the requisite standard. We can say, though, that she should pursue a charge only if she has sufficient, admissible evidence that the person committed the crime to constitute at least a case to answer: evidence sufficient for the court to conclude that he did commit the offence, unless he offers counter-evidence that creates a reasonable doubt.

Being put on trial is in many ways burdensome. Some of the burdens are material, some psychological; even if adequate legal aid is available, there are (for both guilty and innocent) unavoidable costs in time and energy, and the psychological burdens of a trial and of anxiety about its outcome.[25] There is also the moral burden of being formally accused of a criminal wrong. Prosecutors must be slow to impose such burdens on anyone until there is sufficient evidence that he committed the crime to justify doing so. If there is such evidence, it becomes legitimate to require the suspected person to answer in the appropriate forum. The prosecutor can look him in the eye as she charges him, as a fellow citizen who should be ready to answer for himself; she can still claim to accord him the concern and respect due to him as a citizen.

---

[24] See Dale Nance, 'Civility and the Burden of Proof', *Harvard Journal of Law & Public Policy* 17 (1994), 647; Antony Duff, 'Who Must Presume Whom to be Innocent of What?' *Netherlands Journal of Legal Philosophy* 42 (2013), 170, at 174–5, 180–2.

[25] See further Jonathan Rogers, 'Restructuring the Exercise of Prosecutorial Discretion in England', *Oxford Journal of Legal Studies* 26 (2006), 775, at 788–93.

The next question is whether the availability of sufficient evidence of the commission of the offence should be not merely necessary, but sufficient to warrant prosecution; I will turn to that question next, but should first note a possible argument against the claim of necessity. Suppose that a person is widely suspected of a crime, but that there is insufficient evidence to constitute a case to answer: might he not demand to be tried, so that he can publicly clear his name? In a decent polity, he should have no basis for such a claim. A prosecutorial decision not to proceed does often leave the person with the taint of suspected guilt. This is because we often fail to take the PoI that bears on our civic conduct seriously enough; but that failure is encouraged if, for instance, a prosecutor declares that she is not charging a suspect because there is 'insufficient evidence to proceed' with the case.[26] What the prosecutor should say is that the person has no case to answer; when that is said, just as when a court acquits the defendant, his fellow citizens should see that the PoI has not been defeated, and that the once-suspected person must be treated again as innocent (which is why it matters that the verdict is 'Not Guilty' rather than 'Not Proved Guilty').[27] Others might still believe that he is guilty; they might in private conversation say that he is probably guilty, since the PoI applies only to our public, civic lives. But they must, in their civic dealings with the person, treat him as (as if) innocent; if they do so, he can have no grounds for demanding a trial to clear his name.

Suppose, however, that a prosecutor has sufficient, admissible, evidence that a person committed a crime: should she then charge him? Or should she be allowed some discretion not to pursue the case? On a simple reading of the Legality Principle, this question has a straightforward answer: the prosecutor must prosecute whenever she has sufficient evidence. This might seem to be required by the rule of law, and by democratic principles. It is not the role of prosecutors, as unelected officials, to decide when the law should be enforced: once the legislature has made the law, their role is to apply it consistently. My concern here is not with this (over-simple) reading of the Legality Principle,[28]

---

[26] This is a common locution in England, and is often heard as having the same meaning as the police comment after an acquittal that they are not looking for anyone else in connection with the crime: the person is probably guilty, but cannot be proved guilty.

[27] That is why the Scottish verdict of 'Not Proven' is an aberration: see S A Bennett, 'Not Proven: The Verdict' (2002) *Scots Law Times* (News), 96.

[28] See, e.g., Mirjan Damaška, 'The Reality of Prosecutorial Discretion: Comments on a German Monograph' (discussing Weigend, *Anklagepflicht und Ermessen*) *American Journal of Comparative Law* 29 (1981), 119; Antoinette Perrodet, 'The Public Prosecutor', in *European Criminal Procedures*, ed. M Delmas-Marty and J Spencer (Cambridge: Cambridge University Press, 2002), 415; Shawn Boyne's discussion of the erosion of the Legality Principle (for non-felonies) in Germany: in this volume, 148.

but rather with the reasons why a democratic republic should favour an Opportunity Principle, which gives prosecutors some discretion in deciding whether to prosecute, even when they have sufficient evidence; with the proper scope of such discretion; and with the ways in which it should be exercised and made accountable.

I will structure the discussion round the two 'tests' that English prosecutors must apply in deciding whether to prosecute: the 'evidential' test and the 'public interest' test.[29] This is not because I suppose that the English must have it right, but it is a useful way of distinguishing the different kinds of factor that should bear on prosecutorial decisions. The evidential test must, I will argue, be read in substantive rather than in purely formal terms if it is to serve the proper purposes of the criminal law; but this gives prosecutors a distinctive kind of discretion in deciding whether it is satisfied. By contrast, a public interest test, which gives prosecutors a further kind of discretion, is appropriate because they should sometimes have to decide whether the criminal law's purposes are to take priority over a polity's other aims.

3 PROSECUTORIAL DISCRETION (A): THE EVIDENTIAL TEST

The 'evidential test' might seem both straightforward and uncontroversial: prosecutors must, according to the *Code for Crown Prosecutors* (para. 4.4),

> be satisfied that there is sufficient evidence to provide a realistic prospect of conviction against each suspect on each charge. They must consider what the defence case may be, and how it is likely to affect the prospects of conviction. A case which does not pass the evidential stage must not proceed, no matter how serious or sensitive it may be.

For, as suggested in the previous section, it would be improper for the prosecutor to proceed with a case unless she was so satisfied. Matters are not, however, so simple, for two reasons.

The first reason concerns the difference between having sufficient evidence to secure a conviction (which is how the Code puts it) and evidence sufficient to prove the commission of the offence (which is how I put it above): evidence sufficient to prove the commission of an offence might still not suffice for a conviction, because a defendant who is proved to have committed the offence can avoid conviction by offering a defence. According to the Code, if the prosecutor is aware of a likely defence and thinks it unlikely that 'an objective,

---

[29] See www.cps.gov.uk/publications/code_for_crown_prosecutors/ (Code *for Crown Prosecutors*);
Ashworth and Redmayne, *The Criminal Process*, 194–214.

impartial and reasonable' court would convict,[30] she must not proceed, but perhaps sometimes it would be right to proceed. If there is not sufficient evidence to prove the commission of the offence, there is nothing for which the person needs to answer in the court: but if it is proved that he committed an offence, there is something – the offence, as a presumptive public wrong – for which he should answer to his fellow citizens,[31] and the public character of the wrong gives us reason to hold that answering should be in public, i.e. in a criminal trial.

An obvious response to this suggestion is that even if there is such reason for a trial, it is far from conclusive. First, since the prosecutor represents the polity in such matters, we can delegate to her the task of deciding whether a potential defendant can offer such a persuasive defence that there is no need to take the case to trial: that defence is admittedly not offered *in public*, but it is offered to and judged by a public officer. Second, bringing such cases to trial would waste public resources, and impose unnecessary burdens on the defendant. There is force to this response, especially for defendants who were acting as private individuals, but there is still something to be said for the suggestion, at least in the case of public officials. If a police officer has shot someone, it might be clear to the prosecutor that he could successfully plead self-defence; she might be sure, not just she would be unable to disprove the defence, but that it is true – that he did act in self-defence. Nonetheless, there is still reason to take the case to court, not just to avert public anger or anxiety, but to make clear that such actions are presumptive wrongs that must be answered for. The hearing might be brief (we can envisage a practice of agreed 'Not Guilty' pleas, with just a concise presentation of the agreed facts), but it would have significant symbolic value.

The second reason why the evidential test is not straightforward concerns whether we should understand it in formal or in substantive terms. A formal test requires the prosecutor to ask whether she could prove that the potential defendant's conduct fitted the law's formal definition of the crime; by contrast, a substantive test requires her to ask whether his conduct constituted the kind of evil or mischief at which the law is aimed.[32] An example will clarify the issue. When the British government introduced what became the Sexual Offences Act 2003, critics pointed out that ss. 9 and 13 criminalised consensual sexual activity between young people aged fifteen – which, they thought, was

---

[30] *Code for Crown Prosecutors*, para. 4.5; see Ashworth and Redmayne, *The Criminal Process*, 201.

[31] See further Duff, *Answering for Crime*, ch. 9.4.

[32] Compare Jonathan Rogers, 'The Role of the Public Prosecutor in Applying and Developing the Substantive Criminal Law', in *The Constitution of the Criminal Law*, ed. R A Duff et al. (Oxford: Oxford University Press, 2013), 53.

absurd. A minister reassured such critics that was not the Bill's 'intention', and would not be its 'effect': 'we shall be able to trust the Crown Prosecution Service to ensure that intention is followed'.[33] Thus the government was asking the legislature to enact a statute whose offence definitions were avowedly over-broad, since they defined as criminal types of conduct that there was no intention to treat as criminal, and to rely on prosecutors to use their discretion to put that intention into effect.

Suppose that two young people aged fifteen engage in 'sexual touching', and satisfy the definition of the offence of 'sexual activity with a child'. The matter comes to the attention of the police, who (from moralistic enthusiasm) send the case to the CPS; the prosecutor, in line with the government's expressed intention, decides not to prosecute. On a formal reading of the evidential test, it is satisfied: the young people's conduct satisfied the statutory definition of the offence; the decision not to proceed must be based on a judgment that it would not be in 'the public interest' to do so. On a substantive reading of the test, it is not satisfied: it is clear from the Act's legislative history that the law was not intended to capture this kind of conduct as a criminal wrong.

Why should it matter which interpretation of the evidential test we adopt if the prosecutor drops the case in either event? It matters because the interpretation determines what is said to the people concerned, and to the polity. On the formal reading, what is said is that the young people are provably guilty, convictable, of a criminal wrong, but for other reasons to do with the public interest, they are not to be prosecuted. On a substantive reading, what is said is that though their conduct satisfied the formal definition of the offence, they were not guilty of a real criminal wrong. The latter message is surely what the prosecutor should communicate, to the two young people and to the polity.

This is to suggest that the evidential test should be read as if the criminal law included a version of the Model Penal Code's *De Minimis* provision,[34] that courts should dismiss a case if the defendant's conduct did not 'cause or threaten the harm or evil sought to be prevented by the law'; so too, I suggest, a prosecutor should take the evidential test to be failed if the conduct did not constitute the kind of mischief at which the law in question was aimed. The point is not that, in such cases, the potential defendant has a defence; that would be to say that he committed a real offence, for which he must offer an exculpatory answer. The point is, rather, that in such cases, no real offence is committed.

---

[33] Hansard vol. 409, 15 July 2003, col. 248; Paul Goggins, a Home Office Minister.

[34] American Law Institute, *Model Penal Code* § 2.12. See Douglas Husak, 'The *De Minimis* "Defense" to Criminal Liability', in Husak, *The Philosophy of Criminal Law* (Oxford: Oxford University Press, 2010), 362.

This suggestion might seem objectionable for two reasons. First, that it would condone legislative carelessness: it encourages legislatures to enact over-broad offence definitions, relying on prosecutors to do what should be a legislative job, of defining offences precisely. Second, it is undemocratic (at least when prosecutors are not elected): the specification of criminal wrongs is a matter for elected legislatures, not for unelected prosecutors.

The first objection has force, since what is at stake is not just legislative carelessness, but the rule of law and the danger of excessive prosecutorial power. Legislatures can be too ready to enact over-broad criminal offences in order to (be seen to) make sure that they capture all the conduct that should be criminal, and to leave it to police and prosecutors to apply the law more accurately.[35] But this makes the law, as formally published, uncertain and unclear, and gives prosecutors a dangerous power to coerce citizens whose conduct satisfies the definition of the offence. However, this problem is to some extent unavoidable, since we cannot expect legislatures, however committed to the rule of law, to be able to define offences so precisely that they capture only such conduct as does 'cause or threaten the harm or evil sought to be prevented'. Legislation must consist either in 'rules', which do specify in precise descriptive terms the conduct to be criminalised, or in 'standards', which use concepts whose application requires normative judgment (or in a blend of rules and standards).[36] Standards, if properly applied, can capture all and only the conduct that constitutes the mischief against which the law is aimed, but to determine whether the evidential test is satisfied, the prosecutor must make a normative judgment about whether the defendant's conduct violated the standard. By contrast, it is a more straightforward matter for a prosecutor to decide, without the need for normative judgment, that there is sufficient evidence that a person violated a rule. But rules that are not radically under-inclusive are over-inclusive:[37] if they are wide enough to capture even most of the conduct against which the law is aimed, they will also capture some conduct that does not cause the relevant mischief. If prosecutors are to avoid prosecuting some whose conduct does not merit it, they must exercise a normative discretion to weed out such cases. This is not to give legislatures carte blanche to enact criminal statutes in vague or over-inclusive terms; they could do more than they often do to make their laws clear, precise, and narrowly focused on the mischief at which they are aimed. Even a conscientious legislature must, however, rely on prosecutorial

---

[35] For just two of many examples, see Terrorism Act 2000; Offensive Behaviour at Football and Threatening Communications (Scotland) Act 2012.

[36] See Peter J Schlag, 'Rules and Standards', *UCLA Law Review* 33 (1985), 379.

[37] Frederick Schauer, *Playing by the Rules* (Oxford: Oxford University Press, 1993), 31–44.

discretion to weed out cases that satisfy the '*de minimis*' test – and thus on prosecutors to be able to discern the mischief at which the law is aimed.

This leads to the second objection, that it is undemocratic to allow such wide discretion to unelected officials. It might be tempting to reply to this objection by extending Dworkin's account of judicial discretion to prosecutors, to say that they must strive towards a Herculean exercise in interpretation that makes best sense of the statutory material with which they have to deal.[38] However, even those who have sympathy for a Dworkinian account of adjudication should hesitate to extend this to prosecutors – and it does not address the accountability issue. Some might see this as an argument in favour of elected prosecutors, whose accountability is assured in the same way as that of legislators – through the ballot box; to which the familiar response is that justice is ill served by prosecutors who are subject to the vagaries of electoral politics.[39] What is needed is some other mechanism of accountability; I will return to this issue later, after discussing the second English test – the 'public interest' test.

4 PROSECUTORIAL DISCRETION (B): THE 'PUBLIC INTEREST' TEST

A prosecutor should regard the evidential test as satisfied only if she is confident that she has sufficient evidence to convince a court that the person committed a real criminal offence – the kind of wrong at which the relevant statute is aimed. If the test is satisfied, this creates a presumption in favour of prosecution: to define a type of conduct as criminal is to declare that it merits the kind of formal calling to account, and condemnation, that the criminal trial provides.[40] But that presumption is, on the common law understanding of the prosecutor's role, defeasible; the prosecutor should not proceed if it is not in 'the public interest' to do so. But what counts as 'the public interest' here, if not the interest in having crimes prosecuted?

The *Code for Crown Prosecutors* (para. 4.12) lists some of the considerations relevant to the public interest.[41] Most concern the crime's seriousness, or the suspect's culpability (if guilty). But they include the crime's impact 'on the community';[42] whether prosecution might adversely affect the victim's health;

---

[38]   See Ronald Dworkin, *Law's Empire* (London: Fontana, 1986).
[39]   Michael Tonry, 'Prosecutors and Politics in Comparative Perspective', in *Prosecutors and Politics*, 2–4. But see Angela Davis' and Jonathan Simon's papers in this volume.
[40]   See *Code for Crown Prosecutors*, para. 4.8.
[41]   More detailed guidance is given for particular offences: see Ashworth and Redmayne, *The Criminal Process*, 204–9.
[42]   And see www.cps.gov.uk/publications/prosecution/rrpbcrbook.html#a36 (the CPS guide on 'racist and religious crime'): one factor is whether 'the offence is widespread in the area where it is committed'.

whether it would be 'proportionate' (understood in terms of cost-effectiveness); and whether prosecution would make it necessary to make public details 'that could harm sources of information, international relations or national security'.[43]

This list blends factors internal and factors external to the criminal law. Some factors are ones that traditionally figure in sentencing, concerning culpability and harm. Are prosecutors here usurping the sentencer's role? Perhaps not: we could instead see this either as applying the *De Minimis* principle, or as a matter of proportionality. The Model Penal Code's *De Minimis* clause requires courts to dismiss a case if the defendant's conduct did 'cause or threaten the harm or evil' at which the law is aimed, but 'only to an extent too trivial to warrant the condemnation of a conviction';[44] since any conviction is an onerous matter, it might be reasonable sometimes to judge that though the person committed the substantive offence, that commission was not serious enough to deserve such a result. Proportionality, on the other hand, takes us beyond the realm of criminal law narrowly understood, into factors that concern the criminal law's role in the polity's wider structure.

Proportionality is not now a matter of the proportionality of such a response to the crime in question – whether a conviction would be disproportionately harsh. The proportionality is between the costs of prosecution and the good that prosecution is to achieve: is prosecuting in this case worth the cost? This might seem an improper consideration, at least for those who see the prosecution and punishment of the guilty as a *demand* of justice, but it is an inevitable and appropriate consideration. No one can seriously hold that we must prosecute and punish *all* those who commit public wrongs, whatever the cost; even if justice demands that we do so, the demands of justice must compete with other demands on the polity's resources, and we have to ask whether meeting such demands would violate other important values. Such issues arise at every stage of the implementation of criminal law. They arise in legislation,[45] when legislators must ask not only whether a kind of conduct constitutes a public wrong that they therefore have reason to criminalise, but whether it is a wrong of such a kind that that reason is a *good enough* reason. They arise when resources are allocated to police and to the prosecutorial service:

---

[43] I cannot discuss the role (if any) the victim's wishes about prosecution should play: see www .cps.gov.uk/legal/d_to_g/domestic_abuse_guidelines_for_prosecutors/#a24 (the CPS guide on prosecuting domestic abuse), and n. 42 above; see also Michelle Dempsey, *Prosecuting Domestic Violence* (Oxford: Oxford University Press, 2009).

[44] *Model Penal Code* § 2.12; see n. 34 above.

[45] See, e.g., Jonathan Schonsheck, *On Criminalization* (Dordrecht: Kluwer, 1994); Moore, *Placing Blame*, ch. 18; Douglas Husak, *Overcriminalization: The Limits of the Criminal Law* (Oxford: Oxford University Press, 2007).

what resources should we allot to the tasks of detecting, prosecuting, and punishing crime? They arise when resources are allocated within those services: police and prosecutors must, given limited resources, decide which kinds of cases to prioritise. And they arise when individual prosecutors have to decide whether to pursue particular cases: they must make prudent use of the resources at their disposal, which might involve deciding not to pursue some cases that satisfy the evidential test, because it would be too costly to do so.

Some of those costs, of prosecution as well as of punishment, fall on the defendant.[46] We must ask not merely whether the penal consequences would be harsher than his crime warrants, if he is guilty, but also whether it is reasonable to impose such costs on a person who must, so far, be presumed to be innocent. We must ask a similar question about the victim: would the prosecution have a disproportionately 'adverse effect on the victim's physical or mental health'? The point in both cases is that we can reasonably ask citizens to bear certain burdens for the sake of pursuing criminal justice, including those involved in being summoned as a witness, or as a juror, and those that fall on defendants, and on victims.[47] However, there is a limit to the burdens that it is reasonable to expect citizens to bear, which can give prosecutors a further public interest reason not to pursue a case.

The burdens of conviction will, the prosecutor must suppose, fall only on the (provably) guilty, but even these can give her reason not to pursue the case: not because they would be disproportionate to the crime (a matter falling under a *De Minimis* principle), but as a matter of mercy. Mercy, as something distinct from justice, is a consideration that can sometimes irrupt into the criminal process. The suspect would, if guilty, deserve to be convicted and punished; that would be a proportionate response to his crime that could not be faulted from the perspective of criminal justice. But sometimes another perspective is more pressing, more appropriate; if, for instance, he is suffering a terminal illness, his, and our, attention might be more properly focused not on his crime, but on his illness. That could give a sentencer good reason to exempt a convicted offender from further punishment;[48] and it could also give a prosecutor reason not to prosecute.

---

[46]   See at n. 25 above.

[47]   See Sandra Marshall, '"It Isn't Just About You": Victims of Crime, Their Associated Duties, and Public Wrongs', in *Criminalization: The Political Morality of the Criminal Law*, ed. R A Duff et al. (Oxford: Oxford University Press, 2014), 291.

[48]   See Antony Duff, 'Mercy', in *Oxford Handbook of Philosophy of Criminal Law*, ed. J Deigh and D Dolinko (Oxford: Oxford University Press, 2011), 467.

More generally, 'public interest' factors are best understood as factors lying outside the strict confines of the criminal law, which can count against the demands of criminal justice; once we accept that those demands cannot be absolute, we must accept that sometimes they must be weighed against and may be outweighed by other concerns of the polity. Prosecutors should not, because we collectively should not, strive to 'do justice though the heavens fall': they, and we, should perhaps accept as an absolute that we must not convict or punish those whom we know to be innocent, but not that we must try to convict and punish all the guilty.

Two further questions now arise. First, to what factors may prosecutors attend once they look beyond the limits of the law? Second, how can they be democratically accountable for the ways in which they exercise this discretion?

As to the first question, anxiety about the dangers of prosecutorial discretion might grow if we understand their activities in the light of Dempsey's 'normal correspondence thesis' – that 'if a person can realize a value through her action, then normally she will have a reason so to act as to realize that value'.[49] We might then imagine prosecutors (ab)using their office to pursue any political or moral ends that they take to be good. Matters are not as bad as that, however, for a variety of reasons.

First, as public officials, they must act in the light only of values that belong to the public realm, the *res publica*, of the polity; this limits the range of substantive values to which they may attend in any particular polity, and requires them to deliberate on the basis not of their own individual or personal values, but of the polity's self-defining public values.

Second, the operation of the English 'public interest' test implies that the public interest functions not as a goal generating positive reasons for prosecution, but as a side-constraint on prosecutions whose 'justifying aim' is internal to the criminal law. This suggests a normative structure for prosecutorial decisions analogous to that which Hart suggests for punishment:[50] prosecution has a positive justifying aim of calling alleged wrongdoers to public account, which provides reasons to prosecute; but the pursuit of that aim is subject to various side-constraints, including the constraint that it should not be pursued if doing so would seriously harm 'the public interest', understood as including the polity's other public goods.

---

[49] Dempsey, *Prosecuting Domestic Violence*, p. 83. She later argues that, as a conceptual matter, there might be some values that a prosecutor, given her distinctive bureaucratic role, *cannot* realize (at 87–91), but the only value that seems to be thus ruled out is that of retribution.

[50] See H L A Hart, 'Prolegomenon to the Principles of Punishment', in Hart, *Punishment and Responsibility*, 2nd ed. (Oxford: Oxford University Press, 2008) 1.

Or should we go further, and allow that some public goods can generate positive reasons to prosecute? Suppose that a prosecuting authority decides to pay special attention to crimes of domestic abuse, or crimes of racial hatred, on the grounds that it is valuable to send a clear public message about such crimes, and thus reassert the values that they violate? Or suppose a prosecutor focuses on certain kinds of assault because they have been more prevalent in the local community, so that there is a perceived need to reassure the public, or to send a strong deterrent message to potential offenders? This could mean, if prosecutors have any say in the allocation of investigative resources, devoting more resources to investigating such crimes, and bringing prosecutions that might not otherwise have been brought. The evidential test would still be required; only the provably guilty would be prosecuted. But some might be prosecuted who would, absent that 'public interest' concern, have escaped prosecution. Could this be a proper use of the prosecutor's discretion?

One worry about this would concern retributive justice: for one effect of such a practice can be that of two convictable offenders who commit similar crimes, with equal culpability, one might be prosecuted on such public interest grounds, whilst the other is not. Perhaps, however, this is not a major worry: the one who escapes is lucky, in the way that many who escape prosecution are lucky to do so; or the one who is prosecuted is unlucky, but he can hardly complain about being prosecuted for a crime he committed, so long as the prosecution is not motivated by malicious or discriminatory considerations.

Another worry, however, concerns the range of considerations that would be allowed as relevant. It is one thing to say that the prevalence of a certain type of crime, or the need to send a clear message about domestic abuse or racial crime, can provide a reason to prosecute: but what, for instance, of the fact that prosecuting will contribute to reducing unemployment (a public good) by preserving jobs in the criminal justice system? That is surely not a reason to prosecute.[51] That is why we might hesitate to apply Dan Richman's question directly to the activities and decisions of individual prosecutors. A prosecutor who asked 'What can I do to promote citizenship within a liberal democracy?',[52] in deciding whom to charge with what, would surely be transgressing the proper bounds of her role; her job is not to promote or defend democratic citizenship, but to do criminal justice.

There are two ways in which this sort of worry can be met. The first is to recognise that Richman's question is normally to be asked not directly by

---

[51]   Compare Nils Christie, *Crime Control as Industry* (3rd ed.; Routledge, 2000).
[52]   Richman asks 'What role should prosecutors play in promoting citizenship within a liberal democracy?' (this volume, p. 40).

individual prosecutors, but at the stage of designing a prosecutorial system: we need to define the prosecutorial role, within the system of criminal law, in a way that will serve the proper ends of a democracy, by serving the proper ends of the criminal law within such a polity. Thus when it is suggested that we should ask, not about the relationship or contribution of prosecutors to democracy, but about their relationship to such distinctively legal values as the rule of law,[53] the point should not be that we ought to think about the rule of law *rather than* about democracy; it should be that a prosecutorial practice can best serve democracy by promoting and protecting such distinctive values as the rule of law.

As Richman argues, and as I argued earlier, a central way in which prosecutors can serve the rule of (democratic, republican) law is by calling to account citizens who are accused of public wrongs. We must still ask whether, in deciding whom to prosecute, prosecutors should be allowed or required to apply a (positive) public interest test as well as an evidential test – to see the public interest as providing reason to prosecute cases that might not otherwise be prosecuted. However, secondly, we can now argue that the only kind of 'public interest' that can provide legitimate reason to prosecute is a reason that concerns the distinctive goods that the criminal law should serve and protect, and that the alleged crime attacked. If we ask what could justify a policy of focusing prosecutorial resources on crimes of racial hatred, or on domestic violence, or on police conduct towards members of particular racial groups,[54] the most plausible answer is that such policies can serve the rule of law principle of equality before the law by focusing on kinds of crime that have too often been ignored, and that are typically committed by the more powerful against members of civically vulnerable groups.[55] By contrast, although reducing unemployment is a public good, it is not one that concerns the criminal law, or that is connected to the character of the crimes that prosecutors are to pursue.

The upshot of this discussion is that when, having satisfied herself that the evidential test has been met, the prosecutor asks whether prosecution would be 'in the public interest', she may attend only to a narrow range of factors, of

---

[53] As Norman Abrams suggested in discussion.

[54] See Davis' discussion in this volume of prosecutorial responses to police violence against African American citizens. Such decisions are most likely to be legitimate, in rule of law terms, if they are policy decisions rather than ad hoc decisions about particular cases, and if they are made collectively rather than individually (compare William Simon's account of a 'post-bureaucratic' model in this volume).

[55] Compare Richman's suggestion, in this volume, that prosecutors can serve democracy in part by 'Targeting Illegitimate Exercises of Power' (53–7).

the kind indicated in the last paragraph, as public interest considerations favouring prosecution, but to a wider range of factors as public interest factors arguing against prosecution. These include the effects of prosecution on both potential defendants and victims, and other costs of prosecution; they could also include, for instance, any impact on national security or on the security of confidential sources.[56]

Before we consider how the use of this kind of discretion could be made accountable, an example should illustrate some of the issues here. It is a crime under English law to assist a suicide – though prosecutions require the consent of the Director of Public Prosecutions.[57] In a number of publicised cases, people helped their loved ones travel to the Swiss Dignitas clinic to secure the kind of assisted death that was legally unavailable in Britain; such assistance clearly satisfied the statutory definition of the crime, but in no case did the DPP approve a prosecution. This was, however, a matter of *ex post* discretion: those contemplating such assistance had to hope that the DPP would exercise his discretion not to prosecute them.

Unhappy with this situation, Debbie Purdy asked the DPP to tell her what factors would be taken into account in a decision about whether to prosecute a case of assisting suicide, so that she and her husband could know in advance whether he might be prosecuted if he helped her travel to the Dignitas clinic as her multiple sclerosis worsened. When the DPP refused to do this, she went to court, and the House of Lords backed her: the DPP had 'a duty to clarify his position', and must 'promulgate an offence-specific policy identifying the facts and circumstances which he would take into account in deciding' whether to prosecute.[58]

The DPP then published a *Policy for Prosecutors in Respect of Cases of Encouraging or Assisting Suicide*, listing sixteen 'public interest factors tending in favour of prosecution', and six 'tending against prosecution' (paras. 43, 45). This certainly enables those contemplating giving assistance to another's suicide to predict whether they will face prosecution: someone who, acting from compassion and without any prospect of material gain, provided modest help to another who was bent on suicide could be confident that he would not be prosecuted.

What is much less clear, however, is just how the grounds for not prosecuting should be interpreted. Is non-prosecution an exercise of mercy towards those who commit the crime in such difficult circumstances, and who are no

---

[56] As the *Code for Crown Prosecutors* allows: para. 4.12(g).   [57] Suicide Act 1962, s. 2.
[58] R *(Purdy)* v. *Director of Public Prosecutions* [2009] 3 WLR 403; see Antony Duff, 'Criminal Responsibility and the Emotions', *Inquiry* 58 (2015), 189.

doubt still afflicted by grief for the loved one whom they helped? Or does it mark a recognition of compassion as a kind of excuse, similar in its logic to duress – that compassion, in such circumstances, can have a compelling effect that negates or radically mitigates culpability? Or is it an application of a *De Minimis* test – that such assistance, though it satisfies the formal definition of the offence, does not cause or constitute the kind of mischief against which the law is aimed?[59] That third reading, on which this kind of assistance is portrayed as not being (really) criminal, might not at first seem very plausible, but it is suggested by some of the Law Lords' comments in *Purdy*, which implied that the reason for requiring the DPP to publish his policy was to enable law-abiding citizens to work out what they may legitimately do.[60]

The third reading, however, highlights some of the problems of prosecutorial discretion in a democratic polity. The legislature has not just failed, but has explicitly refused, to enact legislation that would permit assisting another's suicide:[61] how could it be proper for the DPP to, in effect, legalise certain kinds of assistance? We might argue that what the law aims to protect is not 'the sanctity of life' as such, but such goods as autonomy and dignity – goods that are sometimes served, rather than violated, by assisting another's suicide. However, it would be impossible to enact a statute that allowed only those kinds of assistance, without creating risks of vulnerable people being or feeling pressured into 'requesting' assistance in dying; so the law must be defined in over-broad terms, and we must trust prosecutors to use their discretion to apply it only to cases that do involve the relevant mischief. If this is what the DPP is doing, however, he is doing it without the kind of explicit guidance from Parliament that is available in other cases;[62] how can it be proper for an unelected official to take on this kind of role in determining the 'real' meaning or purpose of criminal legislation?

More generally, how can the exercise of the kind of discretion I have argued prosecutors should exercise be consistent with the values of a democratic polity? They must, on this account, sometimes determine whether conduct that formally satisfies the definition of a criminal offence really does produce the kind of mischief at which the law is aimed; they must decide whether it is

---

[59] See at nn. 34, 44 above.

[60] See, e.g., [2009] 3 WLR 403 at paras. 40 (Lord Hope), 59 (Lady Hale), 83–6 (Lord Brown). Similar remarks can be found in the later case of *Nicklinson v. Ministry of Justice* [2015] AC 657, concerning the position of healthcare professionals who might assist a suicide – though in both cases, the court was also at pains to insist that it was not for the DPP, or for the court, to change the law on assisted suicide.

[61] Most recently when the House of Commons rejected the Assisted Dying (No. 2) Bill in September 2015, by a large majority (of 212).

[62] See at nn. 32–4 above.

in 'the public interest' to prosecute someone who can be proved to have committed a criminal offence – a decision which is surely political rather than legal, but how can a democracy allow such officials such power?

5 PROSECUTORIAL ACCOUNTABILITY: TO WHOM, AND HOW?

Discretion is most troubling not only when it is un- or under-constrained, but when it is unaccountable. The discretion that prosecutors should, I have argued, enjoy is constrained,[63] but is still troubling unless they can be appropriately accountable for their exercise of it. So we must ask what kinds of accountability are appropriate to a democratic polity. As noted above,[64] we should resist the temptation to think that the only accountability appropriate to a democracy is democratic accountability through the ballot box, making the post of prosecutor an elected office. In a system in which prosecutors are elected, and prospects of any systemic reform are slim, the electoral process might, in the short term, 'present[] the best opportunity for holding prosecutors accountable';[65] but given the familiar pressures and distortions of electoral politics, we would in principle do better to seek other modes of accountability for prosecutors. The modes of accountability available and appropriate for prosecutors (and other criminal justice officials) in a democracy are indeed the same as those that are available and appropriate for other public officials whose decisions can have seriously adverse impacts on people: tax and immigration officers, for instance, and those dealing with welfare eligibility. I will mention some of these briefly, since they are described in more detail elsewhere in this volume,[66] before focusing on an issue that has a particular significance for prosecutors.

Individual prosecutors are accountable within their profession.[67] The prosecuting service can be held accountable for its policies and general practices by an inspectorate, and by the legislature. Prosecutors can, in limited ways, be called to account by individual citizens: in England, victims can seek an independent review of decisions not to prosecute;[68] and anyone with standing can seek judicial

---

[63] It is a species of what Dworkin called 'weak', as opposed to 'strong' discretion: they are bound by standards that are not of their own making; but the application of the standards requires judgment. See Ronald Dworkin, 'The Model of Rules I', in Dworkin, *Taking Rights Seriously*, 2nd ed. (London: Duckworth, 1978), 14.

[64] See at n. 39 above.

[65] Angela Davis in this volume, p. 209; see also David Alan Sklansky, 'The Changing Political Landscape for Elected Prosecutors', *Ohio State Journal of Criminal Law* 14 (2016).

[66] See especially the chapters by Dan Richman (s. III), William Simon, Mathilde Cohen, and Shawn Boyne.

[67] See Ashworth and Redmayne, *The Criminal Process*, 181–3, 220–3.

[68] See www.cps.gov.uk/victims_witnesses/victims_right_to_review/index.html.

review of prosecutorial decisions about policies for particular types of crime, and about particular cases. Two questions about such provisions are, first, who should have the standing to seek judicial review – should it only be the victim, at least when the review sought is of an individual decision, or should any concerned citizen have standing on the grounds that crimes, as public wrongs, are every citizen's business?[69] Second, what standard should the court apply in reviewing the decision? English courts are reluctant to interfere with prosecutorial discretion: an application can succeed only if the court finds the prosecutor's decision to be one that no reasonable prosecutor would have adopted.[70]

It is of course hard for complainants to mount applications for review without knowing the prosecutor's reasons for adopting the policy or making the decision, which opens the way to a further, less institutional mode of accountability. If a prosecutor publishes her reasons for her decisions, this is a way of 'accounting' for those decisions.[71] A problem with this practice is that it can expose those about whom decisions are made to public prejudice: if a prosecutor explains why she decided, on public interest grounds, not to prosecute this person, others will take it that the evidential test is satisfied, and that the person is probably guilty of the offence.

If we consider prosecutorial policies, rather than individual decisions, other modes of accountability are available. Policies can be subject to ex-ante public consultation;[72] and it is of course open to legislatures to enact statutes that overturn a prosecutorial policy.

One could envisage other modes of extra-systemic accountability that would introduce a more directly democratic dimension. If we are serious about participatory democracy, and if we take seriously the idea that the criminal law is our law, why should prosecutors not have to (if challenged) explain their decisions at meetings of concerned citizens? This would avoid the problems inherent in electing prosecutors, since it would involve deliberation rather than simple voting. But it raises larger issues about the proper way for a democracy to organise its criminal law. How far should we try to insulate criminal law and penal policy from direct political or popular influence, given familiar worries about 'penal populism'?[73] A related question

[69]   See *R v. Metropolitan Police Commissioner ex parte Blackburn (No.1)* [1969] 2 QB 118.
[70]   *Associated Provincial Picture Houses v. Wednesbury Corporation* [1948] 1 KB 223.
[71]   Thus the DPP has published the reasons for not prosecuting in some cases of (apparent) assisted suicide: www.cps.gov.uk/search.asp?mode=allwords&search=suicide&submit. x=0&submit .y=0&submit=Search.
[72]   As the DPP does in England: www.cps.gov.uk/consultations/index.html.
[73]   See Nicola Lacey, *The Prisoners' Dilemma: Political Economy and Punishment in Contemporary Democracies* (Cambridge: Cambridge University Press, 2008). See also Pettit's discussions of the importance of 'contestation' in a republican democracy: Philip

concerns the extent to which prosecutorial policies can be local. If prosecutors are, in theory, applying a criminal law that is the common law of the whole polity, how far are they entitled to attend to the more local concerns of particular communities in determining 'the public interest'? I cannot pursue these issues here, but want instead to turn to a different aspect of prosecutorial accountability, accountability to the person facing prosecution, and to the issue this raises in societies that are not merely non-ideal, but systemically unjust.

Penal theorists ask whether it is possible to do penal justice in contexts of social injustice: should the fact that defendants in criminal courts have suffered serious social injustice render it illegitimate to convict or punish them? A background assumption is that we cannot theorise criminal law in isolation from those broader political structures of which it is part: in asking whether the conviction and punishment of a defendant is just, we cannot attend simply to the criteria specified within the criminal law, but must also attend to the relationship between that structure and its wider context. Discussions of this issue often focus on whether the victims of such injustice have any obligation to obey the laws of the society that wrongs them, or on whether such background social injustice should constitute a justification or an excuse.[74] But a further question concerns the standing of the court, and of the polity in whose name it acts, to call such defendants to account.

The criminal process is a process of calling to account or answer: the defendant is called to answer to his fellow citizens, as a responsible citizen, through the court. Responsibility and answerability are relational concepts: we are responsible *to* specifiable people or bodies who have the standing to call us to account.[75] The importance of this point for criminal trials can be shown by considering a defendant who challenges the legitimacy of the trial by arguing that he is not responsible to, or answerable before, this court.

There are various legally recognised grounds on which a defendant can demand not just an acquittal, but dismissal of the case:[76] bars to trial given which the court can neither convict nor acquit him, because it cannot try him. Some concern whether this court has jurisdiction, i.e. whether it has the legal standing to try him, but we should also recognise the possibility of an extra-legal challenge of this kind – a challenge to the political or moral authority of the court to try him. Suppose a defendant comes from a distinctive racial or

Pettit, *Republicanism: A Theory of Freedom and Government* (Oxford: Oxford University Press, 1997), 183–200; *On the People's Terms*, 215–8, 225–9.

[74] See William Heffernan and John Kleinig (eds), *From Social Justice to Criminal Justice: Poverty and the Administration of Criminal Law* (Oxford University Press, 2000).

[75] See further Duff, *Answering for Crime*, ch. 1.   [76] See Duff, *Answering for Crime*, ch. 8.

religious group that has suffered, and still suffers, systematic kinds of social injustice which amount, in effect, to excluding their members from many of the rights and benefits of citizenship: a group whose members have not been treated with equal concern and respect by their fellow citizens or by the state; even if they are willing to look their fellow citizens confidently in the eye as equals, they find that their fellows in the more dominant groups are not willing to look them in the eye with a respectful recognition of fellowship.[77] He now finds himself on trial – summoned to answer, to his fellow citizens, on a charge of public wrongdoing. He might properly reply to the summons not by answering to the charge, or answering for his conduct, but rather by challenging the court's right, and the polity's right, thus to call him to account; the polity that has so far failed, and continues to fail, to treat him as a citizen, cannot legitimately now call him to answer, as a citizen to his fellows.[78]

If this challenge is sound, it appears to present the prosecutor with problems familiar to any official in an unjust political system.[79] She cannot simply say that this is not her concern, that she need only attend to her role within the criminal justice system: for what is challenged is the justice of that system, and thus of her role in it. Should she nonetheless continue to do her prosecutorial job, on the grounds that although the present system is unjust, there is as yet no practicable alternative? Or should she resign, or refuse to prosecute such cases as an act of civic disobedience? Or should she seek to subvert the system from within? Or could she argue that, since injustice cannot be in 'the public interest', she should exercise her legitimate discretion and decide not to prosecute in such cases? That might look like a route to legal and political chaos, but by attending to another aspect of relational responsibility, we can see both a way in which the prosecutor's position is more difficult than that of some other officials in unjust systems, and a possible (though challenging) way forward.

The responsibility relationship, understood as a matter of answerability, must (if it is to be one of equal respect) be two-way: if I claim the right to call you to answer, I must be ready to listen to, and perhaps be persuaded by, your

[77] There are many accounts of this kind of systemic injustice: for recent examples, see Michelle Alexander, *The New Jim Crow: Mass Incarceration in the Age of Colorblindness* (The New Press, 2010); Amy Lerman and Vesla Weaver, *Arresting Citizenship: The Democratic Consequences of American Crime Control* (University of Chicago Press, 2014); Joshua Page and Joe Soss, *Criminal Debts: Predatory Government and the Remaking of American Citizenship* (University of Chicago Press, forthcoming), on 'indentured citizenship'.

[78] See Antony Duff, 'Blame, Moral Standing and the Legitimacy of the Criminal Trial', *Ratio* 23 (2010), 123.

[79] See Kimberley Brownlee, 'Responsibilities of Criminal Justice Officials', *Journal of Applied Philosophy* 27 (2010), 123.

answer. I must also be ready to answer to you if you call me to answer – particularly for my demand that you answer to me. Now when we, collectively, summon someone to trial as a defendant, we must summon him as a citizen, to whom we still owe equal concern and respect: but that means that we must also be ready to answer to him, both for this demand that he answer to us for his alleged crime, and for our collective failure to treat him in other ways as a fellow citizen – for the social injustice that he has suffered and still suffers at our collective hands. This puts the prosecutor on the spot. Her role is to call the defendant to answer, in the polity's name; if he now demands, with justice, that the polity must also answer to him before it can hold him to account, what can she say?

She cannot deny the legitimacy of his demand; she cannot look him honestly in the eye and say that whilst he must answer to the polity for his alleged crimes, his fellow citizens are not answerable to him for the injustice he has suffered. Perhaps, however (and this is how the challenge of social injustice might generate an enriched account of the prosecutor's role), she can answer his demand in a way that restores the legitimacy of the trial. For what undermines the standing to call another to account is not merely the fact of having wronged him, but that fact *together with* a refusal to answer to him for that wrong. We can thus restore our standing to call to account a defendant who has suffered serious injustice at our collective hands if we can show a readiness to answer to him for that injustice; we can then look him in the eye as a fellow citizen to whom we stand in the appropriate relationship of mutual responsibility.

Why should this be part of a prosecutor's role? Because it is the prosecutor who demands that the defendant answer to the polity, by charging him; so it falls naturally to her to answer his counter-demand that the polity answer to him. Now it would be relatively easy to answer that demand if she could simply appeal to a constitutional division of labour, and of the fora in which different kinds of demand are to be made and answered. She could simply say that while the polity should be ready to answer to the defendant for the social injustice that he has suffered, the criminal court is not the appropriate forum for such answering: the court's job is to deal with the particular charge that he faces; there are other fora, those of political life and activity, in which the polity can be called to account for such injustices. There would be force to this reply if, but only if, the defendant did have effective access to such fora; if, but only if, he could be told that the polity is ready to answer, or is already answering, to him in ways that recognise and address the injustices that he has suffered. But suppose that (as seems likely in our present situations) such a 'division of labour' answer cannot be honestly given, that the prosecutor cannot assure the defendant that there are effective fora outside the court in which he can pursue his challenge: what then could she say?

Suppose that we do not believe that the polity is so corrupted by systemic injustice that it cannot now claim to operate a legitimate system of criminal law at all; suppose we think that we must maintain a system of criminal law, even though the preconditions of social justice on which it depends for its legitimacy are not satisfied, and that we cannot simply exempt from the criminal process alleged offenders who have suffered systematic injustices;[80] how can we render the criminal process even imperfectly legitimate in relation to such alleged offenders? Only, it seems, by providing some way within the trial process for the defendant's challenge to be not only heard, but also responded to – a response that must be more than empty words. Since it is the prosecutor who, in our collective name, calls the defendant to answer, it should be the prosecutor who initially makes that response (though the court, which passes judgment and, if the defendant is convicted, passes sentence, will also need to affirm the response). But how could this be done – given that the court lacks the power to begin materially to remedy the systemic injustices that ground the defendant's challenge? At the least, what is needed is a formal, public recognition of the relevance of the defendant's challenge, an explanation of why the trial must still go ahead, and an indication of what the court can and should do – in its judgment, in sentencing, and in what it publicly says – to address the challenge. The voice of the defendant who wants to challenge the trial's legitimacy must be heard, whether he speaks for himself or through counsel, and it must be responded to by those who claim to speak for the polity – responded to in a way that shows it to be taken seriously.

One objection to such a suggestion is that it would privilege defendants over others who have suffered similar injustices – in particular, perhaps, the victims of the crimes with which the defendants are charged, who have often themselves been excluded from full citizenship in the same way as the defendants.[81] Such an objection would have real force if I was presenting the criminal trial as *the* forum in which such matters of social injustice should be addressed, but that is not my suggestion. A polity does need to provide fora in which citizens, especially those who suffer serious injustice, can make their voices heard, and can pursue real change, but the criminal trial is not such a forum. The criminal trial has a limited (but, I have argued, important) role as the forum in which alleged public wrongdoers are called to answer. It must also then allow those who are thus called to answer to answer by querying its legitimacy,

---

[80] See Antony Duff, *Punishment, Communication and Community* (Oxford University Press, 2001), ch. 5.

[81] Thanks to Dan Richman for this objection.

not because this is the best or most appropriate forum in which to discuss issues of social justice, but because when we call someone to answer, we must be ready to listen to his answer, and, if necessary, to answer to him.

The other initial objection to my suggestion is that this kind of procedure would be quite inadequate as a way of addressing or responding to the systemic injustice that so many of the defendants in our criminal courts have suffered: it might provide a ritual of recognition and acknowledgement, but such rituals lack the kind of material and political power that is really needed.[82] In one way, this objection is well-founded: the kind of systemic injustice with which we are concerned here cannot be remedied or lessened by this kind of addition to the criminal trial. But we should not expect such remedies to flow from the criminal trial; this is one of the many ways in which the criminal law and the criminal process can play only a limited role in the life of a polity, and can be expected to achieve only very limited goals. It is also true that this kind of ritual could easily be or become a *mere*, empty ritual. Prosecutors would develop a standard script for responding to such defendants' claims; the words would be said, but they would not be taken seriously, and would not connect to any changes outside the courtroom.

Nonetheless, first, rituals *can* be taken seriously, and can (if connected to genuine efforts towards material change) play a significant role in the life of a polity: they can display and (re)affirm a collective recognition of important values – and, especially in the context of the criminal law and the criminal trial, a recognition of civic fellowship.[83] Second, to emphasise a point made earlier, the reason for suggesting such a ritual is not that this is a particularly good way of addressing the problems of social injustice – it is not; the reason is rather that if the trial is to have even an imperfect legitimacy as a process through which a citizen is called to answer to his fellows, it must give the defendant space to object that the polity lacks the standing thus to call him to answer.

Much more would need to be said (much more than I can say here) to flesh out this so-far gestural suggestion. I will conclude with just three comments.

First, to say that the defendant must be able to object to the trial in this way, and that such objections must be heard and responded to, is not to say that they must always be accepted as justified: sometimes the objection will be ill-founded, or at least arguable, and the prosecutor must have the right to respond accordingly. We should not expect the court to settle the issue by

---

[82] Thanks to Sharon Dolovich and Máximo Langer for pressing this objection.

[83] Compare Shadd Maruna, 'Reentry as a Rite of Passage', *Punishment and Society* 13 (2011), 3, on how those who have served prison terms can be welcomed back, both materially and symbolically.

determining whether this defendant has suffered such injustice that the legitimacy of his trial is undermined, but, I have been suggesting, what affirms or restores the trial's legitimacy is the very fact that the objection is seriously heard.

Second, if we ask what more the court might be able to do, if such an objection is raised and is not manifestly unfounded, we might think of other institutional possibilities outside the criminal process: for instance, the creation of a Social Justice Commission to which claims of injustice of this kind could be referred by the criminal courts, thus providing a more effective forum in which such claims can be made and explored.

Third, I have said nothing about whether or how considerations of social injustice might figure in sentencing, since my focus has been on the prosecutorial rather than the sentencing role. Sometimes, of course, the unjustly disadvantaged context from which the crime flowed constitutes an ordinary mitigating factor,[84] as qualifying either the seriousness of the crime or the culpability of the offender: but even when this is not so, even when such injustice is cited not as a mitigating factor, but as undermining the legitimacy of the trial, the court might show its recognition of the force of a defendant's objections by reducing his sentence. Since we collectively have less right, or less certain standing, to call the defendant to answer in this way, we should mark our recognition of this by imposing a less severe sentence. However, I cannot discuss this possibility further here.

The final part of this chapter has been speculative and gestural, but the problem it addresses is one that we cannot avoid when we discuss the role of prosecutors in a democracy. For they cannot, I have argued, be seen simply as functionaries whose job is to apply the criminal law as they find it, and prosecute those whose conduct seems to satisfy the law's formal offence definitions. They must sometimes ask whether the potential defendant's conduct did cause or constitute the kind of mischief at which the law is aimed – using their discretion to interpret the law in the light of the purposes that can be attributed to it. They must sometimes use their discretion to decide whether prosecution is in the public interest – or whether the demands of other public goods or values must in a particular case outweigh the demands of penal justice. And, I have suggested, they cannot ignore the question of whether the polity in whose name they speak and act really has the standing (political as well as legal) to call this defendant to account; they should be ready to answer, in our collective name, a defendant's objection that standing has been undermined by the systematic injustices that he has suffered at our hands.

---

[84] See Heffernan and Kleinig (eds), *From Social Justice to Criminal Justice*.

2

Accounting for Prosecutors

by Daniel C. Richman*

I INTRODUCTION

What role should prosecutors play in promoting citizenship within a liberal democracy? And how can a liberal democracy hold its prosecutors accountable for playing that role? While these fundamental questions, regularly posed of the police,[1] are asked all too rarely of prosecutors, answering them requires a lot of framing and bracketing.

Particularly when thinking about prosecutors, we ought not assume that manifestly democratic processes – say, elections – are the best institutional design for promoting liberal democratic values. Better to follow the policing literature,[2] start with those values – political representativeness, a commitment to anti-subordination or (as Ian Shapiro calls it) non-domination,[3] and due process of law – and then consider how prosecutors can promote them.

* Paul J. Kellner Professor of Law, Columbia Law School. Thanks to Alexandra Bowie, Shawn Boyne, Devon Carbado, Beth Colgan, Angela Davis, Sharon Dolovich, Antony Duff, Michael Farbiarz, Robert Ferguson, Michael Graetz, Remy Grosbard, Kevin Grossinger, Jackie Hodgson, Olati Johnson, David Kessler, Máximo Langer, Adriaan Lanni, Jen Laurin, Jerry Lynch, Ed Rubin, Sarah Seo, Ian Shapiro, William Simon, David Alan Sklansky, Eric Talley, Sherrod Thaxton, Loic Waquant, and attendees at the 2016 UCLA Prosecutors and Democracy Workshop and a Columbia Law School workshop.

[1] See Diarmaid Harkin, Simmel, *The Police Form and the Limits of Democratic Policing*, 55 Brit. J. Criminol. 730–46 (2015); see also Andy Aitchison, Jarrett Blaustein, *Policing for Democracy or Democratically Responsive Policing? Examining the Limits of Externally Driven Police Reform*,10 Eur. J. Criminol., 496 (2013).

[2] See Trevor Jones, Tim Newburn, & David J. Smith, *Policing and the Idea of Democracy*, 36 Brit. J. Criminol. 182 (1996); see also Peter K. Manning, *Democratic Policing in a Changing World*, 7 (2010) (suggesting that idea that police should be "part of producing a democratic state ... is getting the entire argument backward. It is a democratic state and culture that produce democratic policing and, and there is no evidence that the contrary can result").

[3] Ian Shapiro, *Democratic Justice* (1999); see also Ian Shapiro, *The Real World of Democratic Theory* (2011).

But first comes the challenge of avoiding parochialism when identifying what prosecutors do. Are they freewheeling political actors exercising judicially unreviewable discretion? Subordinated functionaries exercising highly scrutinized professional judgment? Prosecutors play extraordinarily varied roles across liberal democracies, linked only by some shared duty to assess the fitness of criminal cases for adjudication and to shepherd fit cases through the process. Anne van Aaken usefully sets out the basic role of a "procuracy":

> (i) it has the competence to gather information on the behavior of criminal suspects, or to instruct the police to gather more information; (ii) on the basis of that information it has the competence to indict a suspect; (iii) during a trial it represents the interests of the public.[4]

These officials are variously housed in the executive, the judiciary, or a distinct branch of government,[5] but functionally they occupy the space between "police" and "courts."

This intermediary role provides a methodological point of departure. Others have focused on the police when exploring how democratic criminal justice institutions must "balance the goals of coercion and responsiveness," protecting the citizenry while "still maintaining the core conditions of democracy."[6] To the extent that policing relies on the promise or threat of criminal adjudications, the work on democratic policing by David Bayley, David Alan Sklansky, Peter Manning,[7] and others offers a valuable starting point for thinking about prosecutors. My goal here, however, is to peel off the distinctive contributions of prosecutors, distinguishing those from their subsidiary duties.

I will begin, in Part II, by considering the role prosecutors can play in constructing and sustaining democratic citizenship. This is a story about account giving and account demanding. Not only do prosecutors present narratives of criminality, but they are also uniquely positioned to hold those who exercise illegitimate power to account and to promote the accountability of other actors in the criminal justice system.

---

[4] See Anne van Aaken, et al., The Prosecution of Public Figures and the Separation of Powers. Confusion within the Executive Branch – A Conceptual Framework, 15 *Constitutional Political Economy*, 261, 264 (2004).

[5] Michael Tonry, *Prosecutors and Politics in Comparative Perspective*, 41 *Crime and Justice*, 1–33 (2012).

[6] Amy Lerman and Vesla M. Weaver, *Arresting Citizenship: The Democratic Consequences of American Crime Control*, 61 (2014) [hereinafter *Lerman & Weaver, Arresting Citizenship*].

[7] David H. Bayley, *Changing the Guard: Developing Democratic Police Abroad* (2005); David Alan Sklansky, *Democracy and the Police* (2008) [hereinafter Sklansky, *Democracy and the Police*]; Manning, *supra* note 2.

This vision of prosecutorial contributions comes with an expository bias, because it risks normalizing the outsized role played by prosecutors in the United States. One can counteract the bias by remembering to ask whether other state actors are better equipped, institutionally or as a matter of democratic legitimacy, to perform those functions. Yet, for better or worse (and especially because I would have it anyway), an American bias makes sense here.

To be sure, the American prosecutorial "establishment" has been the subject of extensive, and frequently well-grounded, criticism. Many, most notably Bill Stuntz,[8] have written about the "pathological politics" that have led legislators to delegate outlandish authority to U.S. prosecutors. Most outsiders (and many insiders) find the American reliance on elected or politically connected prosecutors odd, even ridiculous – a fact that itself highlights the varied and contestable "modes" of public accountability in this area.[9] Overshadowing all is also the extraordinary U.S. incarceration rate, which John Pfaff has convincingly shown to be driven, at least at the margins, by prosecutorial decision making.[10] Yet while no one is keen to admit borrowing anything from the United States in this area, the American model of the prosecutor as the effective and discretion-exercising gatekeeper of criminal adjudications seems to be spreading internationally.[11] So too is interest in pursuing the kinds of crimes – ranging from domestic violence to political corruption – that, as will be seen, the police cannot easily pursue without prosecutorial assistance that pushes beyond more limited notions of the prosecutorial role.

A final justification for normalizing a maximal conception of the prosecutorial role – at least as a conversational starting point – rests on my interest in institutional alternatives: to the extent that other regimes neither assign nor license prosecutors to play a role they can play in the United States, it would be analytically useful to hear who, if anyone, plays it and the rationales for that assignment.

---

[8] See William J. Stuntz, *The Collapse of American Criminal Justice* (2011); William J. Stuntz, *The Pathological Politics of Criminal Law*, 100 Mich. L. Rev. 505 (2001).

[9] See Michael W. Dowdle, *Public Accountability: Conceptual, Historical, and Epistemic Mappings*, 1, 14, in *Public Accountability: Designs, Dilemmas and Experiences* (Michael W. Dowdle ed., 2006) [hereinafter Dowdle, Public Accountability].

[10] John Pfaff, *The Micro and Macro Causes of Prison Growth*, 28 Ga. St. Univ. L. Rev. 1 (2012); see also John Pfaff, *Locked In: The True Causes of Mass Incarceration and How to Achieve Real Reform* (2017).

[11] See Erik Luna & Marianne Wade, *Prosecutors as Judges*, 67 Wash. & Lee L. Rev. 1413, 1531 (2010); see also Máximo Langer, *From Legal Transplants to Legal Translations: The Globalization of Plea Bargaining and the Americanization Thesis in Criminal Procedure*, 45 Harv. Int'l L.J. 1 (2004).

Part III turns to how a liberal democracy that relies on prosecutors to hold others accountable can ensure that prosecutors are themselves held to account. The accountability of prosecutors in a democracy certainly need not be achieved through direct elections. Indeed, one might argue that only prosecutors highly insulated from direct political responsibility can really promote democratic values. Still, notwithstanding Ed Rubin's Occam-like analysis of what "accountability" entails,[12] the breadth of my normative vision of what prosecutors should do keeps me from simply valorizing fine-grained bureaucratic control (of the sort one finds in France, Germany, and Japan – to name just three paradigmatic cases).

So then, how can I specify the optimal regime of prosecutorial accountability? I can't and don't want to. Once one recognizes the value trade-offs that must inevitably be made across institutional designs, optimality becomes elusive. A large part of the problem is that those features well suited to advancing one project won't be so well suited for advancing another. Jerry Mashaw credits Gunther Teubner with identifying the fundamental "regulatory trilemma": "We demand that regulatory institutions be simultaneously coherent (the rule of law or regularity norm), effective (a variant of the efficiency norm), and responsive (open to the influence of social demands and cultural understandings." Yet "virtually any attempt to reinforce one of these demands works to limit the capacity of the regulatory institution to satisfy another."[13] This dilemma looms large when one thinks about prosecutors. But accountability remains critical. After noting the limitations of specific accountability paradigms, Part III turns to cross-cutting institutional design and legal regime considerations that might, when balanced, foster the legitimacy without which prosecutors can't, and shouldn't be allowed to, do their jobs.

II CONSTRUCTING AND SUSTAINING DEMOCRATIC CITIZENSHIP

Before considering how prosecutors can shape society, one ought to first nail down the role of criminal law – the principal instrument of prosecutorial action – in a liberal democracy. Permit me to bracket this critical question, however, not just because of limited space, but in deference to Ricardo's Law of Comparative Advantage; I'd much prefer to stand on the shoulders of

---

[12] Edward Rubin, *The Myth of Non-Bureaucratic Accountability and the Anti-Administrative Impulse*, 52, *in* Dowdle, Public Accountability, *supra* note 9.

[13] Jerry L. Mashaw, *Accountability and Institutional Design: Some Thoughts on the Grammar of Governance*, 115, 154, *in* Dowdle, *Public Accountability*, *supra* note 9.

Antony Duff, Lindsay Farmer, and others who have done exceptional work on it.[14] For now, I assume that the penal statutes prosecutors enforce are within the range of possibilities in a tolerably well-functioning liberal democracy.

The focus here is, first, on the peculiar role of prosecutors in account telling and account holding, how they set the terms of effective criminalization and build narratives of criminality. Thereafter, I turn to how, in playing that role, they obtain a privileged vantage point within the criminal law enforcement system that allows them to make demands upon other institutions to promote the collective account-holding project.

A Constructing Effective Narratives of Criminality

In their distinct role as the translators of general penal provisions into particularized criminal charges, prosecutors both turn law into action and narrate the circumstances under which they hold defendants to account. Whether or not prosecutors see themselves as constructing democratic citizenship when doing so, that is a foreseeable result of their actions.

1 Turning Generalized Penal Laws into Action within the Courtroom

The mere passage of penal legislation can have a transformative expressive effect.[15] Moreover, one has only to look at cities where minor drug offenses, though not necessarily charged in court, structure the rationales for police activity on the street,[16] to see how criminal law can actively shape citizenship (i.e. who gets stopped and who worries that he'll be stopped) without adjudication. Yet whether because actual enforcement gives meaning to what otherwise would be empty legislative posturing, because the police eventually lose authority when the people they arrest never get charged, or simply because the formal characterization of a specific act or person as "criminal" is highly consequential, prosecutors – as adjudicative gatekeepers – potentially

---

[14] Antony Duff, "Responsibility, Citizenship and Criminal Law, 125–50," in *Philosophical Foundations of Criminal Law* (R.A. Duff & Stuart Green, eds. 2011) [hereinafter Duff, *Responsibility, Citizenship and Criminal Law*]; Antony Duff, *Discretion and Accountability in a Democratic Criminal Law* (in this volume); Lindsay Farmer, *Making the Modern Criminal Law: Criminalization and Civil Order* (2016); see also Sharon Dolovich, *Legitimate Punishment in Liberal Democracy*, 7 Buff. Crim. L. Rev. 307 (2004); Tommie Shelby, *Punishment, Condemnation, and Social Injustice* (unpublished draft) (discussing justifiable enforcement in an unjust society).

[15] See Dan M. Kahan, *Social Influence, Social Meaning, and Deterrence*, 83 Va. L. Rev. 349 (1997).

[16] See Amanda Geller, *Pot as Pretext: Marijuana, Race and the New Disorder in New York City Street Policing*, 7 J. Emp. Legal Stud. 591 (2010).

play an outsized role in translating criminal "law on the books" to criminal "law in action."

Given the absence of any stable transnational definitions of precisely who the police are and what they do, I suppose a prosecutor could play a perfectly serviceable role within a liberal democracy without adding more value to case-processing than a notary adds to a real estate transaction. All the action could be within the police, with the prosecutor simply filing formal charges selected and prepared by others. But the virtually universal reliance on lawyers to perform this gatekeeping function (at least for serious offenses) highlights the non-ministerial role prosecutors are expected to play in performing the translation function. As the link between the police and the adjudicative process, prosecutors are responsible for ensuring that a defendant gets the legal process that the law has deemed his "due" and that liberal democracies value at their core.[17] By proceeding against a defendant only where the evidence supports a charge and where other legal prerequisites have been met, prosecutors help ensure that the criminal law in action is faithful to the substance of legislated penal statutes and to the values underlying the larger criminal law project.

Such is the purely "professional" component of the prosecutorial contribution to the democratic order – "professional" in the narrow sense of law experts drawing on their training and experience to stitch together facts and determine whether they fit the definition of a crime.[18] Beyond that is a distinctively "political" component – "political" not necessarily in the sweeping sense of "policy-making," but in the more limited sense of playing an assigned role in a polity over and above the one a "mere" lawyer might play.

The extent and nature of that political contribution varies across systems, but inevitably entails a modulation of the penal sanctions that the legislature ostensibly mandated for provable conduct. For now, I will be open as to the nature, formality, or legitimacy of this modulation. Broad notions of "prosecutorial discretion" over what charges they need bring and against whom allow American prosecutors to effectively "define" criminal law to be well short of that ostensibly set by statute.[19] Conversely, through the cases they take and the way they frame the facts, American prosecutors regularly push the law beyond

---

[17] See Archon Fung, *Practical Reasoning About Institutions: Governance Innovations in the Development of Democratic Theories*, 2–4 (2006) (unpublished manuscript); see also Hung-En Sung, *Democracy and Criminal Justice in Cross-National Perspective: From Crime Control to Due Process*, 605 Annals, Am. Acad. Pol. & Soc. Sci. 311, 315 (May 2006).

[18] Hung-En Sung, *supra* note 17, at 315. ("A commitment to professionalism and respect for expertise provide the foundation for an increased insulation of criminal justice operations from political interferences and populist demands.")

[19] See Gerard E. Lynch, *Our Administrative System of Criminal Justice*, 66 Fordham L. Rev. 2117 (1998) [hereinafter Lynch, *Our Administrative System*]; Máximo Langer, *Rethinking Plea*

its initially assumed limits.[20] Elsewhere, to various degrees, one finds recognition of prosecutors' de jure or de facto ability to moderate the severity of penal consequences in the interests of efficiency, justice, or some combination of the two. Even where the "principle of legality" – as opposed to those of "opportunity" or "expediency" – is unmuted, distinctions in the zeal with which evidence is gathered and investigatory and adjudicative resources committed will exist (whether recognized or disregarded).

Whether authorized to or not,[21] prosecutors will inevitably shape the application of criminal law to the polities they serve and – to varying extents across regimes – write their enforcement agendas into the dockets they manage. They also may (or should) take a peculiar ownership in the punitive outcomes of their work. The police who apprehend a suspect surely have views on whether and how much he should be punished – views that prosecutors are bound to take into account.[22] I suspect, however, that, absent some immediate public safety issue, prosecutors, being far more involved in adjudication, take a greater interest in the *quantity* of punishment than cops, since granular issues of individual desert are more likely to have been developed in conjunction with judicial processes that follow arrest. Prosecutors' institutional proximity to the judicial process may also come with a special capacity to spearhead diversionary programs that reduce the punitive effects of police enforcement practices.[23]

The mediating effect played by prosecutors can have a social valence beyond advancing enforcement preferences and modulating punishment. To the extent there is any play in the adjudicative joints, they will also be able to exacerbate or mitigate the influence of racial, social, or political inequality on criminal justice outcomes. The nature of this capability will vary, as legal or institutional factors promote or undermine "blind justice." Particularly in adversarial systems (and again my U.S. bias shows here), the

---

    Bargaining: The Practice and Reform of Prosecutorial Adjudication in American Criminal Procedure, 33 Am. J. Crim. L. 223 (2006).

[20] See Daniel C. Richman, Kate Stith, & William J. Stuntz, *Defining Federal Crimes* (2014).

[21] See Paul Marcus & Vicki Waye, *Australia and the United States: Two Common Criminal Justice Systems Uncommonly at Odds*, Part 2, 18 Tulane J. Int'l & Comp. Law 335, 353 (2010) (noting that in Australia, concerns about "horse trading" in plea bargaining have spurred concerns that offenders "are not receiving their 'just deserts'").

[22] See Daniel Richman, *Prosecutors and Their Agents, Agents and Their Prosecutors*, 103 Colum. L. Rev. 749 (2003).

[23] Mary Fan, *Street Diversion and Decarceration*, 50 Am. Crim. L. Rev. 165, 181 (2013) (noting that "American diversion programs, like treatment courts, have largely relied on the decision-making of non-police actors further down the criminal processing timeline – especially prosecutors," but arguing for more police initiatives in this direction); see also Bronwyn Naylor & Adam Fletcher, *A Justice Reinvestment Approach to Criminal Justice in Australia* (March 2013).

quality of publicly provided defense counsel[24] may have determinative, cascading effects on adjudicative outcomes. Yet, whether prosecutors take ownership of the adjudicative process or are simply critical contributors to it, their work will have distributional effects that they can either consider or ignore. Indeed, because disadvantaged groups may simultaneously be both over- and under-policed, I use the term "modulate," rather than "moderate," as intervention can lead across cases to both more and less punitive outcomes.[25]

My use of "modulate" also reflects the dependency of prosecutorial activity on the work of other criminal justice components, especially the police and the courts. Perhaps one reason the scholarly literature has paid more attention to "democratic policing" than "democratic prosecuting" is that a lot of what prosecutors do is interstitial, dampening the zeal of some (units or individuals) and spurring others on.

2 Presenting Authoritative Accounts of Criminality

To maintain a transnational focus, I will not say much about how prosecutors can affect the imposition of punishment on those they bring into the adjudicative process. In the United States, of course – particularly where prosecutors have discretion over whether to bring charges with mandatory sentencing terms – their ability to shape criminal justice outcomes is at a zenith.[26] Even when prosecutors lack that formal power and when judges have sentencing discretion, prosecutors' control over the information that flows to judges and the extent to which judges defer to them can have a similar effect.[27] Suffice it to say that prosecutors who can control or substantially affect adjudicative outcomes will have a far greater influence on criminal law in action than those who are primarily gatekeepers.

Even when they act as "mere" gatekeepers, however, one ought not minimize how prosecutors shape democratic citizenship. Gatekeeping entails not merely the decision about putting criminal defendants "in jeopardy" and to what extent; it is also a pivotal part of the process wherein the state authoritatively

---

[24] A quality that itself may depend on prosecutorial political advocacy, see *infra* text accompanying notes 121–2.

[25] That such modulating efforts can come from police investigators as well is illustrated by the powerful story of a few Los Angeles homicide detectives committed to making "black lives matter." Jill Loevy, Ghettoside (2015). And I wouldn't be surprised to read similar accounts of dogged cops elsewhere.

[26] See William J. Stuntz, "Bordenkircher v. Hayes: Plea Bargaining and the Decline of the Rule of Law," in *Criminal Procedure Stories* (Carol Steiker, ed. 2003); Máximo Langer, *Rethinking Plea Bargaining: The Practice and Reform of Prosecutorial Adjudication in American Criminal Procedure*, 33 Am. J. Crim. L. 223 (2006).

[27] See José Cabranes & Kate Stith, *Fear of Judging: Sentencing Guidelines in the Federal Courts* (1998).

announces who is, after due process, to be treated as a "criminal." Indeed, it is through this condemnation that, as Emile Durkheim and others have pushed us to realize, a society defines itself.[28]

Moreover, prosecutors do not silently preside over gates, for the essence of their job is to explain *how* the law has been violated. As Jerry Mashaw has noted, inherent in the adjudication process is not just the application of norms, but the creation of them.[29] In addition to holding people accountable in the "modulated" process already described, prosecutors model accountability through the narrative that the law requires them to tell. Indeed, the very mechanism for holding defendants to account requires the presentation of a narrative (an account) that helps construct the socio-legal environment.

To be sure, in numbers and ubiquity, the police surely loom larger than prosecutors as civic educators. As Ian Loader writes: "The police send authoritative signals to citizens about the kind of political community of which they are members, the manner in which that community is governed, and the place they occupy in its extant hierarchies."[30] Yet we cannot ignore the way the adjudicative process – and not just its outcomes – teaches citizens about "the political world they inhabit."[31] It is not just the announcement of the charges – to which the political and institutional status of the prosecutor might lend special resonance and volume – but the manner in which the charges are proved: the evidence presented and the inferences urged.

Malcolm Thorburn has highlighted how, in contrast to criminal law theorists like H. L. A. Hart, for whom "the point of the criminal trial is simply to determine whether or not the accused deserves to be punished," Antony Duff has put the trial center stage. For Duff, "[t]he criminal trial is a place where members of a political community come together to engage in discussion about moral wrongdoing."[32] In a trial-driven world, Duff's dialogic account is thus particularly useful for distinguishing the distinctive contribution of prosecutors from that of the criminal law project more generally.

---

[28]   See Frédéric Mégret, *Practices of Stigmatization*, 76 J. *Law & Contemp. Probs.* 287 (2013); Emile Durkheim, *Division of Labor in Society*, 40–3 (W.D. Halls, trans. 1984).

[29]   Jerry L. Mashaw, *Accountability and Institutional Design: Some Thoughts on the Grammar of Governance*, 115, 130, in Dowdle, *Public Accountability, supra* note 9.

[30]   See Ian Loader, *In Search of Civic Policing: Recasting the "Peelian" Principles, Crim. Law & Philos.* at 2 (2014); see also Sklansky, *Democracy and the Police, supra* note 7.

[31]   Lerman & Weaver, *Arresting Citizenship, supra* note 6, at 10; see also id. at 111 (suggesting that "criminal justice contact rivals other more traditional politically socializing experiences and venues for civic education," and that "this socialization, unlike other interactions with the government, cleaves custodial citizens from the broader democratic polity").

[32]   Malcolm Thorburn, *Calling Antony Duff to Account*, 9 *Crim. L. & Philos.* 737, 744 (2015); see also Duff in this volume. Compare H. L. A. Hart, *Punishment and Responsibility* (1968).

Yes, I realize that in some countries (like mine), trials are rare. The truncated adjudication characteristic of plea bargaining often renders the authoritative information ostensibly promised by criminal proceedings thin and formulaic – sometimes with only a passing relationship to historical fact. A world without trials is thus one without much moral dialogue about wrong-doing. Of course in theory, the judge presiding over the plea allocutions and sentencings that replace trials could still ensure a "communicative interaction between the accused and his accusers."[33] Indeed, in Germany, where plea agreements are becoming more prevalent,[34] the Federal Constitutional Court recently demanded that judges push far beyond a defendant's plea-bargained based confession in order to determine his true culpability.[35] At least in the United States, though, the churn of business in busy courtrooms will likely turn the dialogues that Duff celebrates into generic scripts.[36]

Still, when there *are* trials or sustained judicial inquiries, the condemnation sought by prosecutors and the manner in which they seek it will probably have a texture and nuance that provide an instrument for social definition going beyond the "criminal" label. Whether conducted in an accusatory system or an inquisitorial system, trials have a performative and narrative aspect.[37] Particularly in an adversarial system, the prosecution's "case" ends up being a story it tells – a story that may draw on existing narrative tropes, but that inevitably reinforces, legitimates, and extends them.[38] What gets left out can matter as much as what is filled in, as happens, for example, when a prose-cutor, for ease of proof or because the extra sentencing exposure seems unnecessary, leaves out the bias aspect of what "ought" to be understood as a hate crime.[39]

---

[33] Thorburn, *supra* note 32, at 744.

[34] Regina E. Rauxloh, *Formalization of Plea Bargaining in Germany: Will the New Legislation Be Able to Square the Circle*, 34 Fordham Int'l L. J. 296, 297 (2011).

[35] Alexander Schemmel, Christian Corell & Natalie Richter, *Plea Bargaining in Criminal Proceedings: Changes to Criminal Defense Counsel Practice as a Result of the German Constitutional Court Verdict of 19 March 2013?*, 15 German L.J. 43 (2014).

[36] Kimberley Brownlee, *The Offender's Part in the Dialogue*, in *Crime, Punishment, & Responsibility: Festschrift for Antony Duff*, 54 (R. Cruft, M. Kramer & M. Reiff, eds. 2011).

[37] See Greta Olson, "Narration and Narrative in Legal Discourse, sec. 2," in *The Living Handbook of Narratology* (Peter Hühn, ed. May 2014) ("'Narration' in legal discourse most commonly denotes the contest of stories that transpires in adversarial or, with different actors, in inquisitorial trials."); see also Robert P. Burns, *A Theory of the Trial* (1999); Lisa Kern Griffin, *Narrative, Truth, and Trials*, 101 Geo. L.J. 281 (2013).

[38] Defense narratives can have similar effects. See Anne M. Coughlin, *Excusing Women*, 82 Cal. L. Rev. 1, 6 (1994). ("The battered woman syndrome defense rests on and reaffirms [an] invidious understanding of women's incapacity for rational self-control.")

[39] Avlana Eisenberg, *Expressive Enforcement*, 61 UCLA L. Rev. 858, 889 (2014).

Perhaps the prosecutor will construct a narrative not just of the "crime," but of the defendant. In common law countries, a prosecutor's move in that direction will be in tension with liberal criminal law's limited interest in delving the depths of personal culpability[40] and with rules of evidence designed to restrict fact-finder attention to the charged offense. At sentencing, however, broader inquiries may take center stage, and whether a prosecutor pitches the defendant as a citizen who erred or a miscreant who needs to be put away can (depending on the sentencing scheme) make all the difference.

Through trials, prosecutors can teach jurors, witnesses, and other lay (or official) participants about the fairness, or lack thereof, of the criminal justice process. Indeed, education through jury service is an oft-cited goal in Japan's recent (albeit limited) move toward the use of juries in the most serious criminal cases. There, the idea was "to incorporate sound common sense into the deliberative process, increase public understanding of Japan's judicial system, promote civic responsibility, and enhance the tools of democracy available to the citizenry."[41] Those attending (or merely attending to) the trial can also learn more case-specific "truths" about how the world works, lessons – about, say, who "really" is a victim and who "deserves" punishment.[42] The extent to which prosecutors drive this "educational" process varies across systems, as does whether it amounts to a real education or dangerous self-corroboration. Regardless, over time (and perhaps with media help), such stories will take a life of their own and shape social norms.[43]

Of course, defendants receive an education as well. As Ben Justice and Tracey Meares observe, "for an increasing number of Americans, the criminal justice system plays a powerful and pervasive role in providing a formal education in what it means to be a citizen."[44] The lessons that prosecutors

---

[40]   See Marie-Eve Sylvestre, *Rethinking Criminal Responsibility for Poor Offenders: Choice, Monstrosity, and the Logic of Practice*, 55 McGill L. J. 771 (2010).

[41]   Matthew J. Wilson, *Japan's New Criminal Jury System: In Need of More Transparency, More Access, and More Time*, 33 Ford. Int'l L. J. 487, 493 (2010).

[42]   See Candida L. Saunders, *The Truth, The Half-Truth, and Nothing Like the Truth: Reconceptualizing False Allegations of Rape*, 52 Brit. J. Criminol. 1152 (2012) (exploring judgments of U.K. front-line law enforcement professionals as to rape allegations); see also Louise Ellison & Vanessa E. Munro, *Turning Mirrors into Windows? Assessing the Impact of (Mock) Juror Education in Rape Trials*, 49 Brit. J. Criminol. 363 (2009).

[43]   For an extreme version of this larger social influence, see Adriaan Lanni's exploration of the effect on civic norms of trial speeches at Athenian trials. *Law and Order in Ancient Athens* (2016).

[44]   Benjamin Justice & Tracey Meares, *How the Criminal Justice System Educates Citizens*, 651 Annals, Amer. Acad. Pol. & Soc. Sci. 159, 160 (2014); see also Vesla M. Weaver & Amy Lerman, *Political Consequences of the Carceral State*, 104 Am. Pol. Sci. Rev. 817 (2010) (providing evidence indicating that criminal justice contact has a large, negative effect on voting, involvement in civic groups, and trust of government).

"teach" can go beyond the specific social norms implicated by the charged conduct. What a serious criminal prosecution amounts to, at least in the United States, is an effort to detach a defendant from society, not just as a physical matter, but as a political one.[45] These citizenship lessons reach, and affect the lives of, not just convicted defendants, but those around them.[46]

To what extent should a democratic prosecutor self-consciously promote the range of epiphenomenal externalities that attend a criminal conviction? When American prosecutors deliberately tease apart what ostensibly looks like a bundled conviction outcome – bargaining around immigration consequences for individuals,[47] or around the collateral consequences of corporate convictions[48] – are they circumventing legislative intent, or sensitively navigating a legislative menu? Even when prosecutors purport to stay within the four corners of their adjudicative assignment, should we encourage reflection on larger audience responses, or regret it? My instinct is always on the side of self-reflection, but Duff is surely right to worry about maximal self-consciousness at the individual level.[49] For now, let us simply recognize the social consequences of the prosecutorial project, whether appreciated or not.

B Holding More than the Usual Suspects Accountable

The point of departure for the foregoing section had the prosecutor deciding how to proceed when the police have presented her with a suspect. This

---

[45] Duff, *Responsibility, Citizenship and Criminal Law, supra* note 14, at 143 ("In penal theory, some argue that those who commit crimes lose their standing as citizens, so that we can treat them in ways in which we could not treat citizens, and deny them the respect and concern that we owe to citizens; such a view finds formal legal expression in the loss of the right to vote (a central aspect of citizenship) suffered during their incarceration by those serving prison terms in Britain, and for life by convicted felons in some American states."); see also Pamela S. Karlan, *Convictions And Doubts: Retribution, Representation, And The Debate Over Felon Disenfranchisement*, 56 *Stan. L. Rev.* 1147(2004); Loïc Wacquant, *Deadly Symbiosis*, 3 *Punishment & Society* 95, 112 (2001) (noting "convicts are subjected to ever-longer and broader post-detention forms of social control and symbolic branding that durably set them apart from the rest of the population"); Joshua Kleinfeld, Two Cultures of Punishment, 68 *Stan. L. Rev.* 933, 948–74 (2016) (exploring ways in which America has embraced exclusionary forms of punishment).

[46] See Traci R. Burch, *Effects of Imprisonment and Community Supervision on Neighborhood Political Participation in North Carolina*, 651 *Annals, Am. Acad. Pol. & Soc. Sci.* 184, 185 (2014). ("The criminal justice system has the power to shape not only the political participation of current and former felons but also the participation of the people who live around them because criminal justice interactions are demographically and geographically concentrated.")

[47] See Paul T. Crane, *Charging on the Margin*, 57 *Wm. & Mary L. Rev.* 775 (2016).

[48] See Daniel Richman, *Corporate Headhunting*, 8 *Harv. L. & Pol'y Rev.* 265, 278–9 (2014) [hereinafter Richman, *Corporate Headhunting*] (arguing for experimentation with sanction decoupling).

[49] See RA Duff, this volume.

section considers how prosecutors, because of their adjudicative function, are
uniquely positioned not simply to seek the accountability of those presented to
them, but to push beyond the frame the police have constructed and to
promote the accountability of others as well, including the police themselves.

1 Promotion of Police Accountability

The role prosecutors play in promoting citizen accountability may be complemented by their influence on the police – the primary point of contact for
citizens with the criminal justice establishment – as monitors and mediators.
One needs to be careful here, as there is tremendous variation across countries –
and within them, at least in the United States – on this potential contribution to
the rule of law and democratic accountability. Jacqueline Hodgson has
explored the limited degree to which the French procureur supervises police
investigations.[50] In England and Wales, it remains to be seen whether the
Crown Prosecution Service ("CPS") has the institutional capacity to push
police forces to build stronger cases.[51] In the United States, the lack of any
hierarchy that would oblige police to attend to prosecutorial preferences (or vice
versa) frequently leads to institutional disjunction, not coordination.[52]

Still, prosecutors' position as gatekeepers of the adjudicative process and
their unique ability to deploy both technical expertise and experience as
repeat players before ultimate adjudicators give them leverage to question
and perhaps change police behavior (at least across those police domains that
rely on the credible threat of adjudicative action). These sources of authority –
whether deployed or not – exist even in the absence of the sort of institutional
clout that prosecutors might gain from political independence (of the sort
wielded by elected district attorneys in the United States). They draw not just
on prosecutor's special knowledge and the reputational bonding that arises out
of their repeat-player status,[53] but on their legal training and acculturation.
Intermediation, after all, is what lawyers are trained to do – between clients
and courts or regulators, between clients, and across institutional cultures. As

---

[50]   See Jacqueline S. Hodgson, *The French Prosecutor in Question*, 67 *Wash. & Lee L. Rev.* 1361,
       1395–6 (2010); see also Jacqueline Hodgson, *The Police, the Prosecutor and the Juge
       D'Instruction: Judicial Supervision in France, Theory and Practice*, 41 Brit. J. Criminol. 342,
       350–1 (2001).
[51]   See House of Commons Justice Committee, The Crown Prosecution Service: Gatekeeper of
       the Criminal Justice System (Ninth Report of Session 2008–9) at 14–5.
[52]   See Daniel Richman, *Institutional Coordination and Sentencing Reform*, 84 *Tex. L. Rev.* 2055,
       2058–60 (2006) (discussing lack of coordination between police and prosecutors in New
       Orleans.).
[53]   Richman, *Prosecutors and Their Agents, supra* note 22, at 782–3.

Sklansky has suggested, intermediation lies at the heart of the prosecutorial function.[54]

Richard Mulgan explains:

> Forcing people to explain what they have done is perhaps the essential component of making them accountable. In this sense, the core of accountability becomes a dialogue between accountors and account-holders ... using a shared language of justification.[55]

The ability of citizens to directly hold police officers "to account" for their granular decision-making varies considerably across polities,[56] and changes with technologies (as has been seen with viral videos in the United States). Even so, the essential opacity of the criminal process substantially limits their ability to do so in even the most open democracies. Prosecutors, however, have a privileged vantage point. From there, they can force police officers to "explain what they have done" – how the arrest was effected, the investigation conducted, and the witness questioned. Even as the questions generally arise in a case-specific context, the answers (and perhaps the motivation for the questions) will often cut across cases. To be sure, the degree to which prosecutorial views – as supplemented by the views of other adjudicatory actors – are internalized by police forces may be a function of, among other things, the extent to which there is mutual dependence (what I have called "team production"[57]) and the political clout of each side. But prosecutors' potential contribution to overall criminal justice accountability ought to be recognized and extended, particularly where, as in England and Wales, the legal architecture is no impediment.[58]

2 Targeting Illegitimate Exercises of Power

Further consideration of the dynamics of interaction between the police and prosecutors should push us to think, not just about how prosecutors can promote police accountability across all case types, but also about how prosecutors can foster the pursuit of one subset of criminal conduct that they are

---

[54] See David Alan Sklansky, *The Nature and Function of Prosecutorial Power*, 117 J. Crim. L & Crim. 473, 502–04 (2017).

[55] Richard Mulgan, *Holding Power to Account: Accountability in Modern Democracies* 9 (2003).

[56] See Monica den Boer & Roel Fernhout, *Policing the Police: Police Oversight Mechanisms in Europe: Toward a Comparative Overview of Ombudsmen and Their Competencies* (2008); National Democratic Institute, *Democratic Oversight of Police Forces: Mechanisms for Accountability and Community Policing* (2005).

[57] Richman, *Prosecutors and Their Agents, supra* note 22, at 809.

[58] See Criminal Justice Joint Inspection, *Joint Inspection of the Provision of Charging Decisions*, 25 (May 2015) (reporting that, outside of the headquarters unit dealing with "the most complex cases," CPS prosecutors were often not giving or being asked for "early investigative advice").

peculiarly capable of addressing – the illegitimate exercises of power that disrespect the individual autonomy at the heart of liberal democracy.

Sklansky has powerfully argued that "'democratic policing' should mean . . . making the police as effective as possible in combating unjustified patterns of private domination and unthreatening as possible as a tool of official domination."[59] For their part, prosecutors can help free citizens from the subordination that is antithetical to a liberal democracy merely by avoiding illegitimate self-aggrandizement[60] and working with the police to shepherd appropriately made criminal cases through the adjudicative process. Yet prosecutors can do far more than that, and, should they rise to the challenge, can play a distinctive role in combatting illegitimate domination.

A great deal of regular police work can relieve citizens of illegitimate exercises of power. Any city dweller can tell you how the wide berth given to the menacing street tough narrows when a cop appears. Yet, some of the worst exercises of illegitimate power take more than a cop's quick glance to be recognized as such. These are situations where a prosecutor's slow second look can make a big difference in uncovering and pursuing these exercises.

Consider the difference between extortion and robbery. In a robbery, "the threat, the point at which the threatened act will occur, and the consent all happen around the same time. The robber says 'your money or your life,' and the victim, fearing immediate harm, hands over his wallet."[61] A police officer encountering this scene will quickly figure out what is happening, and if she can't, the victim will explain. Extortion is very different. Here the bad guy may say "make regular payments to me or I will hurt you and your family." When the victim pays, the transaction will look pretty ordinary; the police officer who encounters it will have no reason to think otherwise, and, in all too many cases, the victim won't explain.[62] Indeed, the worse – the more serious and the more enduring – the exercise of illegitimate power, the more "natural" the transaction will look and the less likely the victim will be to tell the police about it. Indeed, some "victims," might not even feel victimized, like those who make payoffs to public officials – payoffs that are ultimately included in the contract price, which in turn is often paid by the state and its taxpayers.

Then there are instances of private oppression that might occasion a call to the police and a response, but that won't make it through the adjudication process without special attention. This is the world of domestic violence, where, if a case

---

[59]　Sklansky, *Democracy and the Police, supra* note 7, at 127.

[60]　For a horrendous example of illegitimate prosecutorial domination, see Nancy King's story of *Duncan v. Louisiana,* in Criminal Procedure Stories (Carol Steiker, ed., 2003).

[61]　Daniel C. Richman, Kate Stith, & William J. Stuntz, *Defining Federal Crimes* 270 (2014).

[62]　Id.

ever makes it to trial, the defendant's chief witness will often be the victim herself, and the prosecution's case will have to be made through evidence collected with an eye to just such an asymmetric adjudication.[63] Avlana Eisenberg has found similar dynamics at work in hate crime investigations, where, in the absence of prosecutorial prodding, police officers regularly avoid considering motive, looking only to physical harm.[64] It is also the world of organized crime.

Perhaps every case of domestic violence, gang intimidation, or official corruption does not threaten democracy. But impunity does. These are the offenses where the harm goes well beyond the injury suffered from specific acts, and where the exercise of illegitimate power can cripple the ability of victims and those around them to flourish as individuals and citizens. Because what makes these exercises of power particularly insidious is that their illegitimacy won't be conspicuous to outsiders, these are precisely the cases unlikely to be successfully developed and pursued without prosecutors taking the lead.

Let me not overstate the point. Can one envision that the same kind of dedicated detective work that one sees in homicide dramas (pick your country), and sometimes in real life, can build domestic violence and hate crime cases and doggedly pursue organized crime and corruption cases? Of course, especially if one considers the wide range of institutional arrangements across jurisdictions and assumes the requisite resource commitments. Police departments with hate crime units are more likely to follow through on their institutional commitment to bias cases,[65] and the same dynamics can be expected with domestic violence, and perhaps even organized crime. Still, the pressures on police forces with patrol and crime control responsibilities are indefeasible, and all too often – particularly when murder has not occurred and victims are not complaining – come at the cost of the intensive police work needed to investigate crimes not in plain view.[66]

These are pressures that prosecutors are well positioned to counter and compensate for. There is evidence that they can do just that, if properly

---

[63] See Andrew R. Klein, *National Institute of Justice, Practical Implications of Current Domestic Violence Research,* 43–44 (June 2009); see also Jill Theresa Messing, *Evidence-Based Prosecution of Intimate Partner Violence in the Post–Crawford Era: A Single-City Study of the Factors Leading to Prosecution,* 60 *Crime & Delinq.* 238 (2014).

[64] Avlana Eisenberg, *Expressive Enforcement,* 61 *UCLA L. Rev.* 858, 885–6 (2014).

[65] Id. at 885; see also Jennifer Balboni & Jack McDevitt, *Hate Crime Reporting: Understanding Police Officer Perceptions, Departmental Protocol, and the Role of the Victim: Is There Such a Thing as a "Love" Crime?,* 3 *Just. Res. & Pol'y* 1 (2001).

[66] For a sense of how the pressures to do street enforcement drain intensive investigation resources, even in homicide cases, see Loevy, *supra* note 25; Jeffrey Fagan & Daniel C. Richman, *Understanding Recent Spikes and Longer Trends in American Murders,* 117 *Colum. L. Rev.* 1235 (2017).

supported. In the United States, studies have found that a combination of "no drop" policies and a high degree of coordination between police and specialized prosecutors is the key to increasing the success of domestic violence prosecutions.[67] In England and Wales, in the face of "disappointingly mixed reports about the extent to which [police] forces and the CPS are pursuing evidence-led prosecutions" in domestic violence cases, authorities have highlighted the gap between articulated prosecutorial needs and police investigative efforts.[68] In Germany, on the other hand, where an overwhelming proportion of domestic violence cases end up dismissed, a 2004 report faulted the police for not gathering adequate evidence and prosecutors for being too prone to abide by victim inclinations to drop.[69]

In domestic violence cases, prosecutors' unique competence lies in their ability to preserve what might be unstable evidence of criminal conduct, with an eye to the demands of an especially challenging adjudicative process. In cases involving more organized criminal conduct, their unique competence lies in their deployment of the adjudicative process itself to investigate and prove criminal conduct. Again, with due recognition of my American bias, I make only a provisional claim about how organized criminal activity and particularly corruption can most productively be pursued. The claim, though, is that enforcers can go after embedded criminal activity only if they can obtain closely held private information from those with their own criminal culpability, and that the only effective "currency" is leniency in adjudicative outcomes. Prosecutors' adjudicative role thus makes them necessary actors in this investigative process – which often will proceed in grand juries, the special province of U.S. prosecutors[70] – and their efforts will determine how high up a criminal hierarchy penal sanctions can go.

Certainly the use of deal-brokered accomplice testimony has become (for better or worse) a hallmark of U.S. organized crime and corruption prosecutions.[71] Indeed, my sense is that some of the interest in "American style"

---

[67] Klein, *supra* note 63, at 45.

[68] HM Inspectorate of Constabulary, *Everyone's Business: Improving the Police Response to Domestic Abuse*, 102–3 (2014). The interaction between police and prosecutors in domestic violence cases, particularly in the face of "attrition" has be the subject of sustained attention by U.K. authorities. See HM Inspectorates of Crown Prosecution Service and Constabulary, *Violence at Home: A Joint Thematic Inspection of the Investigation and Prosecution of Cases Involving Domestic Violence* (Feb. 2004).

[69] Federal Ministry for Family Affairs, *Senior Citizens, Women, and Youth, Working Together to Combat Domestic Violence: Cooperation, Intervention, Research*, at 17 (2004).

[70] See Daniel Richman, *Grand Jury Secrecy: Plugging the Leaks in an Empty Bucket*, 36 Am. Crim. L. Rev. 339 (1999).

[71] See Daniel Richman, *Cooperating Clients*, 56 Ohio St. L. J. 69 (1995); see also Alexandra Natapoff, *Snitching: Criminal Informants and the Erosion of American Justice* (2011).

prosecutions – in Brazil, for example – comes from a desire to replicate U.S. tactics in such cases.[72] And Shawn Marie Boyne reports that even in Germany, where "there is still widespread denial … regarding the use of 'confession agreements' in major crime cases," deals are regularly made and are of particular use in corruption cases.[73] She also notes that, even though most cases in Germany start with a police investigation whose matured fruits will only thereafter be sent to prosecutors, the very nature of economic crime and corruption cases requires considerable prosecutor–police cooperation from the start.[74]

Mind you, the claim is not that prosecutors are inherently white knights questing to relieve subordination in the home or on gang turf and ready to target those who would abuse the democratic process for private ends. Nor is it that criminal law is necessarily the best vehicle for furthering these goals. Rather, I merely suggest that if criminal sanctions are going to be used, prosecutors will have to play an outsized role in the process – certainly larger than the one they play in "regular" episodic criminal cases and at least as large as that normally played by the police. In contrast to street crimes, if prosecutors are not spearheading the pursuit of, say, corruption, those cases are unlikely to happen.

3 Prosecutors and Legislative Accountability

The accountability that prosecutors can bring to the police will play out at both the retail and wholesale levels. When a prosecutor questions the legality of an arrest or the sufficiency of the evidence the police provide to support formal charges, the iterated nature of this kind of case can lead to broader policy discussions or disputes. How about other branches of government? To what extent should prosecutors be able to hold legislators' feet to the fire on criminal justice issues?

In theory, were criminal justice outputs sufficiently valued and closely monitored by the elected officials responsible for constructing and funding the operative legal regime, a high degree of insulation from politics would not impair the democratic prosecutorial mission, and could indeed promote it. Not only is there always a risk of institutional self-dealing, but the separation of everyday politics from the administration of criminal justice can further rule-of-law values at the heart of democratic liberalism.

---

[72] See Will Connors & Luciana Magalhaes, *How Brazil's "Nine Horsemen" Cracked a Bribery Scandal*, Wall St. J. Apr. 6, 2015; see also OECD, *Phase 3 Report on Implementing the OECD Anti-Bribery Convention in Brazil* (Oct. 2014), at 40–1.

[73] Shawn Marie Boyne, *The German Prosecution Service* 138 (2013).   [74] Id. at 129.

When it comes to institutional self-dealing, the United States provides a dramatic object lesson. Many have noted how the federal Justice Department regularly proposes and shapes the legislative products of Congress.[75] Federal prosecutors also shape the effective scope of legislation through the cases they choose to pursue and the legal interpretations they promote through carefully chosen facts.[76] Yet more notable than the influence of one co-equal political branch on another at the federal level has been the sustained and successful efforts of local prosecutors to block and advance criminal justice measures in their statehouses. Michael Campbell, for example, has given a powerful account of how, between 1989 and 1993, Texas prosecutors blocked sentencing reform and pushed for prison expansion. He notes:

> Texas prosecutors were influential because they provided an important link between state and local politics, and because prosecutors have specialized skills linked to their position as legal experts and political actors. They operated as an important interpreter of popular demands, and as a powerful voice in opposing legal changes that would limit their discretion.[77]

That prosecutors – working within a plea-bargaining regime that allows them to use the threat of harsher sentences and expansive liability theories to induce defendants to give their trial rights – have endeavored to reduce judicial sentencing discretion is not particularly surprising, however regrettable.[78] More disheartening, at least from a democracy-promoting perspective, has been their opposition to (or simply tepid support for) the adequate funding for indigent defense schemes.[79] Prosecutorial involvement in the larger political process thus can come with real costs to liberal values.

---

[75]   See Rachel E. Barkow, *Prosecutorial Administration: Prosecutor Bias and the Department of Justice*, 99 *Va. L. Rev.* 271 (2013); Daniel Richman, *Federal Sentencing in 2007: The Supreme Court Holds – The Center Doesn't*, 117 *Yale L.J.* 1374, 1388 (2008) [hereinafter Richman, Federal Sentencing in 2007].

[76]   Daniel Richman, *Federal Criminal Law, Congressional Delegation, and Enforcement Discretion*, 46 *UCLA L. Rev.* 757, 762–3 (1999); see also Dan M. Kahan, *Is Chevron Relevant to Federal Criminal Law?*, 110 *Harv. L. Rev.* 469, 479–80 (1996).

[77]   Michael C. Campbell, *Ornery Alligators and Soap on a Rope: Texas Prosecutors and Punishment Reform in the Lone Star State*, 16 *Theoretical Criminol.* 289, 290 (2011); see also Jonathan Simon, *Governing through Crime* (2007) (arguing that "prosecutorial complex" has been the driving force in criminal justice governance).

[78]   See R. Michael Cassidy, *(Ad)ministering Justice: A Prosecutor's Ethical Duty to Support Sentencing Reform*, 45 *Loy. U. Chi. L. J.* 981 (2014).

[79]   For an insightful exploration of the political economy of indigent defense funding in the United States, see Darryl K. Brown, *Epiphenomenal Indigent Defense*, 75 *Mo. L. Rev.* 907 (2010); see also Lawrence C. Marshall, *Gideon's Paradox*, 73. *Ford. L. Rev.* 955, 961 (2004) (quoting a Georgia prosecutor "who opposed an indigent defense-funding measure on the

That said, prosecutorial insulation from the political process when those within it do not adequately attend to the health of the criminal justice system comes with a different set of costs. For a sense of these costs, one needs only to look at instances where the insulation of prosecutors has left them unable to prevent their work from being undercut, even nullified by political actors. Carlo Rossetti reports that in Italy, when a "tiny group of magistrates" brought major corruption cases, those just ended up on the long queue of cases awaiting trial, subject to legislated deadlines for disposal of cases that gave the targets of long corruption probes "de facto impunity."[80] In England and Wales, the CPS's lack of political clout has come with an underfunding that surely has system-wide effects.[81] The abuses of lobbying power ought not blind us to the role prosecutors can play as engaged and knowledgeable reform leaders.

III ACHIEVING DEMOCRATIC FUNCTIONALITY AND ACCOUNTABILITY

Having explored some of the ways in which prosecutors can contribute to a well-functioning democracy, one can easily jump to a number of basic questions. First, to what extent do we want prosecutors to play these roles? Second, are other institutions better suited to play each role, and why? And third, what institutional design trade-offs might both serve these goals and ensure prosecutorial accountability? I can't image any categorical answers to these questions, which all involve foundational political choices and require engagement with the entire socio-legal structure in which the criminal justice regime, and the prosecutorial establishment in particular, is enmeshed.

Yet once again, shielded by Ricardo's law, let me go straight to the third question. And on even this, I start with critical caveats that (I hope) excuse the level of abstraction (and, again, the American bias) with which I proceed. Even as I talk generally about institutional characteristics, I'll give scant attention to the precise institutional designs that generate them. This sweep is in part dictated by an interest in trans-jurisdictional breadth. But it is also dictated by a lack of

---

ground that 'it was the greatest threat to the proper enforcement of the criminal laws of this state ever presented.'"). For a burden-increasing proposal designed to recruit prosecutors to lobby for indigent defense funding, see Adam M. Gershowitz, *Raise the Proof: A Default Rule for Indigent Defense*, 40 Conn. L. Rev. 85, 119 (2007).

[80] Carlo Rossetti, *The Prosecution of Political Corruption: France, Italy and the USA – A Comparative View*, 13 Innovation 169, 173 (2000).

[81] See Owen Bowcott, *Crown Prosecution Service Chief Inspector Signals Concern over Funding: Kevin Mcginty Says Cuts Can Leave Agencies Unable to Function, amid Fears Criminal Justice System Cannot Sustain Its Schedule*, The Guardian, Sept. 23, 2015.

correspondence between de jure and de facto features of prosecutorial regimes. When trying to take "systematic stock" of prosecutorial independence transnationally, for example, van Aaken et al. found that the correlation between de jure and de facto indicia of prosecutorial independence (i.e. tenure and formal accountability to political hierarchs vs. actual forced retirements, and changes in legal foundations for the prosecution of crimes) was "slightly negative."[82] Indeed, they found a slight correlation between de jure prosecutorial independence and higher levels of perceived corruption.[83] And they suggest that "this finding reflects reversed causality: Due to gentle pressure to fight corruption, many governments have passed fresh legislation granting their prosecutors more formal independence. Yet, formal legislation often remains unenforced."[84]

Permit me, then, to provisionally speculate in general terms about the coherence of various institutional design features with the various democracy-advancing roles that prosecutors might play. Put differently, let me return to the question of how to promote democratic accountability for prosecutors within existing structures. I'll first note the limitations of specific accountability paradigms and then step beyond them to explore cross-cutting institutional design and legal regime considerations.

A Accountability Paradigms and Their Limitations

Mulgan has usefully set out several accountability typologies: "legal (external with high control), political (external with low control), bureaucratic (internal with high control), professional (internal with low control)."[85] Each of these, to varying extents and in varying combinations, has been extended to prosecutorial establishments. The United States is somewhat of an outlier in its reliance on fragmented authority and direct political accountability, with most liberal democracies relying on a mix of legal and bureaucratic mechanisms.

Does an embrace of the full measure of contributions that prosecutors can make to democracy necessarily imply preference for a particular kind of prosecutorial establishment and blend of accountability typologies? I'm not sure. Here, the "regulatory trilemma" identified by Teubner appears in the tradeoffs required when we balance regularity against effectiveness against responsiveness.[86] Consider the most dramatic project from Part II, the crusading prosecutor committed to curing democracy deficits by taking on

---

[82] Anne van Aaken, et al., *Do Independent Prosecutors Deter Political Corruption? An Empirical Evaluation across Seventy-eight Countries*, 12 Am. L. & Econ. Rev. 204, 220 (2010).

[83] Id. at 223.   [84] Id. at 229.   [85] Mulgan, *supra* note 55, at 31.

[86] See *supra* text accompanying note 13.

entrenched interests in government or at its periphery. The stuff of legends, movies,[87] and sometimes reality. Such a figure is unlikely to step out of a bureaucracy tightly tethered – by culture, hierarchy, regulation or some combination thereof[88] – to a central authority anchored in the political status quo.[89] One would not expect grand corruption to be a central interest of this bureaucracy, and in France (to take one example) it hasn't been.[90]

Move to a different project, and the analysis changes radically. Even when maximally pursued, grand corruption cases are but a small part of the prosecutorial diet. In most cases, the project of punishment modulation becomes most salient, and bureaucratic regularity has considerable appeal. Indeed, the very notion of a prosecutor playing a self-conscious democracy-promoting role may be anathema to those looking for consistency, professionalism, and compliance with positive law.

Even were we to select only for the crusading project, I'm not sure what the optimal prosecutorial arrangement would be. Rossetti attributes the zeal of the Italian judges and prosecutors who pursued corruption in the 1990s to their constitutionally secured independence, which "protects them from arbitrary interference by the executive and legislative branches."[91] DiFederico, on the other hand, questions the attribution of anticorruption zeal to the independence and low democratic accountability of Italian prosecutors, noting that prosecutors were similarly insulated during a long

---

[87] My favorite film example is the "examining magistrate" in Costa Gavras's Z. See Robert L. Waring, *Picturing Justice: Images of Law and Lawyers in the Visual Media, Z*, 30 *U.S.F. L. Rev.* 1077 (1995).

[88] Mirjan Damaška noted long ago that the real limits on prosecutorial discretion in Europe have come less from the external legal system but rather from internal organizational structures and norms – hierarchical, centralized supervision of the prosecutorial corps and a professional emphasis on consistent, uniform decision-making. See generally Mirjan Damaška, *Structures of Authority and Comparative Criminal Procedure*, 84 *Yale L.J.* 480, 503–4 (1975).

[89] See Anne van Aaken, et al., *supra* note 4 at 262 (noting recent scandals involving possible pressure by the executive on prosecutors pursuing corruption cases in Germany, Italy and Israel, and arguing that "[a] procuracy depending on the executive can not only lead to higher levels of crimes but can have far-reaching effects on the legitimacy as well as on the stability of the state").

[90] See Jacqueline Hodgson, *French Criminal Justice: A Comparative Account of the Investigation and Prosecution of Crime in France* 80 (2005) (noting that while the "historical accountability of the *parquet* to the Minister of Justice is claimed as a form of democratic accountability," it "also offers the potential for political interference in a way that does not guarantee, but undermines, the independence of the *parquet* and serves to protect favoured individuals from legal scrutiny"); see also Rossetti, *supra* note 80, at 174. ("In recent years French magistrates met with a number of difficulties and obstacles in cases involving the government, the public administration, and especially state-owned banks. Interference by the government prevented the magistrates from reaching the upper ranks of the government system implicated in a conspiracy to defraud the state.")

[91] Rossetti, *supra* note 80, at 169.

period of inactivity.[92] Indeed when prosecutors are too well insulated, citizen voices against impunity – a possible wellspring of zeal and democratic commitment – will also be muted. It was just such voices, from local anti-corruption groups, that prodded local prosecutors in Indonesia into action, according to a recent World Bank study.[93] (This is not to say that those voices were enough. The study also tells how local Indonesian anticorruption movements had trouble sustaining public pressure as cases inched through the legal process and how they had scant influence once cases moved up to the centralized appeals process.[94])

Fear not, appreciating how public pressure can galvanize prosecutors into action does not lead me to support prosecutorial elections, even in service of the crusading project. After all, the politics that drive prosecutorial elections will usually be those in which a corrupt elite is enmeshed. Even the pursuit of sex abuse cases within a specific community can fall victim to political expediency.[95] Whether or not the prosecutor has any further political ambitions (and an important subset do), virtually all will have political affiliations that give pause to those looking for magisterial purity. Even if one assumes that the claims of partisan targeting that will inevitably attend prosecutions frequently lack foundation, the risk that both real and perceived that criminal cases will be treated as an extension of partisan warfare is real, and has become a standard American trope.[96]

Indeed, I would go further and suggest that in the country where prosecutorial elections are the norm – to the understandable dismay of most domestic and comparative scholars[97] – embrace of them as instruments of democratic accountability and non-bureaucratic zeal has been at best half-hearted. Many have cogently argued that the dominant American approach offers the worst of all worlds. Because the elections are generally not seriously contested, they offer little in the way of accountability, yet the populism they inject into the process still impedes the thoughtful exercise of prosecutorial

---

[92]   Giuseppe Di Federico, *Prosecutorial Independence and the Democratic Requirement of Accountability in Italy: Analysis of a Deviant Case in a Comparative Perspective*, 38 Br. J. Criminol. 371, 383 (1998).

[93]   Taufik Rinaldi, Marini Purnomo & Dewi Damayanti, *Fighting Corruption in Decentralized Indonesia (World Bank Case Studies on Handling Local Government Corruption)*, at 8 (May 2007).

[94]   Id. at 8, 71.

[95]   See Ray Rivera & Sharon Otterman, *For Ultra-Orthodox in Abuse Cases, Prosecutor Has Different Rules*, NY Times, May 10, 2012 (reporting on Brooklyn District Attorney Charles Hynes's treatment of sex abuse cases within a Jewish community).

[96]   See Sanford C. Gordon, *Assessing Partisan Bias in Federal Public Corruption Prosecutions*, 103 Am. Pol. Sci. Rev. 534 (2009).

[97]   Michael Tonry, *Prosecutors and Politics in Comparative Perspective*, 41 Crime and Justice 1 (2012).

authority.[98] But it bears remembering that the idea behind the move to popular elections – widespread in the second quarter of the nineteenth century – was more defensive than offensive: to deflect efforts of governors and legislators to use appointments for political patronage.[99] Such defensiveness is somewhat of a theme across American prosecutorial establishments. In the federal system, for instance, the relative independence of appointed U.S. attorneys from the political hierarchs in Washington has been (regularly, but not always) fostered by Congress less in the interest of controlling the districts themselves than to prevent the President and his circle from exercising such control.[100] Note how this theme accepts and perhaps even reinforces a regime in which prosecutorial discretion is at its apogee. Rather than rein in prosecutors – through legislative specificity, closer judicial supervision, or binding executive guidelines – the institutional design project has been more to prevent the political deployment of the office by other hubs of governmental power. And that project has been hostage to contingency and history, as we discovered when President George W. Bush tried to cull his United States attorneys.[101]

It is hardly a defense of the American embrace of direct political accountability to observe that it furthers negative goals that are different from those ostensibly targeted. But in the end, my expository goal is also negative. I have simply taken a handful of many possible democracy-promoting projects for prosecutors and suggested why it may be difficult, even with that limited focus, to figure out the optimal institutional arrangements to promote them. I've considered only the choice between a politically insulated bureaucracy and elected political hierarchs. Just think how hard the equation gets if we also consider different doctrinal approaches to prosecutorial decision-making – "principle of legality" vs. the "principle of opportunity" – or different modes of fact-finding, adversarial vs. inquisitorial. One would then have to account for path-dependent and historically contingent traditions that foster institutional cultures. And then, if the goal is really to have a tournament of systems, one would have to look at the entire array of ways that prosecutors might promote

---

[98] See, e.g., Ronald F. Wright, *How Prosecutor Elections Fail Us*, 6 *Ohio St. J. Crim. L.* 581, 583 (2009) (noting, of elections: "First, they do not often force an incumbent to give any public explanation at all for the priorities and practices of the office. Second, even when incumbents do face challenges, the candidates talk more about particular past cases tha[n] about the larger patterns and values reflected in local criminal justice."); see also Russell M. Gold, *Promoting Democracy in Prosecution*, 86 *Wash L Rev* 69, 71 (2011). ("Lack of a meaningful political check on prosecutors diminishes popular sovereignty.")

[99] See Michael J. Ellis, Note, *The Origins of the Elected Prosecutor*, 121 *Yale L.J.* 1528 (2012).

[100] Richman, *Federal Criminal Law, supra* note 76, at 808–9.

[101] Daniel Richman, *Political Control of Federal Prosecutions: Looking Back and Looking Forward*, 58 *Duke L.J.* 2087, 2105–8 (2009).

democracy, opine on the efficacy with which each system promotes each goal, and devise some global means of balancing. Perhaps someone can actually do this. I lack the data, competence, and inclination.

So where does this leave us? Even as various states reassess aspects of their legal regimes and institutional structure, path dependency limits formal change – particularly in an area where informal adaptation is usually more convenient to insiders. If we are to be attentive to ways in which liberal democracies can support prosecutors, as well as vice versa, better that we speak of the principles that ought to guide change or stability across diverse institutional arrangements, rather than celebrate or condemn particular regimes.

B Principles Cutting across Accountability Typologies

When assessing the normative promise of institutional arrangements, we should heed Andreas Schedler's reminder:

> Holding power accountable does not imply determining the way it is exercised; neither does it aim at eliminating discretion through stringent bureaucratic regulation. It is a more modest project that admits that politics is a human enterprise whose elements of agency, freedom, indeterminacy, and uncertainty are ineradicable; that power cannot be subject to full control in the strict, technical sense of the word.[102]

Mindful of this counsel, I will offer a few modest principles with application across diverse prosecutorial regimes. Obviously incomplete, the list is, at best, a good first step.

1 Language of Rationality and Equality

At a bare minimum, those exercising power need to be able to explain themselves – give an "account" – to someone, somehow. There are also normative constraints on what those explanations can be – one being that the language sound in rationality and equality. Any prosecutorial establishment must, as Jerry Mashaw has put it, give "operational content" to the "public reason approach" that provides legitimacy to those "modern states characterised by both democratic aspirations and a heavily administrative institutional structure."[103] And the public reasons offered need to themselves be true to democratic values.

---

[102] Andreas Schedler, *Conceptualizing Accountability* 14, in *The Self-Restraining State: Power and Accountability in New Democracies* (Andreas Schedler, et al. eds. 1999).

[103] Jerry L. Mashaw, *Public Reason and Administrative Legitimacy*, 11, 13 in *Public Law Adjudication in Common Law Systems: Process and Substance* 11, 13 (John Bell et al. eds., 2016).

If, like Edward Rubin, one defines accountability "as the ability of one actor to demand an explanation or justification of another actor for its actions, and to reward or punish the second actor on the basis of its performance or explanation,"[104] we can easily see how a highly bureaucratic system, with line actors acting at the direction of and under the hierarchal control of supervisors who themselves are similarly accountable, can limit the reasons a line prosecutor may give and formally preclude the exercise of "discretion."[105] Yet the challenges of ex ante specification are endemic (though perhaps not unique) to penal systems and particularly great when the "principle of legality" requires the pursuit of every makeable case.

Canonical and bureaucratic restriction of the language of prosecutorial justification may thus drive the action underground, with mixed normative results. Consider Germany. As Shawn Boyne explains:

> [A] significant part of a German prosecutor's initial training involves one-on-one training in the art of documenting actions taken on a case file. Not only does this one-on-one training ensure that prosecutors accurately and consistently document the history of a case in the case file, the training systematically conveys the routines of organizational practice to newcomers entering the organization ... In theory, any prosecutor could pick up another prosecutor's file and immediately understand the case.[106]

Such documentation may come with risks of, indeed an invitation to, disingenuity. In a plea for more candor about prosecutorial discretion in Germany and elsewhere, Erik Luna has noted that "some European systems have ... preserved orthodox interpretations of the legality principle only by denying the existence of prosecutorial power."[107] This quiet opacity has upsides; Luna suggests that "mandatory prosecution" (a principle that Germany has relaxed only for low-level or juvenile cases[108]) – might be seen as a "necessary fiction" that "maintain[s] prosecutorial independence from the political process and [] protect[s] prosecutors from charges of arbitrary decisionmaking."[109] Yet Thomas Weigend properly notes how the

---

[104] Edward Rubin, *The Myth of Non-Bureaucratic Accountability and the Anti-Administrative Impulse*, at 52, in Dowdle, *Public Accountability*, at 9.

[105] See also Edward L. Rubin, *Discretion and Its Discontents*, 72 Chi.-Kent L. Rev. 1299 (1997).

[106] Shawn Boyne, *Procedural Economy in Pre-Trial Procedure, Developments in Germany and the United States*, 24 S. Cal. Interdisc. L. J. 329, 353 (2015).

[107] Erik Luna, *Prosecutor King*, 1 Stan. J. L. & Crim. Policy 48, 81 (2014).

[108] Boyne, *supra* note 106, at 339.   [109] Id.

move ends up shielding the prosecutor from personal responsibility,[110] with a consequent loss of even conversational accountability.

In such circumstances, perhaps bureaucratic accountability mechanisms can profitably be supplemented with political ones. In recognition of the democracy deficit endemic to bureaucratic hierarchies, the Venice Commission has noted the increasing use of "prosecuting councils" across Europe. It observes:

> If they are composed in a balanced way, e.g. by prosecutors, lawyers and civil society, and when they are independent from other state bodies, such councils have the advantage of being able to provide valuable expert input in the appointment and disciplinary process and thus to shield them at least to some extent from political influence. Depending on their method of appointment, they can provide democratic legitimacy for the prosecution system.[111]

If the characteristic fault of German prosecutors is to deny that there is any discretion to explain, that of American prosecutors – and it is probably more grievous – is to offer scant explanation for starkly discretionary decisions. Here, what can often be a substantial absence of bureaucratic accountability – particularly in county-based state systems, but to varying extents everywhere – is justified (such as it is) by reference to a political accountability far more direct than a "prosecuting council."

To some extent, the direct (or in the federal system, indirect) electoral accountability of U.S. prosecutors can lead to public reasoning about priorities and policies. But public discourse in the United States about prosecutorial choices is limited. The limited nature can be attributed to the opacity of the plea bargaining process; a doctrinal framework that frees prosecutors from ever explaining why charges were not brought;[112] and a lack of legislative specificity about cases that can be brought. Yet discourse is limited even for those cases that go to trial by evidentiary rules that preclude the presentation of a great deal of information considered in the decision to charge. Moreover, as anyone familiar with the "politics of crime" in the United States knows,[113] wildly swinging

---

[110]   Id. (citing Thomas Weigend, *A Judge by Another Name? Comparative Perspectives on the Role of the Public Prosecutor, in The Prosecutor in Transnational Perspective*, 391 (Erik Luna & Marianne Wade, eds., 2012)).

[111]   European Commission of Democracy Through Law (Venice Commission, Report on European Standards as Regards the Independence of the Judicial System: Part II – The Prosecution Service, Study No. 494/2008 (Adopted 2010), at 34.

[112]   See Daniel C. Richman, Old Chief v. United States: Stipulating Away Prosecutorial Accountability?, 83 *Va. L. Rev.* 939 (1997) [hereinafter Richman, *Old Chief*].

[113]   See Michael C. Campbell, *Are All Politics Local? A Case Study of Local Conditions in a Period of "Law and Order" Politics*, 664 Annals, Am. Acad. Pol. & Soc. Sci. 43 (2016);

electoral politics will often undercut the ability of prosecutors to promote reasoned local conversations (even when they are interested in doing so).[114]

Americans could, of course, ask more of prosecutors in the courtroom. Indeed, cogent arguments have long been made for empowering judges – as either a statutory or constitutional matter – to demand justifications for charging and plea bargaining decisions.[115] Formal authority in this regard might simply complement the soft power that trial judges frequently deploy – to various extents in various jurisdictions: the ability to sternly peer from the bench, say that the prosecutor "must be joking," and ensure that the prosecutor who "doesn't get with the program" regrets it. Yet the general reluctance of appellate courts and legislators to give judges de jure authority is not just a matter of separation of power formalism, but deep-seated (however contestable) concerns about institutional competence.

Would the accountability of American prosecutors be usefully enhanced if they no longer had absolute immunity to constitutional tort suits for conduct relating to their adjudicatory decision-making?[116] I suspect not, since only the most egregious and provably illegal conduct provides the basis for relief in suits when immunity is "qualified" – as it is for the police or for prosecutors acting in an investigative capacity.[117] I would also want a better sense of what the noise-to-signal ratio would be, were this litigation avenue opened up. That said, egregious prosecutorial conduct has occurred with sad regularity. At the very least, placing prosecutors on equal footing with the police and dispensing with the need to distinguish between advocacy and investigative work by prosecutors would eliminate the distortions in constitutional tort law created when the interconnectiveness of prosecutorial and police activity is ignored and when those seeking relief for wrongful convictions have to focus on police conduct.[118] Since wrongful conviction cases can spark reform outside the courts even when unsuccessful within them, it is particularly important to get the whole story across all relevant institutions.

Katherine A. Beckett & Theodore Sasson, *The Politics of Injustice: Crime and Punishment in America* (2003); Jonathan Simon, *Governing Through Crime* (2009).

[114] See Rubin, *supra* note 12, at 57 (on deficiencies of local politics as accountability mechanism).

[115] See Darryl K. Brown, *Judicial Power to Regulate Plea Bargaining*, 57 Wm. & Mary L. Rev. 101 (2016).

[116] See *Van de Kamp v. Goldstein*, 555 U.S. 335 (2009); Jennifer E. Laurin, *Prosecutorial Exceptionalism, Remedial Skepticism, and the Legacy of Connick v. Thompson*, in *National Police Accountability Project, Civil Rights Litigation Handbook*, 29–70 (2011).

[117] See *Stinson v. Gauger*, 799 F.3d 833 (7th Cir. 2015).

[118] See John C. Jeffries, Jr., *The Liability Rule for Constitutional Torts*, 99 Va. L. Rev. 207, 220–31(2013).

That electoral accountability may contribute little to public reasoning and courts may lack much formal power to demand rationales does not mean that American prosecutors are not subject to other, more sustained and granular pressures to explain their actions. As a descriptive matter, there are a variety of other accountability mechanisms that demand attention and that, as a normative matter, might be strengthened – mechanisms not unique to American prosecutors but, in absence of the top-down bureaucratic dialogue seen elsewhere, are of particular importance in the United States.

My claim is not that the mesh of networked institutions in which prosecutors in the United States (and perhaps elsewhere) do their work necessarily provides low-visibility channels for reasoned justification and democratic legitimacy, but that it can. Just as prosecutors can monitor the police, so too can the police monitor prosecutors and ask them to explain their adjudicatory positions.[119] To the extent that the police are, by structure or task, bound to the citizenry they serve, we should expect some of their accountability to carry over to prosecutors who depend on police work. Indeed, the lack of a hierarchical relationship between police and prosecutors, combined with their distinct professional cultures, might provoke more reasoned deliberation than otherwise. Sure, beat cops usually don't second-guess charging decisions, even when made by rookie (or overly jaded) prosecutors. But the iterated nature of their interaction, and their distinct chains of command, brings the possibility of a dialogue that may even enrich public debate.[120]

Iterated interaction between police and prosecutors is not unique to liberal democracies. The same creative tensions presumably arise in authoritarian states, without necessarily contributing to democratic accountability. What distinguishes the interactions in a liberal democracy is the nature of the institutions involved, with the possibility that police and prosecutors there have diverse political anchors that bring a dialogic richness (perhaps with expletives) to their conversations. What also distinguishes them is that, in an open society and a media interested in crime news,[121] these arguments easily spill into public discourse. Similar provocation for public reasoning may – for

---

[119] See *supra* section II.B.1; Richman, *Prosecutors and Their Agents*, *supra* note 22; see also Richman, *Federal Sentencing* in 2007, *supra* note 75 (explaining how the federal system is enmeshed in local systems).

[120] See Catherine M. Coles, *Community Prosecution, Problem Solving, and Public Accountability: The Evolving Strategy of the American Prosecutor*, 17 (2000) (giving example of Indianapolis prosecutor speaking of his rivalry with police department as democratic competition for community favor).

[121] For a nice taxonomy of media coverage and its limits, see Stephanos Bibas, *Prosecutorial Regulation, Prosecutorial Accountability*, 157 U. Pa. L. Rev. 959, 983–8 (2009).

some offenses – come from victims, should they get an adequate forum – whether formally in court (as in some continental systems) or less formally, in communities and the media.

Then there are defense lawyers. Notwithstanding the absence of strong adjudicative controls over prosecutorial decisions, one might also imagine that, in an adversary system, defense counsel might still do yeoman service in pushing prosecutors to explain, if not justify, their discretionary decisions. Indeed, Jerry Lynch has provocatively imagined a world in which plea dispositions emerge out of textured discussions that reflect a "common law" across cases.[122]

The last two paragraphs were pretty tentative, however, as was Lynch's insightful piece. Foundational to the accountability narratives just adumbrated are vigorous institutional players and what Mulgan called a "shared language of justification."[123] This means there must be thoughtful collaboration between police and prosecutors, fora where victims and affected community can listen and speak, and well-resourced defenders. If American prosecutors are to have a claim to democratic legitimacy through this networked accountability, these mechanisms need strengthening. The German prosecutor bound by the principle of legality will justifiably be hard-pressed to explain her exercise of discretion. The American prosecutor with sweeping discretion both as a matter of law and practice lacks this excuse. Yet, all too often, she deploys lame mantras of "prosecuting to the full extent of the law."[124]

Note how a key aspect of the American accountability narrative – and this is a common thread in all adversarial systems – requires prosecutors to exert their political power to support defense institutions, especially for the indigent, who comprise a majority of criminal defendants. The same independence that insulates prosecutors from other executive and legislative actors thus finds a modicum of justification when deployed to support a countervailing source of accountability, for the legitimacy of prosecutorial power in part demands that they be able to explain themselves to their adversaries. Moreover, the sense of a joint project cutting across legal roles promotes a professional accountability that cuts across cases. As Mulgan notes, professional accountability, while potentially flowing from formal disciplinary mechanisms, can also arise from the way members of a profession are "answerable to each other through shared networks and collegial relationships."[125]

---

[122] See Lynch, *Our Administrative System, supra* note 19. [123] Mulgan, *supra* note 55, at 9.

[124] See, e.g., Richman, *Corporate Headhunting, supra* note 48, at 269 (discussing DOJ stance on prosecuting corporate executives).

[125] Mulgan, *supra* note 55, at 34; see also Mashaw, *Accountability and Institutional Design, supra* note 13, at 124–6 (discussing "social accountability"); Richman, *Old Chief, supra* note 112 (discussing professional basis for prosecutorial accountability).

This answerability across institutional divides is quite different from transparency. Transparency, of course, is a critical democratic norm, and calls for "the broad visibility of government decision making" have been a powerful and understandable part of recent criminal justice critiques.[126] Still, formal transparency is not an unalloyed good, particularly if it provides levers for less engaged, and perhaps overly punitive, actors to intervene in downstream decision-making. Such is the lesson of federal sentencing history between 1989 and 2007.[127] Such has also often been the experience in the United States when, to promote consistency within a jurisdiction or an office, bureaucratic promulgations have limited line prosecutor options. While transparent governance does not have an inherent punitive tendency, when coupled with punitive politics, it has ratcheting effects. When looking across systems, we would thus do well to think more about promoting a "shared language of justification" for use across a variety of institutional interactions, even those the public cannot and should not know about.

2 Scale of Accountability

Although often lost in discussions of democratic accountability, any inquiry into the relationship of prosecutors to democracy needs to consider scale. How big need the polity in whose name the prosecutor acts be? And need that polity be the same one that produces the criminal laws being enforced?

Duff gracefully explains how one "distinctive and proper purpose" of "our criminal law" is to "call someone to account," a process that requires a "normative community to which both called and callers can be said to belong."[128] But why can't the community in whose name a defendant is called and the prosecutor is doing the calling be unrepresentative, even peculiar, elements of the larger polity whence come the laws themselves? Niki Lacey and David Soskice have cogently argued that local autonomy has been a key driver of over-punitiveness in the United States.[129] Still, the division

---

[126] See Sklansky, *Democracy and the Police, supra* note 7, at 91; Erik Luna, Transparent Policing, 85 *Iowa L. Rev.* 1107 (2000).

[127] Richman, *Federal Sentencing in 2007, supra* note 75.

[128] Duff, *Responsibility, Citizenship and Criminal Law, supra* note 14, at 126.

[129] Nicola Lacey & David Soskice, *Why are the Truly Disadvantaged American, When the UK is Bad Enough? A Political Economy Analysis of Local Autonomy, in Criminal Justice, Education, Residential Zoning* 29, 35 (2013) (unpublished manuscript), at 29, 35 (2013 draft) (arguing that "diffusion and localisation of democracy has been one of the most powerful institutional factors in shaping America's distinctive patterns of crime, punishment, segregation and indeed social inequality" and that "more centralised systems avoid the negative externalities of local decision-making characteristic of the US").

of law-making vs. law-applying authority embodied in the county-based system offers, what, in theory at least, could be a productive blending of small vs. larger community norms. Moreover, one might imagine that, however selected, a local prosecutor – anchored by the local nature of so much criminal enforcement – will provide just this blending. Perhaps at some point local variation is an affront to the norm of equal citizenship. Yet one can also embrace the inevitable variation of a loosely linked "federal" system and make that variation itself a feature of the membership that a citizen enjoys.

Even in far more centralized and bureaucratized France, Jacqueline Hodgson and Andrew Roberts tell us:

> [I]t is recognised that the prosecutor's discretion is an important part of adapting prosecution policy to local conditions and concerns – an example of the influence that certain social and systemic pressures in the broad surround can have on subjective decision-making. The aim may be to manage the flow of cases, charging some offences at a lower level so that they remain in a mid-level court and are not subjected to the lengthy instruction procedure ... Or the aim may be to respond to local mores and expectations.[130]

Yet considerations of scale – which may depend on a polity's embrace of local "responsiveness" and tolerance for national disparities – must be balanced against "capacity." With respect to norm generation, this will always be a contestable measure. One person's "community" is bound to be another's "unrepresentative pocket." Moreover, there will be more objective, or at least exogenous, aspects to capacity that implicate the permissible scale for the administration of justice in a liberal democratic polity. Recent reports from Ferguson, Missouri,[131] and elsewhere drive the lesson home. If a political unit is not big enough to supply adequately trained police and prosecutors or support a court system not constrained to self-finance, it needs to be right-sized (to draw on a current managerial trope).

The institutional design "solution" may lie in overlapping jurisdictions, with more ostensibly responsive local establishments balanced by national or subnational (but supra-local) prosecutors whose deficiencies with respect to local knowledge and communal preferences find compensation in a perspective less tethered to local leaders and pathologies. Even as I am reluctant to valorize

---

[130] Jacqueline Hodgson & Andrew Roberts, *An Agenda for Empirical Research in Criminal Justice: Criminal Process and Prosecution*, at 22 (2010 draft).

[131] U.S. Dep't of Justice, Civil Rights Div., *Investigation of the Ferguson Police Department* (2015) (highlighting focus of Ferguson law enforcement on generating revenue).

the American federal system – whose floating federal "responsibilities"[132] bring their own accountability challenges – the gains when one prosecutorial level is able to hold another's feet to the fire are undeniable. This may play out in policy decisions – as when one prosecutor publically questions the priorities and decisions of another – or corruption cases against prosecutors themselves and their allies.

Note that the value of a second level of prosecutors is not just a matter of perspective but institutional capacity. If prosecutors are to make a sustained contribution to democracy – one that goes beyond shepherding cases through the adjudicative process – they need the capability to either investigate or cause the investigation of the crimes that don't involve manifest disorder of the sort that attracts police attention. I hesitate to specify the institutional arrangements that would best foster prosecutorial attention to domestic violence, corruption, and other such cases that strike at the heart of individual autonomy and political functionality. One can imagine, in theory, a wide range of possibilities – including overlapping jurisdictions (Robert Cover spoke of the "complex concurrency" of the American system[133]), dedicated police-prosecutor squads, and the like. Indeed, even though a prosecutorial office is freer to invest investigative and adjudicative resources in this critical subset of cases when it is not constrained by the principle of legality, some combination of political will and institutional accounting can perhaps obtain the same result where that principle is respected. Theory, though, has its limits, and if care is not taken, these cases can easily get slighted.

3 Information Use/Collateral Consequences

Another principle requiring translation across different prosecutorial orders goes not to which cases will be brought, but how all adjudicated cases will be received. What volume control will there be on prosecutorial articulations of criminality? Perhaps there should be an "acoustical separation" that, by dampening how prosecutors can construct citizenship, might compensate for deficiencies in their accountability?[134] This dampening could limit the

---

[132]   Daniel C. Richman & William J. Stuntz, *Al Capone's Revenge: An Essay on the Political Economy of Pretextual Prosecution*, 105 *Colum. L. Rev.* 583 (2005).

[133]   Robert M. Cover, *The Uses of Jurisdictional Redundancy: Interest, Ideology, and Innovation*, 22 *Wm. & Mary L. Rev.* 639, 646 (1981); Daniel C. Richman, *The Changing Boundaries Between Federal and Local Law Enforcement*, in 2 *Criminal Justice 2000: Boundary Changes in Criminal Justice Organizations* 81 (2000).

[134]   Meir Dan-Cohen, *Decision Rules and Conduct Rules: On Acoustical Separation in Criminal Law*, 97 *Harv. L. Rev.* 625 (1983).

social and political meaning of a decision to prosecute that ends in a criminal conviction.

Some aspects of this meaning are endogenous to a polity's criminal process – the definition of an offense, the mode of proof, and the nature and severity of the sentence. Affecting all will be the legitimacy of the state generally and of its authority to punish specifically.[135] Important aspects of a conviction's meaning, however, are exogenous to the adjudicative process and are subject to regulatory decisions (or non-decisions) that can substantially limit a prosecutor's power to shape the social order. A well-functioning democratic order would attend to these regulatory decisions, which optimally would reflect a polity's considered judgment both about authority already delegated to prosecutors and the degree to which it should be extended to other domains.

Americans have been coming to grips with the authority – by default or otherwise – that has been effectively given to prosecutors by laws and rules that make criminal convictions into automatic triggers for a slew of "collateral" consequences. Frequently, convicted felons in the United States will lose the ability to vote, even after they are released from prison. In Europe and elsewhere, debate rages about whether those incarcerated should lose the right even while serving their sentence. An accountability lens offers no clearer resolution of these issues than it does on the qualitatively different issue of sentence severity. Powerful arguments that it is a grievous category mistake to deprive convicted offenders of basic citizenship rights may, for some, find answer in a communitarian logic.[136] Yet an accountability lens highlights the fact that the United States, where prosecutors are the least susceptible to granular accountability for their charging decisions, is also the least attentive to the weight that other authorities give those prosecutorial interventions post-conviction.

There is no grand paradox here. The fragmentation of governmental authority in the United States and the status accorded prosecutors goes far to explain the cascading (and often personally devastating) consequences that attend an adjudicated decision to charge, with legislators and regulators quick to pile on. Indeed, a political status perspective may explain the degree to which the United States (as a fragmented collective) allows the articulations of

[135] See Shelby, *supra* note 14 (explaining how the second can (somewhat) exist in the absence or weakness of the first).

[136] See John Finnis, *Prisoners' Voting and Judges' Powers*, 13 (2015) (unpublished draft). ("Allowing serious criminals to vote during incarceration under sentence says to the law-abiding that their vote does not count very much, and says to the criminal that his own vivid defiance of the communal project of self-government (so far as that project called upon him to respect his victim) leaves his right to continued participation in that project unimpaired, entirely unimpaired.")

its prosecutors to shape the rest of a defendant's life. That, combined perhaps with different views about the "ownership" of information about public (including criminal) processes, may explain the very different approaches to criminal records information in the United States and Europe. As James Jacobs has comprehensively shown, while "American criminal records are exceptionally public, exceptionally punitive, and exceptionally permanent,"[137] the European Union and its member states, by contrast,

> treat individual criminal history information as personal data that the individual has a right not to have disclosed by government personnel or by private parties. Consequently, police records do not circulate at all, court records are not open for public examination and (except in Sweden) private firms are not permitted to sell criminal record information to employers, even if they could obtain it."[138]

Still, the diversity in criminal information regimes – and in the varying degrees to which prosecutors are allowed to construct citizenships – usefully pushes us to think harder about the relationship between prosecutors' accountability and their authoritative narrative power.

IV CONCLUSION

The role of prosecutors in a liberal democracy entails standing apart from the polity, speaking for and to it, and being true to its laws and values. One might see this as an existential dilemma, but I prefer to take it as a law and institutional design challenge – a challenge that probably does not have a single optimal solution (or at least one constitutionally attainable across all jurisdictions). Above all, it is a challenge to reason: to hold people and institutions to account, and to be able to give an account of oneself.

Prosecutors in the United States have been rightfully pressed in recent years to give a better account of themselves, but so too have prosecutors in other countries. Before resorting to transplantation or even just intellectual valorization, more thought should be given to the trade-offs inherent in each set of institutions. The quiet claim here is not that any particular prosecutorial

---

[137] Kevin Lapp, *American Criminal Record Exceptionalism*, 14 *Ohio St. J. Crim. L.* (2016) (forthcoming) (drawing on James Jacob, *The Eternal Criminal Record* (2015), to argue that "American criminal record exceptionalism functions as an inexpensive way to sort and inflict punishment by devolving a great portion of the work to private actors and the general public").

[138] See James B. Jacobs & Elena Larrauri, *European Criminal Records and Ex-Offender Employment*, Oxford Handbooks Online.

establishment necessarily must trade off one democratic citizenship enhancing project for another. That a prosecutor has a sustained commitment to going after corruption and domestic violence should not insulate her from challenges that, for example, she is doing a poor job at modulating punitive outcomes. Still, unless we think beyond basic typologies, variations in institutional design will determine the likelihood that different projects will be pursued and with what effectiveness. As jurisdictions contemplate reform, they should therefore consider not just what is missing, but what they might lose.

3

The Democratic Accountability of Prosecutors in England and Wales and France: Independence, Discretion and Managerialism

Jacqueline S. Hodgson

I. INTRODUCTION

Across Europe, North and South America, the role of the prosecutor is evolving, acquiring greater powers and responsibilities within existing functions, as well as changing more fundamentally as a criminal justice actor, increasingly responsible for the disposition as well as the prosecution of cases, and for the development and implementation of criminal justice policy. This raises important issues about the prosecutor's status, accountability and independence. As the state's representative in the prosecution of offenses under criminal law, the prosecutor is required to be independent to ensure the fair and consistent application of the law, but also to be accountable in some way to the democratic institutions she so publically represents. Independence and accountability are configured differently, depending on where the prosecutor is located within the legal and political landscape. She may function within an executive line of appointment and accountability, and so might be expected to promote government policy; she may be independent of ministerial hierarchies and so able to develop alternative agendas through the structures of the prosecution service itself; she may be rooted in the infrastructure of local politics, developing criminal responses adapted to local needs; and, she may be elected on a local political platform, with populist rather than centralized accountability.

Understandings of these contrasting forms of accountability as either democratic, or as inappropriately political,[1] are located within broader legal and

---

[1] See, for example, Michael Tonry, "Prosecutors Politics in Comparative Perspective," in *Prosecutors and Politics: A Comparative Perspective*, ed. Michael Tonry (Chicago: University of Chicago Press, 2013), 1.

political cultures. In England and Wales, for example, an important dimension of the judiciary's role in upholding the rule of law is their ability to call politicians to account in the exercise of their legal powers. In France, by contrast, as a republic, the moral and political authority of the state is paramount, understood as representing the will of the (sovereign) people. The unelected judiciary remains subordinate to political power within this "statist" tradition, reflected in the hierarchical accountability of the French prosecution service to the Minister of Justice and in the constitutional status of the judiciary as an authority, rather than a power.[2]

The level at which prosecutors are accountable (as well as to whom they are accountable) is also likely to determine whether or not we consider it a good thing; the implementation of broad prosecution policies disseminated through guidance or internal hierarchies is experienced and understood differently from interventions or instructions in individual cases. The professional status and training of the prosecutor is also important – whether her role is characterized as a partisan advocate or a more neutral judicial figure has the potential to shape the prosecutor's work and may color our view of her relationship to those to whom she must account. Central to these debates is the relationship between independence and accountability, and the nature and extent of prosecutorial discretion – how it is shaped, regulated and defined within law; how the prosecutor understands the limits of the various roles that she plays; and the structures of political, professional, judicial and constitutional authority within which discretion is exercised.

This paper considers the changing role and power base of the prosecutor, with particular focus on her relationship with the police, on whom she depends for the investigation and evidence gathering that will form the basis of the decision to prosecute. It examines the contrasting ways in which prosecution policy is developed and executed in England and Wales and in France, its relationship to the public and to the executive and the importance of the professional role and status of the prosecutor in defining her relationship with political hierarchies and so democratic accountability. It also reflects on the importance of the individual prosecutor as an independent professional – the extent to which she is a cog in the machine of national policy, is driven by bureaucratic and managerialist imperatives or she enjoys individual discretion

---

[2] In 1958, the judiciary was demoted from a *pouvoir* to an *autorité*, recognizing the fact that the state makes the law, but judges simply apply it. They lack the status of a "power," as this would rival that of the state and so challenge the sovereign will of the people. Although the judicial authority enjoys a degree of autonomy, this is regarded by some as serving to legitimate, rather than to act as any check upon the actions of the state. See Jean-Claude Magendie and Jean-Jacques Gomez, *Justices* (Paris: Atlas Economica, 1986), 18–20; Sudhir Hazareesingh, *Political Traditions in Modern France* (Oxford: Oxford University Press, 1994), 173.

rooted in her professional expertise and ideology. This analysis is comparative, but the nature of the prosecution function, including democratic accountability and the exercise of discretion, does not depend simply on the procedural roots of a jurisdiction, but on a range of factors, albeit that some of these may be more strongly associated with the adversarial or inquisitorial tradition.

II THE ORIGINS OF THE POLICE-PROSECUTOR RELATIONSHIP

The prosecution function is made up of relationships with, and dependencies on, a range of legal and non-legal actors – from suspects, witnesses and victims, to judges, police officers and defense lawyers. Perhaps most important among these is the relationship with the police as the front line gatherers and producers of evidence. Public prosecutors in England and Wales and in France have seen their role expand in a variety of ways. This has changed aspects of their relationship with the police with whom they work and on whom they depend in different ways to carry out the criminal investigations and evidence gathering that will underpin the prosecution case. France and England and Wales do not share the same historical criminal procedural model and the police-prosecution relationship is structured differently, reflecting different histories and political and procedural values. Aside from the adversarial and inquisitorial roots of the two systems which characterize the prosecutor in England and Wales as a party to the case, and her French counterpart as a more neutral judicial officer whose prosecution role also includes one of investigation, the office of prosecutor in the two jurisdictions has evolved at different points in time and in response to different circumstances.

A *France*

In France, the current role of the public prosecutor (the *procureur*) developed during the twentieth century alongside a practice of official police enquiries that later became known as the *garde à vue*.[3] Existing outside any formal legal regulation, this procedure often resulted in the arbitrary detention of individuals and it was only formally legally regulated in 1958. Defense lawyers had been permitted access to the case dossier and to be present during the interrogation of the accused by the *juge d'instruction* (the investigating judge) during the *instruction* investigation from 1897. This was not well-received by many who feared this would undermine the effectiveness of the *instruction* as a search for the truth.

---

[3] The role has existed in different guises for centuries.

[B]y obliging the *juge* to warn the accused at his first formal questioning that he is free to say nothing, by imposing the presence of a lawyer at all following interrogations, by, above all, constraining the *juge* to give the case file to the defence lawyer the day before every interrogation, this law paralyses the action of the judge who can barely hope, even himself, to discover the truth.[4]

In response, in order to avoid the *instruction*, the police and the *procureur* developed an alternative procedure for the detention and questioning of suspects in order to bypass any involvement of the defense lawyer in the investigation.[5] This proved to be an effective strategy; the procedure became formalized into the *garde à vue* in 1958, but lawyers remained absent until 1993, a century after their arrival in the *instruction*.[6]

This is in many ways a familiar story of how the strengthening of what we would now think of as due process or fair trial rights within one part of the criminal process, leads to the removal or the undermining of protections in another. In England and Wales, for example, the suspect's right to custodial legal advice following section 58 of the Police and Criminal Evidence Act 1984 was then used as justification for the removal or weakening of other defense safeguards, such as the attenuation of the right to silence.[7] In Scotland, at the same time that suspects were granted access to custodial legal advice following

---

[4] Herbert Halton, "Etude sur la procédure criminelle en Angleterre et en France" (Thèse, Faculté de Droit de Paris, 1898), 69 cited by Denis Salas, "Note sur l'histoire de l'instruction préparatoire en France," in *La mise en état des affaires pénales: Rapport de la Commission Justice Pénale et Droits de l'homme*, Annexe 2, ed. Mireille Delmas-Marty (Paris: La Documentation Française, 1991), 248.

[5] Jacqueline S. Hodgson, *French Criminal Justice: A Comparative Account of the Investigation and Prosecution of Crime in France* (Oxford: Hart Publishing, 2005), 117.

[6] Suspects were permitted to see a lawyer for 30 minutes, after 20 hours of detention in *garde à vue* from 1993. In 2000, access was permitted from the start of the *garde à vue* and finally, after the Grand Chamber judgment of the European Court of Human Rights in *Salduz v. Turkey*, Application No. 36391/02 November 27, 2008, suspects now have access to a lawyer for a 30 minute consultation during the police interrogation – though the lawyer's role is greatly restricted to that of passive observer. See Jacqueline S. Hodgson, "Making Custodial Legal Advice More Effective in France: Explores the Challenges in Accessing a Lawyer When in Police Custody," *Criminal Justice Matters* 92, no. 1 (2013): 14; Jodie Blackstock, et al., *Inside Police Custody: An Empirical Account of Suspects' Rights in Four Jurisdictions* (Antwerp: Intersentia, 2014); Jacqueline S. Hodgson, and Ed Cape, "The Right to Access to a Lawyer at Police Stations: Making the European Union Directive Work in Practice," *New Journal of European Criminal Law* 5, no. 4 (2014):450.

[7] Adverse inferences may be drawn from silence in some circumstances under s.34 of the Criminal Justice and Public Order Act 1994. By attaching a penalty to the exercise of the right, its value is significantly undermined.

the decision in *Cadder*,[8] which held Scotland to be in breach of Article 6 of the European Convention on Human Rights (ECHR) by preventing suspects in police custody from accessing legal counsel, the period of police detention was doubled from six to 12 hours.[9]

It is also significant as a redistribution of judicial and political power within the criminal justice process, as the *procureur* and the *juge d'instruction* are both judicial officers, but sit within different structures of accountability and therefore at different points within the constitutional separation of powers. The *juge d'instruction* is independent of the executive, cannot be moved to a different office and cannot be given either oral or written instructions. Her independence is guaranteed by the constitution and she is not subject to the authority of the Minister of Justice. The *procureur* belongs to a different branch of the judiciary (the so-called standing, rather than the sitting judiciary) and is hierarchically accountable to the Minister of Justice, a political appointee of the government. She is responsible for delivering the government's criminal justice policy and must act within the guidelines set by her superiors and the Ministry circulars. Her accountability to a democratically elected Minister is seen as an important guarantor of her independence – she may not pursue her own policies, but must act within the law. Severing the "umbilical cord" between the *parquet* and the Minister of Justice has been the subject of decades of discussion and whilst lobbied for by the *parquet* (the collective term for *procureurs*) and made the subject of a parliamentary Bill, recent reform attempts seem unlikely to attract the necessary political support.[10]

For North American scholars, this may seem unremarkable, to have independence guaranteed directly, or indirectly, through the electorate. At the federal level, the Attorney General and district US Attorneys are political appointees of the President's party and the 2,300 state prosecutors are elected mostly at county level and operate a wide variety of policies and practices, according to local political conditions. In France, complete independence from the executive is understood to risk unfettered power and the *gouvernement des juges*, where judicial power exceeds that of the elected state.[11] To the English lawyer, however, accountability to the executive does not guarantee

---

[8] *Cadder v. HM Advocate* [2010] UKSC 43, which followed the European Court of Human Rights case of *Salduz v. Turkey*, Application No. 36391/02, Grand Chamber judgment, November 27, 2008.

[9] Section 14 of the Criminal Appeal (Legal Assistance, Detention and Appeals) (Scotland) Act 2010. The custody officer may extend detention for a second 12-hour period.

[10] The proposal also failed in 1998. To succeed, it requires a three-fifths majority in the Congress (the union of both parliamentary chambers, the *Assemblée* and the *Sénat*), which seems unlikely as the current government has only a slim majority in the former and is in the minority in the latter.

[11] Hodgson, *French Criminal Justice*, 77.

independence, but risks political interference. This concern is not without merit, as we have seen countless French scandals in which the executive, often under the direction of the President, has exerted pressure on the judicial system to protect its own patrons and supporters.[12]

The trajectory of the development of the *garde à vue* procedure as a means of supplanting the *instruction* has continued, and investigation under the supervision of the *procureur* now overshadows completely the *instruction*; less than two percent of cases are dealt with in this way. The *procureur's* growth in investigative power in the face of an increasingly due process *instruction* model is also significant as a shift away from an independent judicial investigation, to one which is ultimately accountable to the executive, including until recently, the power of the Justice Minister to issue written orders to *procureurs*. The hierarchy of the *parquet* and the culture of instruction and subordination are part of the prosecutor's career, as well as her daily practice. Promotion is based on an evaluation of the *procureur* that includes her "capacity to implement penal policies" and "to be part of the hierarchical relationship"; loyalty and conformity are rewarded, whilst independence is penalized.[13] The structure of the *parquet* has also ensured that the President and the Minister of Justice have a key role in the selection and promotion of *procureurs*, cultivating a culture of patronage and dependence that, even with the removal of written orders, has been hard to break.[14]

This tension between the two models of investigation and loci of power is reflected in government reform agendas that seek to bolster the power of the *procureur* (and so the executive) to the detriment of the more politically independent *juge d'instruction*. The most recent enquiry to recommend the effective abolition of the *juge d'instruction* in her current role, placing the *procureur* in charge of all criminal investigations, was the Léger Commission, reporting in 2009.[15] The recommendation (reflecting then President Sarkozy's premature announcement, some nine months before the Commission reported in September 2009, of his intention to abolish the office of *juge d'instruction*) was undercut, however, by the decision of the European Court of Human Rights in *Medvedyev v. France*[16] and then *Moulin v. France*,[17] in which it was held that the

---

[12] Hodgson, *French Criminal Justice*; Jacqueline S. Hodgson, "The French Prosecutor in Question," *Washington & Lee Law Review* 67, no. 4 (2010): 1361–1411.

[13] Mathilde Cohen, "The Carpenter's Mistake? The Prosecutor as Judge in France" (this volume).

[14] See the observations in Pierre Truche, *Rapport de la commission de réflexion sur la Justice* (Paris: La documentation Française, 1997).

[15] Philippe Léger, *Comité de réflexion sur la justice pénale* (Paris: La documentation Française, 2009).

[16] Application No. 3394/03, Grand Chamber Judgment, March 29, 2010.

[17] Application No. 37104/06, November 23, 2010.

procureur was not a judge for the purpose of Article 5 of the ECHR because she is a party to the case as a prosecutor and is not independent of the executive.

Recent legislation reducing police accountability and increasing the *procureur's* power to authorize certain investigative measures has also been controversial. Following the terrorist attacks in Paris in November 2015, emergency measures were put in place which lacked the usual safeguards of judicial guarantees in the exercise of intrusive powers. Although intended to be time limited and exceptional, the government has now sought to place these measures on a statutory footing. The proposed legislation includes greater powers for the *procureur* to authorize wire taps and electronic data capture, investigations that may currently be authorized only by the more independent sitting judiciary.[18] In this way, greater power to authorize measures that infringe on the liberties of the individual is being assigned to the public prosecutor, whose line of accountability ends with the Minister of Justice. At the same time, the Bill sets out the professional orientation of the *procureur* in more strongly "judicial" terms, with a new addition to Article 39 of the *code de procédure pénale*, requiring that the *procureur*:

> checks the legality of the means implemented by [police officers], the proportionality of investigative acts with regards to the nature and gravity of the offence, the opportunity to carry out the investigation in this or that direction, as well as the quality of its content. He ensures that investigations are aimed towards the determination of the truth and that both inculpatory and exculpatory evidence are collected, in the respect of the rights of the victim and of those of the suspect.
>
> (Article 22 of the Bill)

Parliament seeks to increase the power of the prosecutor, whilst also strengthening her apparent neutral and independent judicial ideology. But the expression of her professional role in terms similar to that of the *juge d'instruction* is somehow unconvincing. The simple addition of a new clause to the *code de procédure pénale* changing the description of the prosecutor's role will not in itself transform the ideology or practices of the profession.[19] The fact remains that authority is seeping away from the politically independent *juge d'instruction* to the *procureur*. Moreover, the legal rhetoric of independence is not supported by any change in the structure of prosecutorial accountability, which remains with the executive.[20]

---

[18] Projet de loi no. 3473. This power is proposed in cases of organized crime and terrorism.

[19] The reform is inspired by the recommendation of Jacques Beaume, *Rapport sur la procédure pénale* (Paris:Ministère de la Justice, 2014), 30.

[20] Controversially, Article 18 of the Bill goes further still and provides the police with the authority to detain and question individuals for up to four hours without any judicial oversight.

B England and Wales

In contrast to the *procureur's* long history within French criminal procedure, the Crown Prosecutor in England and Wales is a relatively new function, established under the Prosecution of Offences Act 1985. Prior to the establishment of the Crown Prosecution Service (CPS), there was no public prosecutor in England and Wales. The police were responsible for criminal prosecutions, which they brought either in person, or through locally instructed prosecuting solicitors. This meant that there was no unified, centralized national prosecution policy. In their review of criminal procedure arrangements, the Philips Commission (reporting in 1981) noted that police-prosecution practices varied across the country, resulting in inconsistent levels of charging and the prosecution of weak cases unsupported by sufficient evidence.[21] The police were too close to cases and unable to make the legal and forensic judgments required.

The Commission recommended the establishment of a national public prosecution service headed by the Director of Public Prosecutions (DPP) in order to address these issues and to professionalize the prosecution of crime. A key feature of the new CPS was their independence from the police investigation phase. Under the former arrangement, prosecuting solicitors worked for, and were consulted by, the police in around three-quarters of police forces,[22] but had only an advisory role. They were bound to follow the instructions of their client, the police, and the prosecution process was under the control of the chief officer of police. With the establishment of the CPS, the initial charging decision remains that of the police, but cases then pass to a Crown Prosecutor to assess the strength of the evidence and to determine the final charge to be prosecuted. This means that the decision not to charge remains with the police, but cases where prosecution is anticipated are subject to review by the CPS who determines whether to prosecute the case as charged, prosecute a lesser offense or discontinue the prosecution. In many areas, former prosecuting solicitors were appointed as Crown Prosecutors. However, this loss of power from the police to the newly independent CPS was not well-received by officers who continued to

---

Detention is permitted of those for whom "there are serious reasons to think they represent a threat for the security of the state or that they are in direct and not coincidental relation with such people" – without informing the *procureur*. When acting in this administrative, rather than judicial, capacity, the police are under the hierarchy of the Minister of Interior.

[21] Royal Commission on Criminal Procedure (1981), Cmnd 8092, chaired by Sir Cyril Philips.

[22] Statement of the then-Home Secretary, William Whitelaw HC Deb, November 20, 1981, vol. 13, c532.

investigate and gather evidence, but could no longer control the prosecution process.[23]

Removing from the police the decision to prosecute and making it entirely a CPS judgment addresses the problem identified by the Phillips Commission, but the Philips principle, as it is generally known, goes further than this; it sees the separation between the investigation and prosecution phases as crucial to ensuring the independence of the Crown Prosecutor's decision. This might be criticized as a narrow construction of prosecutorial independence on at least two counts. First, it casts the police as gatekeepers to the prosecution process; where the police decide not to pursue a case, other than in some specified circumstances, the CPS will have no involvement or knowledge of the investigation. They are unable to prevent the police from discontinuing investigations where the evidence is strong, or where there may be a strong public interest in prosecution. Second, although hailed as a new Ministry of Justice type role, the independence of the Crown Prosecutor function has been limited by their reliance on the police for the information on which their prosecution decision will be based. It might be argued that greater involvement in the investigative phase could produce better quality evidence and so a better-informed prosecution decision; the Crown Prosecutor would be less captive to the police view of the case.

This is very much the approach of the French model, in which the role of the public prosecutor, the *procureur*, is not separate from, but is inextricably linked with that of the police investigation. This stems in part from the different understanding of the prosecution process, which in France includes the investigation phase carried out under the judicial supervision and direction of either the *procureur* or the *juge d'instruction*, but it also allows the prosecutor to orient the enquiry from a legal perspective. In England and Wales, whilst the Crown Prosecutor may be consulted by the officers prior to charge, it is fundamental to the understanding of their roles as independent of one another that she is not an authority over the police and that there is a separation of the prosecution function from that of investigation. The *procureur*, on the other hand, is a direct authority over officers as they investigate the case and, in particular, during the detention and questioning of the suspect during *garde à vue*.

So, we have two very different models – one in which the prosecutor has no power over the police investigation and charging process, understood as a

---

[23] The CPS deals with the prosecution of cases investigated by the police. Prosecutions are also brought by other agencies such as Her Majesty's Revenue and Customs, the Serious Fraud Office and the Health and Safety Executive.

necessary function of prosecutorial independence, and the other in which the prosecutor is a judicial authority over the police, responsible for the investigation and prosecution of crime. In the latter, prosecutorial independence from the police might be understood through the power to require them to act in certain ways, in contrast to the Crown Prosecutor's dependence on police-generated evidence. In my own fieldwork, French officers expressed admiration for what they saw as the far greater autonomy enjoyed by the police in England and Wales. In France, questions of independence and accountability center on the relationship with the Ministry of Justice rather than the police; the French prosecutor's independence as a judicial officer implementing government policy is understood to be guaranteed by the Minister, a member of the executive. Yet, as we shall see, this constraint on power through ministerial democratic accountability carries with it the risk of political interference and so the potential to compromise the independence of the *procureur*. In England and Wales, the CPS was established in order to ensure the independence of the prosecution function from that of the police and it is this relationship that has attracted the greatest attention.

III THE CHANGING SHAPE OF THE PROSECUTOR'S ROLE

The roles of prosecutors in both jurisdictions have expanded in recent years, driven principally by a desire to improve efficiency by increasing the number of out-of-court case disposals and by speeding up the process of case disposition in general. In England and Wales, the prosecutor's function at the local level has been strengthened, providing her with greater powers of case disposition, but also a new role in mandatory charging advice and decision-making. At the national level, the DPP has developed a policy-making role through the issuing of guidance on charge and prosecution in a range of cases (such as domestic abuse and assisted suicide) to be implemented uniformly through local Crown Prosecution offices. Although she still lacks authority over officers and any powers of direction or instruction, the Crown Prosecutor now works more closely with the police and this has been the explicit aim of successive reviews of the CPS and the criminal justice process.

In France too, the *procureur* now enjoys greater powers to authorize and oversee criminal investigations, as well as an increased range of case disposition options, including a guilty plea procedure where a reduced sentence is offered. This is one of a range of new procedures in which the defense is now explicitly written into the process and the judge's role has diminished in favor of a more party-centered approach. However, while the DPP in England and Wales has begun to develop national prosecution policy in a range of offense areas, this remains strictly Ministry of Justice territory in France. The French prosecutor's policy role, in contrast, has developed through engagement with local political and criminal justice actors. Relationships with the police are also changing in different ways. As noted above, the *procureur*'s role has developed hand-in-hand with that of the police, and the practice of dealing with cases in real time in order to speed up decision-making has led to yet closer working relationships. In contrast to England and Wales, however, where the prosecution is being encouraged to work more closely with the police, this has become a cause for concern and a recent review of the *parquet* recommended that prosecutors place some distance between themselves and officers, in order to preserve their independence.[24] As power shifts away from the *juge d'instruction* and towards the *procureur*, this also represents a shift in the political accountability and dependence of criminal justice, away from the judiciary and towards the executive. The counterbalance within the French criminal process is increasingly provided (in theory at least) by the defense, rather than by the judiciary. These are very different roles, however – constitutionally, professionally and in their criminal justice function.[25]

In addition to relationships with other criminal justice actors, these changes in role and function have also impacted on the organization of prosecution work – the degree of professional autonomy and discretion that she enjoys; the extent to which work is becoming standardized and delegated; and the extent to which her decision-making is regulated within pre-defined structures set by politicians, or the internal hierarchy of senior prosecutors. Lines of accountability intersect with changes in the professional role of the prosecutor, and the boundaries between local and national politics, as well as the policy role of the prosecution hierarchy itself, have shifted.

A England and Wales: The CPS

The role of the CPS has evolved since its creation 30 years ago, from the powers of individual prosecutors, to the nature of the DPP's role in guiding and steering the organization. In contrast to France, where national prosecution policy is part of the political agenda set by the Minister of Justice, disseminated down through the prosecution hierarchy, in England and

---

[24] The English Crown Prosecutor is not an authority over the police, so closer relationships are not seen to threaten independence in the same way.

[25] See, for example, Jacqueline S. Hodgson, "Constructing the Pre-trial Role of the Defense in French Criminal Procedure: An Adversarial Outsider in an Inquisitorial Process?" *International Journal of Evidence and Proof* 6, no. 1 (2002a): 1–16; Hodgson, *French Criminal Justice*, ch. 4.

Wales, the DPP has developed this role. In addition to guidance on charging, prosecution, evidentiary matters, protocols on serious investigations, guidance based on case law and what must be proved in court, cautions and diversion away from trial, the DPP has established policies on the prosecution of particular offenses such as domestic violence and assisted suicide. These are important supplements to legislation and case law, as the policies on prosecution will determine how the law develops subsequently. Many of these guidelines are preceded by a public consultation, the responses to which are published.[26] They range from the prosecution of child sexual abuse, to prosecution for perverting the course of justice and charging in rape and domestic violence cases. The stimulus for these guidelines is often a high-profile case that has not gone well, or to provide certainty where there is a legislative gap, such as in the case of encouraging or assisting suicide.[27] This is an interesting alternative to more traditional democratic routes such as legislative guidance or policy disseminated by a government minister, as happens in France. The DPP is appointed by and responsible to the Attorney General, whose office advises the government and represents the public interest in a range of capacities. This creates a less direct line of political accountability and one which, by convention, is "exercised very sparingly, and not used to further the narrow political interests of the government and its supporters."[28]

At the other end of the organization, individual Crown Prosecutors have, on the face of it, been given more power as they now make charging decisions in many instances that were formerly determined by the police.[29] Although the CPS is divided into 13 areas across England and Wales, each led by a Chief Crown Prosecutor, charging advice and decisions are taken by CPS Direct for the most part, with Area Crown Prosecutors being involved in some early investigative advice and charging. The police are able to contact CPS Direct through a single national telephone number and officers speak to the next available prosecutor. Although discussions take place over the telephone, evidence is transmitted electronically, as are decisions, providing an accessible case record from the outset. In theory, this places prosecutors closer to police officers in case building, and in advising on charge and evidence, but a recent Joint

---

[26] The guidance on the prosecution of assisted suicide followed a web consultation which elicited 4,700 responses.

[27] All of the CPS guidance is published in its website. See, for example, The Director of Public Prosecutions, *Policy for Prosecutors in Respect of Cases of Encouraging or Assisting Suicide* (London, 2014), www.cps.gov.uk/publications/prosecution/assisted_suicide_policy.html.

[28] Antoinette Perrodet, "The Public Prosecutor," in *European Criminal Procedures*, ed. Mireille Delmas-Marty and John Spencer (Cambridge: Cambridge University Press, 2002), 422.

[29] See CPS, *The Director's Guidance on Charging 2013*, 5th edition (London, 2013), www.cps.gov.uk/publications/directors_guidance/dpp_guidance_5.html.

Inspectorate Report suggests that there is still some way to go in making this an effective working relationship.[30] It found one-third of the cases in which the police brought charges should have been dealt with by the CPS; one-tenth of the cases dismissed by the CPS should have been decided by the police; and the police decision to charge was incorrect in eight percent of cases.[31]

Whilst officers are free to consult the CPS in any case, this is mandatory for more serious and complex cases.[32] This change was made on the recommendation of the enquiry headed up by Lord Justice Auld with the aim of creating closer working relationships between police and prosecutors so that weak cases could be weeded out earlier, and ensuring that more recorded crimes resulted in a conviction or some other form of case disposal. The police tendency had been to overcharge, with high numbers of judge-ordered and judge-directed acquittals. This may be because the police adopt a more subjective and less formal and legalistic approach, or because they anticipate that more evidence will emerge justifying the higher charge – or it may also flow from the differences in charging standards; the police are not required to take account of public interest considerations, but this is written in to CPS guidance. After piloting the procedure in 2002, legislation amended the Police and Criminal Evidence Act 1984 (PACE) to transfer charging decisions from the police to the DPP, through local Crown Prosecutors. Under section 37A(1) PACE, the DPP now has the power to issue guidance to police custody officers on how to facilitate the Crown Prosecutor's charge decision. Crown Prosecutors now direct (rather than advise) officers on formal cautions, warnings and reprimands. The CPS guidance, in contrast, requires decisions to be based on a review of the evidence, not on an oral report. The Attorney General and the DPP regard this shift in roles as the most significant change in the relatively brief history of the CPS, expanding the CPS role and limiting constabulary independence as set out in *ex parte Blackburn*.[33]

---

[30]   HMIC, *The Joint Inspection of the Provision of Charging Decisions* (London, 2015), www.jus ticeinspectorates.gov.uk/hmic/wp-content/uploads/joint-inspection-of-the-provision-of-char ging-decisions.pdf, which was carried out jointly by Her Majesty's CPS Inspectorate and Her Majesty's Inspectorate of Constabulary.

[31]   Ibid., para. 1.12.

[32]   CPS, *Director's Guidance*, para. 7 states that early investigative advice (EIA) may be provided in serious, sensitive or complex cases and it should always be utilized in cases involving death, rape or other serious sexual offenses. HMIC, *Joint Inspection*, para. 6.4 found that EIA is well-established in the CPS Headquarter units (such as counter terrorism), but not in local areas. Officers were uncertain as to what was available and the Joint Inspectorate found that only two out of 13 rape cases and one out of 21 cases involving other serious sexual offenses in their sample had sought EIA (paras. 6.5–6.7).

[33]   *R v. Commissioner of Police of the Metropolis, ex parte Blackburn* [1968] 2 QBD 118. Lord Denning stated that whilst every police officer is under a duty to enforce the law of the land, they are wholly independent of the executive and not subject to the orders of the Secretary of

One perhaps unexpected consequence of this different way or organizing charge and prosecution is that the process is more closely regulated both for prosecutors and the police. Crown Prosecutors have a range of legal guidance that they must follow, such as when to apply the Full Code Test, or the Threshold Test;[34] when to characterize offenses within certain categories such as homophobic violence or domestic abuse, and so follow the charging guidance on these and other offenses.[35] The result is that prosecutors are less reliant on their own professional discretion as lawyers following an evidential and public interest test. Instead, they are required to justify their decisions and their application of specific criteria through detailed record-keeping that is subject to later review. This forms part of the file that will be passed to those working at the next stage of the prosecution process. Other than in serious, complex and sensitive cases where early investigative advice (EIA) should be sought, no single Crown Prosecutor is responsible for a case;[36] the file will pass through numerous sets of hands, with the result that case ownership is difficult to establish. This more bureaucratic model shares many of the features of an inquisitorial model.[37]

The other aspect that is significant in this way of organizing work, driven also by the constant need to work within a smaller budget, is the increased use of non-professionally qualified staff. Section 7A of the Prosecution of Offences Act 1985 empowers the DPP to designate Crown Prosecutor powers and rights of audience to non-legal staff, and to determine their training. A significant proportion of prosecution work, including bail decisions and guilty pleas, is now carried out at court by associate prosecutors (APs). These are typically experienced former administrators within the CPS who have undergone one week's training on criminal law and one week on

State: "The responsibility for law enforcement lies on him. He is answerable to the law and to the law alone" (769 *per* Lord Denning, M.R.).

34   The Threshold Test may be applied where the suspect "presents a substantial bail risk if released and not all the evidence is available at the time when he or she must be released from custody unless charged. The Threshold Test may be used to charge a suspect who may be justifiably detained in custody to allow evidence to be gathered to meet the Full Code Test realistic prospect of conviction evidential standard." CPS, *Director's Guidance*, para. 11.

35   CPS, *Domestic Abuse Guidelines for Prosecutors* issued by the DPP www.cps.gov.uk/legal/d_to_g/domestic_abuse_guidelines_for_prosecutors/; CPS, *Guidance on Prosecuting Cases of Homophobic and Transphobic Crime* issued by the DPP, www.cps.gov.uk/legal/h_to_k/homophobic_and_transphobic_hate_crime/; For the full range of legal guidance issued to the CPS, see www.cps.gov.uk/legal/.

36   There should be "continuity of prosecutor" where the CPS has provided EIA. CPS, *Director's Guidance on Charging*, para. 7.

37   Jacqueline S. Hodgson, "Hierarchy, Bureaucracy and Ideology in French Criminal Justice: Some Empirical Observations," *Journal of Law & Society* 29, no. 2 (2002b): 227.

criminal procedure.[38] The widespread use of these APs is indicative of the level of routinization that now characterizes criminal justice in the courts in England and Wales. It also creates a tier of CPS staff that is further removed from the usual lines of accountability.

In addition to stronger powers in charging decisions, Crown Prosecutors are now empowered to issue conditional cautions with punitive (rather than rehabilitative or reparative) conditions attached. Although a relatively minor measure used infrequently,[39] this nonetheless represents a transfer of power from the judiciary to the CPS. The Attorney General has described this as the offender's choice, with the benefit of legal advice, but this is a weak notion of consent in a criminal process that makes guilty pleas the norm, enforced through a series of systematic and institutional pressures. Neither can basic constitutional principles be traded off for efficiency. This is a punishment (rather than a prosecution diversionary measure) and its administration by a prosecutor (lacking even the basic judicial status of the French *procureur*) does not offer Article 6 ECHR fair trial guarantees.[40] This increased power in the criminal process, and in the disposition of cases in particular, places accountability for the prosecutor's exercise of her discretion further under the spotlight.

B *France: The* Parquet

In England and Wales, the story has been the gradual transfer of power from the police to the public prosecutor. In France, power has shifted from the judge to the *procureur* (who has always exercised the same powers as the

---

[38] For further detail and the selection and training of Aps, see CPS, The *CPS Annual Report and Accounts 2014–15*, Annex E (London, 2015), www.cps.gov.uk/publications/docs/annual_report_2014_15.pdf.

[39] Out-of-court disposals issued by the CPS at the pre-charge stage (a simple caution, conditional caution, reprimand, final warning or offense to be taken into consideration) accounted for 0.6 percent of the 500,000 cases prosecuted in 2014/15 (CPS, *Annual Report and Accounts 2014/15*). The numbers have declined, but were never more than 2.4 percent in 2008/09 (CPS, *CPS Annual Report and Resource Accounts 2010/11*, Annex B, London, 2015), www.cps.gov.uk/publications/reports/2010/annex_b.html). Recorded crime has declined steadily over the last decade from around 6 million in 2004 to around 4 million in 2014, a decrease of one-third (see Figure 1), see Office for National Statistics, *Crime in England and Wales: Year Ending December 2015* (London, 2015), www.ons.gov.uk/peoplepopulationandcommunity/crimeandjustice/bulletins/crimeinenglandandwales/yearendingdecember2015. Prosecutions have halved in the same period from over one million to 500,000.

[40] This is what Andrew Ashworth calls the borderlands of fair trial. See Andrew J. Ashworth, "Manslaughter: Direction to Jury – Diminished Responsibility," *Criminal Law Review* October (2006): 88.

police), avoiding the lengthy pre-trial *instruction* and reducing the use of formal prosecution and the court disposition of cases in favor of a more speedy process handled by the prosecutor.[41] These include warnings (*rappels à la loi*), mediation, reparation and rehabilitation schemes, but more significantly also the imposition of fines or community work (*compositions pénales*). There is also a range of rapid trial procedures, including the guilty plea procedure, the *comparution sur reconnaissance préalable de culpabilité* (CRPC).[42] The criminal response rate measured as a percentage of recorded crime where the offender is identified and there is evidence for prosecution stands at 91 percent. 40 percent of these are dealt with by some form of alternative to prosecution, 5 percent by *composition pénale* and 46 percent by going to trial or *instruction*.[43] Even those cases going to trial are often channeled through procedures such as *comparution immédiate* that are within the control of the *procureur*. This places the *procureur* in a key position, determining the disposition of nearly half of all cases.

It is perhaps assumed that these measures ease the pressure on the courts by diverting cases away from trial, but the effects of these changes are not uniform across France. For example, comparing two court regions, Aubert demonstrates that whilst official figures suggest consistent results, in Bobigny, these procedures are used to deal with cases that are not a local priority, but in Bordeaux, they are used to deal with cases that would not have been prosecuted, thus having a net-widening effect.[44] Official statistics show that over the last decade, the *procureur* has dealt with greater numbers of cases, but the courts continue to try between 12 and 13 percent of recorded crime, or between 45 and 46 percent of prosecutable offenses. The increased workload of the *procureur* has not been to reduce the court's docket, but to provide a response to cases that would otherwise have been dismissed. Dismissals have halved from 25 percent of prosecutable crime to 12 percent, while cases settled by the

[41] Antoine Garapon, *La prudence et l'autorité: l'office du juge au XXIe siècle*, Rapport de l'IHEJ (Paris: Ministère de la Justice, 2013), 107 describes the *procureur*'s role as no longer being that of determining whether to prosecute or to drop a case. She now has a range of options allowing her to satisfy the broader demand for a criminal "response." This range of case pathways, from sanctions to punishments, to compensation and mediation, are often referred to as the "third way."

[42] For further discussion, see Jacqueline S. Hodgson, "Guilty Pleas and the Changing Role of the Prosecutor in French Criminal Justice," in *The Prosecutor in Transnational Perspective*, ed. Erik Luna and Marianne Wade (Oxford: Oxford University Press, 2012), 116–134.

[43] Ministère de la Justice, *Une réponse pénqle pour 91% des auteurs d'infractions* (Paris, 2015), www.justice.gouv.fr/budget-et-statistiques-10054/infostats-justice-10057/une-reponse-penale-pour-91-des-auteurs-dinfractions-28451.html.

[44] Laura Aubert, "Systématisme pénale et alternatives aux poursuites en France: une politique pénale en trompe-L'œil," *Droit et Société*. 74, no. 1 (2010): 17–33.

prosecution have risen from 28 percent of prosecutable offenses to 44 percent.[45]

The function of the *procureur* is no longer principally that of accuser, but now includes responsibility for the management of caseloads and the disposition of a significant proportion of criminal cases. Justice has moved out of the courtroom and into the office of the *parquet*. This, of course, renders justice less visible as these procedures are not open to the public. There is no judge present (she will approve the procedure later, without even the presence of the *procureur*), only the accused's lawyer, but her role as potential negotiator and party to the case means that she cannot fulfill that same function provided by independent judicial oversight. Traditionally, the *magistrat* has been seen as the first defender of the rights of the accused, but the *procureur* lacks the independence of the *juge d'instruction* and this is no substitute for active defense rights. The prosecutor's role is to ensure that the suspect's rights are respected throughout the criminal procedure, not to actively challenge the legality of actions or to champion the rights of the accused.

The nature of the *procureur*'s supervision of the police has also changed in some respects. As she has gained more power and responsibility, her supervision has become more intrusive. However, just as earlier research noted the bureaucratic nature of the *procureur*'s supervision of the police investigation,[46] contemporary forms of oversight remain overly focused on detail and procedure, rather than with strategic oversight. The "real time" procedure of *traitement en temps réel* (TTR) provides a good example of this. Designed to ensure that decisions re prosecution are made faster, this procedure requires the *procureur* to base her decision on the oral account provided on the telephone by the officer; the prosecutor will have seen neither the case file nor the accused. This has been criticized by the Beaume review as being too involved and intrusive,[47] turning the *procureur* into a form of "supercop" and so threatening her independence. The prosecutor's role is not to oversee the daily conduct of affairs, but to ensure the legality and proportionality of police measures and to supervise the general direction and quality of the investigation. However, Mouhanna criticizes the standardizing effect of this procedure,

---

[45] Ministère de la Justice, *Statistiques: Activité des parquets des TGI* (Paris, 2015), www.justice .gouv.fr/statistiques.html and Ministère de la Justice, *Chiffres Clés de la Justice 2015* (Paris: Directeur de la publication, 2015), www.justice.gouv.fr/publication/chiffres_ cles_20151005.pdf.

[46] Hodgson, *French Criminal Justice*, ch 5.

[47] Police officers are angry at the time they have to wait to get through to the *parquet* office on the telephone; prosecutors are frustrated that they are now less available for the more serious and long-term investigations. Jacques Beaume, *Rapport sur la procédure pénale*, 28.

as prosecutors orient cases towards police standard documentation and high rates of prosecution.[48] The more closely involved in the investigation she is, the less the *procureur* can claim impartiality.

As in England and Wales, these changes have an impact on the nature of the prosecutor's way of working. In France, the *procureur* has increasingly become an administrator or manager, responsible for the effective management of caseloads and accountable for the nature and level of response to criminal cases.[49] The corresponding increase in the auditing of their work, however, is experienced by *procureurs* less as a means of ensuring an appropriate criminal response and more as a way of managing the *parquet* itself.[50] This came to a head in January 2016 when 86 percent of the 168 *procureurs* in France decided not to produce their usual annual report for the Minister of Justice, but a less detailed version that would not include tables of figures that had to be produced by hand, as they did not have the technology to produce the required statistics.

Neither are the *procureur*'s fellow judicial officers immune from this bureaucratic, rather than democratic, accountability. Justice is measured by quantitative standards that focus on the avoidance of delay above all else, and so the number of cases processed.[51] There is frustration with these managerialist imperatives to move cases along quickly and to involve prosecutors in minor cases that are easily oriented, leaving a gap where they are needed in more serious and complex cases. The TTR, for example, is also characterized as part of a trend to move to a faster procedure that depends on an oral account, resulting in a less-considered review of the written evidence. This further undermines the professional identity of the judiciary, requiring decisions to be governed by economic, rather than judicial, imperatives.[52] Furthermore, the responsibility placed on prosecutors to set clear justice priorities and ensure that cases are disposed of rather than discontinued, is in direct tension with the

---

[48] Christian Mouhanna and Benoit Bastard, "Procureurs et substituts: l'évolution du système de production des décisions pénales," *Droit et Société* 74, no. 1 (2010):35–53.

[49] As in England and Wales, these methods that require prosecutors to manage caseloads as quickly, efficiently and inexpensively as possible are drawn from the world of business and the language of productivity, and so are alien to those in the judicial world. Garapon, et al., *La prudence et l'autorité*.

[50] Philip Milburn, et al., *Les procureurs: Entre vocation judiciaire et fonctions politiques* (Paris: Presses universitaires de France, 2010), 94–95.

[51] Court areas and even individual judicial officers are measured by their productivity, by the fruits they bear. This emphasis on efficiency and reducing delay has resulted in the number of cases dealt with increasing by one-fifth in the last decade. Garapon, et al., *La prudence et l'autorité*, 70, footnote.101.

[52] Garapon, et al., *La prudence et l'autorité*.

budgetary constraints they face. It is a familiar story; prosecutors are required to do more with less, wrapped in the euphemistic rhetoric of efficiency.

One aspect of managing these growing caseloads more efficiently (that is, more cheaply) is to delegate work. This is a feature of much modern professional life, from health, to education, to justice, as a rational response to increased demands and accountability, at the same time as budgets are shrinking. In England and Wales, criminal defense lawyers engaged in the mass delegation of criminal work to trainee solicitors and clerks in the 1980s and 1990s, with the result that their businesses thrived, but clients' interests were subordinated to profit.[53] As noted above, a good deal of magistrates' court work, the responsibility of Crown Prosecutors, is now assigned to non-legally trained Associate Prosecutors. Delegation is also a feature of the modern French prosecution function. Many aspects of the *procureur*'s work are now carried out by mediators and associate prosecutors (*délégués du procureur*) who are typically former police officers or gendarmes. They operate a policy of auto prosecution with procedures such as the *composition pénale* and *ordonnance pénale*. Taken together with this increasing culture of accountability, this offers a reshaped picture of the profession – one in which decisions about the procedure to follow are more standardized and less within the professional discretion of the *procureur*, whose role is becoming less judicial and more administrative.[54] The *procureur* is at the center of criminal justice decision-making, but much of this is carried out in more standardized and pre-determined ways. If the mainstay of judicial safeguarding and accountability is increasingly subject to the administrative demands of the executive, this has important implications for the balance of power within criminal justice.

The *procureur*'s role as local policy maker has also become significant. In addition to the top-down hierarchical structures of policy and accountability associated with classic inquisitorial-type procedures,[55] the *procureur* now works with the police, local government, customs and border police to set priorities and to develop effective ways of handling cases. The TTR, for example, began as a local pilot, but was then rolled out nationally. Historically, local security matters would have been the concern of local government (the *préfet*), but the *procureur* is now a visible part of civil society and local political life and her role within local policy-making has developed as a demand of a more security-oriented civil society. Although the *procureur*

---

[53] Mike McConville, et al., *Standing Accused: The Organisation and Practices of Criminal Defence Lawyers in Britain* (Oxford: OUP, 1994).

[54] See also Garapon, et al., *La prudence et l'autorité*, 110.

[55] Hodgson, "Hierarchy, Bureaucracy and Ideology," 227–257.

has welcomed this, confident that she is able to differentiate her judicial role clearly from that of the more political *préfet*, her *magistrat* colleagues are less convinced. There is a certain paradox in that it is her judicial status that defines her role, and the necessity for that role, within local politics, yet the further enmeshed within the local political administration the *procureur* becomes, the weaker her status as *magistrat* in the eyes of her judicial colleagues.[56]

This paradox is situated within a wider debate as to whether the *procureur* should retain the status of *magistrat* along with *juges du siège*, or whether her role as investigator and enforcer of government policy sets her apart. For their part, *procureurs* fear professional relegation to the rank of functionary and positioning within a hierarchy headed by the Minister of Interior. They see a government that determines the *parquet*'s role against its will and an alliance between judges, lawyers and parliament to impose a more accusatorial procedure in which the *procureur* role will narrow to that of simply the accusing party and her judicial role will necessarily wither away. Given the tiny minority of criminal matters now dealt with by the *juge d'instruction* and the omnipresence of the *procureur* in the investigation and prosecution of crime, the prospect of her turning into a *superpolicier* would remove the current guarantees of independence and protection of rights and freedoms in favor (in theory, at least) of a more European rights-based approach.[57] This would require a much improved and developed criminal bar, which currently is playing catch-up with the growth in suspects' rights and which has yet to be recognized as a serious guarantor of justice either by the judiciary or the government.[58]

In addition to, and often in tension with this more local role, the *parquet* also receives directives and circulars from her own hierarchy, coming down from the Minister of Justice – but also from the Minister of Interior. These are of such a quantity that 80 percent of cases now fall within priority areas for action.[59] There has also been something of an explosion of criminal

---

[56] Milburn, et al., *Les procureurs*, 137.

[57] The Beaume Report warned against the *procureur* becoming a kind of supercop operating more as a superior police officer than a judicial authority. See Beaume, *Rapport sur la procédure pénale*, 28.

[58] Jacqueline S. Hodgson, "The Role of Lawyers During Police Detention and Questioning: A Comparative Study," *Contemporary Readings in Law and Social Justice* 7, no.2 (2015): 47–56; Cape and Hodgson, "The Right of Access to a Lawyer"; Hodgson, "Custodial Legal Advice," 14–15; Jacqueline S. Hodgson, "Safeguarding Suspects' Rights in EU Criminal Justice: A Comparative Perspective," *New Criminal Law Review* 14, no. 4 (2011): 611–665; Hodgson, "Constructing the Pre-trial Role, "1–16.

[59] Milburn, et al., *Les procureurs*, 92.

legislation and prosecutors report difficulty in keeping abreast of the range of procedures now in place for different offense types. As a result, *procureurs* are overloaded with sometimes contradictory demands, and report feeling torn between their response as professionals, their role in shaping local criminal justice and security policy, and the demands of an executive (which increasingly includes the Minister of the Interior, as well as the Minister of Justice) keen to secure electoral success. An example of the tension created by these executive orders is the circular issued by the Minister of Interior inviting the *parquet* to contribute to an interministerial initiative to increase the number of identity checks carried out on the outskirts of schools. This was not coordinated with local policies, nor did it take account of local conditions. Only later was a circular from the Justice Minister issued, corroborating these instructions.[60] The prosecutor's role in safeguarding individual freedoms, and as a local criminal justice policy actor, have become important modes of retaining her professional role and autonomy, and of resisting pressure on the *parquet* from the state to be instrumental in putting into effect its repressive criminal justice agenda.[61]

IV THE RELATIONSHIP BETWEEN INDEPENDENCE AND DEMOCRATIC ACCOUNTABILITY

Discussion of concepts such as independence, accountability and democracy are riddled with difficulties. On the face of it, they appear to be positive, just as unaccountability, dictatorship and a lack of independence appear to be negative. But these are not universal concepts that mean the same thing wherever they appear; they are at times interlinked and are highly context-dependent. As discussed above, prosecutorial independence and accountability are shaped in part by different historical and professional factors, but also by the balance of roles and responsibilities between legal actors,[62] by the nature of prosecutorial discretion, the procedural tradition (itself connected to the political culture, as noted by Damaška),[63] and even relations with the media.[64] In comparing the different constructions of prosecutorial independence, Di Federico characterizes the process as one of accommodating two conflicting values at the operational level:

---

[60] Milburn, et al., *Les procureurs*, 93.   [61] Milburn, et al., *Les procureurs*, 101–102.

[62] Hodgson, *French Criminal Justice*, ch. 3, especially pp. 79–85 on the contrasting roles of *juge d'instruction* and *procureurs* and their assertions of independence in response to political pressure.

[63] Mirjan Damaška, "Structures of Authority and Comparative Criminal Procedure," *Yale Law Journal* 84 (1975): 480–544.

[64] Hodgson, *French Criminal Justice*, 82–83; Éric Zemmour, "Justice et médias, les nouveaux aristocrates de la Ve," *Pouvoirs* 99 (2001): 163–170.

On the one hand, there is awareness that public prosecution contributes substantially to the definition and implementation of criminal policy. This requires that mechanisms be devised to ensure that the active role played in that crucial area be somehow directed and controlled in the context of the democratic process. On the other hand, the need to guarantee that public prosecution be exercised with rigour, consistency and fairness makes it necessary to ensure that too close a tie with the political process be not unduly used by the existing majority to influence the conduct (actively or by omission) of public prosecution for partisan purposes; more generally to ensure that citizens be treated equally.[65]

In the US, the role of prosecutors in the "definition and implementation of criminal policy" is "directed and controlled in the context of the democratic process" through the election of prosecutors in the locality where they serve. This populist model is criticized by some, such as Michael Tonry, as being "lawless" because prosecutors "exercise their enormous power over citizens' lives without being accountable to anyone but the electorate."[66] In Italy, in contrast, "absolute priority is given to the value of independence"[67] with no relevance accorded to democratic accountability to either an electorate or political power.[68] This is explained in part by the historical and political context of the prosecution function. Political independence and autonomy were considered paramount in establishing the prosecution function after World War II in order to avoid the political discrimination experienced during the Fascist period. This was accompanied by a principle of mandatory prosecution to avoid any arbitrary or political exercise of power. The result has been, argues Di Federico, the unjustified aggrandizement of the status of the profession and the exercise of discretion in a fragmented way that reflects personal and local preferences, rather than equal treatment before the law or any form of democratic accountability.[69]

---

[65]   Giuseppe Di Federico, "Prosecutorial Independence and the Democratic Requirement of Accountability in Italy," *British Journal of Criminology* 38 (1998): 373.

[66]   Tonry, *Prosecutors and Politics*.

[67]   Di Federico, "Prosecutorial Independence and the Democratic Requirement," 375.

[68]   See also Carlo Guarnieri, "Prosecution in Two Civil Law Countries: France and Italy," in *Comparing Legal Cultures*, ed. David Nelken (Aldershot: Dartmouth Pub Co, 1997), 183–193; Carlo Guarnieri, and Patrícia Pederzoli, *The Power of Judges: A Comparative Study of Courts and Democracy* (Oxford: Oxford University Press, 2002).

[69]   He quotes (1998: 380) Giovanni Falcone, the judge who prosecuted, and ultimately was assassinated by, the mafia in 1992: "How can it be conceivable that in a liberal democratic regime we do not yet have a judicial policy, and everything is left to the *absolutely irresponsible decisions* of the various prosecutors' offices and often even to the personal decisions of their members? In the absence of institutional controls on the activities of public prosecutors, [there is] the peril that informal influences and hidden connections with hidden *loci* of power

In England and Wales and in France, this balance is struck in different ways. In France, prosecutors are not elected, but they sit in a direct hierarchical structure of authority with the Justice Minister at the apex. This might be described as a kind of second-tier democratic input, through the filter of an already-elected government. This has the advantage of uniformity and coherence, and perhaps the expertise and professionalism of government, but risks the imposition of the will of presidents and prime ministers on matters of justice, potentially compromising the independence of decision-making. The *procureur* is also increasingly implicated within local civil society, working alongside local politicians to shape local criminal justice policy. In England and Wales, prosecutors are neither elected, nor do they sit within a political/ judicial hierarchy. There is a more indirect political accountability through the politically appointed DPP and the Attorney General, with a high degree of professional autonomy, albeit increasingly regulated through prosecution guidance and charging standards issued by the DPP. The professional status and the legal and political histories of prosecutors in England and Wales and France are different, as are their models of democratic accountability and the relationship to prosecution policy.

A *The* Parquet: *Democratic Accountability through Hierarchy*

The solution in France has been to maintain a clear link with the executive, ensuring that the prosecutor acts within the sphere determined by a democratically elected politician. This is achieved through a mixture of Ministry directives and policy guidance from within the hierarchy of the *parquet* itself. For prosecutors, this provides a broad context, allowing individuals to provide responses that are adapted to the locality and the individual, without undermining the fundamental principle of democratic accountability. As one senior *procureur* explained it:

> Of course there are problems of standardization ... you cannot follow the same *politique pénale* everywhere because the cases are different, the populations are different, the problems are different ... In one instance you will prosecute far more offenders than in another, because there is less delinquency ... A uniform system of justice, which is delivered in the same way

might influence their activities. It seems to me that the time has come to rationalise and coordinate the activities of public prosecutors rendered de facto unaccountable by a fetishistic conception of the principle of mandatory criminal prosecution." Giovanni Falcone, *Interventi e Proposte* (1982–92) (Milan: Sansei, 1994), 173–174.

everywhere and so which does not take account of differences, would effectively be a non-democratic system of justice.

[A6][70]

However, some have also criticized the broad discretion that this allows.

> Justice varies in different regions. You will not be prosecuted for some offences in some places – which basically means that you can commit more crime in the city. I saw a case in the Alps when a person was prosecuted for letting out his cattle. They said it was a breach of public order there – but I think hitting your wife is worse than that, yet it is not prosecuted [here]. I think they prosecute minor offences to justify their existence.
>
> [*Procureur*, Site D][71]

This runs the risk of going beyond applying central policy in a way adapted to local or individual needs, and undermining the democratic line of accountability.

> In this way, transgression of the same law leads to sanctions in one place, to total impunity in another. Diverted from its objective, as soon as what should and should not be sanctioned is translated into something over which there is total choice, the discretion to prosecute runs the not insignificant risk of resulting in unacceptable distortions in crime control between different jurisdictions; and that would go way beyond what could be justified by the criminal policy legitimately followed by each *parquet* according to its particular local conditions.[72]

In my own research, it was clear that these differences extended beyond court areas, to the exercise of individual discretion in a way considered by some to undermine democratic and hierarchical accountability. Some *magistrats* denied any personal choice in the application of the law.

> The one thing I am afraid of is to have a moment of emotion. Sometimes, when I have a person before me, I try to make them face up to their responsibilities and when I see him leave [my office for court] I know that he is going to get four or six months in prison and sometimes that breaks my heart. But I have a responsibility, a *politique* to respect and I apply it.
>
> [A2][73]

---

[70] *Procureur adjoint*, interviewed in field site A, quoted in Hodgson, *French Criminal Justice*, 230.

[71] Hodgson, *French Criminal Justice*, 231. [72] Magendie and Gomez, *Justices*, 102.

[73] Junior *procureur*, interviewed in site A, quoted in Hodgson, *French Criminal Justice*, 232–233.

Others recognized the inevitability of individual discretion, unconstrained by broader policy.

> The fact that the evidence must all be in writing does not prevent us from having a significant amount of leeway. It is procedural, but it does not prevent us from reacting ... I am not at all tolerant of sexual offences, but I had a colleague who just didn't give a damn. It depends on your personality.
>
> [A4][74]

This was also corroborated by police officers we surveyed.

> The policies or decisions of certain *magistrats* are, in identical circumstances but in different places, often different. The differences in treatment are sometimes surprising, at the heart of the same jurisdiction. The personal involvement of some *magistrats* is difficult to manage. This subjectivity, without basis, is experienced quite negatively by police personnel.
>
> [Police questionnaire respondent 5][75]

In this way, the exercise of prosecutorial discretion at the regional and individual level can conflict with the application of criminal justice policy set by the Ministry of Justice, and so undermine democratic accountability. On the other hand, it might be argued that local differentiation better serves local needs, especially given the *procureur*'s role developing policy and new initiatives alongside local political and criminal justice actors. This might be seen as a form of local democracy shaping the prosecution function.

However, there is also broad discretion at the individual level. This includes the unfettered discretion enjoyed by the *procureur* in middle-ranking offenses (*délits*) concerning whether or not to open an *instruction* investigation, or to deal with the investigation herself. There is no legal guidance and so prosecutors may exercise their discretion to keep the investigation under their power, a decision that will necessarily deprive the accused of the due process rights that she would be afforded during the *instruction*. The courts have been inconsistent on this issue and what should or should not motivate the decision to retain a case within the jurisdiction of the *procureur* – a trial court first striking out such a procedure in 2012, but the *Cour de Cassation* in 2013 upholding it as not in any way infringing the accused's right to a fair trial on the grounds that these rights would be available once at trial, so the accused was not disadvantaged. However, there is a world of difference between enjoying access to the dossier, being able to request investigative acts and

---

[74]   Junior *procureur* interviewed in site A, quoted in Hodgson, *French Criminal Justice*, 234.
[75]   Quoted in Hodgson, *French Criminal Justice*, 234.

having the benefit of legal assistance and representation all as pre-trial rights, rather than simply at trial.

A different kind of threat to prosecution and democracy in France is also represented by the executive itself. Historically, executive control of the *parquet* extended to instructions in individual cases, transforming executive or democratic structures of accountability into unacceptable opportunities for political interference.[76] Rather than ensuring the consistent and impartial application of the law, instructions in individual cases enabled the government of the day to protect favored individuals from scrutiny, undermining the independence of the *procureur* and of the law. Orders were given to delay or to dismiss cases that may have "unfortunate and unforeseen consequences for a number of political representatives," as this was considered necessary to protect the interests of the state.[77] Many of these incidents involved senior politicians seeking to keep cases away from the independent *juge d'instruction* (over whom they exercise no control) and under the authority of the more politically malleable *procureur*. Even where cases have been investigated by the *juge d'instruction*, the *procureur*'s lack of political independence has been of concern. In 2009, at the close of investigations into former French President, Jacques Chirac, for the misuse of public funds and breach of trust, the *procureur* recommended that no prosecution be brought on the grounds that there was insufficient supporting evidence. The *juge d'instruction*, Xavière Simeoni, disagreed and in a 215-page report, she set out why she considered that at least 21 of Chirac's associates were not in fact genuine employees.[78] In December 2011, Chirac was convicted and given a two-year suspended prison sentence.[79]

Furthermore, whilst directives and policy guidance are in written form, affording a degree of transparency, instructions in individual cases were oral and secret. Even following reforms that required instructions to individual *procureurs* to be in writing, prosecutors reported continuing to receive oral instructions from their superiors, acting as a conduit for the Minister. Given

[76] Hodgson, *French Criminal Justice*, 80–85.

[77] Former Justice Minister, Henri Nallet, discussed in Hodgson, *French Criminal Justice*, 81.

[78] Hodgson, "The French Prosecutor in Question," 1382.

[79] "Jacques Chirac condamné à deux ans de prison avec sursis," *Le Monde*, last modified December 15, 2011, www.lemonde.fr/societe/article/2011/12/15/verdict-attendu-dans-l-affaire-d es-emplois-fictifs-de-la-ville-de-paris_1618652_3224.html. For a chronology of events from the start of investigations in 1999, the constitutional reform giving him presidential immunity while in office, the criminal investigation and the reimbursement of funds to the office of the mayor of Paris, see "Chronologie: Affaire Chirac: 12 ans de procédure," *Le Nouvel Observateur*, accessed December 15, 2011, www.tempsreel.nouvelobs.com/societe/20111215 .OBS6852/chronologie-affaire-chirac-12-ans-de-procedure.html.

the controlling influence on the *procureur*'s career exercised by the hierarchy headed by the Justice Minister, the historic culture of obedience and subordination was difficult to break in practice.[80] Legislation in 2013 now forbids the Minister of Justice from issuing any instructions to prosecutors in individual cases.

B The CPS: Accountability and Policy from Within

CPS accountability is very different from that of the French *procureur*. Crown Prosecutors are not under the direct authority of the Justice Minister, even through local internal hierarchies as in France, and as discussed above, the executive's relationship with the prosecution and the judiciary is also different. The executive hierarchy within which the *parquet* sits is regarded as a legitimate form of democratic accountability in France. As a republic, the state represents the will of the people. In England and Wales, this would be considered political interference with the criminal process. Whilst in France, the State is and represents the public interest, "Common law countries [. . .] regard the public interest as an interest separate from that of the state – moreover, an interest which is often in direct conflict with the interest represented by the government."[81] Representing or acting in the public interest is an important aspect of democratic accountability and this has been incorporated into the development of prosecution policy, principally through an open and transparent process of public consultation. After concerns were raised about the democratic legitimacy of the DPP setting out prosecution policy on assisted suicide, the practice of public consultation around CPS policies was instituted, with the results being published on the CPS website.[82] This would not be regarded as legitimate in France, where the public interest is understood as something different from and greater than the sum of private interests.[83] For the CPS in England and Wales, however: "The frequency with which the public's views are sought provides some assurance that the current public interest factors carry with them their acceptance and support."[84]

---

[80] Truche, *Rapport*.
[81] Vera Langer, "Public Interest in Civil Law, Socialist Law, and Common Law Systems: The Role of the Public Prosecutor," *American Journal of Comparative Law* 36 (1988): 279–280.
[82] See CPS, "Consultations," The Crown Prosecution Service, www.cps.gov.uk/consultations/index.html.
[83] Laurène Soubise, "Prosecutorial Discretion and Accountability" (PhD Thesis, University of Warwick 2016), 131.
[84] Roger Daw and Alex Solomon, "Assisted Suicide and Identifying the Public Interest in the Decision to Prosecute," *Criminal Law Review* (2010): 737–743.

Although the CPS works with local police in order to provide information on high-volume and priority crimes, it does not actively shape local policy. Guidance on a range of issues, procedures and offenses is set nationally by the DPP, and CPS case record-keeping reflects this explicitly, especially in key areas such as domestic violence and rape, where different procedures must be followed, evidence thresholds may differ and police-CPS consultation is required. However, the accountability of prosecutors themselves is not centralized. The organization of the CPS into charge teams, magistrates' court teams, Crown Court teams, rape and serious sexual offenses teams and so on reflects the segmentation of the criminal justice process, but also means that it is rare for one single prosecutor to have ownership of the case file. A series of decisions and reviews take place at each stage and so accountability itself is fragmented, limited to a specific range of actions at different points in the process. At the other end of the scale, the work of the CPS as a whole is subject to oversight. Cases are reviewed and decision-making is audited by national inspectorates, and performance targets are set nationally and locally.

We have seen that French prosecutors are subject to a form of macro democratic accountability from the Minster of Justice, but individual decisions are subject to little scrutiny. This stems from the legal cultural understanding of the application of law as an objective process, which leads to a logical and inevitable conclusion. Reasons are not, therefore, considered necessary, shielding the decision of the individual prosecutor from review. In the criminal process in England and Wales, the existence of discretion is recognized explicitly and so is more closely regulated. In contrast to the mass of DPP policy guidance for Crown Prosecutors, and requirements to demonstrate compliance by case record-keeping, the *procureur* enjoys almost unfettered discretion to determine how to proceed with a case. With more regulation comes the possibility of review, as there are clear criteria against which to measure the proper exercise of prosecutorial discretion. This transparency of decision-making lends legitimacy to the work of the CPS and provides the possibility for public challenge, but can be experienced by prosecutors as a constraint on the exercise of their professional judgment.

V CONCLUSION

In both jurisdictions, the prosecutor's role in determining the prosecution, treatment and disposition of criminal cases is now significant. There has been a shift away from judicial processes (and so from the corresponding safeguards of transparency and publicity) towards pre-trial prosecution determinations that are designed to be faster and cheaper, and so more efficient. Mechanisms of accountability need to reflect these changes in the prosecution function in order to maintain the legitimacy of the criminal process. However, given differences in legal and political culture, as well as the role and functions of the public prosecutor in France and in England and Wales, we might not expect the same mechanisms of democratic accountability to be in place. Indeed, the concept itself is interpreted differently through the broader question of what is understood to be democratic – whether this engages the state or the public – and the nature of prosecutorial accountability – whether this operates at the level of national or local policy, or of the individual case decision. In both jurisdictions, democratic accountability for prosecution policy more broadly is regarded in positive terms. It encourages uniformity and consistency and so fairness in the application of the law.[85] Operating at the level of individual cases, however, it is the reverse. It seeks to impose differential treatment on an individual, undermining the consistency and independence of the law, replacing it with political favoritism and advantage.

There are also clear differences in the nature of local and national models of democratic accountability. In France, there is a tension, and even a contradiction, between the demands of local and national democracy as it relates to the prosecution function. Locally, the *procureur* is closely associated with the *préfet*, a government appointed head of local police and security. She works with the local political administration and other agencies in order to develop local criminal justice policy and responses to crime. However, at the same time, she is subject to targets and a variety of output measures set by the Justice Minister. Garapon et al. (2013) talk about a different kind of democratization of justice, in which the government is implicated in everything, including advancing the rights of victims; ensuring that more cases are disposed of; an explosion of criminal legislation; and setting targets re cost-saving, reducing delays, case management and overall measures of efficiency. The result is that prosecutors and other judicial officers are governed more by economic imperatives than judicial reasoning. The need to comply with these national policies and target outputs, together with nationally determined budget constraints, creates a conflict of interests for the *procureur* and undercuts her ability to set workable local policies and targets.

The different procedural traditions of England and Wales and of France also affect the relationship between prosecutorial independence and democratic

---

[85] Fairness is also a problematic concept and this account of fairness may be contested; absolute uniformity may appear unfair in some circumstances, as expressed by some of the *procureurs* quoted above. The concept of adaptation – where the criminal response or the sentence is adapted to the offender – is important in French criminal justice. This form of discretion tempers the harsh rigidity of uniformity, but sits comfortably within the professional ideology of the *juge*. Jacqueline S. Hodgson and Laurène Soubise, "Understanding the Sentencing Process in France," *Crime and Justice* 45, no. 1 (2016).

accountability. The inquisitorial framework of the French criminal process vests greater power in the *procureur* than is enjoyed by the Crown Prosecutor, and together with her judicial status, this relegates the defense to a relatively marginal role, suggesting that the concentration of authority that independence implies should be tempered by a democratic steer. Even with recent reforms that allow the defense a greater opportunity to participate in the investigation and trial of cases, the defense remains in a weak position from which to call the prosecutor to account. The judicial status of the *procureur* is understood to justify the concentration of power and of trust in the office of prosecutor; as a *magistrat*, she represents the public interest and ensures compliance with due process safeguards. Who better to entrust with the impartial application of the law? Yet, she is not a judicial officer for the purpose of Article 5 ECHR and in practice, her judicial status has been found to clothe in neutrality a police and crime control orientation.

Whilst the democratic accountability of the *procureur* is understood to be provided through the hierarchical organization of the *parquet*, with the Justice Minister at its head, in England and Wales, the democratic accountability of the CPS lies more in the public's participation in the development of prosecution policies (developed by the DPP rather than a politician) and in the possibility of review. The autonomy of the Crown Prosecutor is limited, however, by the plethora of policy guidelines that must be followed and by the rigid division of case processing into pathways and stages. Discretion is defined and regulated and so subject to later scrutiny. The picture is very different in France. By denying the existence of a broad discretion, even in the face of the accepted practice of ensuring that the criminal response is "adapted" both to the offender and the locality, the French *procureur* enjoys a high level of professional autonomy in her decision-making. Despite the generally bureaucratic nature of inquisitorially rooted procedures,[86] paradoxically, it is in England and Wales, and not in France, that the individual accountability of the public prosecutor is greater.

Bibliography

Ashworth, Andrew J. "Manslaughter: Direction to Jury – Diminished Responsibility." *Criminal Law Review* October (2006): 88.

---

[86] Mirjan R. Damaška. *The Faces of Justice and State Authority: A Comparative Approach to the Legal Process* (Yale: Yale University Press, 1986); Hodgson, *Hierarchy, Bureaucracy and Legitimacy*.

Aubert, Laura. "Systématisme pénale et alternatives aux poursuites en France: une politique pénale en trompe-L'œil." *Droit et Société.* 74, no.1 (2010): 17–33.

Beaume, Jacques. *Rapport sur la procédure pénale.* Ministère de la Justice, 2014.

Blackstock, Jodie, Cape, Ed, Hodgson, Jacqueline, Ogorodova, Anna, and Spronken, Taru. *Inside Police Custody: An Empirical Account of Suspects' Rights in Four Jurisdictions.* Antwerp: Intersentia, 2014.

Cohen, Mathilde. "The Carpenter's Mistake? The Prosecutor as Judge in France." (this volume).

CPS. "Consultations." The Crown Prosecution Service. www.cps.gov.uk/con sultations/index.html.

CPS. *Domestic Abuse Guidelines for Prosecutors.* www.cps.gov.uk/legal/d_to_ g/domestic_abuse_guidelines_for_prosecutors/.

Di Federico, Giuseppe. "Prosecutorial Independence and the Democratic Requirement of Accountability in Italy," *British Journal of Criminology* 38 (1998): 373.

Garapon, Antoine, Perdroille, Sylvie, Bernabé, Boris, and Charles, Kadri. *La prudence et l'autorité: l'office du juge au XXIe siècle* Rapport de l'IHEJ. Ministère de la Justice, 2013.

Guarnieri, Carlo and Pederzoli, Patrícia. *The Power of Judges: A Comparative Study of Courts and Democracy.* Oxford: OUP, 2002.

Guarnieri, Carlo. "Prosecution in Two Civil Law Countries: France and Italy." In *Comparing Legal Cultures,* edited by David Nelken, 183–93. Aldershot: Dartmouth Pub Co, 1997.

Hazareesingh, Sudhir. *Political Traditions in Modern France.* Oxford: Oxford University Press, 1994.

HMIC. *The Joint Inspection of the Provision of Charging Decisions.* HMIC. London, 2015. www.justiceinspectorates.gov.uk/hmic/wp-con tent/uploads/joint-inspection-of-the-provision-of-charging-decisions.pdf.

Hodgson, Jacqueline S. "Constructing the Pre-trial Role of the Defence in French Criminal Procedure: An Adversarial Outsider in an Inquisitorial Process?" *The International Journal of Evidence & Proof* 6, no.1 (2002a): 1–16.

Hodgson, Jacqueline S. "Hierarchy, Bureaucracy, and Ideology in French Criminal Justice: Some Empirical Observations." *Journal of Law and Society* 29, no. 2 (2002b): 227–257.

Hodgson, Jacqueline S. *French Criminal Justice: A Comparative Account of the Investigation and Prosecution of Crime in France.* Oxford: Hart Publishing, 2005.

Hodgson, Jacqueline S. "The French Prosecutor in Question." *Wash. & Lee L. Rev.* 67 (2010): 1361–1412.

Hodgson, Jacqueline S. "Safeguarding Suspects' Rights in EU Criminal Justice: A Comparative Perspective." *New Criminal Law Review* 14, no. 4 (2011): 611–665.

Hodgson, Jacqueline S. "Guilty Pleas and the Changing Role of the Prosecutor in French Criminal Justice." In *The prosecutor in Transnational Perspective*, edited by Erik Luna and Marianne Wade, 116–134. Oxford: Oxford University Press, 2012.

Hodgson, Jacqueline S. "Making Custodial Legal Advice More Effective in France: Explores the Challenges in Accessing a Lawyer When in Police Custody." *Criminal Justice Matters* 92, no. 1 (2013): 14–15.

Hodgson, Jacqueline S. "The Role of Lawyers During Police Detention and Questioning: A Comparative Study." *Contemporary Readings in Law and Social Justice* 7, no. 2 (2015): 47–56.

Hodgson, Jacqueline S., and Cape, Edward. "The Right to Access to a Lawyer at Police Stations: Making the European Union Directive Work in Practice." *New Journal of European Criminal Law* 5, no. 4 (2014).

Hodgson, Jacqueline S. and Soubise, Laurène. "Understanding the Sentencing Process in France." *Crime and Justice* 45, no. 1 (2016).

Langer, Vera. "Public Interest in Civil Law, Socialist Law, and Common Law Systems: The Role of the Public Prosecutor." *American Journal of Comparative Law* 36 (1988): 279–280.

Léger, Philippe. *Comité de réflexion sur la justice pénale.* Paris: La documentation Française, 2009.

Magendie, Jean-Claude and Gomez, Jean-Jacques. *Justices.* Paris: Atlas Economica, 1986.

McConville, Mike, Hodgson, Jacqueline, Bridges, Lee, and Anita, Pavlovic. *Standing Accused: The Organisation and Practices of Criminal Defence Lawyers in Britain.* Oxford: Oxford University Press, 1994.

Milburn, Philip, Kostulski, Katia, and Salas, Denis. *Les procureurs: entre vocation judiciaire et fonctions politiques.* Paris: Presses universitaires de France, 2010.

Ministère de la Justice. *Chiffres Clés de la Justice 2015.* Directeur de la publication. Paris, 2015. www.justice.gouv.fr/publication/chiffres_cles_20151005.pdf.

Ministère de la Justice. *Statistiques: Activité des parquets des TGI.* Ministère de la Justice. Paris, 2015. www.justice.gouv.fr/statistiques.html.

Ministère de la Justice. *Une réponse pénale pour 91% des auteurs d'infractions.* Ministère de la Justice. Paris, 2015. www.justice.gouv.fr/budget-et-statistiques-10054/infostats-justice-10057/une-reponse-penale-pour-91-des-auteurs-dinfractions-28451.html.

Le Monde. "Jacques Chirac condamné à deux ans de prison avec sursis." Last modified December 15, 2011. www.lemonde.fr/societe/article/2011/12/15/verdict-attendu-dans-l-affaire-des-emplois-fictifs-de-la-ville-de-paris_1618652_3224.html.

Mouhanna, Christian and Bastard, Benoit. "Procureurs et substituts: l'évolution du système de production des décisions pénales." *Droit et Société* 74, no. 1 (2010): 35–53.

Le Nouvel Observateur. "Chronologie: Affaire Chirac: 12 ans de procédure." www.tempsreel.nouvelobs.com/societe/1920111215.OBS6852/chronologie-af faire-chirac-12-ans-de-procedure.html.

Office for National Statistics. *Crime in England and Wales: Year ending December 2015.* London, 2015. www.ons.gov.uk/peoplepopulationandcom munity/crimeandjustice/bulletins/crimeinenglandandwales/yearending december2015.

Perrodet, Antoinette. "The Public Prosecutor." In *European Criminal Procedures*, edited by Mireille Delmas-Marty and John R. Spencer, 422. Cambridge: Cambridge University Press, 2002.

Salas, Denis. "Note sur l'histoire de l'instruction préparatoire en France." In *La mise en état des affaires pénales: Rapport de la Commission Justice Pénale et Droits de l'homme*, edited by Mireille Delmas-Marty, Annexe 2,248. Paris: La Documentation Française, 1991.

Soubise, Laurène. "Prosecutorial Discretion and Accountability: A Comparative Study of France and England and Wales." PhD Thesis, University of Warwick 2016.

The Director of Public Prosecutions. *Policy for Prosecutors in Respect of Cases of Encouraging or Assisting Suicide.* London, 2014. www.cps.gov.uk/publica tions/prosecution/assisted_suicide_policy.html.

Tonry, Michael. "Prosecutors and Politics in Comparative Perspective." In *Prosecutors and Politics: A Comparative Perspective*, edited by Michael Tonry, 1. Chicago: University of Chicago Press, 2013.

Truche, Pierre. *Rapport de la commission de réflexion sur la Justice.* Paris: Documentation française, 1997.

Zemmour, Éric. "Justice et médias, les nouveaux aristocrates de la Ve." *Pouvoirs* 4 (2001): 163–170.

4

The French Prosecutor as Judge. The Carpenter's Mistake?

Mathilde Cohen*

INTRODUCTION

On the eve of the opening of a new Paris courthouse in 2017, a controversy rages in French legal circles. Will the French judiciary repeat the "carpenter's mistake" yet again? This expression refers to the traditional spatial arrangement whereby French prosecutors are seated on a raised platform at the level of judges, well above the ground level where the defense and the victim's lawyers stand.

If a courtroom's physical organization is a sign system through which a society conveys a conception of the relationship between judges, prosecutors, defendants, and others involved in the justice system, then the "carpenter's mistake" is suggestive of French prosecutors' peculiar position. Their location in the courtroom is a physical reflection of their institutional status. The French judicial function is defined more broadly than in the United States, encompassing two types of "*magistrats*": the prosecutors and the judges.[1] Statutorily as well as sociologically, prosecutors *are* judges, having attended the same national school for the judiciary, enjoying the same civil servant status, sharing the same office spaces, budget, and staff, and being able to transfer back and forth throughout their career between judgeships and prosecutorial posts.[2] How does this unusual institutional design impact the relationship between prosecutors and democracy?

* Associate Professor of Law and Robert D. Glass Scholar, University of Connecticut School of Law and Research Fellow, CNRS. I would like to thank all the prosecutors and judges who agreed to be interviewed for this project. I am also grateful to Beth Colgan, Elizabeth Emens, and Daniel Turbow, as well as participants at the UCLA "Prosecutors and Democracy" workshop for their comments and suggestions. For excellent research assistance, I thank Joshua Perldeiner.
1 *See generally* JACQUELINE S. HODGSON, FRENCH CRIMINAL JUSTICE: A COMPARATIVE ACCOUNT OF THE INVESTIGATION AND PROSECUTION OF CRIME IN FRANCE 65–72 (2005) (presenting the structure of the French judiciary and prosecutors' status within that structure).
2 *See* Richard Vogler, *Criminal Procedure in France, in* COMPARATIVE CRIMINAL PROCEDURE, section 6.2.1, 62 (John Hatchard, Barbara Huber, & Richard Vogler, eds, 1996). In practice, however, the majority of high-level prosecutors spend almost their entire career working as prosecutors rather than judges. *See* FLORENCE AUDIER ET AL., LE MÉTIER DE PROCUREUR DE

In France as elsewhere, prosecutors and their offices are seldom conceived as agents of democracy. A distinct theoretical framework is missing to conceptualize the prosecutorial function in democratic states committed to the rule of law. What makes prosecutors democratically legitimate (or not)? Can old and new democratic theories help break down the different dimensions along which prosecutors could be held democratically accountable?[3] Beyond the broad commitment to rule by the majority, democratic theory involves a number of notions in theoretical tension concerning the proper function and scope of power, equality, freedom, justice, and interests. To evaluate French prosecutors' democratic pedigree, I do not commit to any particular conception of democracy. Rather I pick and choose between various conceptions of democracy which seem most pertinent to prosecutors' position in the democratic state. These include liberal democracy, classical separation of powers doctrine, deliberative democracy, and critical race theory. Based on these democratic paradigms, I examine four ways in which prosecutors could be viewed as democratic actors: via selection through a popular or autonomous process, separation of powers principles, deliberative decision-making norms, or representation through diversity. These four categories do not exhaust the field, as other possibilities exist, such as participatory democracy, which may call for the intervention of actors others than prosecutors in prosecutions, minimalist conceptions of democracy, whereby prosecutors' powers should be reduced significantly, or democracy as general will, in which the prosecutor's job would be to foster the common good.

My hypothesis is that in the French context, prosecutors' professional status and identity as judges determines, to a great extent, whether and how they can be considered democratic figures. As members of the judiciary, they share in a number of the French bench's democratic shortcomings – bureaucratic recruitment, minimal reason-giving, and insufficient diversity, to name but a few. The institutional factors that distinguish prosecutors from judges, most significantly the pervasive role of the executive in prosecutors' transfers and promotions as well as governmental interventions in prosecutorial decisions challenge the notion of a democratic prosecutor. At the same time, prosecutors' self-image as judges may to some extent preserve their independence. Having gone through the same curriculum and training and seeing judges as colleagues create a common professional ethos. Prosecutors' occupational ideology casts

---

LA RÉPUBLIQUE OU LE PARADOXE DU PARQUETIER MODERNE, Rapport GIP 16, 95–6 (2007) (noting that only 13 percent of prosecutors serve as judges in the course of their career).

[3] For a comparative take on prosecutors' accountability, *see* Ronald F. Wright & Marc L. Miller, *The Worldwide Accountability Deficit for Prosecutors*, 67 WASH. & LEE L. REV. 1587 (2010).

them as "impartial accusers"[4] or "advocates of the law"[5] who disinterestedly apply criminal statutes for the "public good"[6] rather than parties responsible for presenting the case against individuals suspected of breaking the law. Identifying as judges who enjoy more functional and decisional independence motivates prosecutors to achieve greater *external* autonomy from the executive branch and *internal* autonomy from their own rigid hierarchy.

In terms of methodology, I engage with the theme of prosecutors and democracy using a particular case study – France – combining democratic theory with original qualitative data. Qualitative research methods proved essential to exploring the hypothesis that French prosecutors' professional identity impinges upon their democratic pedigree. The contours of their occupational subculture are neither discernible in black letter law nor in the doctrine. They can only be drawn by collecting prosecutors and judges' own representations of their job and its democratic meaning for the society they live in. In that sense, the chapter looks at empirical answers to theoretical questions not usually treated as having empirical answers.[7] It assumes that hard questions of democratic theory have practical counterparts which role-agents must solve for themselves within the confines of their particular institutions.

The heart of the data consists in court observations and semi-structured interviews with *magistrats* and other professionals gravitating around the judiciary. From September 2015 to June 2016, I conducted courtroom observations during public hearings as well behind the scenes in back offices.[8] The courtroom observational data spans over 40 hearings held in four urban locations. I carried out 35 interviews: 26 with *magistrats* and 9 with other legal actors, be they working in law enforcement, applicants to the judiciary and the professors teaching them, or defense attorneys.[9] Among the 26 *magistrats*, 14 had served

---

[4] Interview with 13, Chief Prosecutor (2015).   [5] Interview with 2, Senior Prosecutor (2016).

[6] Interview with 12, Senior Judge (2015).

[7] I already used this combination in my previous work, *see, e.g.,* Mathilde Cohen, *Reason Giving in Court Practice: Decision-makers at the Crossroads,* 14 COLUM. J. EUR. L. 257 (2008) and Mathilde Cohen, *Ex Ante versus Ex Post Deliberations: Two Models of Judicial Deliberations in Courts of Last Resort,* 62 AM. J. COMP. L. 401 (2014).

[8] Prosecutors were involved in a range of activities, including: talking to the police over the phone, conducting police custody renewal hearings, arraignments, staff meetings to strategize about the day's difficult cases, etc.

[9] The interviews typically lasted 45–120 minutes, during which I took detailed notes. Some of them were recorded and transcribed. All the interviews were conducted in French and later translated by me. The interviews covered a wide variety of topics, including the judges and prosecutors' own backgrounds and professional developments, the process by which they had attained their current post, their vision of the prosecutor's office and its relation with judges, on the one hand, and the executive power, on the other hand, budgetary constraints, the routine of their work, the relationship between law and politics, and issues of ethics and discipline.

as judges for their entire career, 6 as prosecutors only, 5 as both judges and prosecutors, and one was still a trainee-*magistrat* wishing to embark on the prosecutorial track.[10] I enlisted the initial couple participants through existing contacts I had within the French legal community. Other participants were recruited using a snowball technique.[11] Within the constraint of snowball sampling, I strived to select a sample of *magistrats* representative of the current French judiciary in terms of prosecutors versus judges.[12]

The chapter has five Parts. After reviewing in Part I French prosecutors' selection and promotion mechanisms, Part II examines the question of separation of powers in the criminal justice system. Part III turns to prosecutors' deliberative practices and Part IV reflects on their lack of diversity as a failure in representative democracy. Part V concludes that despite the various democratic critiques which can be formulated against the prosecutor's office, French prosecutors engage in *de facto* forms of independence.

I BUREAUCRATIC SELECTION AND POLITICAL PROMOTIONS

A nation's system for selecting prosecutors is demonstrative of its vision of democratic governance. In most democratic countries, prosecutors' democratic pedigree stems from a recruitment and promotion process that aspires to democratic legitimacy, not only *ab initio*, but also throughout their tenure. Two selection methods are typically favored: popular elections and independent appointment commissions which aim at insulating the functions of appointment, promotion, and discipline from partisan politics. The underlying idea is that in a country where citizens enjoy political liberties, if elections are free and participation is widespread – or if the appointment mechanism is transparent and gives a voice to civil society – then public officials such as prosecutors will be more likely to act in the best interest of the people. Selection procedures which allow for appraisal of incumbents' performance, holding them accountable for the results of their past actions, e.g., through retention elections or re-appointment, also appear more democratic than lifetime tenure. At the same time, accountability based on reelection and re-appointment could conflict with prosecutors' independence. Can

---

[10] To maintain confidentiality, I do not include information that would identify the interviewees personally as the source of a comment, such as their title and the name and location of their court.

[11] *See generally* PRANEE LIAMPUTTONG, QUALITATIVE RESEARCH METHODS (2009).

[12] In 2014, 33.04 percent of the 7,726 members of the judiciary served as prosecutors while 66.96 percent served as judges. *See* CONSEIL SUPÉRIEUR DE LA MAGISTRATURE, RAPPORT D'ACTIVITÉ 2014 25 (2014).

one be a truly independent prosecutor if one fears being fired or demoted? The hope is that such procedures incentivize prosecutors to apply the criminal law according to public priorities and values even if in practice, they have been shown to be unreliable democratic guarantees.[13]

If selection were a litmus test for democratic pedigree, French prosecutors would fare poorly given the bureaucratic nature of their recruitment and the politicization of their transfers and promotions. They are neither democratically elected nor appointed through a non-partisan commission. Initial recruitment is identical to judges'; aspirants are typically selected in their early twenties through competitive examinations for admission to the Judiciary School, the *École nationale de la magistrature* ("ENM"). The entrance exam consists in anonymous written essays followed by a series of oral tests. The *magistrats* I talked to viewed the exam as eliminating political considerations and personal favoritism, in line with the egalitarian aspirations of the French Republic. An appellate judge described it as a "republican exam … a recruitment procedure which gives satisfaction because it has a republican legitimacy based on competence."[14] Yet, as I argue elsewhere, this purportedly meritocratic and unbiased selection mechanism results in massive class and race inequities, as it implies familiarity with a typically white middle-class culture and comportment.[15] Once admitted into the Judiciary School, trainee-*magistrats* receive a generalist instruction in the many functions of the judiciary, which include prosecutorial positions as well as generalist and specialized judgeships. Upon graduation, the new *magistrats* choose their first assignment as a judge or prosecutor based on availability as well as on their school ranking. From their initial post, they can later transfer to prosecutorial position or to a judgeship and vice versa.

The selection of prosecutors is removed from partisan politics, but transfers, promotions, and removals are not.[16] There is a split between judges and prosecutors. Judges manage their own affairs through the High Council of the Judiciary (*Conseil supérieur de la magistrature* or "CSM"), an independent

---

[13] The election of prosecutors in the U.S., in particular, has been the subject of numerous critiques. *See, e.g.,* Ronald F. Wright, *How Prosecutors Fail Us*, 6 Ohio St. J. Crim. Law 581 (2009).

[14] Interview with 7, Court of Appeals Judge (2016).

[15] *See* Mathilde Cohen, *Judicial Diversity in France: The Unspoken and the Unspeakable, Law & Social Inquiry* (forthcoming, 2018). *See also* Pierre Bourdieu & Monique de Saint Martin, *Agrégation et ségrégation. Le champ des grandes écoles et le champ du pouvoir*, 69 Actes de la recherche en sciences sociales 2 (1987) (critiquing elite French schools and public institutions' purportedly meritocratic admissions process).

[16] Tenure in the French context means that *magistrats* cannot be removed from office except for gross abuse of their authority.

commission composed of judges, lawyers, and outside political appointees, which has final decision-making on judicial promotions and removals. By contrast, the Council's role is much more limited when it comes to prosecutors as the Ministry of Justice largely determines their career, including promotion, transfer, discipline, and removal from office, which has led the European Court of Human Rights, in a series of cases, to criticize French prosecutors' subordination to the executive.[17] High-level prosecutors are appointed directly by the French cabinet (*Conseil des ministres*) with no Council involvement whatsoever.[18] As a retired chief prosecutor explained, "for very important positions, the Ministers decide ... I'd even add, for very, very, important positions, occasionally the Ministry of Justice calls the *Élysée* [i.e., the French white house] saying 'the Paris chief prosecutor must be appointed, we'd like X, what do you think?'"[19]

Does this subordination to political authorities pose a threat to the democratic character of the prosecutor's office? Can prosecutors who are dependent in some way upon the person who appoints them be relied upon to deliver independent decisions? Further empirical research is needed to answer this question. To be sure, current transfer and promotion mechanisms perpetuate the risk of "telephone justice," whereby Ministry bureaucrats orally instruct prosecutors on what to prosecute and how – a practice theoretically outlawed, but which may not have totally disappeared, as an appellate court chief judge reports,

> in principle, it should no longer occur, but it's certain that the Minister of Justice, via intermediaries, continues to follow sensitive cases. So she'll be informed of what is going on ... One way for the prosecutor's office to resist is to pass on the information or not pass on the information, waiting for the decision to be made so as to report an already-made decision. That can be a way to escape orders.[20]

This brief presentation of transfers and promotions raises the next question: if French prosecutors are neither selected nor promoted through democratic procedures, is their independence preserved through other mechanisms, such as separation of powers?

---

[17] ECHR, Medvedyev v. France, N°3394/03, July 10, 2008; ECHR, Medvedyev v. France, N° 3394/03, March 29, 2010; ECHR, Moulin v. France, N°37104/06, November 23, 2010.

[18] The High Council of the Judiciary does play a role when it comes to lower-level prosecutorial positions by giving non-binding advice on the Ministry of Justice's nominees.

[19] Interview with 1, retired Chief Prosecutor (2015).

[20] Interview with 6, Appellate Court Chief Judge (2015).

II SEPARATION OF POWERS

Separation of powers between executive, legislative, and judicial bodies is meant to guarantee individual freedom and prevent abuse of power. Should those making investigative, charging, and advocacy decisions be separated from those who make adjudicative decisions? Prosecutors usually belong to the executive, not the judicial, branch, but French prosecutors stand in a bizarre institutional configuration. They are officially members of the judiciary, but report to the executive branch.

A *Prosecutors and the Judicial Branch*

Does the fact that French prosecutors and judges are colleagues within the same organization pose the risk of commingling the functions of investigation and adjudication? Judges and prosecutors not only share the same professional status, but also the same office spaces, support staff, and budget. Far from being spatially segregated within court buildings, their offices are often adjacent. In a few courts, prosecutors have their own floors, but more often than not, their offices are integrated with judges'. A retired prosecutor summed up the situation quoting the following adage: "single corps, single courthouse," before adding that prosecutors and judges working on related issues are sometimes purposefully assigned neighboring offices to facilitate contact.[21] For example, a single building may bring together all the court members working on criminal cases: prosecutors, investigative magistrates,[22] and judges presiding over criminal trials. The two groups interact on a daily basis behind closed doors, inevitably discussing cases. The chief judge of a large appellate court who visited several foreign courts shared her comparative insights, "in Hungary, there was such a separation that the prosecutor could not speak with the presiding judge in the corridor because one may have feared some sort of collusion between them. They absolutely did not discuss outside of the public hearing. As for us, it's the exact opposite. We [judges and prosecutors] talk all the time. We each assume our responsibility and may reach different decisions, but there's a constant open dialogue."[23]

---

[21] Interview with 1, retired Chief Prosecutor (2015).
[22] The investigative magistrates (*juges d'instruction*) are specialized judges tasked with conducting the investigative hearings preceding major criminal trials. They only intervene for the investigation of the gravest crimes, that is, in 1.28 percent of prosecutable offenses. *See* MINISTÈRE DE LA JUSTICE, LES CHIFFRES-CLÉS DE LA JUSTICE 14 (2015).
[23] Interview with 6, Appellate Court Chief Judge (2015).

For the longest time, this proximity had a symbolic translation in the hearing ritual as prosecutors and judges used to enter and exit the courtroom from same door, a practice now abandoned because it gave the appearance of improper intertwining. While the outward exhibition of judges and prosecutors' union was effaced, its practical and decisional manifestations were not. Judges and prosecutors share the same finances, which can create tensions and impinge on case management. Every French court is governed by a dyad composed of a chief judge and chief prosecutor who must jointly agree on resource allocations. This diarchy leads to conflicts ranging from the mundane to the serious. A senior judge who served as a chief judge confided:

> what is very problematic is that a chief judge manages his tribunal with a chief prosecutor. All decisions must be taken jointly. For example, you buy three computers: you give one to the judges, one to the prosecutors, but who gets the third one? ... If there aren't enough judges, another question is whether we'll cancel civil or criminal hearings. Will the administrative staff support prosecutors or judges?[24]

Agreeing on the number and type of hearings to apportion to criminal prosecutions is particularly troubling from a separation of powers standpoint. By negotiating this allocation with their prosecutorial counterparts, chief judges become involved in shaping prosecutorial choices. One of prosecutors' prerogatives is to screen complaints and sort out cases for types of prosecution, from fully-fledged criminal trials to expedited trials to a variety of alternative dispute resolution processes. When a chief judge decides to ration criminal hearings (or to provide more of them), she indirectly encourages certain prosecutorial policies. As a recently retired appellate court chief judge explained,

> The prosecution's position ... tends to be: "I need more hearings. I prosecute a lot and these prosecutions deserve to be examined through hearings, rather than ADR" ... And the position of judges is to say: "I can't grant you as many hearings as you request because I have other imperatives and my imperatives are to process civil cases, family cases, small claims, social security, labor disputes, etc. ... Besides, perhaps you, the prosecutor's office, ought to diversify your prosecutorial arsenal."[25]

The issue of hearing allocation is particularly contentious. Perhaps because of their professional identity as judges, prosecutors remain attached to traditional trials even though expedited trials and alternative dispute resolution are gaining ground. In 2014, of the 1.3 million offenses deemed prosecutable, 4.7

---

[24] Interview with 10, Senior Judge (2015).   [25] Interview with 17, retired Chief Judge (2015).

percent were processed through guilty pleas on the model of plea bargaining, 12 percent through penal orders (*ordonnance pénale*), 5.3 percent through settlements (*compositions pénales*), and 38.2 percent were resolved through other alternative dispute resolution mechanisms such as warnings, mediation, court-mandated courses, and treatment programs.[26] Membership in the judiciary, therefore, has profound implications for prosecutorial autonomy, limiting prosecutors' control over the type of actions they can choose, and pushing them toward ADR as a way to save resources for civil proceedings. But prosecutors must also contend with another meddling influence in their decision-making: the executive branch.

B Prosecutors and the Executive Branch

1 External Hierarchy

According to the French Constitution, the head of the executive branch, the President of the Republic, is the guarantor of the justice system's independence.[27] In the French republican ideology, the executive is supposed to protect citizens from excesses of unelected judges rather than judges protecting citizens from the executive, as in the Anglo-American tradition. This is a post-Revolutionary legacy. Of all the institutions of the Old Regime, the multitudinous courts that existed before 1789 with overlapping jurisdictions and quasi-legislative powers were among the most disparaged. By contrast, the judiciary established by the revolutionaries was characterized by its centralization and subordination to other branches of the government. Old Regime prosecutors, who had enjoyed some degree of freedom from the king, were abolished and replaced under Napoléon by a docile corps of bureaucrats.[28] Ever since, the structure of the prosecutor's office remained highly hierarchical. All prosecutors are accountable to the Minister of Justice as well as to their immediate superiors.

The subordinated network of prosecutors is tasked with carrying out governmental policies. In traditional French statist and centralized fashion, the Ministry of Justice defines priorities of nationwide applicability known as "penal policies" (*politique pénale*) accompanied by quantified objectives.[29] These guidelines trickle down the prosecutorial structure via circulars as well as yearly meetings with supervisors relaying the directions locally. Until 2013, the Minister of Justice was entitled to give written instructions in individual

---

[26] See Ministère de la Justice, *supra* note 22, at 14.   [27] Fr. Const. Article 64.
[28] Jean-Marie Carbasse, Histoire du Parquet 16–7 (2000).
[29] See Code de Procédure Pénale [C. pr. pén.] Article 30 (Fr.).

cases such as ordering the prosecution of a given person.[30] In theory, the discontinuation of a prosecution could not be ordered, but in practice, demands to close cases of political allies were frequent. According to sociologists Philip Milburn and Christian Mouhanna, sanctions for the failure to follow ministerial instructions take various forms, from being summoned to the Ministry for disregarding national orientations, to improvised inspections following a high-profile prosecution, to the transfer of refractory prosecutors.[31] In addition, the professional misconduct charge of "insubordination" can result in discipline and sanctions.[32]

Giving and following instructions is such an entrenched characteristic of the prosecutors' office that it turns up in the performance evaluation system. Junior prosecutors are dependent upon senior prosecutors in a career system in which high-level prosecutors evaluate and grade lower-level prosecutors every other year. Evaluations and grade become part of prosecutors' individual files, which are the basis for future transfers, promotions, or disciplines. Evaluators use a standardized performance appraisal form. Submission and compliance are explicitly valued and serve as measures of professional achievement. To evaluate prosecutors with managerial responsibilities, central criteria include the "capacity to conduct penal policies" and "to be part of the statutory hierarchical relationship." Reciprocally, line prosecutors are evaluated based on their "capacity to implement penal policies" and "to be part of the statutory hierarchical relationship."[33] In short, those determining promotions are explicitly instructed to reward loyalty and conformity and to penalize independence.

2 Internal Hierarchy

The strong internal hierarchy among prosecutors reinforces their external subordination to the executive branch. The prosecutors I interviewed insisted that a defining feature of their professional identity is the *collective* nature of

---

[30]   *See* statute n°2013–669 of July 25, 2013, codified at C. PR. PÉN. ARTICLE 30.

[31]   Philip Milburn & Christian Mouhanna, *Présentation*, 74 DROIT & SOCIÉTÉ 7, 15 (2010).

[32]   Few prosecutors have been disciplined merely for failing to follow hierarchical orders, the charge being often associated with other types of misconduct. *But see* July 16, 2004 *Avis Motivé* in CONSEIL SUPÉRIEUR DE LA MAGISTRATURE, RAPPORT ANNUEL 2003–2004 178–82 (2004) (reprimanding a deputy prosecutor for preventing his superior from "controlling" his requisitions and for himself refusing to exercise his hierarchical control over line prosecutors). *See also* decree of December 22, 1958, Article 45 (providing that sanctions for misconduct include reprimand, reassignment to a different position, withdrawal from certain functions, demotion, compulsory retirement, and removal).

[33]   These criteria are laid out in an internal document distributed to all high-level judges and prosecutors who evaluate their junior colleagues.

the job, contrasted to the solitary work of judges. Asked about the defining feature of his time in the prosecutor's office, a former prosecutor turned judge replied, "first of all, my experience of the prosecutor's office is an experience of collective life one does not find in judgeships."[34] Group decision-making in a highly stratified system, however, may reinforce pressure toward conformity. As I was able to see for myself, the default day-to-day work of handling ongoing investigations takes place in an open space office layout. Prosecutors overhear one another talking to the police over the phone and making on the spot investigative or prosecutorial decisions. They constantly chat with one another, commenting on their investigations and asking for feedback. Supervisors present in the room inform superiors immediately if any unusual or sensitive investigation comes up.

For instance, during my observations, a juvenile case generated frenzy in the office. A couple of weeks after the November 2015 Paris attacks, a teenager wrote on President François Hollande's Facebook page that he wanted to "exterminate all French Jews." The line prosecutor who received the case turned to colleagues for guidance. They agreed that the statement constituted the crimes of "apology of terrorism," "incitation to racial hate," and "death threats." Since the attacks, the state of emergency was placed and the Ministry of Justice had ordered zero tolerance on terror threats, leading the supervisor present in the room to conclude that charges should be brought as soon as possible. The group was unsure of the victim's identity, however. Was it the French state? The Jewish community? This hesitation prompted the supervisor to call the chief prosecutor's aide on her cell phone for directions.

A functional equivalent of the executive branch's right to order prosecutions is the chief prosecutors' right to substitute prosecutors working on a specific case. Trial courts' chief prosecutors (the *"procureurs de la République"*) have full discretion to organize their office as they sees fit, moving line prosecutors around from post to post and reclaiming or re-allocating cases at any time.[35] As a former prosecutor quoted above recounted, "I have seen chief prosecutors repossess a case ... The chief prosecutor said 'no I don't agree with you, hand over the file. I will make the charging decision.'"[36] Each *procureur de la République* is assisted by deputy and line prosecutors who have little room to exercise independent judgment, hence, perhaps, their official title, "substitutes of the prosecutor" (*substituts du procureur*). The *substituts* are interchangeable pawns acting in the name of the chief prosecutor rather than in their own. The

---

[34] Interview with 12, Senior Judge (2015).
[35] CODE DE L'ORGANISATION JUDICIAIRE, ARTICLE R.311–35.
[36] Interview with 12, Senior Judge (2015).

threat of constant mutability discourages them from expressing their personal
convictions when they are contrary to their superiors' instructions.

After having examined prosecutors' position from a separation of powers
perspective, the next Part turns to their deliberative practices.

III DELIBERATION

Deliberative democracy is a contested concept, but at its core is the idea that
decisions made by state authorities must be justified by reasons, or at least
contestable. This ensures that citizens are treated not merely as passive subjects to be ruled, but as autonomous agents who take part in the governance of
their own society, directly or through their representatives.[37] Do prosecutorial
decisions meet these conditions?

A *Reason-giving*

French prosecutors, like their American counterparts, have very limited obligations to give reasons. Most strikingly, they do not need to justify the decision
to prosecute by bringing formal charges or by orienting a case toward ADR.

In only three circumstances are prosecutors under a legal duty to give
reasons: 1) when they decide not to prosecute;[38] 2) when they extend a suspect's
police custody or request the pre-trial detention of a suspect;[39] and 3) for the
most serious crimes, when they respond to the investigative magistrate's conclusions and propose a set of charges.[40] In the first couple scenarios, reason-
giving is purely boilerplate; prosecutors check boxes on fill-out forms such as
"insufficient evidence," "amnesty," or "irregular procedure" when closing a
case. When prolonging custody or requesting pre-trial detention, pre-printed
reasons include the need for the police to continue investigating, ensuring the
presence of the suspect at arraignment, preventing the destruction of evidence, etc. Though formulaic, these reasons are a step forward; boxes to be
checked are more informative than no boxes to be checked. The third form of
reason-giving, reserved to the few serious cases deferred to a *juge d'instruction*,[41] presents prosecutors with the only sustained justificatory obligation in
their professional life. After the *juge d'instruction* completes her investigation,
the prosecutor drafts a detailed memo, ranging from 4 to 800 pages depending

---

[37] *See generally* Amy Gutmann and Dennis Thompson: Why Deliberative Democracy?
(2004) (providing an exposition of deliberative democracy and its application to practical
problems).

[38] C. pr. pén. Article 40–2.   [39] C. pr. pén. Article 137–4.

[40] C. pr. pén. Article 175.   [41] *See supra* note 22.

on the complexity of the case, reviewing the evidence and recommending whether or not to charge, what to charge, and whether to send the case to the *tribunal correctionnel*, composed of professional judges only, or to the *cour d'assises*, where professional judges sit with lay assessors.

These three reason-giving requirements are primarily addressed to colleagues and superiors rather than the public, the accused, and the victims. One would expect that the decision to drop a case was justified for the benefit of the victim, who is often the person soliciting law enforcement. Yet, prosecutors can choose not to by checking the apposite box on the pre-filled form: "do not give notice to the victim." More surprising yet, the alleged perpetrator does not receive a copy of the decision to close a case. One of the defense attorneys I interviewed complained that the only way for the accused to find out why the case was dropped is to "go to the *Renseignements* [the internal intelligence agency] and request a copy ... It's totally archaic."[42] Archaic or not, the question which interests us is whether the need to resort to the secret services is a sign of democratic failure. Though neither available to the public, the accused, nor the victim, these reasons have the merit of existing. They may prove efficacious internally, be it as precedents for future cases, arguments for political action, or record for review purposes.

Rather than a tool for external accountability toward parties and the public, the pre-printed reason-giving form functions principally an internal accountability mechanism. One of the Ministry of Justice's proclaimed goals is for prosecutors to provide a "penal response" to all prosecutable offenses. As a result, prosecutors use the form to justify *to their supervisors* the termination of prosecutions (which occurred in 11.5 percent of the cases in 2014).[43] Similarly, the duty to justify the prolongation of police custody as well as pre-trial detention operates as an internal rather than external accountability mechanism. I observed five police custody prolongation hearings conducted over videoconference.[44] In all instances, the prosecutors neither introduced themselves nor explained the purpose of the hearing and the custody when interrogating the suspects, leading to confusion as to their role and identity. One of the suspects concluded the hearing by saying, "Thank you, Mr. Judge," betraying the mistaken assumption that he was talking to a judge. Two other suspects consistently addressed the prosecutor as "Chief," suggesting awareness that they were speaking to a higher authority of sorts, but raising doubt as to whether they were informed of the nature of the hearing. The recipient of the boilerplate statement of reasons in the form of checked boxes is

---

[42] Interview with B, Defense Attorney (2015).
[43] MINISTÈRE DE LA JUSTICE, *supra* note 22 at 14.
[44] Fieldwork Observations (2015 and 2016).

neither the detained individual nor the public (the form is not a public document), but rather the specialized judge responsible for decisions on release and detention (*juge de la liberté et de la détention*).

The third form of mandatory reason-giving benefits parties more directly, given that both the defendant and the victim (represented as a "civil party")[45] obtain a copy of the prosecution's memo. Yet, the prosecutor's argument is aimed at persuading the *juge d'instruction* rather than explaining the charges to the accused or the public (in fact the document is not publicly available and I was only able to familiarize myself with its content and format by asking my research subjects for copies). The prosecutor's hope, when drafting this type of memo, is that the *juge d'instruction* will agree on whether to charge, what to charge, whether to charge in a *tribunal correctionnel* or in a *cour d'assises*, whether to allow defendants to enter diversion programs, etc. This memo too represents an internal form of accountability, which leaves out parties and the general public.

The only form of reason-giving geared toward external accountability is found at trial. Prosecutors' statements at trial are public and provide some measure of justification for prosecutions. Their explanatory power, however, varies considerably from trial to trial and prosecutor to prosecutor, depending on a host of factors, from the specifics of the case to the individual style of prosecutors. As one interviewee remarked,

> The caricature of the prosecutor is the guy seated through the entire hearing who brusquely stands up when his turn comes to say just four words before sitting down again: "Application of the law," that is, I will leave the case to the judges' appreciation. For repetitive cases such as driving offenses, it is very common. It's also more prevalent among senior prosecutors. At the beginning young prosecutors strive to argue, but they soon find out that it's a waste of time for recurrent cases.[46]

In addition to engaging in these different forms of reason-giving, prosecutors' decisions present varying degrees of contestability.

B Contestability

As a complement or alternative to reasoned deliberation, some theorists have proposed that the contestability of public decisions allows citizens to maintain a democratic government.[47] The idea is that unreviewable power and absolute

---

[45] C. PR. PÉN. ARTICLE 2 (in all criminal proceedings, those injured as a result of a criminal act may intervene by interposing a claim for civil relief, becoming known as "civil parties").

[46] Interview with 1, retired Chief Prosecutor (2015).

[47] *See* Philip Pettit, *Republican Freedom and Contestatory Democratization* in DEMOCRACY'S VALUE 163 (Ian Shapiro & Casiano Hacker-Cordon, eds., 1999).

discretion are incompatible with democracy outside of the most dire of emergencies. If citizens have the ability to challenge public decisions, however, they keep public officials in check, preventing them from slipping into the arbitrary power and from advancing their own interests or those of the powerful. Are prosecutorial decisions contestable? Few legal checks exist to police-prosecutorial decisions ex ante, judges generally lacking the power to monitor and control the work of prosecutors before charging decisions are made.[48] French rules of evidence are far less constraining than Anglo-American rules, providing prosecutors with more leeway in their handling of the investigation and their rapport with the police.[49] It is the criminal process triggered by prosecutors' indictments that determines whether the decision to prosecute was warranted based on the evidence.

By contrast, the decision *not* to prosecute is open to pre-trial review. The process is non-judicial, resembling a superior audit. The *Code de procédure pénale* provides that, "any person who denounced the facts" can appeal the decision to close the case to one of the 36 chief prosecutors (*procureurs généraux*).[50] According to a former chief prosecutor, "the chief prosecutor requests the file, reexamines it, and sometimes in these situations he instructs the line prosecutor who closed the case to prosecute, saying 'I disagree with your closure decision' ... In general the line prosecutor anticipates this and prosecutes even before the appeal has been examined."[51] Preemptive correction by subordinates without any finding that they have erred or committed a fault is symptomatic of the hierarchical nature of the system. Subordinates have all the incentives to adjust decisions of their own initiative to avoid conflict and maintain a good working relationship with their supervisors. Who benefits from this limited right to contest prosecution terminations? All the actors who share in the prosecutorial function due to their capacity to trigger criminal proceedings, that is, the victims, but also the various authorities who initiate cases: the police, administrative agencies, social workers, and NGOs. There is no equivalent right for the accused to contest charging decisions, despite the plausibility of scenarios in which political forces push indictments in cases lacking legal or factual merits.

The French case illustrates the distance between the deliberative democracy ideal and the prosecutorial function as it manifests itself in many democratic states, divorced from the values of citizen participation and generally

---

[48] By contrast, investigative judges' (*juge d'instruction*) decisions are subject to review by a special judicial panel known as the *chambre de l'instruction*.

[49] C. PR. PÉN. ARTICLE 427 (stating the principle of freedom of proof or evidence by all means in criminal law).

[50] C. PR. PÉN. ARTICLE 40.3.   [51] Interview with 1, retired Chief Prosecutor (2015).

unconcerned with reason-giving and contestability. Could a more diverse corps of prosecutors generate more responsive, community-oriented prosecutorial roles? As the next Part argues, another angle to assess the relationship between prosecutors and democracy is the idea of representative bureaucracy.

IV DIVERSITY

Theoretical discussions of representative democracy have traditionally focused on the formal procedures of authorization and accountability within nation states, that is, on what Hanna Pitkin calls "formalistic representation."[52] However, such a focus is not satisfactory in diverse societies where segments of the population are systematically underrepresented in positions of power and overrepresented among those accused in the criminal justice system. The concept of representative bureaucracy can be mobilized to assess the relationship between prosecutors and democracy.[53] The notion of representative democracy should be extended to include the demographic representation of citizens in key public offices. Representative bureaucracy suggests that a public workforce representative of the people in terms of race, ethnicity, gender, and sexual orientation, but also socio-economic status, regional origin, abilities and disabilities, helps ensure that the interests of all groups are considered in decision-making processes. Are more diverse prosecutorial offices less susceptible to bias? Social scientists are divided on the issue, but there is strong evidence indicating that they are.[54] One way in which prosecutors could be agents of democracy, therefore, would be by engaging in both passive and active representation whereby they would not only more closely match the population on various dimensions of diversity, but also be attuned to the rights and needs of those they "look like" or represent.[55]

France is a heterogeneous society characterized by widespread diversity along multiple axes. However, prosecutors and judges are a homogeneous group. Drawn from the elite stratum of society concentrated in the Paris region, they are strikingly under-representative of racial, ethnic, and sexual minorities,

---

[52] Hanna Fenichel Pitkin, THE CONCEPT OF REPRESENTATION 11, 89 (1967).

[53] *See* DONALD KINGSLEY, REPRESENTATIVE BUREAUCRACY: AN INTERPRETATION OF THE BRITISH CIVIL SERVICE (1944) (articulating the notion of a representative bureaucracy in the context of the British civil service during the Second World War).

[54] *See* KATHERINE J. BIES, ET AL., STUCK IN THE '70S: THE DEMOGRAPHICS OF CALIFORNIA PROSECUTORS 14–16 (2015) (reviewing the literature on the effects of diversity in prosecutorial agencies).

[55] Another complementary approach would be to train prosecutors along the lines of what Angela Davis has proposed in the U.S. context. *See* Angela J. Davis, *In Search of Racial Justice: The Role of the Prosecutor,* 16 N.Y.U. J. LEGIS. & PUB. POL'Y 821 (2013).

as well as low-income citizens and rural regions. Women dominate the French judiciary overall, but men remain overrepresented among prosecutors. About 63.05 percent of the combined judges/prosecutors are female,[56] but only 39 percent of prosecutors are female, versus 56 percent of judges.[57] The (real or imaginary) gendering of judgeships and prosecutorial posts explains this discrepancy. Working as a prosecutor is harder on those with caregiving responsibilities, who tend to be female, as the job calls for long, often unpredictable hours, constant availability over the phone when on-call, as well as night and weekend shifts. The hierarchized and collective nature of the day-to-day work, defined by constant interactions with the police, foster a masculinized professional ethos. Throughout my research, I was struck by the gendered language used by research subjects. Time after time, they used feminine-coded adjectives to describe judicial assignments as "solitary," "bureaucratic," or "passive," in contrast to prosecutors' work, which was depicted as "collegial," "dynamic," and "active." Practical constraints as well as cultural constructions collude to perpetuate a gender imbalance among prosecutors.

Ascertaining the racial and ethnic background of judges, prosecutors, and defendants is an arduous task in the French context as no official data on race and ethnicity are collected.[58] In the supposedly "universalist" French tradition, not only the state, but also French social scientists tend to deny the reality of race and ethnicity.[59] The collection of so-called "ethnic statistics" is generally prohibited, perpetuating the invisibility of minorities and obscuring the reality of systemic discrimination and other forms of oppression.[60] The biographical directory of French judges and prosecutors (*"annuaire de la magistrature"*) includes their name, date and place of birth, educational background, professional background prior to entering the judiciary, if any, and a chronological list of posts occupied. Nothing is known about their race or ethnicity. This façade of color-blindness covers a deep hypocrisy, however. Journalists and activists have

---

[56] CONSEIL SUPÉRIEUR DE LA MAGISTRATURE, *supra* note 12, at 28.

[57] Cécile Petit, *État des lieux des femmes dans la magistrature* (2004) (unpublished paper), *available at* www.administrationmoderne.com/pdf/activites/compterendu/cr_fmagistrature .pdf. *See also* AUDIER ET AL., *supra* note 2, at 44 (reporting that about 46 percent of male graduates of the Judiciary School land a prosecutor position right after graduating, compared to 38 percent of females).

[58] David B. Oppenheimer, *Why France Needs to Collect Data on Racial Identity . . . in a French Way*, 31 HASTINGS INT'L & COMP. L. REV. 735 (2008).

[59] *See* Cécile Laborde, *The Culture(s) of the Republic: Nationalism and Multiculturalism in French Republican Thought*, 29 POL. THEORY 716 (2001) (describing French republicanism's "ethical universalism," which is committed to cultural nationalism and hostile to multiculturalism).

[60] The French census includes data about nationality and country of birth, but not race and ethnicity.

long denounced the police and secret services' collection of racial and ethnic data on certain categories of offenders.[61] The judiciary's own database of offenders, "*Cassiopée*," contains a number of race-neutral data – name, place of birth, nationality, language, dialect, name of parents, domicile – which taken together give prosecutors an inkling of suspects' likely racial identification.

By most accounts, there are enormous disparities between the race, ethnicity, and social class of criminal defendants and prisoners, on the one hand, and that of judges and prosecutors, on the other hand. Based on my fieldwork, it appears that judges and prosecutors are overwhelmingly middle-class whites of Christian backgrounds. A retired chief prosecutor with intimate knowledge and experience of the justice system estimated that on the 7,726-member corps of judges and prosecutors, "not more than twenty" are black.[62] Asked about diversity in her court, the chief judge of a large appellate court responded, "there are no foreigners," before correcting herself, "they [the judges and prosecutors] are French."[63] As I explain elsewhere, many of the *magistrats* I interviewed lumped together race, ethnicity, and nationality, betraying the assumption that Frenchness is inseparable from whiteness.[64] Several *magistrats* noted that among the younger generations, a few "*beur*" (i.e., a colloquial term to designate French born people of North African descent) could be found. By contrast, Maghrebi, black, or Eastern European males from working-class and underprivileged backgrounds make up the majority of the accused, a fact reflected in the prison population.[65] In his 2015 study of a prison in the suburbs of Paris, anthropologist Didier Fassin was able to "visualize the astonishing presence of minorities."[66] According to him, black and Arab men represented two-thirds of the prisoners' population, closer to three-quarters of those below the age of 30. Other researchers have documented the fact that minorities and second-generation immigrants are more likely to be confined than whites and those of French descent.[67]

---

[61] *See, e.g., SOS Racisme accuse les RG d'avoir constitué un fichage ethnique des délinquants*, LE MONDE (August 23, 2006) (reporting on SOS Racisme's – one of France's leading anti-racist organizations – condemnation of the collection of racial and ethnic data by the *Renseignements généraux*) *See also* ALAIN BAUER, FICHIERS DE POLICE ET DE GENDARMERIE: COMMENT AMÉLIORER LEUR CONTRÔLE ET LEUR GESTION? 21 (2006) (discussing the police's use of racial and ethnic data).

[62] Interview with 1, retired Chief Prosecutor (2015).

[63] Interview with 6, Appellate Court Chief Judge (2015). [64] *See* Cohen, *supra* note 15.

[65] DIDIER FASSIN, L'OMBRE DU MONDE: UNE ANTHROPOLOGIE DE LA CONDITION CARCÉRALE (2015).

[66] *Id.*

[67] Sociologist Farhad Khosrokhavar, using parents' nationality as a proxy, found that those who had parents born in the Maghreb made up 39.9 percent of prisoners aged 18–24 and 35.4

Judiciaries of similarly situated societies such as England have identified the lack of diversity in the judicial ranks as a major social justice problem undermining public confidence in the justice system.[68] French judges and prosecutors are more reticent to acknowledge the problem. While gender and socio-economic inequalities are no longer taboo,[69] racial discrimination and oppression goes unmentioned. In 2008, the Judiciary School created a special preparatory course (the *"classes préparatoires Égalité des chances"*) to foster a "diverse recruitment" into the judiciary, by which it means socio-economic and geographic diversity. Applicants must either prove financial hardship or reside in urban areas defined by the government as high-priority targets due to economic impoverishment, violence, and unemployment. The stated goal is *not* to foster racial and ethnic diversity; as a prep course professor noted, it would be "impossible, it's against the French Constitution ... because of the way in which we interpret the anti-discrimination principle in the Constitution we can't have ethnic statistics, etc."[70] Though minorities are underrepresented and whites overrepresented among French prosecutors, neither the idea of representative bureaucracy nor the benefits of diversifying prosecutor's offices are on the agenda. So long as the judiciary will solely be interested in fostering socio-economic, geographic, and gender diversity, it will perpetuate a formalistic notion of representative democracy, which blithely ignores unwarranted racial, ethnic, as well as sexual orientation disparities in public institutions.

To summarize the chapter so far, the French prosecutor's office's design and functioning appears misaligned with a variety of goals which democratic theorists have assigned to a democratic state, from bureaucratic recruitment, to opaque transfer and promotion mechanisms, to erratic separation of powers, to sparse reason-giving, to lack of diversity. There may be nothing specific to the French case in that prosecutorial agencies elsewhere may share many of these shortcomings. Yet, as the next and final Part argues, what is specific about the French case is that prosecutors have found a variety of methods to

percent of prisoners aged 25–39. *See* Farhad Khosrokhavar, L'ISLAM DANS LES PRISONS 279–80 (2004). *See also* CATHY LISA SCHNEIDER, *POLICE POWER AND RACE RIOTS: URBAN UNREST IN PARIS AND NEW YORK* 131, 193 (2014) (reporting an assessment of the Versailles prison as composed of 90 percent black and Arab inmates).

[68] Erin Delaney, *Searching for Constitutional Meaning in Institutional Design: The Debate over Judicial Appointments in the United Kingdom*, 14 INT'L J. CONST. L. (2016).

[69] The High Council of the Judiciary publishes yearly gender statistics, which document females' continued underrepresentation in high level posts. As of 2014, 63.05 percent of the combined judges and prosecutors were females, but only 12 of the 36 appellate courts' chief prosecutors are women. *See* CONSEIL SUPÉRIEUR DE LA MAGISTRATURE, *supra* note 12, at 28.

[70] Interview with C, prep course Professor (2016).

resist the hierarchical structure in which they are embedded, by relying in part on their status of *magistrats* akin judges.

V *DE FACTO* INDEPENDENCE?

On the ground, prosecutors have developed several approaches to counteract hierarchical and political pressures, including peer-mediated corrections, specialization, and unionization.

A *Peer Review*

The French judiciary represents somewhat of an anomaly from a theory of organizations perspective. Bureaucracies are generally assumed to be goal-driven organizations whose members are tasked with common aims. Contrary to that view, the French judiciary includes within the same structure two sets of bureaucrats functionally pitted against one another: judges and prosecutors. Prosecutors are not only embedded in teams of prosecutors, but also in broader teams including judges. Their discretion is therefore not only bounded by rules of criminal procedure, but also by these two sets of colleagues. The missions of judges and prosecutors are distinct and, to a large extent, antagonistic. Prosecutors are advocates, indicting and prosecuting, while judges are supposed to be disinterested adjudicators. Avoiding an entangling alliance between the two functions seems essential to the democratic functioning of the justice system. Yet in practice, entanglement itself – in the form of joint membership in a unified professional body – may act both as a check on prosecutorial discretion and an impetus for prosecutorial independence.

How does belonging to the same corps promote independence? A few of the prosecutors I interviewed emphasized that going through the same training and professional experiences as judges acculturates them into judicial ethics, which they come to identify with. As a high-level prosecutor explained, "just by investigating, regardless of whether or not we will end up indicting, we infringe upon individual liberties, we infringe upon people's reputations, we create a host of constraints, and we must do so with an extremely rigorous ethics, and I believe that that of judges isn't the worst."[71] Prosecutors see themselves as sharing a judges' distinctive professional ethos in that they are first and foremost public servants tasked with protecting the general interest, not advocates. They insist that they are not a typical party to the criminal trial,

---

[71] Interview with 15, Senior Prosecutor (2015).

but a "very peculiar party." As another high-level prosecutor declared, "what is asked from the prosecutors is that no consideration other than the necessity to defend the general interest and prosecute crimes interfere with their decision. That's impartiality."[72] This judicial posture is a powerful tool for individual prosecutors to resist internal and external interference in their decision-making. When asked about whether his supervisors or the Ministry bureaucrats intervened in his cases, a judge who had served as a prosecutor answered negatively, "I was coming from a judgeship. Perhaps it's a question of character. When I made a decision, the decision was made."[73]

Belonging to the same corps as judges also not only fosters independence, but it may also limit prosecutorial discretion through internal norms of collegiality and peer review. As discussed above,[74] prosecutors' decisions are not technically subject to judicial review, but professional membership in the judiciary creates an institutional check on discretion. Prosecutors and judges belong to the same state-sanctioned elite; they studied together, transfer from one position to the other, eat lunch together, and are sometimes coupled,[75] all factors driving them to get along. A former judge who never served as a prosecutor pointed out that "being in the same building, one is constrained to take into account what the other will say. It's very different from what I observed abroad where the prosecutor is an external partner. Our institutional positioning is very different."[76] Another judge, who served as a prosecutor, recalls his trial experience: "You are there to show your colleague on the bench what you would do if you were in his shoes. And it's extremely helpful for a judge. He needs this."[77] The two groups trust one another quasi-instinctively, being controlled by the same powerful educational and institutional norms. At the same time, their professional goals often conflict so they must make conscious efforts to avoid dissatisfying the other camp. For example, prosecutors engage in self-censuring behaviors such as refraining from prosecuting cases that lack sufficient factual basis, investigating and paying attention to both inculpatory and exculpatory evidence, and volunteering to share information with the defense during the pre-trial phase as a showing of good faith.[78]

---

[72] Interview with 13, Chief Prosecutor (2015).   [73] Interview with 12, Senior Judge (2015).

[74] *Supra* Part III.B.

[75] To obtain assignments in the same court, a common strategy for married or partnered *magistrats* is for one to serve as a judge and the other as a prosecutor, given the unlikelihood of securing two judgeships at the same time.

[76] Interview with 5, retired Chief Judge (2015).   [77] Interview with 12, Senior Judge (2015).

[78] According to one of the defense attorneys I interviewed, the prosecution has no duty to share its file with the defense during the pre-trial phase, but often does so as to "look good."

Having served as a judge earlier on in one's career, prosecutors say, helps one to anticipate when a case will hold up to judicial scrutiny and when to engage in preventative rectification. I witnessed a colorful illustration of this self-censorship. Over several days, the police called the prosecutor's office I was observing about a dentist accusing a former patient of harassment and death threats. The alleged perpetrator was held in custody for 48 hours. What evidence did the police gather during that time? Flowers, chocolates, and text messages ("I've been loving you for two years" or "I want to take you out to dinner"). Finally, upon learning that the suspect, a Russian citizen with very little French, could not have been meaningfully interrogated without an interpreter, one of the prosecutors on call ordered his immediate release, ironizing: "Sending flowers, of course, is a form of violence. We'll look good, I can tell you. These are shitty procedures."[79] After hanging up the phone, furious, he exclaimed that his "colleagues" – the judges – would laugh at him and his office if charges were brought.

The familial and professional bond between judges and prosecutors operate as checks on discretion in a Goffmanian sense.[80] Prosecutors do not attempt moves that may lead to losing face in front of colleagues. Tellingly, few things irritate prosecutors more than being rebuked by judges who never served as prosecutors, and therefore, they claim, lack the ability to identify with their perspective. The same prosecutor who dropped the spurned lover's case became enraged, a couple hours later, when the judge on call that day for authorizing pre-trial detention (*juge des libertés et de la détention*) released three suspects. He wanted them in custody so that they could be tried through an expedited proceeding the next day. Upon hearing of their release, he burst out: "See, that's what happens when we have incompetent civil judges on call on weekends as *juge des libertés et de la détention*. To be sure they never served as prosecutors or they would know better. If X [one of the suspects, a repeat DUI offender] kills a child tomorrow, I'll call the media to tell them it's the judge's fault!"

As this acting out suggests, judges and prosecutors, though officially colleagues, are also in competitive relationships. Implicit in the disgruntled prosecutor's charge was the reality that the justice system is often the target of media and political attacks, with judges and prosecutors attempting to pass the buck to one another. Their rivalry can be beneficial, however, fostering prosecutorial

---

79 Fieldwork Observations (2015).
80 *See* Erving Goffman, *On Face-Work*, in SOCIAL THEORY: THE MULTICULTURAL READINGS 338 (Charles Lemert, ed., 2010, [1955]) (laying out some of the ways in which people present a face or image of the self in social relationships).

independence and accountability. Prosecutors do not have the monopoly on prosecutions. The most serious crimes are in principle investigated and prosecuted by investigative magistrates (the *juges d'instruction*), who represent a significant check on prosecutorial discretion. Should a prosecutor's office try to sweep a case under the rug, e.g., because it implicates public officials, well-known figures, or the police, or is likely to have a high media impact, the victims and a number of NGOs[81] can initiate criminal proceedings by referring the case directly the *juge d'instruction*, bypassing the prosecutor's office altogether.[82] This eventuality is dreaded as a source of great embarrassment for prosecutors whose lack of independence would be exposed for the bench and the general public to witness. The overlapping competence between *juges d'instruction* and prosecutors, therefore, acts as a powerful motivation for the latter to strive to be independent decision-makers, lest they be ridiculed in the profession and in the media.

B *Policy-making and Specialization*

Localism and specialization may further *de facto* independence in the hyper-centralized and hierarchized French context where requests for information emanating from the Ministry of Justice or high-level prosecutors are frequent.

1 Bottom-up Policy-making

Prosecutorial discretion varies depending on the size of a court. In small courts relying on fewer than five prosecutors, the head prosecutor intervenes in the majority of the cases. In medium to large courts, line prosecutors enjoy broader responsibilities and more leeway; only in sensitive or very serious cases will supervisors be involved from the beginning, leaving room for local policy-making as well as decision-making free of political interference to develop.[83] Localism has democratic effects in that it produces greater independence from the executive and introduces an element of citizens' participation in the criminal justice system, but it may also have undemocratic consequences in increasing prosecutorial discretion.

Localism facilitates participatory democracy through community involvement in the justice system. A high-level prosecutor who spent most of his career lobbying for greater prosecutorial independence through decentralization and local initiatives explained that since the 1990s, penal policies increasingly

---

[81] Such as anti-racist organizations, violence against women groups, victims' association, anti-drug groups, child protection groups, etc.

[82] C. PR. PÉN. ARTicle 85.   [83] *See* AUDIER ET AL., *supra* note 2 at 130.

developed bottom-up. Through local partnerships with a range of actors, including the *préfets* (the state's representative at the local level), the police, educators, and social workers, prosecutors expanded their role far beyond the sole prosecution of cases.[84] They increasingly enlist public actors as well as the civil society in the definition and implementation of penal priorities. Partnerships such as *"contrats de ville"* or the *"maisons de justice et du droit"* were established to foster cooperation between judges, prosecutors, elected officials, and social workers with the goal to prevent crimes, develop ADR, and assist victims by offering free legal clinics. According to this pro-decentralization prosecutor, the introduction of "real-time" processing of delinquency (the so-called *traitement en temps réel* or "TTR") strengthened prosecutors' supervision of the police, all the while affording them a deeper grasp of the realities of crime. Prosecutors now process every single case signaled by the police though a telephone monitoring system. They direct investigations and order, renew, or revoke suspects' custody, deciding whether or not to prosecute in real time as the information flows in through telephone communications. As a judge argued, these constant interactions with investigators and offenders made prosecutors prized experts on the nation's social problems, systematically consulted by legislators and other agencies for major reform projects.[85]

The flipside of this accrued independence is the potential broadening of prosecutorial discretion. The *traitement en temps réel* system operates as an emancipatory mechanism from the Ministry of Justice and the *procureurs généraux*, allowing line prosecutors to develop the expertise and fine-grained knowledge of their fieldwork necessary to generate independent penal policies. At the same time, it resulted in widening disparities between different prosecutor's offices and among prosecutors within each office. It expanded prosecutions to behaviors previously not taken to court – petty offenses such as traveling on public transportation without a valid ticket, smoking pot, or congregating in a building's communal parts. The police officer I interviewed believes that prosecutors now enjoy too much individual discretion, even though he and his colleagues use this excess to their advantage. When they need to secure prosecutorial authorization for an action, their first step is to find out which prosecutors are on call. Depending on the answer, they delay or accelerate the investigation so as to connect with those prosecutors perceived as more accommodating, rather than "the bougie, squeamish female prosecutors who do not understand the realities on the ground"[86] – a characterization which reflects the enduring masculine coding of the prosecutorial function, as discussed above.

---

[84]   Interview with 15, Senior Prosecutor (2015).   [85]   Interview with 24, Senior Judge (2015).
[86]   Interview with Police Officer (2015).

To counterbalance the broadened discretion brought about by real-time processing, a supervising prosecutor explained that when she was appointed, her first priority was to push for more uniformity in prosecutorial responses to police investigations.[87] She wanted to avoid the precise situation described by the police officer whereby some prosecutors gain a reputation for leniency while others are shunned as fastidious and difficult to deal with. Her strategy to check line prosecutors' discretion while setting clearer boundaries with the police was to establish clear recommendations for prosecutorial response to offenses. She consulted with the entire staff, compiling charts and tables indicating the orientation to adopt for all standards categories of offenses and offender profiles. The new guidelines were shared with the police as well as youth organizations, social workers, and other local actors. While non-binding, they represent an effort to balance independent and local decision-making with bounded discretion.

2 Caseloads and Specialization

In 2014, 4,621,486 criminal cases were processed by the French criminal justice system, of which over three million were closed due to the lack of identifiable perpetrator or for insufficient charges or evidence.[88] Still, 1,327,980 were disposed of, be it through trial, ADR, or dismissal after an initial proceeding had begun.[89] That same year, there were 1,919 prosecutors working in the country. On average, each prosecutor was responsible for processing 728 cases in addition to the hundreds of cases dismissed yearly.

Criminal caseloads are so high that they necessitate the *de facto* specialization of prosecutors, resulting in relative spheres of autonomy from the executive.[90] With the exception of prosecutors assigned to the generalist department of real-time case processing and for those in supervisory positions or in offices so small that everyone is a generalist, prosecutors specialize based on offense categories or, more rarely, territory.[91] Mid-size offices include separate prosecutorial departments for areas such as juvenile delinquency, organized crime, economic and financial crimes, and drugs. The largest offices include hyper-specialized divisions in matters such as terrorism, maritime pollution, tax fraud, or public health. Geographic specialization is becoming the norm in large urban areas where some prosecutors concentrate on a particular neighborhood. They become the point person for that district, responsible for investigating and

---

[87] Interview with 22, Chief Prosecutor (2016).

[88] MINISTÈRE DE LA JUSTICE, *supra* note 22, at 14.   [89] *Id.*

[90] Christian Mouhanna, *Les relations police-parquet en France: Un partenariat mis en cause?* 58 DROIT & SOCIÉTÉ, 505, 512–3 (2004).

[91] *Id.*

prosecuting offenses committed there, as well as coordinating the office's interactions with elected officials and civil society representatives.

Similar to bottom-up policy-making, caseloads and specialization are ambiguous in terms of democratic effects; while creating areas of decision-making free from political and hierarchical interferences, they yield new opportunities for prosecutorial discretion. Line prosecutors increasingly play a triage and filtering role. Their basic job is to sort out criminal complaints into three piles: those for which formal charges will be brought through a trial proceeding, those which will be dealt with through ADR, and those which will be dropped. This classification is informed by the nationwide *"politique pénale"* dictated by the Ministry, but prosecutors enjoy a significant margin of discretion. The French prosecutorial tradition is based on the so-called principle of *"opportunité des poursuites"* (discretionary prosecution), rather than the legality principle. This implies that prosecution itself may be subordinated to considerations of expediency. But in practice, since the revival of the punitive model in the 1990s combined with the victims' rights movement, prosecutors are encouraged to bring charges for all prosecutable offenses. The major change, however, is that the range of penal responses has diversified with the growing use of mediation (*médiation*), settlement (*composition*), expedited adjudication without hearing (*ordonnance*), and the introduction of a plea-bargaining-like procedure (*comparution sur reconnaissance préalable de culpabilité* or CRPC) in 2004. Prosecutors enjoy less discretion than before as to *whether or not* to prosecute, but more discretion as to *how* to prosecute.

This discretion is all the more insulated from accountability that caseloads are high (there aren't enough resources to oversee decisions with such a volume of cases) and prosecutors are specialized (monitoring is harder when decisions involve content expertise). Greater independence may come at the expense of increased discretion in the case of localism and specialization. As the next section argues, a final factor in French prosecutors' structural independence is unionization.

C Unionization

Do unions foster prosecutors' autonomy from their internal hierarchy as well as from other branches of government or do they compromise their independence by officializing their politicization? Unions are powerful forces in the French judiciary, with nearly two fifth of judges and prosecutors unionized. The *magistrats* can choose among several unions, including the leading *Union syndicale des magistrats*, a center-right organization first established in 1945,[92] the left-wing *Syndicat de la magistrature*, created in 1968 as an instrument of anti-elitism and hierarchism at a time when the French judiciary was a highly conservative force,[93] and *Force Ouvrière Magistrats*, a Trotskyist group founded in 1990. Here again, prosecutors' status as judges may be an advantage from a democracy perspective. As a judge and union member herself explained, "young prosecutors aren't always comfortable with the idea of joining a union; they worry that it may conflict with their duty of loyalty toward the hierarchy."[94] But many unionize while still at the Judiciary School or when they occupy a judicial post, i.e., before their appointment as a prosecutor. Still others make the leap inspired by their colleagues on the bench. In her view, if the two sets of professionals were split, prosecutors would be far less likely to unionize.

Unions cater to both judges' and prosecutors' interests, but they have been particularly active in pushing for greater prosecutorial independence both at the individual and collective level. At the individual level, unions assist judges and prosecutors threatened with discipline by their hierarchy. Though this assistance role is not specific to prosecutors, it is particularly crucial given prosecutors' unique vulnerability to being disciplined for insubordination. The *Syndicat de la magistrature* lobbied for years for the *magistrats* to acquire broader rights in disciplinary proceedings. Thanks to the union's battle, the *magistrats* accused of professional misconduct are now entitled a copy of their file during the pre-trial phase. But they continue to be deprived of the right to counsel during the initial investigation. As a former manager of the Ministry of Justice's division in charge of investigating accusations of judicial and prosecutorial misconduct (*Inspection générale des services judiciaires*) told me, "if judges and prosecutors obtained these guarantees, all civil servants would need to be treated the same, which would be unmanageable."[95] In his view, judges and prosecutors are no different than other civil servants such as teachers, police officers, doctors, nurses, or secretarial staff. He dismissed the argument that they should be entitled to special due process guarantees in virtue of the democratic need for prosecutorial independence from the executive.

Though the *Syndicat de la magistrature* lost the right to counsel battle, according to another judge, who belongs to a union, "a number of *magistrats* unionized during the Sarkozy era to protect themselves."[96] They hoped that

---

[92] *See* BENOÎT GARNOT, *HISTOIRE DE LA JUSTICE. FRANCE, XVIE-XXIE SIÈCLE* 309 (2009) (recounting the history of the union).

[93] *See* Willem de Haan et al., *Radical French Judges: Syndicat de la Magistrature*, 16 J.L. & SOC'Y 477, 479 (1989) (presenting the role of the union within the judiciary).

[94] Interview with 24, Senior Judge (2015).   [95] Interview with 8, Senior Prosecutor (2015).

[96] Interview with 24, Senior Judge (2015).

membership would shield them from media fire or investigation should they make a decision unpopular with the executive. According to her, the unions' protective effect is not "clear" in practice, but membership nonetheless provides a number of benefits, in particular the rare opportunity for prosecutors to meet and discuss issues of common interest. As a conservative high-level prosecutor conceded, not himself a union member and who admitted to feeling queasy about unions, "we need to regroup."[97] Unions engage in the public debate in multiple ways, from commenting on bills pertaining to the prosecutor's office and criminal procedure, to organizing yearly congresses addressing a variety of themes (ranging, in the past few years, from compulsory mental health care to "jihadist terrorism"), to issuing reports and press releases. To illustrate, a few days after the November 2015 Paris attacks, the leftist *Syndicat de la magistrature* published a press release protesting the government's use of the state of emergency to stifle civil liberties.

Unions have been particularly vocal in claiming greater independence for prosecutors. A recurrent demand is the insulation of the transfer and promotion system from the executive branch. In 2010, the *Syndicat de la magistrature* published a detailed report[98] denouncing the government's political appointment of high-level prosecutors close to the presidential camp.[99] The report also condemned the dismissal and forced transfer of prosecutors who had either refused to follow executive orders or criticized governmental policies.[100]

In sum, though unions may introduce elements of partisan politics in the judiciary, they represent an important outlet for prosecutors to meet and discuss the nature of their office within the democratic state. Notably, through unionization, prosecutors have obtained additional guarantees of independence.

CONCLUSION

The new courthouse, which will open in the northwest of Paris, will perpetuate the "carpenter's mistake." Despite the protestations of the Paris bar, prosecutors will remain at the same level as the judges' bench, above the

[97] Interview with 8, Senior Prosecutor (2015).
[98] SYNDICAT DE LA MAGISTRATURE, LA SITUATION DU MINISTÈRE PUBLIC FRANÇAIS (Feb. 23, 2010).
[99] For instance, a former President Sarkozy disciple, Philippe Courroye, was appointed chief prosecutor of the Nanterre tribunal despite the High Council of the Judiciary's negative advice.
[100] Thus in 2009, Marc Robert, the Riom chief prosecutor, was transferred to the *Cour de cassation* after having voiced concerns regarding the suppression of a local trial court and the proposed reform of the *juges d'instruction*. Robert was also lobbying for a more independent status for prosecutors.

table reserved for defense attorneys. Is the carpenter's "mistake" truly a mistake, however? As this chapter has shown, this symbolism is descriptively accurate in its representation of prosecutor-judges' relationships. Is it normatively correct as well? Prosecutors' status as judges has advantages and disadvantages from a democratic theory perspective. By self-identifying first and foremost as generalist *magistrats* susceptible to serve both as judges and prosecutors, prosecutors secure a measure of independence from the executive and embed themselves in peer accountability. At the same time, judges and prosecutors' common status poses a separation of powers issue, raising the specter of a criminal justice system united to secure as many convictions as possible at the expense of defendants.

The professional status of prosecutors as *magistrats* is a profoundly divisive issue within the French judiciary. In the past decades, there have been calls for splitting the corps into two distinct and autonomous agencies. But opponents fear that separation would result in a prosecutor's office being wholly subservient to the executive. This debate and its figurative manifestation as a carpentry dilemma reveal the instability of prosecutors' professional self-definition. French prosecutors aspire to a democratic role in the state as independent public servants disinterestedly serving the law. Yet, their growing awareness of alternative institutional designs for prosecutorial offices, combined with skyrocketing caseloads amid budget cuts and unfilled prosecutorial vacancies, puts them at odds with this self-presentation. The corps is in a state of perpetual soul-searching, as evidenced by the close to yearly reports commissioned by the Ministry of Justice on criminal justice reform. Until there is real political will to overhaul the system, carpenters will remain unemployed in courtrooms.

5

German Prosecutors and the Rechtsstaat

Shawn Boyne*

> To influence an investigation because its possible result might not seem opportune is an intolerable interference with the freedom of justice.
>
> – German Federal Prosecutor Harald Range[1]
>
> (the day before he was fired)

I INTRODUCTION

During the past two decades, scholars, politicians, and legal practitioners in the United States have criticized American prosecutors for adopting a "conviction mentality" that diverges from their ethical duty to pursue justice. Most notably, critics have alleged and, in some cases shown, that prosecutors have suppressed exculpatory evidence, applied the law selectively,[2] used their sentencing leverage to force plea bargains, and may even have helped fuel America's incarceration epidemic. These criticisms locate the origin of these problems in prosecutors' lack of accountability,[3] the inefficiency of

---

* Professor of Law, Indiana University Robert H. McKinney School of Law. The author wishes to thank Angela Davis, Thierry Delpeuch, Antony Duff, Jacqueline Hodgson, Maximo Langer, Daniel Richman, Jacqueline Ross, and David Alan Sklansky, as well as the participants in the workshops at UCLA Law School and the University of Illinois College of Law for their comments on an earlier draft. I would also like to gratefully acknowledge the research assistance of Carolin Maria Obermaier.

1 "Federal Prosecutor Range Criticizes 'Political Influence' on Investigation," *Deutsche Welle*, August 4, 2015. www.dw.com/en/federal-prosecutor-range-criticizes-political-influence-on-inv estigation/a-18625429.
2 Angela J. Davis, *Arbitrary Justice: The Power of the American Prosecutor* (New York: Oxford University Press, 2007), 4.
3 See, e.g., Hon. Alex Kozinski, "Criminal Law 2.0," *Georgetown Law Journal Annual Review Criminal Procedure.* 44 (2015): iii, viii. Accessed March 14, 2016, www.georgetownlawjournal .org/files/2015/06/Kozinski_Preface.pdf.

elections,[4] non-transparent decision-making processes, and prosecutors' desire for political gain.[5]

These criticisms have spawned a number of proposals designed to hold prosecutors more accountable including: documenting misconduct,[6] strengthening internal decision-making guidelines, increasing the transparency of the discovery process, and stiffening disciplinary consequences.[7] However, solving the problem may require that reformers find ways to change the organizational culture of prosecution offices. Decades ago, William Pizzi chastised prosecutors and police for the emphasis placed on "winning" that is embedded in their organizational cultures.[8] The assumption underlying many of these proposals is that, by increasing transparency and strengthening prosecutors' democratic accountability, we can curb the inequitable use of prosecutorial discretion and limit prosecutorial misconduct.

In contrast, if there has been any criticism of German prosecutors, that criticism focuses on prosecutors' proclivity to dismiss charges or defer prosecution and under-prosecute certain types of cases.[9] This is particularly true with respect to corporate corruption cases where weak laws and personnel constraints often lead prosecutors to conclude weak "confession agreements" with powerful corporate actors.[10] Scholars and human rights groups, as well as the media, have also criticized prosecutors for their failure to prosecute perpetrators of the Holocaust,[11] individuals who commit hate crimes,[12] as well as crimes against women. In addition, parliamentary bodies on the *Länder* level have

---

[4] Ronald F. Wright, "How Prosecutor Elections Fail Us," *Ohio State Journal of Criminal Law* 6 (2009): 509–606.

[5] Glenn Harlan Reynolds, "Ham Sandwich Nation: Due Process When Everything Is a Crime," *Columbia Law Review Sidebar* 113 (2013): 102.

[6] Center for Prosecutor Integrity, *Registry of Prosecutorial Misconduct*, accessed March 15, 2016, www.prosecutorintegrity.org/registry/database/.

[7] Center for Prosecutor Integrity, *An Epidemic of Prosecutor Misconduct* (2013), Appendix B, accessed March 15, 2016, www.prosecutorintegrity.org/wp-content/uploads/EpidemicofProsecutorMisconduct.pdf.

[8] William T. Pizzi, *Trials without Truth* (New York: NYU Press, 1999).

[9] See Shawn Marie Boyne, *The German Prosecution Service: Guardians of the Law?* (Heidelberg: Springer, 2013).

[10] Ibid., 119–144. See also, David Crawford and Mike Esterl, "Siemans Settlement Sets off Criticism of German Inquiries," *The Wall Street Journal*, October 8, 2007, accessed May 30, 2016, www.wsj.com/articles/SB119179176083751435.

[11] "'Hurried Action': Germany Criticized for Late Push on War Criminals," *Der Spiegel Online*, May 13, 2013, accessed January 15, 2016, www.spiegel.de/international/germany/law-experts-criticize-german-authorities-for-late-push-on-nazi-crimes-a-899445.html.

[12] "The State Response to Hate Crimes in Germany," *Human Rights Watch*, December 2011, accessed January 17, 2016, www.hrw.org/news/2011/12/09/state-response-hate-crimes-germany.

alleged that politicians have sought to use their political influence to subvert the prosecution of individual cases.

Still, in contrast to the current robust criticism concerning prosecutorial overreaching in the U.S., the German prosecution service is not under fire for over-prosecuting cases. This lack of criticism is due to several striking differences not only between the institutional role played prosecutors in both countries, but also between each state's vision of governance, democratic accountability, and the law itself. Perhaps, most tellingly, the judges and the prosecutors themselves, as well as the European Parliament, have launched the most visible calls for reform of the prosecution service.[13] Moreover, the current generation of would-be reformers aim not to make prosecutors more accountable, but rather to increase their political independence.

The divergent directions of these calls for reform in Germany and the U.S. contradicts the narrative that, despite differences between the adversarial and inquisitorial traditions, there are significant points of convergence between prosecutorial practices in both countries. To cite several examples, although Germany was once hailed as the land without plea-bargaining,[14] today "confession-bargaining" is used to settle a rising percentage of criminal cases.[15] Second, despite the fact that the German legislators sought to ban prosecutorial discretion by requiring prosecutors to file charges in all cases where sufficient evidence of a crime existed, today prosecution is mandatory only in a large percentage of felony cases.[16] From the U.S. side, calls for the increased use of internal bureaucratic controls, which are prevalent in Germany's hierarchical prosecution service, have increased on both the federal and state levels.[17] Also, although American prosecutors do not enjoy the protection of lifetime tenure, more and more prosecutors in the U.S. see their position as a lifetime career rather than as an interim stepping-stone. Finally, there are increasing calls for American prosecution

---

[13] See, e.g., "Threats to the Rule of Law in Council of Europe Member States: Asserting the Parliamentary Assembly's Authority," Committee on Legal Affairs and Human Rights, Doc 13713, *Council of Europe*, February 18, 2015, pp. 11–13, accessed February 28, 2016, www.asse mbly.coe.int/nw/xml/XRef/Xref-XML2HTML-en.asp?fileid=21564&lang=en.

[14] John H. Langbein, "Land without Plea Bargaining: How the Germans Do It," *Michigan Law Review* 78 (1979): 204.

[15] Regina E. Rauxlouh, "Formalization of Plea Bargaining in Germany: Will the New Legislation Be Able to Square the Circle?," *Fordham International Law Journal* 34 (2011):296.

[16] Thomas Weigend, "Is the Criminal Process about Truth?: A German Perspective," *Harvard Journal of Law & Public Policy* 26, No. 1 (Winter 2003): 157–174.

[17] See, e.g., Marc L. Miller and Ronald F. Wright, "The Black Box," *Iowa Law Review* 94: 125, 179–181 (2008); Lauren-Brooke Eisen, Nicole Fortier, and Inimai Chettiar, *Federal Prosecution for the 21st Century*, Brennan Center for Justice at New York University School of Law (2014), accessed June 7, 2016, www.brennancenter.org/sites/default/files/publications/Federal_Prose cution_For_21st_Century.pdf.

offices to introduce performance measures that aim to promote fairness and foster integrity.[18]

The existence of these superficial similarities, however, obscures deeper and more durable differences between the two systems. These differences are not fully captured by analyses that argue that adversarial systems are becoming more inquisitorial and inquisitorial systems have adopted some adversarial procedures. Although a significant body of scholarship in the field of comparative criminal procedure has focused on the functional, normative, and institutional differences between adversarial and inquisitorial systems, this chapter aims to break new ground by exploring the tension between democratic accountability and independence that undergirds the institutional position of German prosecution offices within an inquisitorial framework.

This chapter details the tension between prosecutors' institutional position as members of the executive branch and their statutory commitment to finding the truth. In particular, it begins to examine the extent to which politics shapes prosecutorial decision-making and asks the question: does political accountability strengthen or weaken prosecutors' commitment to the rule of law? This chapter will begin by describing the structure and role of the German prosecution service. In Part II, I will discuss some ways in which politics may usurp a prosecutor's commitment to the law. Part III will examine how the European Union is seeking to increase prosecutorial independence. In Part IV, I explore the politics behind the firing of Harald Range – the former Chief Federal Prosecutor. Finally, in Part V, I will discuss whether and how the principle of democratic accountability fits the German criminal justice system.

II INTRODUCTION: LAW AND STATE

A *Preliminary Comparisons*

According to the German criminal code, German prosecutors are apolitical figures who function as second judges in Germany's inquisitorial criminal justice system. As unelected bureaucrats with life tenure, they are positioned to function relatively free from political influence. According to German law, the prosecution service is independent of both the police as well as the judiciary.[19] Although prosecutors are bound to follow the orders of their

---

[18] John Worrall and M. Elaine Nugent-Borakove (eds.), *The Changing Role of the American Prosecutor* (Albany: SUNY Press, 2014), 94–97.

[19] Sects. 150 and 151, GVG (Courts Constitution Act), May 9, 1975.

superiors in the Ministry of Justice, with few exceptions, their superiors cannot order individual prosecutors to handle an individual case in a specific manner. In addition, while American prosecutors often use the media to boost their own visibility and standing with the electorate, German prosecutors as a whole prefer anonymity. For these reasons, it is tempting to classify German prosecutors as apolitical legal technocrats.

In contrast to the majority of District Attorneys in the U.S., Germany's top office prosecutors do not campaign for office. Instead, the prosecution service is staffed with civil servants, many of whom spend their careers never seeking promotion to the next higher position, that of a department manager. Although Germany's federal prosecutors may take on more high-profile cases, most prosecutors work at the state, or *Länder*, level under the authority of the *Länder*-level Ministries of Justice. Although a change in the political leadership at the Federal or State level will usher in change at the top levels of the Ministry, the leadership changes within the prosecution service are largely insensitive to electoral results. Yet, despite the stark differences between the institutional positions of German and American prosecutors, prosecutorial decision-making in Germany is not immune from political influence. The origins of that influence date back to the creation of the service itself.

Indeed, the subordinate position of the prosecution service within the Ministries of Justice is no accident. Ironically, the prosecution service's structure and role dates back to a mid-nineteenth-century political compromise. On one side of the compromise were liberal reformers, who wanted a new institution to reign in the court police forces that functioned with no real oversight.[20] On the other stood officials loyal to the Prussian King who sought to undercut the judiciary's power and independence.[21] In 1847, the forces reached a compromise in which Germany removed the prosecution function from the judiciary and created a separate prosecution service. Even though today the prosecution service stands under the direct control of the federal and state-level Ministries of Justice, legal scholars disagree about the prosecution service's precise institutional position. Although prosecutors are part of a distinct hierarchical structure, part of their statutory mandate is to function as "second judges" who are beholden only to the law. Moreover while Ministry officials and senior prosecutors oversee prosecutorial decision-making, that supervision is bounded by statutes that seek to preserve prosecutors' duty of

---

[20] Eberhard Siegismund, "The Public Prosecution Office in Germany: Legal Status, Functions, and Organization," *120th International Senior Seminar Visiting Experts' Papers* (UNAFEI) 2001, 59, accessed June 6, 2016, www.unafei.or.jp/english/pdf/PDF_rms/no60/cho3.pdf.

[21] Peter Collin, "Die Geburt der Staatsanwaltschaft in Preußen." *Forum Historiase Iuris* 12 (12. März 2001), para. 28, accessed June 6, 2016, www.forhistiur.de/2001-03-collin/.

objectivity.[22] Because of this dual executive and judicial role, some scholars claim that the service is its own separate institution within the criminal justice system.[23] Others position the service in an intermediate position in between the executive and judicial branches.[24]

Part of the problem is that neither the Federal Constitution, nor the Constitutions of the *Länder*, specify precisely where the prosecution offices fit within the State's constitutional structures. However, Article 92 of the German Constitution (*Grundgesetz*) only grants full decision-making independence to the judicial branch. Most German legal practitioners believe that "the Prosecution Services are criminal justice authorities within the executive whose individual agents exercise their power in non-political fashion."[25]

As a result of their position within the executive branch, German prosecutors have sometimes struggled to balance their loyalty to the state with their normative mandate to find the objective "truth." Although many of the battles over prosecutors' decision-making independence take place away from the public eye, in 2015, one of these battles made the headlines when the Federal Minister of Justice fired Germany's top Federal Prosecutor, Harald Range. More commonly, politics plays a subtler role, influencing personnel moves or discrete, discretionary decisions. However, because prosecutors are protected by life tenure, most members of the prosecution service are fiercely independent and seek to serve the law, rather than politics. Despite this commitment to the law and to objectivity, the law itself does not shield prosecutors from all political influence.

B Bureaucratic Structure

Like the United States, Germany is a federal system. As a result, there is both a federal prosecution service located in Karlsruhe as well as independent prosecution services organized at the level of the sixteen *Länder*. However, the jurisdiction of federal prosecutors in Germany is much more circumscribed than their American counterparts. Germany's federal prosecutors concentrate their practice on crimes against the state and crimes against humanity. The

---

[22] Ekaternia Trendafilova and Werner Róth, "Report on the Public Prosecution Service in Germany," in *Promoting Prosecutorial Accountability, Independence and Effectiveness. Comparative Research*. Ed. Open Society Institute (Sofia: Open Society Institute, 2008), 237, citing German Code of Criminal Procedure (StGB) Sect. 160, accessed June 7, 2016, www.opensocietyfoundations.org/sites/default/files/promoting_20090217.pdf.

[23] Ibid., 237, citing Werner Beulke, *Strafprozessrecht* (2006), marginal no. 88.

[24] Ibid., 237, citing H.H. Kuehne, *Strafprozesslehre*, marginal no. 61; Karl Peters, *Strafprozess. Ein Lehrbuch*, § 23II.

[25] Trendafilova and Róth, *Report on the Public Prosecution Service in Germany*, 237.

office also represents the State in cases before the Federal Court of Appeals.[26] The office is led by the Federal Prosecutor General who is nominated by the Minister of Justice, appointed by the President, and then confirmed by the Federal Legislature.[27] Federal prosecutors have no authority over state prosecutors. State prosecutors report to the Minister of Justice at the *Länder* level rather than to the Federal Ministry of Justice. In some ways, the German system resembles the structure of the federal system in the United States[28] in that the head of the Ministry of Justice on the federal and state levels is chosen by the Chancellor (*Bund*) and the Minister-Presidents of the *Länder* respectively.

On the *Land* level, in most states, the state-level Minister of Justice appoints the state's regional prosecutors who are known General Public Prosecutors (*Generalstaatsanwälte*). In other states, the State Ministry of Justice works with a judicial selection committee to recommend candidates for consideration. Although the Minister may deviate from the committee's recommendations, that rarely happens in practice. Up until recently, the Minister of Justice could remove the General Prosecutor in four states for political reasons.[29] However, during the past fifteen years, all of Germany's Federal States have now abolished that possibility.[30]

In addition to appointing the Prosecutor Generals, the Ministry of Justice sets overall prosecution priorities, allocates budget dollars, and makes the key promotion decisions within the prosecution offices. In contrast to the United States, where voters in most states elect attorney generals on the state level and district attorneys on the local level, in Germany, the occupants of those key positions are chosen by the Ministry. However, because Ministers of Justice on the federal and state level are politicians who represent a party in the governing coalition, it would be naive to believe that those politicians do not try to influence decision-making in key cases. Some of this influence is decidedly positive. For example, if the Ministry of Justice decides to highlight a new prosecution priority or to set guidelines specifying when cases may be dismissed.

---

[26] Gwladys Gilliéron, *Public Prosecutors in the United States and Europe: A Comparative Analysis with Special Focus on Switzerland, France, and Germany* (Switzerland: Springer 2014), 243, citing GVG Sect. 142 (1).

[27] GVG Sect. 149.

[28] Sara Sun Beale, "Prosecutorial Discretion in Three Systems: Balancing Conflicting Goals and Providing Mechanisms for Control," in *Discretionary Criminal Justice in a Comparative Context*, eds. Michele Caianiello and Jacqueline Hodgson (Durham, North Carolina: Carolina Academic Press, 2015), 27–58.

[29] Trendafilova and Róth, *Report on the Public Prosecution Service in Germany*, 220.

[30] Christian Rath, "Wie unabhängig sind Staatsanwälte?," *Vorwärts*, August 6, 2015, accessed June 7, 2016, www.vorwaerts.de/artikel/unabhaengig-staatsanwaelte.

Despite the fact that the prosecution service is subordinate to the Ministry of Justice, the prosecution service has developed its own organizational culture. While there have been at least two periods in German history where prosecutors repeatedly equated the public interest with political ends,[31] in recent decades, that organizational culture has nurtured a strong sense of prosecutors' quasi-judicial identity. Still, as members of a hierarchically ordered bureaucracy, prosecutors' allegiance to the law is subject to organizational priorities and incentives.

C The Rechtsstaat and Prosecutors' Fidelity to the Law

In contrast to the American adversarial system, where prosecutors function as a party to the criminal proceeding, in the German system, most prosecutors are not invested in "winning a case." While judges lead the presentation of evidence at trial, ideally, prosecutors function like second judges and join the judge(s) in questioning witnesses. The prosecutor's main role is to work with the police to prepare the case file that the court will use to conduct the trial. Unlike their American counterparts, they do not bear the burden of proof at trial, but they are free to proffer their own sentencing recommendations. Even in that role, they are charged with viewing the evidence through an objective lens. For example, in their closing statements, prosecutors are charged with presenting the facts both for and against a defendant.[32] They may reach their own opinion about the defendant's guilt or innocence. Prosecutors are also free to ask the court to acquit the defendant or to file an appeal on the defendant's behalf.[33] Unlike American prosecutors, who may define their individual success in major cases in terms of "winning" trials and "putting the defendant away," German prosecutors seldom view cases and their own agency in the instrumental terms of winning and losing. Instead, their role is to find the truth.[34]

---

[31] When the service was first created in 1847, the institution functioned as an arm of the state. Glenn Schram, "The Obligation to Prosecute in West Germany," *The American Journal of Comparative Law* 17: 627 (1969). When the National Socialist Party came to power in 1933, the prosecution service was at the forefront of enforcing the regime's brutal policies against so-called enemies of the state. See Ingo Müller, *Hitler's Justice: The Courts of the Third Reich* (Cambridge: Harvard University Press, 1991).

[32] Sects. 160(2) and 296 (2) StPO.   [33] Sect. 296(2) StPO.

[34] Prosecutor Interview [12CJ], November 29, 2005 (discussing a case where she asked for an acquittal after listening to witness testimony at trial). Between 2006 and 2010, I interviewed over one hundred prosecutors and judges. To protect their anonymity, each prosecutor is represented by a unique code.

This commitment to objectivity and to the law itself is deeply rooted in the German conception of the State. Although the word, *Rechtsstaat*, is often translated as the law-governed state, the German ideal differs from its American counterpart. Rooted in the civil law tradition, it not only embodies the concept that the power of the state is constrained by law, but more importantly, it means that the state acts in a lawful (*rechtlich*) way. Any action undertaken by the state must be based on law. To emphasize this point, every citizen has the right to challenge the constitutionality of a government action before the Federal Constitutional Court. The language and currency of the state is the law. It is the medium through which the State governs.[35] Ideally, the law constrains state action to prevent arbitrary decision-making and to guarantee certainty and predictability.

As an organized entity, the state is limited not only by law, but also by the fundamental principles of legality.[36] The state is not a purely political entity that can pursue policies that dispense with the law. It follows then that, as agents of the state, prosecutors view their role in less instrumental terms than American prosecutors. The ideal German prosecutor is a "guardian of the law" and, by implication, a pillar of the *Rechtsstaat*. Because prosecutors may form their own opinion about the evidence presented at trial and even move for an acquittal, their commitment to objectivity as well as their professional outlook straddles the executive and judicial functions. For the most part, prosecutors judge their performance not by their conviction rate or the length of the defendant's sentence, but by whether they applied the law correctly in a particular case.[37] In contrast to American prosecutors who function as a party, German prosecutors are obliged by law to investigate the facts both for and against the defendant.[38]

Although it is tempting to elide the concepts of *Rechtsstaat* with the concept of the rule of law, a key difference between the two is the location of the law in reference to the state. In a rule of law state, the law stands above the state and constrains the sovereign's discretionary power.[39] Moreover, as the final arbiter of the meaning of the law, the judiciary functions as its primary guardian. In contrast, in the German *Rechtsstaat*, the law originates with the legislature. It

---

[35] Martin Krygier, "Rule of Law (and Rechtsstaat)," *University of New South Wales Faculty of Law Research Series* No. 53 (October 2013): 6, accessed June 12, 2016, www.law.bepress.com/cgi/viewcontent.cgi?article=1052&context=unswwps-flrps13.

[36] T. R. S. Allan (1998). Rule of law (Rechtsstaat). In *Routledge Encyclopedia of Philosophy* (1998). London: Routledge, DOI: 10.4324/9780415249126-T022-1, accessed November 30, 2015, www.rep.routledge.com/articles/rule-of-law-rechtsstaat/v-1/.

[37] Senior Prosecutor Interview [7GC], April 6, 2006.   [38] Sect. 160, Para. 2 StPO.

[39] Krygier, "Rule of Law (and Rechtsstaat)," 5.

is not above the state, but rather part of the state's structure as well as its product.[40] One could argue that the legislature, courts, and prosecutors serve as the guardians of the law in the German system. The birth of the Federal Constitutional Court in the post-war era and the post-war Constitution's embrace of human dignity have not only added a layer of control over state power, but have also embedded a commitment to social welfare in the structure of the State.[41]

D The Civil Code as a Constraint

Civil law systems rely on two mechanisms for ensuring that prosecutors are accountable[42] – a penal code that strives to limit prosecutors' decision-making choices and the principle of mandatory prosecution.[43] Although the demise of legal formalism put to rest any idea that common law principles might form the basis of a legal science in the United States,[44] Germany's legal theorists have long lauded the theoretical structure of German criminal law as a scientific achievement.[45] By limiting prosecutors' charging choices, the criminal code aims to limit prosecutorial discretion.[46]

The Code of Criminal Procedure attempts to regulate prosecutorial decision-making and mandate prosecutors' fidelity to the law in other ways as well. The core principle at the heart of this effort is the principle of mandatory prosecution, which requires prosecutors to file charges in all cases in which sufficient suspicion exists of a suspect's guilt. Although this positivistic faith in the law's prescriptive force seems less plausible today, the provision's drafters believed that the law alone could prohibit state interference in the administration of justice.[47] Consistent with the civil law tradition, German legal scholars viewed the charging decision as the logical conclusion of a decision-making process in which a legal scientist classified facts within the correct legal categories.

---

[40] Ibid., 5.   [41] Ibid., 9.   [42] Miller and Wright, "The Black Box," 1595.

[43] Ibid., 1595, citing Emilio S. Binavince, "The Structure and Theory of the German Penal Code," *American Journal of Comparative Law* 24 (1976): 601.

[44] Horacio Spector, "The Future of Legal Science in Civil Law Systems," *Louisiana Law Review* 65 (2004): 261.

[45] Markus Dirk Dubber, "*The Promise of German Criminal Law: A Science of Crime and Punishment*," *German Law Journal* 6 (2005): 1051, accessed December 12, 2015, www.german lawjournal.com/pdfsNolO6NoO7fPDF_-Vol_-06_-No_-07_-1049-1073_ArticlesDubber.pdf.

[46] Richard S. Frase and Thomas Weigend, "German Criminal Justice as a Guide to American Law Reform: Similar Problems, Better Solutions," *Boston College International and Comparative Law Review* 18 (1995): 330–337.

[47] Mirjan Damaška, "The Reality of Prosecutorial Discretion: Comments on a German Monograph." *American Journal of Comparative Law* 29 (1981): 125.

According to Germany's prominent nineteenth-century legal theorists, legal decision-making could be stripped of political considerations and reduced to a process of categorizing the facts into the correct legal categories.[48] The theorists who wrote the German criminal code believed that law was a science that could and should exclude political influences.

Although the principle of mandatory prosecution has long been heralded as the cornerstone of German criminal justice, beginning in the 1970s, the principle began to lose some of its prescriptive force. In particular, during the past four decades, in an effort to help prosecutors to handle rising caseloads in an era of flat budgets, German legislators began to carve out exceptions to the principle in non-felony cases. The more significant changes give prosecutors the power to dismiss minor cases not in the public interest,[49] resolve cases with a penal order, and even to enter into a confession agreement after an abbreviated proceeding.[50] As a result of these changes, the prominent German legal scholar Thomas Weigend wrote "[t]oday prosecution is in effect mandatory only with respect to most felonies."[51] Because these changes have widened prosecutors' discretion with respect to less serious crimes, wide variations in case handling practices have developed throughout Germany. As a result, case dismissal rates in minor crime cases vary widely throughout Germany with states in the Northern part of Germany posting the highest dismissal rate and those in the southern part posting the lowest.[52] Even though prosecutors now may use a wide range of disposition options, because the sentencing philosophy of the German system focuses on rehabilitation and eschews long sentences, German prosecutors lack the degree of leverage that American prosecutors enjoy to force a plea.

II BUREAUCRATIC CONTROLS

A *Ministry of Justice*

Despite their role as second judges in the criminal process, as members of a bureaucracy, prosecutors do not function completely independently of bureaucratic control. Although the organizational structure of the prosecution offices is

---

[48] Ibid. [49] Sect. 153 StPO. [50] Sect. 257c StPO.
[51] Thomas Weigend, "The Prosecution Service in the German Administration of Criminal Justice," in *Tasks and Powers of the Prosecution Services in the EU Member States*, ed. P. J. P. Tak, vol. 1 (Nijmegen: Wolf Legal Publishers, 2004), 215.
[52] Beatrix Elsner and Julia Peters, "The Prosecution Service Function within the German Criminal Justice System," in *Coping with Overloaded Criminal Justice Systems: The Rise of Prosecutorial Power Across Europe*, eds. Jörg-Martin Jehle and Marianne L. Wade (Berlin: Springer 2006), 219.

relatively flat, prosecutors are bound to follow the instructions of their superiors. In this regard, there are two different sources of control mechanisms. The Ministry of Justice possesses an external right of instruction (*externe Weisung recht*) vis-à-vis prosecutors and typically would issue these instructions through the General Public Prosecutors. The Ministry's right of instruction stems from the Ministry's responsibility to be accountable to the democratically elected parliament.[53] Typically, the types of "instructions" issued by the Ministry fall into the category of general instructions that guide prosecutors in their handling of certain types of cases, such as domestic violence charges.[54] For example, these general instructions (*Richtlinien*) may detail the recommended disposition practices for certain low-level offenses. Although the instructions are designed to produce uniform case disposition practices throughout a particular state, there are widespread differences in those same practices from state to state.

B General Public Prosecutors

In the United States, the chief way in which prosecutors are held accountable is through the election of district attorneys at the city or regional level. Although German prosecutors are not elected, the key contact point between politicians and civil servants occurs between the Ministry of Justice at the *Land* level and the General Public Prosecutors (*Generalstaatsanwälte*) who serve as the top regional prosecutors. The General Public Prosecutor position is directly accountable to the Ministry of Justice.[55] These individuals may also issue "internal" guidelines to direct the handling of routine cases. In addition, within the prosecution service, superiors exercise supervisory control over their subordinates in the civil service (See Fig. 1).

At the top of the prosecution service, General Prosecutors head regional prosecution offices located in cities that host the regional appellate courts (*Oberlandesgerichte*). In keeping with the character of the prosecution service, the Ministry typically appoints senior civil service members to direct these regional offices. In general, even when there is a change in the political control of the *Land* parliament, the General Public Prosecutor will not change. Typically, the Minister of Justice will only appoint a new top prosecutor when her predecessor retires.[56] However, in at least one city-state that I visited, the political parties in parliament influence the choice of both the General Public Prosecutor and the

---

[53] Volker Krey, *German Criminal Procedure Law* (Vol. 1) (Stuttgart: W. Kohlhammer Publishing Company 2009), 77. Senior Prosecutor Interview [25IFG], April 16, 2008.
[54] GVG, Art. 146 and 147.   [55] GVG Sect. 147.
[56] Justice Ministry Official Interview [9OU], May 15, 2006.

Federal Level

Federal Minister of Justice

Chief Federal Prosecutor

Federal Prosecutors

Land or State Level

State Ministry of Justice

General Public Prosecutor

Leading Office Prosecutors

Department Leaders

Individual Prosecutors

FIGURE 1 **Hierarchical Organization of Prosecution Offices**

city's leading office prosecutor (LOSTA) as well.[57] Typically, the occupants of those positions belong to the same political party as the government.[58]

The bulk of a General Public Prosecutor's supervisory activities is limited to monitoring the progress of the most high-profile cases.[59] Despite the fact that superiors possess the "right of instruction" over their subordinates, the primary control measure is a prosecutor's case processing efficiency, rather than the quality of her decision-making. The exception to this are those cases where superiors require prosecutors to file regular reports with their department leaders and their supervisors in certain cases. In some cases, the supervisors will review the actual investigation file to track a prosecutor's decision-making. Those reports are reviewed and passed up the chain of command. Not only do these reports enable a prosecutor's superiors to track the trajectory of a case, but they also keep them in the loop in case of a media inquiry. Without discounting the possibility that some superiors use supervision practices to monitor politically important cases, one General Public Prosecutor stated:

> [M]y main interest is that a prosecutor's work is reviewed positively, or at least not in a negative way. The preliminary investigation should be calm and without any journalistic hype... [It is not my role to get] into politics and upstage them (I don't feel like it, nor do I have the ambition to do so). The department of public prosecution's work should always be good and technically correct that nobody in the cabinet can talk about it badly.[60]

[57] Ibid.   [58] Ibid.
[59] Ronald F. Wright and Mark L. Miller, "The Worldwide Accountability Deficit for Prosecutors," *Washington & Lee Law Review* 67 (2010):1602.
[60] General Public Prosecutor Interview [6AI], March 6, 2006.

Most of the directives issued by General Public Prosecutors relate not to specific cases, but rather detail how to handle certain types of cases including summary dispositions on certain administrative offenses.[61] One senior prosecutor claimed that the General Public Prosecutor only exercises a control function in important cases and that function is circumscribed by regulations.[62] In most *Länder*, instructions relevant to a specific case occur rarely. For example, one prosecutor reported that, during his ten-year career, the General Public Prosecutor had only "exercised control" on two cases.[63]

C Office Leadership

Each prosecution office is directed by a lead office prosecutor (*Leitender Staatsanwalt* or LOSTA) who has risen through the civil service ranks. Individual offices are organized along department lines typically with different departments managing different types of crimes. The degree of control exercised within the office depends on the preferences of the office prosecutor. This control appears more frequently in high-profile and serious crime cases, where prosecutors may be required to keep their superior apprised of case developments through regular written reports. The top office prosecutor may also issue guidelines on how to handle certain types of cases. In one large office, the top prosecutor required prosecutors to obtain his approval before they filed charges in all murder and large drug cases. Due to the volume of cases, however, a top office prosecutor in a large city "cannot control all the finer points of decision-making."[64] However, if a prosecutor makes a mistake on a major case, "there will be a phone call."[65] Nevertheless, there is a striking variety of control styles in different offices. As one department manager related:

> Who the Lead Office Prosecutor is has a large impact on the organizational culture. [Here] it is very collegial. He doesn't get involved in managing the cases. He believes that the prosecutor who is handling the case, knows the most about the case and should manage it individually. The individual [prosecutor] has a lot of decision-making room. Also he protects their back against the Ministry of Justice and the General Public Prosecutor. This is not the usual practice in Germany.[66]

The nature of the German prosecutor's role in a civil law system facilitates a more detailed case review process than is possible in the United States.

---

[61] Richtlinien für das Strafverfahren und das Bußgeldverfahren (RiStBV).
[62] GVG, Art. 146, 147   [63] Justice Ministry Official Interview [9OU], May 15, 2006.
[64] Senior Prosecutor Interview [25ST], April 16, 2008.   [65] Ibid.
[66] Senior Prosecutor Interview [7GC], April 6, 2006.

Because German prosecutors document the entire investigation, as well as each decision they make in a case, their decisions are transparent to any superior who seeks to review the investigation file. This practice of documentation is ingrained in new prosecutors who must spend nearly six months simply learning how to document their decision-making in the case file by using a unique nomenclature. One casualty of rising caseloads is that supervisors do not have the time to review complete investigation files, unless the case is flagged for review because of the severity of the charges involved. Given that ninety percent of a case file is never reviewed by a superior, prosecutors in most departments believe that they enjoy significant decision-making freedom.[67] However, one could argue that because prosecutors must inscribe every action that they take in a case file which will ultimately go to the court, the potential review of the file by a superior or a judge encourages prosecutors to make responsible decisions. Ironically, lay jurors are not allowed to view a case file.

D *Departmental Supervision and the Quest for Efficiency*

As a general rule, each department is headed by a senior public prosecutor who manages case assignments and possesses oversight responsibility. To be eligible for promotion to the position of department manager, prosecutors must typically complete a rotation at the General Public Prosecutor's Office that involves screening the appeals of case dismissals. By removing potential department leaders from their home office and temporarily placing them in a regional office, the training aims to ensure that all department managers in a particular region possess a uniform view of the control function.

Within each department, the department leader may also set her own controls. For example, in one juvenile crimes department, the department manager decided that all the cases had to be filed within three months of the initial police report.[68] While a department manager may choose to review a prosecutor's court dispositions, that review is limited to determining whether the result was a legally plausible one. In many cases, the department manager will only look at the prosecutor's court file and not the complete investigation file to determine whether the trial result falls within the realm of possibility.

Unfortunately, the most ubiquitous form of supervisory control is not exercised over the quality of prosecutorial decision-making, but rather over prosecutors' case-handling efficiency. Department managers, as well as the top

---

[67] Prosecutor Interview [4GG], January 30, 2006.
[68] Prosecutor Interview [13BR], November 18, 2005.

office prosecutors, receive weekly statistical reports that provide supervisors with a snapshot of each prosecutor's caseload. These reports show how long an investigation has been pending, the number of files that a prosecutor has open, and the prosecutor's case dismissal rates. If a prosecutor's statistics lie outside the norm, the department manager will investigate further. A key control statistic is the age of the case. In one prosecution office that I visited, if a case is older than six months, the prosecutor must explain to her department manager why the case is still pending. When it is older than twelve months, the department manager must report this to the Lead Office Prosecutor. To successfully navigate caseload pressures, prosecutors in many departments must dismiss or defer prosecution in a high percentage of cases. Despite the ubiquity of these productivity measures, supervisors have few tools available to motivate less industrious prosecutors. While the Ministry could fire a prosecutor as the result of a disciplinary proceeding before an administrative tribunal, those proceedings are rare. Indeed, in 2010, supervisors initiated only three proceedings against prosecutors.[69] In two of the cases, the prosecutor was accused of an ethical breach. The remaining case involved a criminal offense.[70] The disciplinary tribunal formally reprimanded two of the prosecutors and reassigned cases away from the third prosecutor.[71]

Despite these controls, the organization's relatively flat structure gives prosecutors considerable decision-making latitude. Because most prosecutors remain as a state prosecutor (*Staatsanwalt*) for their entire career with pay increases based on the length of their service, their main performance incentive is the opportunity to work in particular departments. After approximately ten to fifteen years of service, a small percentage will become department managers (*Oberstaatsanwalt*) and oversee a department. Over the course of their careers, prosecutors may rotate through different departments and handle different types of crimes, but very few prosecutors are promoted to a supervisory level.

E Public Complaints about Case Dismissals

Although citizens do not elect prosecutors, on paper, citizens may challenge a prosecutor's decision to dismiss a case by filing a formal complaint.[72] In those cases, a prosecutor will explain her decision in writing to her department

---

[69] *Report on European Judicial Systems-Edition* 2014 (2012 data): *Efficiency and Quality of Justice* (Strasbourg: Council of Europe Publications, 2014), 363 (Table 11.47), accessed May 13, 2016, www.coe.int/t/dghl/cooperation/cepej/evaluation/2014/Rapport_2014_en.pdf.
[70] Ibid.   [71] Ibid., 369 (Table 11.51).   [72] §172 StGB.

manager. If the department manager believes that the investigation was incomplete, the prosecutor must investigate the case further. The effectiveness of this control mechanism depends on the degree of public involvement in the case and the department leader's open-mindedness.[73] If the manager supports the dismissal decision, the file will then be reviewed by the top office prosecutor. Lastly, if the top office prosecutor agrees with the dismissal, the file will be reviewed by a senior prosecutor in the General Public Prosecutor's Office. If the reviewer recommends that the prosecutor further investigate the case, the General Public Prosecutor's Office will inform the prosecutor what additional investigation is necessary.[74] According to one senior prosecutor who performs this function in a General Public Prosecutor's Office, about ten percent of the cases are reopened.[75] In those cases, the reviewer will typically determine that the prosecutor misinterpreted the requirements of the law or that the police did not interview all of the relevant witnesses.[76] Even if the supervisory prosecutors at these three levels of review support the prosecutor's decision to dismiss the case, the complaining party may still appeal that decision to a judicial body. However, a court may not force a prosecutor to file charges in a case when the prosecutor does not believe that there is sufficient evidence to proceed.[77]

F The Norm of Collective Wisdom

> If you go from a judicial position to the prosecution service, your mind will not adapt to the change. You cannot carry the same perspective of objectivity with you. Your mind is captured by the collegial culture.[78]

In the bulk of their cases, prosecutors enjoy a wide range of discretion. Still, even though changes in the law have widened prosecutorial discretion, informal collegial controls strongly shape decision-making. From the start of their initial three-year probationary period and onwards, prosecutors are trained to seek out the opinion of their colleagues. Indeed, a key aspect of the service's organizational culture is a desire to act within the decision-making norms of a particular office. Most often, this information is not passed top-down through the organization, but rather between groups of prosecutors during informal coffee meetings. During these exchanges, younger prosecutors or prosecutors

---

[73] Senior Prosecutor Interview [7GC], April 6, 2006.
[74] Senior Prosecutor Interview [9OU], May 15, 2006.   [75] Ibid.   [76] Ibid.
[77] Volker Krey, *German Criminal Procedure Law* (Vol. 1)(Stuttgart: W. Kohlhammer Publishing Company 2009), 73.
[78] Appellate Judge Interview [18AB], July 22, 2004.

new to a particular department will discuss charging decisions and investigation strategies. Even experienced prosecutors engage in informal conversations with their colleagues to guide decision-making.[79] These communities of practice play an integral role in ensuring that an individual prosecutor's decision-making conforms to office norms.[80] Because of this collegial culture, German prosecutors are not likely to make a major decision on a case without discussing it with their supervisor or colleagues. To the extent that there is consistency in prosecutors' decision-making practices, that consistency is due to the service's collegial culture. The normative practice of valuing collective wisdom, the prosecution service's flat structure, and the criminal justice system's non-adversarial structure creates an organizational incentive system that does not motivate prosecutors to define themselves by whether or not they secure a front-page conviction. The downside of group collegiality is that individual prosecutors may be less likely to challenge group norms that are outdated or inappropriate.

III THE HAND OF POLITICAL CONTROL: THE MINISTRY OF JUSTICE AND THE PARLIAMENT

A *The Ministry of Justice's Invisible Hand*

As originally designed, the German Code of Criminal Procedure sought to banish arbitrary political interference in the criminal justice system. Even before norms of practice weakened the Principle of Mandatory Prosecution however, prosecutors possessed some flexibility in their investigation and charging decision-making. While that discretion gives prosecutors and judges the ability to ensure that the system is fair, it also invites the delivery of arbitrary justice. The chief complaint from prosecutors is that the *Länder*-level Ministries of Justice sometimes attempt to quash prosecutions for political reasons. Cases that may draw political attention typically involve the investigation of politicians, campaign contributors, or prominent businessmen. Although a prosecutor who receives an instruction that runs counter to their fidelity to the law may request that the instruction be communicated in writing, most political pressure is delivered in the form of phone calls and informal oral suggestions.[81] Although a prosecutor may attempt to come to an

[79] Senior Prosecutor Interview [16PP], May 11, 2006.
[80] Etienne Wenger, "Communities of Practice and Social Learning Systems," *Organization* 7 (May 2000): 229, accessed May 14, 2016, doi: 10.1177/135050840072002.
[81] Senior Prosecutor Interview [5BC], January 16, 2006.

agreement with her superiors,[82] if no agreement is feasible, the Minister of Justice may reassign a case to a different prosecutor.[83]

When a case involves a prominent individual, prosecutors may try to use the principle of mandatory prosecution and the prosecution service's organizational culture to resist political influence. One top office prosecutor told me that when his office opened an investigation into a member of the *Land* cabinet's finances, the Ministry was not pleased.[84] Convinced that the Minister had committed a fraud by accepting unauthorized donations, the office brought the case to court. Although the initial court dismissed the case for lack of evidence, the office appealed the dismissal to over the Ministry's objections.[85] The regional court then reopened the case and ultimately sentenced the Minister to probation and ordered him to pay a fine.

The largest threat to prosecutors' fidelity to the law exists in those states where prosecutors rotate between positions in the judiciary, the Ministry, and the prosecution service at regular intervals. Although prosecutors enjoy life tenure, the Ministry or a prosecutor's superiors may use the prospect of a future rotation to reward or punish prosecutors who honor or rebuff the Ministry's wishes.[86] Although one typically would progress up the ranks to more senior positions during these rotations, one's career may get sidetracked. It is also possible that prosecutors in the states that do not rotate individuals through different positions may find their advancement stymied for lack of "social competence." As a senior prosecutor remarked:

> One of the criteria for promotion is "social competence." If you reject an informal instruction, this could affect [the Ministry's] impression of your social competence. They will not issue a written instruction or take a case away from you. There will no notification in your personnel file. However you will not know what is in their head.[87]

Based on interview data and media reports, prosecutors in Bavaria face the largest political threats to their independence. One reason for this lack of independence is that one political party, the Christian Social Union (CSU), has dominated the political landscape for decades. Prosecutors' actions are constrained for political reasons most often in economic crimes and corruption cases. It manifests either as a failure to devote adequate resources to the

---

[82]   Trendafilova and Roth, "Report on the Public Prosecution Service in Germany," 221 (citing Werner Beulke, *Strafprozessrecht* (2006) at marginal no. 85.

[83]   GVG, Art. 145.   [84]   General Public Prosecutor Interview [11OT], July 15, 2004.   [85]   Ibid.

[86]   Senior Prosecutor Interview [8HL], May 26, 2006.

[87]   Senior Prosecutor Interview [8AQ], May 26, 2006.

prosecution of certain cases,[88] promises of favorable promotions to prosecutors who handle specific cases in a politically palatable manner,[89] or pressure to shut down an investigation.[90]

The most famous example of political retaliation is the prosecutor who filed the initial charges against the former Chancellor Helmut Kohl in 1999. The prosecutor found himself "promoted" to a position of family court judge in a small German town.[91] Although the original prosecutor filed felony-level bribery charges against the former Chancellor, the case ultimately was dismissed under Sect. 153a, which allows prosecutors to dismiss minor cases that are supposedly not in the public's interest to prosecute. The decision to dismiss the case led several German law professors and commentators to charge that the dismissal was inappropriate.[92]

B Parliamentary Oversight

Members of the opposition parties on the federal and state levels may function as a potential check on arbitrary meddling by the Ministry of Justice in a specific case. Because the Ministry of Justice is politically accountable to Parliament, members of Parliament may initiate investigations into particular cases and submit written questions to the Ministry.[93] If a Minister issues an instruction in a high-profile case that falls outside of case-handling norms, an opposition party may launch a legislative investigation.[94] In those cases where a prosecutor's handling of a case attracts negative publicity or rumors of political interference surface, a *Land* parliament may appoint an investigative committee. The investigation will target the Ministry of Justice, rather than the individual prosecutor who handled the case; however, the legislature may obtain a prosecutor's case materials and question witnesses. Inevitably, the committee will ask the prosecutor where she received oral or written instructions from the Ministry

---

[88] David Crawford and Mike Esteral, "GERMANY: Siemens Settlement Sets off Criticism of German Inquiries," *Wall Street Journal*, October 8, 2007, accessed June 21, 2016, www.wsj.com/articles/SB119179176083751435.

[89] Senior Prosecutor Interview, [8HL], May 22, 2006.

[90] Stefan Mayr, "Brisante Aktenvermerke im Fall Schottdorf," *Süddeutsche Zeitung*, January 26, 2015, accessed June 7, 2016, www.sueddeutsche.de/bayern/laboraffaere-brisante-aktenvermerke-im-fall-schottdorf-1.2319780.

[91] Senior Prosecutor Interview [16PP], April 30, 2008.

[92] "Germany's Party Finance Scandal 'Ends' with Kohl's Plea Bargain and Too Many Unanswered Questions," *German Law Journal* 2 (2001), accessed June 7, 2016, www.germanlawjournal.com/index.php?pageID=11&artID=60.

[93] Leading Office Prosecutor Interview [2BN], July 16, 2004.

[94] Federal Civil Service Act, Art. 56(2).d (BBG).

in the case.[95] This possibility alone may discourage some Ministers from ordering prosecutors to handle individual cases in a particular way.[96]

However, while legislative hearings may attract media coverage, the scope of the parliamentary investigation is limited to whether or not the law was followed. Because competitive party politics shapes the use of this control mechanism, a parliamentary investigation may have little to do with whether the prosecutor applied the law correctly. As one example, during my visit to one prosecution office, prosecutors in the office were involved in the parliamentary review of a case in which a suspect murdered a citizen after he had been released from pre-trial detention.[97] According to a senior prosecutor in that office, the opposition party in the state parliament initiated the review just to create an election issue.[98]

The degree of political meddling in prosecutorial decision-making varies from *Land* to *Land*. One senior prosecutor told me that the prosecutors in that office had to be careful about pursuing certain cases because the opposition party actively monitored high-profile cases.[99] In one case in which a prosecutor filed charges against two prominent politicians, Ministry officials reviewed her case report and told the prosecutor to "be sure" that she wanted to proceed.[100] Although the officials claimed that the law at issue was unclear, it is difficult to see how the Ministry's interest in the case was apolitical. Though the prosecutor pressed forward with the charges, a court ended up dismissing the case on legal grounds.[101] Still, the senior prosecutor reported, "[i]t is possible to file political accusations. You will not get fired, but you can be reassigned to another department." Another senior prosecutor was more circumspect about the prospect of political influence, stating "the fact that influence is possible is a problem because it reflects poorly on prosecutors."[102]

The degree of political meddling varies. In one state in particular, several prosecutors cited several cases they had handled in which someone from the General Public Prosecutor's Office had attempted to influence the case outcome at the direction of the Ministry.[103] That intervention may take different forms. For example, in one case in which a senior prosecutor had filed charges against an individual, friends of the defendant filed a complaint with the General Public Prosecutor's (GPP's) office. Rather than directly issue an

---

[95] Trendafilova and Róth, *Report on the Public Prosecution Service in Germany*, 237 fn 83.
[96] Gilliéron, *Public Prosecutors in the United States and Europe*, 282.
[97] Senior Prosecutor Interview [7GC], April 6, 2006. [98] Ibid.
[99] Senior Prosecutor Interview [9BU], May 4, 2005. [100] Ibid. [101] Ibid.
[102] Senior Prosecutor Interview [16PP], April 30, 2008.
[103] Senior Prosecutor Interviews [8AQ] and [8HL] and Group Leader Interviews [8FN] and [8DE], May 26, 2006.

instruction in the case, an official at the GPP's office responded to the citizen's complaint by notifying the defendant's attorney that if the suspect made "such and such a statement" about their intent, it would undercut the prosecutor's ability to show criminal intent and the case would be dismissed.[104] More often, the "instruction" is an informal suggestion. One department manager reported to me that over the course of his three-decade career, he had received many informal instructions.[105]

V CASE STUDIES: TWO ILLUSTRATIONS OF OVERSIGHT

German prosecutors function in a hybrid role. On the one hand, prosecutors are bureaucrats who must answer to their superiors. It is equally true that they are protected civil servants who are embedded in a collegial culture that fosters a norm of non-partisanship and impartiality. When instructions from above serve partisan political interests, rather than comport with prosecutors' decision-making norms, prosecutors may view those instructions not as a form of democratic accountability, but rather as partisan political interference. Parliamentary investigations, often convened by an opposition party, act as an imperfect check against cases of partisan interference. Yet, instructions from above may also fill an important role in cases where prosecutors make decisions that, either undermine basic democratic values or are inconsistent the law's intent. The two cases below highlight how the Ministry's control function may represent questionable political interference or promote democratic accountability.

A *The Schottdorf Investigation*

Over ten years after Munich prosecutors began investigating prominent pharmaceutical executive Bernd Schottdorf, the German media as well as political elites continue to debate whether political influence coxed prosecutors to eventually dismiss the case. Dubbed the "laboratory affair" by the German press, prosecutors initially alleged that Schottdorf's laboratory, as well as hundreds of doctors, had overbilled insurance companies for laboratory testing. During a fifteen-month investigation by a Bavarian parliamentary committee, the committee documented that the Ministry of Justice, as well as the General Public Prosecutor, used several tactics to encourage prosecutors to dismiss the case, including transferring the case to another office, interfering

---

[104] Senior Prosecutor Interview [8AQ], May 26, 2006.
[105] Senior Prosecutor Interview [16PP], May 11, 2006.

with the course of the investigation, and even promoting a key prosecutor handling the case.[106]

Although prosecutors rarely detail the political pressures they face for fear of retribution, during the hearings, a key witness, Christian Schmidt-Sommerfeld, was nearing retirement and did not feel those same restraints. Equally critical, as the current President of Munich's regional court (*Landgericht*), who had previously served as one of Münich's top prosecutors, the witness's credibility could not be questioned. Schmidt-Sommerfeld testified that the General Public Prosecutor had improperly influenced the Schottdorf case in three ways.[107] First, he failed to authorize certain searches sought by the police.[108] Second, he forbade prosecutors from pursuing measures to extend the statute of limitations.[109] Finally, despite the fact that the Münich prosecutor's office started the investigation and had successfully prosecuted a similar case, the General Public Prosecutor transferred the case to the smaller Augsburg office.[110] Other witnesses, such as senior prosecutor Hildegard Bäumler-Hösl and several law enforcement officials, testified that the General Public Prosecutor's Office had at times hamstrung the investigation by cancelling search warrants and denying prosecutors permission to access potential evidence.[111] Moreover, the Minister of Justice transferred the case to Augsburg shortly after the case prosecutor requested that the General Public Prosecutor put his order not to secure a search warrant in writing.[112]

As a prominent party member from Bavaria's dominant political party – the Christian Social Union (CSU) – Schottdorf was politically well-connected to key government officials including the Justice Minister and the General Public Prosecutor. Although one role of the General Prosecutor's Office is to standardize how different prosecution offices handle similar types of cases, in the Schottdorf case, the General Public Prosecutor apparently transferred the cases to ensure that the Augsburg office would dismiss them.[113] Perhaps the most damning evidence that politics subverted the law in this case is that, after

---

[106] Stefan Mayr, "Justiz im Zwielicht,"*Süddeutsche Zeitung*, October 20, 2015, accessed December 1, 2015, www.sueddeutsche.de/bayern/affaere-schottdorf-justiz-im-zwielicht-1.2700023.

[107] Stefan Mayr, "Schwere Vorwürfe gegen Generalstaatsanwaltschaft im Fall Schottdorf," *Süddeutsche Zeitung*, October 13, 2015, accessed November 22, 2015, www.sueddeutsche.de/bayern/einflussnahme-schwere-vorwuerfe-gegen-generalstaatsanwaltschaft-im-fall-schottdorf-1.2690099.

[108] Ibid. [109] Ibid. [110] Ibid. [111] Ibid.

[112] Stefan Mayr, "Justiz im Zwielicht," *Süddeutsche Zeitung*, October 20, 2015, accessed December 1, 2015, www.sueddeutsche.de/bayern/affaere-schottdorf-justiz-im-zwielicht-1.2700023.

[113] Ibid.

the Augsburg prosecutor closed the investigation, the Ministry promoted him to a senior prosecutor position in the General Public Prosecutor's Office.[114]

Based on my interviews, in the states where political influence is commonplace, that influence is typically directed at prosecutors in the economic crimes or corruption departments. The reporting requirements on their own are not evidence that the Ministry intends to steer the case in a particular direction. For example, it would be a mistake, solely based on the Schottdorf case, to conclude that efforts to exert political influence are widespread. However, a good percentage of the prosecutors that I interviewed with over five years of experience had received at least one instruction during the course of their career. Still, even when a supervisor issues an instruction, a prosecutor may disregard the order when the prosecutor disagrees with the instruction.[115] Even when a superior requests a report on a highly-publicized case, the prosecutor may not know the Ministry's impression of the case.[116] Indeed, in all high-profile cases, prosecutors are required to pen regular reports to their superiors to keep them informed. According to one economic crimes prosecutor, the oversight procedure may also have a positive impact: "[w]hen one has to write a report, it influences [your] decision on making an arrest or what witness you decide to take statements from. It also makes you do your job in a more thorough way and to work a bit faster."[117] Moreover, in some cases where supervision is more intense, the purpose of the vertical reporting measures is to keep superiors in the loop and to quiet public outrage about a case.[118]

B Political Accountability and the Public Interest: The Case of Harald Range

As previously discussed, top prosecutors are rarely dismissed. One might expect then that when the Federal Minister of Justice dismissed Range in August 2015, the move would spark widespread condemnation. However, by deciding to investigate members of the press, Range lost a key medium for public support. Also the nation's top prosecutor position is unique under German law as the Federal Prosecutor is a "political civil servant" who, by law, may be sent into temporary retirement at any time. According to the Act Defining the Scope of Civil Servants' Rights and Duties (*Beamtenrechtsrahmengesetz*-BRRG), "political civil servants" must agree with the government's political beliefs and policy goals.[119]

---

[114] Ibid. [115] Senior Prosecutor Interview [10FF], June 28, 2006.
[116] Group Leader Interview [8FN], May 26, 2006.
[117] Prosecutor Interview [12FG], April 24, 2006.
[118] Senior Public Prosecutor Interview [5BC], January 26, 2006.
[119] Beamtenrechtsrahmengesetz, Sect. 31 I (BRRG). [Act Defining the Scope of Civil Servants' Rights and Duties].

Range's political problems began in May 2015 when the head of the power-ful Office of the Protection of the Constitution (BfV),[120] Hans-Georg Maassen, encouraged Range to investigate two journalists from the popular blog, Netzpolitik.org. The blog editors, Markus Beckedahl and Andre Meister, angered Massen by publishing confidential documents obtained from Massen's Office[121] that revealed that the office had opened a new unit to monitor citizens' internet content.[122] While Range had sufficient "initial suspicion" on paper to investigate the bloggers, the confidential information published in the blog had already been widely discussed in Berlin. Moreover, the blog was hardly a mainstream news source with a wide readership.[123]

Equally problematic for Range, the case arose when many Germans were still angry that the U.S. National Security Agency (NSA) had spied on millions of mobile phones of German civilians including the Chancellor's phone. Since the majority of the German public viewed the NSA's surveillance program as out of control,[124] they were not happy that their own government had begun to expand its own internet surveillance. In fact, many members of the public looked at the Netzpolitik revelations with alarm and many took to the street in front of the Ministry of Justice's Berlin headquarters in protest.[125]

Ironically, although the press has often supported prosecutors in cases where political influence threatens to sabotage an investigation, by targeting two journal-ists for investigation, Range lost the support of the press who viewed his actions not as an act of political courage, but rather as an attack on freedom of the press.[126]

In addition to the public outcry, a number of prominent German politi-cians, as well as Europe's Organization for Security and Cooperation, called for Range's resignation.[127] Among the politicians, Renate Künast, a Green

---

[120] Germany's domestic intelligence agency is responsible for protecting the country's internal security.

[121] "German Prosecutors Investigate Internet Journalists for Treason," *Deutsche Welle*, July 30, 2015, accessed December 10, 2015, www.dw.com/en/german-prosecutors-investigate-internet-journalists-for-treason/a-18619254.

[122] Klaus Brinkbäumer, "Berlin's NSA Fears: Treason Investigation Reveals Anxiety at the Top," *Der Spiegel*, August 10, 2015, accessed December 9, 2015, www.spiegel.de/international/germany/german-treason-investigation-reveals-anxiety-among-leaders-a-1047256.html.

[123] Ibid.

[124] Pew Research Center's 2014 Global attitudes Survey, accessed June 20, 2016, available at www.pewglobal.org/2014/07/14/nsa-opinion/country/germany/.

[125] "Thousands March in Berlin over Journalist 'Treason' Claims," *Deutsche Welle*, August 1, 2015, accessed December 10, 2015, www.dw.com/en/thousands-march-in-berlin-over-journalist-treason-claims/a-18621978.

[126] Ibid.

[127] "German Justice Minister Maas Terminates Federal Prosecutor Range," *Deutsche Welle*, August 4, 2015, accessed June 14, 2016, www.dw.com/en/german-justice-minister-maas-terminates-federal-prosecutor-range/a-18625000.

party member and the chair of the Bundestag's legal affairs committee, charged that the investigation "was a disgrace to the rule of law."[128] Even members of the Christian Democratic Party's (CDU) coalition partner, the Social Democratic Party (SPD), criticized Range's actions as the party's deputy chairman maintained that Range "had [sic] gone down completely the wrong track, and had [sic] clearly lost sight of the purpose of his rule."[129] Even the deputy chairman of Range's own party, the Free Democratic Party (FDP), told one newspaper that "[i]f the chief prosecutor ignores the constitutional right of freedom of the press and the task of journalists, then he is the wrong choice for the job."[130]

In retrospect, Range misjudged the extent of his political support. In opening the investigation itself, Range had elected to ignore the counsel of his supervisors in the German Ministry of Justice.[131] Ironically, the fabled principle of mandatory prosecution does not require prosecutors to file charges in all cases. In fact, the law enables the Federal Prosecutor to dismiss an investigation or prosecution "if other overriding interests present an obstacle to prosecution."[132] Here, a desire to protect the freedom of the press overrode the state's interest in prosecuting journalists who did not threaten national security. When the Federal Minister of Justice ordered Range to close the investigation, his penultimate act was to complain to an unsympathetic press about political interference with his decision-making.[133] Rather than paint Range as a champion of prosecutorial independence however, reporters argued that he was a symbol of prosecutorial overreach.[134]

Despite Range's allegations about political interference, his dismissal ultimately stands as a victory for democratic accountability. Ironically, Range's own prior decision-making undercut his claim that his office should function

---

[128] "German Press and Politicians Criticize 'Absurd' Netzpolitik Inquiry," *Deutsche Welle*, July 31, 2015, accessed December 12, 2015, www.dw.com/en/german-press-politicians-criticize-absurd-netzpolitik-inquiry/a-18619716.

[129] "German Politicians Urge Chief Prosecutor to Resign over Treason Probe," *Deutsche Welle*, August 1, 2015, accessed December 12, 2015, www.dw.com/en/german-politicians-urge-chief-prosecutor-to-resign-over-treason-probe/a-18621859.

[130] Ibid.

[131] "German Justice Ministry 'Warned' against Netzpolitik Treason Investigation,'" *Deutsche Welle*, August 3, 2015, accessed December 12, 2015, www.dw.com/en/german-justice-ministry-warned-against-netzpolitik-treason-investigation/a-18623227.

[132] StPO (Code of Criminal Procedure), Sect 153(d).

[133] Frank Jordans, "Top German Prosecutor Fired over Treason Investigation," *Business Insider*, August 4, 2015, accessed March 9, 2016, www.mail.iu.edu/owa/#path=/mail.

[134] "Critics Say Maas Sacked Prosecutor on Political Grounds," *Deutsche Welle*, August 5, 2015, accessed December 12, 2015, www.dw.com/en/critics-say-maas-sacked-prosecutor-on-political-grounds/a-18628274.

independent of politics. Most notably, although Range chose to investigate the U.S. National Security Agency's (NSA) hacking of the Chancellor's phone, he ultimately dismissed that case, citing a lack of evidence.[135] At the time, members of the press charged that that dismissal was motivated by politics rather than by a lack of solid evidence.[136] So, when Range claimed that he was subject to ultra vires political pressures, members of the press, as well as the public, accused Range of being a hypocrite.[137] As the *Deutsche Welle* reported:

> By condemning Maas' intervention in his investigation and invoking the freedom of the judiciary, Range portrayed the dispute as a constitutional battle between politics and the rule of law.
>
> This was disingenuous. Inside Germany, many commentators – not to mention Twitter users – slammed Range's statement as a willful misdirection of his constitutional role. Citing the information on the prosecutor's official website, many pointed out that Range was not an independent member of the judiciary, but a political official, appointed by the Justice Minister and accountable to him. By openly criticizing his boss, therefore, Range was deliberately forcing Maas to dismiss him.[138]

Still, Range's dismissal did not come without pushback. Christoph Frank, the head of the Federation of German Judges and State Prosecutors (*Richterbund*) called the firing a "significant threat" to the rule of law[139] and charged that political influence on prosecutorial decision-making threatened to undermine the public's confidence in the criminal justice system.[140] Berlin's justice senator, Thomas Heilmann, criticized the Justice Minister stating: "I can't accept the behaviour of Minister Maas, . . . [e]ither he understands himself as the supervising authority over the state prosecutors, in which case he should have already intervened two months ago, or he is, like me, of the opinion that

[135]   Melissa Eddy, "Germany Drops Inquiry into Claims U.S. Tapped Angela Merkel's Phone," *New York Times*, June 12, 2015, accessed November 12, 2016, www.nytimes.com/2015/06/13/world/europe/germany-drops-inquiry-us-tapped-angela-merkel-phone.html?_r=0.
[136]   Ibid.
[137]   Ben Knight, "Outrage as Range Turns Netzpolitik Treason Storm into Constitutional Row," *Deutsche Welle*, August 4, 2014, accessed November 13, 2014, www.dw.com/en/outrage-as-range-turns-netzpolitik-treason-storm-into-constitutional-row/a-18626420.
[138]   Ben Knight, "How the World Misunderstood Germany's Netzpolitik Affair," *Deutsche Welle*, August 5, 2015, accessed October 12, 2015, www.dw.com/en/how-the-world-misunderstood-germanys-netzpolitik-affair/a-18630649.
[139]   "Plugging Leaks: Merkel's War on Germany's Press and Parliament," *Der Spiegel*, August 7, 2015, accessed January 13, 2016, www.spiegel.de/international/germany/berlin-goes-after-journalists-to-protect-state-secrets-a-1047265.html.
[140]   Deutscher Richterbund, "Richterbund kritisiert Eingreifen des Bundesjustizministers," *Press Release*, August 4, 2015, accessed November 10, 2015, www.drb.de/cms/index.php?id=917&L=0.

politicians can't decide on political criminal investigations, in which case he shouldn't have been allowed to intervene."[141] In an editorial, the influential German magazine, *Der Spiegel*, took the opposite tack, stating: "something is wrong with a political system when an intelligence service and the judiciary join forces against the media. And when state and federal prosecutors can be instrumentalized for political interests."[142] In that same vein, the Bundestag's legal affairs committee, led by opposition leader Renate Künast, held hearings to investigate the government's role in prosecuting the journalists. Künast herself stated that the charges were "clearly aimed at intimidating media organizations – maybe even parliamentarians."[143]

V LESSONS: PROSECUTORIAL POWER AND DEMOCRATIC ACCOUNTABILITY

A *Lessons from the Case Studies*

As the Range and Schottdorf cases illustrate, the duty of objectivity does not fully protect German prosecutors from political interference. If we compare both cases, the first similarity is that both the Federal Prosecutor, as well as the state prosecutors in Bavaria, were uniquely vulnerable. They either lacked the benefit of life tenure (Range) or their future frequent career rotations were determined by the *Länder*-level Ministries of Justice (Schottdorf). Viewing both cases through the lens of Germany's principle of mandatory prosecution, it seems safe to assume that the prosecutors had sufficient suspicion to investigate the targeted defendants. In the investigation phase of both cases, political actors intervened to stop or hamstring the investigation. In the Range case, the Netzpolitik investigation embarrassed the Ministry of Justice and prompted both the media and the general public to complain. Not only did Range's investigation threaten the freedom of the press, Range was the first Federal Prosecutor in history to accuse the Minister of Justice of interfering in a case for political reasons.[144] Range's insubordination and threats to the freedom of the press led to his dismissal. While it is true that political factors

---

[141] "Critics Hunt Fresh Scalps in Treason Scandal," *The Local De*, August 6, 2015, accessed December 12, 2015, www.thelocal.de/20150806/critics-hunt-fresh-scalps-in-treason-scandal.

[142] Klaus Brinkbäumer, "Berlin's NSA Fears: Treason Investigation Reveals Anxiety at the Top."

[143] Naomi Conrad, "In Berlin, Probe into Netzpolitik Inquiry Drags On," *Deutsche Welle*, August 19, 2015, accessed December 11, 2015, www.dw.com/en/in-berlin-probe-into-netzpoli tik-inquiry-drags-on/a-18658583.

[144] John Blau, "Prosecutor Fired after Targeting Journalists," *Handlesblatt*, August 5, 2015, accessed June 19, 2016, www.global.handelsblatt.com/edition/234/ressort/politics/article/pro secutor-fired-for-targeting-journalists.

led to Range's firing, those factors were congruent with the state's democratic values and the wider public interest.

One cannot draw the same conclusion in the Schottdorf case. Here, political interference undercut the investigation's scope. Political influence acted to undermine the justice system's commitment to the principle of mandatory prosecution to advance the interests of Mr. Schottdorf and his political allies. Because the allegations involved the price-fixing of lab tests, one can argue that the failure to prosecute harmed the wider public interest in reasonable medical costs. Although the Ministers of Justice at the *Bund* and *Land* levels are accountable to parliamentary bodies that may investigate prosecutorial decision-making, those bodies cannot force prosecutors to file charges. Besides, although the investigative hearings in the Schottdorf case uncovered multiple instances of political interference, in some cases, parliamentary hearings themselves may be viewed as a political sideshow that is driven less by the public interest than party politics.

B Drawing Comparisons

The United States was founded on the aspiration that power should flow from the people rather than from a king. However, representative democracy has not always guaranteed that prosecutorial decision-making has been responsive to public values. Even when that decision-making has honored public values, the actions reflected by those values have not always ensured that the system's results are both fair and just. Although elections tie prosecutors to some form of democratic control, they have also encouraged the unchecked growth of prosecutorial power and have sometimes undermined prosecutors' duty to do justice. As Darryl Brown has written: "[p]rosecutorial authority has grown and judicial authority contracted because, in various ways, U.S. criminal process trusts political decision-making over legal regulation."[145]

Although our founders believed that juries would check state power, today, jury trials are rare. At the same time, as citizens and interest groups have demanded greater security, harsh punishments have become more ubiquitous[146] Armed with the prospect of long sentences, American prosecutors enter the plea bargaining process with extraordinary leverage over defendants. This leverage may force defendants to accept a plea rather than risk paying a trial

[145] Darryl K. Brown, *Free Market Criminal Justice: How Democracy and Laissez Faire Undermine the Rule of Law* (New York: Oxford University Press, 2016), 4.

[146] Ibid., 5.

penalty for taking their case to trial.[147] Ironically the election of top prosecutors has led to a system that is "administered less by rules grounded in public values and principles and more by private interests, partisan motivations, and political preferences."[148] This outcome runs counter to the goals of America's nineteenth-century political reformers who, beginning in 1832, "believed that electing prosecutors, rather than appointing them as many still are, would remove them from partisan politics and force them to be accountable to voters and local communities."[149]

In contrast, at its best, the German system trusts fidelity to the principle of mandatory prosecution and the civil legal code over political decision-making. Unfortunately, that commitment to narrow prosecutorial discretion applies today only to serious crimes. Although the Code of Criminal Procedure mandates that prosecutors file charges in all cases where sufficient initial suspicion exists, the introduction of expedited case-handling practices in minor crime cases, as well as confession bargaining, has undercut the law's former prescriptive force. Though that bargaining is more sharply constrained than plea bargaining in America, the increasing use of statistics which measure case processing "efficiency" has led prosecutors to decline to prosecute increasing numbers of cases. For that reason, although prosecutorial discretion in Germany has increased, prosecutorial power has not. In Germany, prosecutors terminate or dismiss many cases and the country's sentencing practices are noticeably more lenient than in the United States. Germany's legal technocrats function largely in anonymity.

Although American prosecutors are often seen as combatants who seek to "win" cases, German prosecutors do not measure their success in convictions and long sentences. Rather than promote their own individual successes, most often German prosecutors seek to function within an envelope of consensual and horizontal decision-making. This commitment to consensus is engrained in new prosecutors during their probationary period and embedded in the service's norms and identity. The service's commitment to objectivity and prosecutors' self-understanding of their quasi-judicial role support an organizational culture that holds most individual prosecutors accountable with the rule of law and cabins decision-making. Although weakened, the principle of

[147] Andrew Chongseh Kim, "Underestimating the Trial Penalty: An Empirical Analysis of the Federal Trial Penalty and Critique of the Abrams Study" (June 23, 2015), *Mississippi Law Journal*, Vol. 84, No. 5, 2015, accessed June 22, 2016, www.ssrn.com/abstract=2635657.

[148] Darryl K. Brown, *Free Market Criminal Justice: How Democracy and Laissez Faire Undermine the Rule of Law*, 2.

[149] Amita Kelly, "Does It Matter that Ninety Five Percent of Elected Prosecutors Are White?" *National Public Radio*, July 8, 2015, accessed July 4, 2015, www.npr.org/sections/itsallpolitics/2015/07/08/420913118/does-it-matter-that-95-of-elected-prosecutors-are-white.

mandatory prosecution still serves as a bulwark against political influence in the *Länder* where prosecutors do not rotate between positions in the service, the Ministry and the judiciary. According to one General Public Prosecutor, "it is this duty that gives the prosecution service its independence."[150]

The subordinate relationship of the prosecution service within the Ministry of Justice is both a source of political accountability as well as a potential source of political influence. There is a widespread assumption among German prosecutors and members of the press that when political figures seek to influence prosecutorial decision-making, it undermines the German principle of legality. Consistent with this sentiment, rather than call for greater democratic input and accountability, the debate about improving prosecutorial performance has included calls that prosecutors enjoy greater independence from executive authority. In fact, German prosecutors have lobbied the Bundestag for greater insulation from political interference in their investigation and charging decisions. In addition, in 2012, the anti-corruption organization Transparency International called on German politicians to grant regional public prosecutors autonomy from their justice ministries "in order to prevent [the] suspicion of political influence."[151] However, there are officials within the Ministry of Justice who believe that because prosecutors are powerful officials, the prosecutors must be subject to some form of control.[152]

These calls to increase prosecutors' political independence resonate with the recommendations of the Council of Europe's Committee of Ministers. As one step toward that goal, Recommendation (2000) 19 instructs members of the government responsible for oversight of the prosecution office to "exercise their powers in a transparent way."[153] Moreover, in cases where the government instructs prosecutors to handle a specific case in a certain way, the Recommendation states that "such instructions must carry with them adequate guarantees that transparency and equity are respected."[154] This same body has also stated that "instructions not to prosecute in a specific case should, in principle, be prohibited."[155] Ironically, in 2012, in response to an information request by the Consultative Council of European Prosecutors, Germany stated:

---

[150]   General Public Prosecutor Interview [11OT], July 15, 2004.
[151]   "84 Recommendations for More Integrity: Transparency Germany Presents Its National Integrity Assessment for Germany," *Transparency International Press Release*, January 19, 2012, accessed June 19, 2016, www.transparency.org/news/pressrelease/20120119_germany_nis.
[152]   Ministry Interview [9RR], June 2, 2006.
[153]   Council of Europe Committee of Ministers, Recommendation Rec (2000)19 of the Committee of Ministers to Member States on the Role of Public Prosecution in the Criminal Justice System. Adopted October 6, 2000. Rec 13(b), accessed December 20, 2015, www.wcd.coe.int/ViewDoc.jsp?id=376859.
[154]   Ibid., Rec 13 (d).   [155]   Ibid., Rec 13 (f).

The prosecution service is by law governed by the principle of legality meaning that there is a duty to investigate whenever there are allegations of a crime committed. Although theoretically the Ministry of Justice could issue orders just as in any other administration, any such intervention would trigger careful public scrutiny. Thus, in practice there are no interventions by the ministry of justice and no interference with the duties assigned by law.[156]

Although that statement may reflect the aspirations of the German system, as long as the Ministers of Justice possess the external right of instruction, it is possible that they will use that power to achieve political aims and to subvert the rule of law. This risk is particularly acute in *Länder*, where a prosecutor's refusal to follow an order might lead to a transfer to a less desirable position. Conversely, the fact that prosecutors in those states that follow all orders may be rewarded with a promotion undermines the collegial decision-making ethos found in most prosecution offices. Ironically, the German prosecution system itself was originally conceived both as an "organ of the state" as well as a "guardian of the law." Although German prosecutors possess wide decision-making latitude and lifetime tenure, the tension between those two missions allows politicians to use their supervisory role to undermine the aims of the system's goal of equality under the law.

BIBLIOGRAPHY

Books

Allan, T. R. S. "Rule of Law (Rechtsstaat) (1998)," *Routledge Encyclopedia of Philosophy*, www.rep.routledge.com/articles/rule-of-law-rechtsstaat/v-1/. DOI: 10.4324/9780415249126-T022-1.

Beale, Sara Sun. "Prosecutorial Discretion in Three Systems: Balancing Conflicting Goals and Providing Mechanisms for Control," *Discretionary Criminal Justice in a Comparative Context*, Caianiello, Michelle and Hodgson, Jacqueline, eds., 27–58. Durham, North Carolina: Carolina Academic Press, 2015.

Boyne, Shawn Marie. *The German Prosecution Service: Guardians of the Law?* Heidelberg: Springer, 2013.

---

[156] Consultative Council of European Prosecutors: Questionnaire with a View of the Preparation of Opinion No. 7 on the Management of the Means of the Prosecution Services (Replies from Germany) (Strasbourg, February 7, 2012), www.coe.int/t/dghl/coopera tion/ccpe/opinions/travaux/OP_7_Germany.pdf.

Davis, Angela J. *Arbitrary Justice: The Power of the American Prosecutor*. New York: Oxford University Press, 2007.

Elsner, Beatrix and Peters, Julia. "The Prosecution Service Function within the German Criminal Justice System" in *Coping with Overloaded Criminal Justice Systems: The Rise of Prosecutorial Power Across Europe*, eds. Jörg-Martin, Jehle and Wade, Marianne L., 207–236. Berlin: Springer 2016.

Gilliéron, Gwladys. *Public Prosecutors in the United States and Europe: A Comparative Analysis with Special Focus on Switzerland, France and Germany*. Switzerland: Springer, 2014.

Müller, Ingo. *Hitler's Justice: The Courts of the Third Reich*. Cambridge: Harvard University Press, 1991.

Pizzi, William T. *Trials without Truth*. New York: New York University Press, 1999.

Weigend, Thomas. "The Prosecution Service in the German Administration of Criminal Justice," *Tasks and Powers of the Prosecution Services in the EU Member States*, Tak, P. J. P., ed., vol 1, Nijmegen: Wolf Legal Publishers (2004): 203–222.

Worral, John and Nugent-Borakove, M. Elaine. (eds). *The Changing Role of the American Prosecutor*. Albany: State University of New York Press (2014): 94–97.

Journals

Binavince, Emilio S. "The Structure and Theory of the German Penal Code," *American Journal of Comparative Law* 24 (1976): 594–601.

Blau, John. "Prosecutor Fired after Targeting Journalists," *Handelsblatt*, August 5, 2015. www.global.handelsblatt.com/edition/234/ressort/politics/ar ticle/prosecutor-fired-for-targeting-journalists.

Brinkbäumer, Klaus. "Berlin's NSA Fears: Treason Investigation Reveals Anxiety at the Top." *Der Spiegel*, August 10, 2015. www.spiegel.de/interna tional/germany/german-treason-investigation-reveals-anxiety-among-lea ders-a-1047256.html.

Collin, Peter. "Die Geburt der Staatsanwaltschaft in PreuBen." *Forum Historiase Iuris* (12 März 2001):1–18. www.forhistiur.de/2001-03-collin/.

Damaška, Mirjan. "The Reality of Prosecutorial Discretion: Comments on a German Monograph," *American Journal of Comparative Law* 29 (1981): 119–138.

Dubber, Markus Dirk. "The Promise of German Criminal Law: A Science of Crime and Punishment," *German Law Journal* 6 (2005): 1049–1071. www .germanlawjournal.com/pdfsNo1O6NoO7fPDF_-Vol_-06_-No_-07_-1049-10 73_ArticlesDubber.pdf.

Eisen, Lauren-Brooke, Fortier, Nicole, and Chettiar, Inimai. "*Federal Prosecution for the 21st Century*," Brennan Center for Justice at New York

University Law School (2014). www.brennancenter.org/sites/default/files/p ublications/Federal_Prosecution_For_21st_Century.pdf.

Frase, Richard S. and Weigend, Thomas. "German Criminal Justice as a Guide to American Law Reform: Similar Problems, Better Solutions," *Boston College International and Comparative Law Review* 18 (1995): 330–337.

Kozinski, Alex. "Criminal Law 2.0," *Georgetown Law Journal Annual Review Criminal Procedure*, 44 (2015): iii–xliv. www.georgetownlawjournal.org/file s/2015/06/Kozinski_Preface.pdf.

Krygier, Martin. "Rule of Law (and Rechtsstaat)," *University of New South Wales Faculty of Law Research Series* No. 53 (October 2013): 1–17. www.law .bepress.com/cgi/viewcontent.cgi?article=1052&context=unswwps-flrps13.

Langbein, John H. "Land without Plea Bargaining: How the Germans Do It," *Michigan Law* Review 78 (1979): 204–225.

Miller, Marc L. and Wright, Ronald F. "The Black Box," *Iowa Law Review* 94 (2008): 127–196.

Rauxlouh, Regina. "Formalization of Plea Bargaining in Germany: Will the New Legislation Be Able to Square the Circle?," *Fordham International Law Journal* 34 (2011): 295–331.

Reynolds, Glenn Harlan. "Ham Sandwich Nation: Due Process When Everything Is a Crime," *Columbia Law Review Sidebar* 113 (2013): 102–108.

Schram, Glenn. "The Obligation to Prosecute in West Germany," *The American Journal of Comparative Law* 17 (1969): 627–632.

Siegismund, Eberhard. "The Public Prosecution Office in Germany: Legal Status, Functions, and Organization," *120th International Senior Seminar Visiting Experts' Papers* (UNAFEI) (2001): 58–76. www.unafei.or.jp/eng lish/pdf/PDF_rms/no60/cho3.pdf.

Spector, Horacio. "The Future of Legal Science in Civil Law Systems," *Louisiana Law Review* 65 (2004): 255–269.

Weigend, Thomas. "Is the Criminal Process about Truth?: A German Perspective," *Harvard Journal of Law & Public Policy* 26, No. 1 (Winter 2003): 157–174.

Wenger, Etienne. "Communities of Practice and Social Learning Systems," *Organization* 7 (May 2000): 225–246. doi:10.1177/135050840072002.

Wright, Ronald F. "How Prosecutor Elections Fail Us," *Ohio State Journal of Criminal Law* 6 (2009): 509–606.

Wright, Ronald F. and Miller, Mark L. "The Worldwide Accountability Deficit for Prosecutors," *Washington & Lee Law Review* 67 (2010): 1587–1620.

Articles Online

Conrad, Naomi. "In Berlin, Probe into Netzpolitik Inquiry Drags On," *Deutsche Welle*, August 19, 2015. www.dw.com/en/in-berlin-probe-into-netz politik-inquiry-drags-on/a-18658583.

Crawford, David and Esterl, Mike. "Siemans Settlement Sets off Criticism of German Inquiries," *The Wall Street Journal*, October 8, 2007. www.wsj.co m/articles/SB119179176083751435.

Der Spiegel Online, May 23, 2013. "Hurried Action: Germany Criticized for Late Push on War Criminals," www.spiegel.de/international/germany/law-experts-criticize-german-authorities-for-late-push-on-nazi-crimes-a-899445. html.

August 7, 2015. "Plugging Leaks: Merkel's War on Germany's Press and Parliament," www.spiegel.de/international/germany/berlin-goes-after-jour alists-to-protect-state-secrets-a-1046265.html.

Deutsche Welle, July 30, 2015. "German Prosecutors Investigate Internet Journalists for Treason," www.dw.com/en/german-prosecutors-investigate-i nternet-journalists-for-treason/a-18619254.

July 31, 2015. "German Press and Politicians Criticize 'Absurd' Netzpolitik Inquiry," www.dw.com/en/german-press-politicians-criticize-absurd-netz politik-inquiry/a-18619716.

August 1, 2015. "Thousands March in Berlin over Journalist 'Treason' Claims," www.dw.com/en/thousands-march-in-berlin-over-journalist-trea son-claims/a-18621978.

August 1, 2015. "German Politicians Urge Chief Prosecutor to Resign over Treason Probe," www.dw.com/en/german-politicians-urge-chief-prosecu tor-to-resign-over-treason-probe/a-18621859.

August 3, 2015. "German Justice Ministry 'Warned' against Netzpolitik Treason Investigation," www.dw.com/en/german-justice-ministry-warned-against-netzpolitik-treason-investigation/a-18623227.

August 4, 2015. "German Justice Minister Maas Terminates Federal Prosecutor Range," www.dw.com/en/german-justice-minister-maas-termi nates-federal-prosecutor-range/a-18625000.

August 4, 2015. "Federal Prosecutor Range Criticizes 'Political Influence' on Investigation," www.dw.com/en/federal-prosecutor-range-criticizes-p olitical-influence-on-investigation/a-18625429.

Eddy, Melissa. "German Drops Inquiry into Claims U.S. Tapped Angela Merkel's Phone," *New York Times*, June 12, 2015. www.nytimes.com/2015/ 06/13/world/europe/germany-drops-inquiry-us-tapped-angela-merkel-phon e.html?_r-0.

German Law Journal 2 (2001). "Germany's Party Finance Scandal 'Ends' with Kohl's Plea Bargain and Too Many Unanswered Questions," www.german lawjournal.com/index.php?pageID=11&artID-60.

Human Rights Watch, December 2011. "The State Response to Hate Crimes in Germany," www.hrw.org/news/2011/12/09/state-response-hate-crimes-germany.

Jordans, Frank. "Top German Prosecutor Fired over Treason Investigation," *Business Insider*, August 4, 2015. www.iu.edu/owa/#path=/mail.

Knight, Ben. "Outrage as Range Turns Netzpolitik Treason Storm into Constitutional Row," *Deutsche Welle*, August 4, 2014. www.dw.com/en/out rage-as-range-turns-netzpolitik-treason-storm-into-constitutional-row/a-18626420.

Deutsche Welle, August 5, 2015. "How the World Misunderstood Germany's Netzpolitik Affair," www.dw.com/en/how-the-world-misunderstood-germa nys-netzpolitik-affair/a-18620649.

Mayr, Stefan. "Brisante Aktenvermerke im Fall Schottdorf," *Süddeutsche Zeitung*, January 26, 2015. www.sueddeutsche.de/bayern/laboraffaere-bri santa-aktenvermerke-im-fall-schottdorf-1.2319780.

Süddeutsche Zeitung, March 17, 2015. "Schwere Vorwürfe gegen CSU-Politiker," www.sueddeutsche.de/bayern/schottdorf-laboraffaere-schwere-v orwuerfe-gegen-csu-politiker-1.2397251.

Süddeutsche Zeitung, March 19, 2015. "Gauweiler nicht mehr Anwalt von Schottdorf," www.sueddeutsche.de/bayern/laboraffaere-in-augsburg-gau weiler-nicht-mehr-anwalt-von-schottdorf-1.2400810.

Süddeutsche Zeitung, October 13, 2015. "Schwere Vorwürfe gegen Generalstaatsawnwaltschaft im Fall Schottdorf," www.sueddeutsche.de/ba yern/einflussnahme-schwere-vorwuerfe-gegen-generalstaatsanwaltschaft-i n-fall-schottdorf-1.2690099.

Süddeutsche Zeitung, October 20, 2015. "Justiz im Zwielicht," www.sued deutsche.de/bayern/affaere-schottdorf-justiz-im-zwielicht-1.2700023.

Süddeutsche Zeitung, December 1, 2015. "Ex-Generalstaatsanwlat bestreitet politischen Einfluss im Fall Schottdorf," www.sueddeutsche.de/bayern/land tag-ex-generalstaatsanwalt-bestreitet-politischen-einfluss-im-fall-schottdorf-1.2762574.

Rath, Christian. "Wie unabhängig sind Staatsanwälte?," *Vorwärts*. August 6, 2015. www.vorwaerts.de/artikel/unabhaengig-staatsanwaelte.

The Local De, August 6, 2015. "Critics Hunt Fresh Scalps in Treason Scandal," www.thelocal.de/20150806/critics-hunt-fresh-scalps-in-treason-scandal.

Trendafilova, Ekaternia and Róth, Werner. "Report on the Public Prosecution Service in Germany," *Promoting Prosecutorial Accountability, Independence and Effectiveness. Comparative Research*. Open Society Institute, ed. Sofia: Open Society Institute, 2008: 213–246. www.opensocietyfoundations.org/sites/default/files/promoting_20090217.pdf.

Press Releases

Richterbund, Deutscher. "Richterbund kritisiert Eingreifen des Bundesjustizministers," *Press Release*, August 4, 2015. www.drb.de/cms/ind ex.php?id=917&L=0.

"84 Recommendations for More Integrity: Transparency Germany Presents Its National Integrity Assessment for German," *Transparency International Press Release*, January 19, 2012, www.transparency.org/news/pressrelease/ 20120119_germany_nis.

Miscellaneous

Center for Prosecutor Integrity, *An Epidemic of Prosecutor MisConduct* (2013): Appendix B, www.prosecutorintegrity.org/wp-content/uploads/Epidemicof ProsecutorMisconduct.pdf.
Registry of Prosecutorial Misconduct, March 15, 2016. www.prosecutorintegrity .org/registry/database.
Consultative Council of European Prosecutors: Questionnaire with a View of the Preparation of Opinion No. 7, replies from Germany (Strasbourg, February 7, 2010), www.coe/int/t/dghl/cooperation/ccpe/opinions/travaux/ OP_7_Germany.pdf.
Council of Europe (2000), Committee of Ministers, *Recommendation Rec (2000)19 of the Committee of Ministers*. www.wcd.coe/int/ViewDoc.jsp? id=376859.
Council of Europe, February 18, 2015, pp. 11–13, "Threats to the Rule of Law in Council of Europe Member States: Asserting the Parliamentary Assembly's Authority, *Committee on Legal Affairs and Human Rights* Doc. 13713. www .assembly.coe.int/nw/xml/XRef/Xref-XML2HTML-en.asp?filei d=21564&lang-en.
Pew Research Center, 2014 Global Attitudes Survey, www.pewglobal.org/2014/ 07/14/nsa-opinion/country/germany/.
Report on European Judicial Systems-Edition 2014 (2012 data): *Efficiency and Quality of Justice* (Strasbourg: Council of Europe Publications, 2014), 363 (Table 11.47), www.coe.int/t/dghl/cooperation/cepej/evaluation/Rappor t_2014_en-pdf.

German Legislation

Civil Servants Framework Act, Sect. 31 (Beamtenrechtsrahmengestez, BRRG).
Code of Criminal Procedure, Sects 153, 153(d), 160(2), 172, 257, 296(2).
Courts Constitution Act, Art. 145, 146, 147, 150, 151, 152 (Gerichtsverfassungsgesetz, GVG), May 9, 1975.
Federal Civil Service Act, Art. 56(2)d (Bundesbeamtengesetz,BBG).
Penal Code, Sect. 172 (Strafgesetzbuch, StGB).

6

The Organization of Prosecutorial Discretion

William H. Simon

Contemporary understanding of prosecutorial discretion is influenced by anachronistic conceptions of judgment and organization. These conceptions have lost ground dramatically in professions like medicine, teaching, and social work. Yet, they remain prominent to a unique degree in law. They are embedded both in the general professional culture and in legal doctrine. Innovative prosecutorial practices have emerged in recent decades, but their progress has been inhibited by attachment to these older conceptions.

The older conceptions understand professional judgment as a substantially tacit and ineffable decision by a single professional grounded in a relatively static and comprehensive discipline. The associated model of organization emphasizes decentralization, pre-entry training and certification, and a reactive, complaint-driven approach to error detection. This view contrasts professionalism to bureaucracy – decision driven by stable, rigid, and hierarchically-promulgated rules. The professions operate in realms where bureaucracy is often ineffective, and the case for professional judgment, traditionally understood, rests in part on the assumption that it is the only alternative to bureaucracy.

Yet, models of judgment and organization that are neither bureaucratic nor traditionally professional have established themselves in many sectors of both the private and public realms. These models, which might be called post-bureaucratic – or in one important variation, experimentalist – see decision as governed by explicit but provisional norms and arising from multidisciplinary group deliberation. They imply forms of organization that combine local autonomy with centralized monitoring, foster continuous learning and revision, and take proactive approaches to error detection and correction.

I appeal in this paper to models of post-bureaucratic or experimentalist organization both to emphasize the extent to which prosecution has lagged other sectors in its understanding of judgment and organization, and to connect the important innovations that have occurred in prosecution to developments in other fields.

The analysis of competing conceptions of organization has implications for the relation of prosecutorial discretion and democracy. Post-bureaucratic organization has two features that promise to enhance democratic accountability – greater transparency and greater potential for stakeholder participation.

I TRADITIONAL PREMISES

The *discretion* part of "prosecutorial discretion" connotes a combination of flexibility and discipline that elides arbitrariness on the one hand and regimentation on the other. Our key paradigm for such activity is the traditional idea of professional judgment.[1]

In the paradigm, judgment is a decision by an individual applying a discrete body of university-based knowledge to a particular situation. The decision is presumptively all-things-considered, taking into account both the full range of knowledge within the professional field (but not beyond the field's boundaries) and all relevant aspects of the particular situation. It is substantially tacit and ineffable; it cannot be explained fully to lay people and its correctness cannot be determined confidently even by peers in a large fraction of instances. And the decision is difficult to observe, in part, because it is so sensitive to myriad particular facts and in part because many of these facts are confidential. The disciplines such judgments implement are understood as stable, and their general effectiveness can only be assessed in informal ways.

This type of judgment implies a distinctive form of organization. Work units tend to be organized by discipline, with workers supervised by members of the same profession and physically separated from people in other fields. Offices tend to be relatively decentralized. Workers are only loosely supervised. Instead, responsibility is assured in substantial part by licensing controls that certify the adequacy of training and ethical disposition on entry. Learning on the job occurs most characteristically through informal association with supervisors and mentors. These mechanisms are supplemented by processes of error-detection and correction that are initiated by complaints. Although the complaint processes are initiated by clients, the key judgments are made by, or

---

[1] See Burton Bledstein, *The Culture of Professionalism: The Middle Class and the Emergence of Higher Education in America* (1976); Talcott Parsons, "A Sociologist Looks at the Legal Profession," in *Essays in Sociological Theory* (Rev. ed 1954).

strongly influenced by, professional peers. Errors are understood as idiosyncratic and are adjudicated and remedied one-by-one.

This vision of professional judgment has been nowhere more entrenched than in law, and in particular in the discussion of prosecutorial discretion. Consider three recent examples: First, an article by Zachary Price on the political and constitutional dimensions of enforcement discretion has received a lot of attention, in part because of its pertinence to various controversial initiatives of the Obama administration, including guidelines for enforcement of immigration, controlled substance, and health care laws. In general, Price views as undesirable, constitutionally suspect, or worse most efforts by prosecutors to discipline or make transparent their enforcement decisions through explicit rules, guidelines, or general norms. His most encompassing objection derives from a conception of law and the separation of powers. It rests on a distinction between "categorical" or "across the board" norms and "individualized" or "case specific" judgments. "Executive nonenforcment discretion extends only to case specific considerations," he insists.[2] This is because wholesale non-enforcement amounts to "making" or "remaking" law, which is a legislative power, while only retail non-enforcement is consistent with the executive function of "applying" the law. If, for example, it is impossible or undesirable to enforce the immigration laws fully against undocumented residents, the executive branch should not specify the criteria it will use to select residents for deportation, but should instead permit such decisions to be made by frontline agents, asylum officers, and administrative law judges with minimal guidance other than the statutes and an informal sense of equity.

The second example is *Connick v. Thompson*, in which the Supreme Court considered a claim that due process required the New Orleans district attorney to train his subordinates about the constitutional duty to turn over exculpatory evidence to the defense. At least one, and perhaps several, prosecutors in the office had violated this duty in connection with a trial of the plaintiff years earlier. At least four other violations by lawyers in the office had been condemned by the courts in the prior ten years. As far as the record showed, the agency did no relevant training. The plaintiffs invoked earlier cases holding that the failure of a police department to provide training in the use of deadly force could violate the Constitution.

Justice Thomas, writing for the Court, rejected the idea that the police cases were relevant to prosecutors. He emphasized that lawyers, to a far greater

---

[2] Zachary Price, *Enforcement Discretion and Executive Duty*, 67 *Vanderbilt L. Rev.* 671, 705 (2014).

extent than police officers, must undergo lengthy education and then demon-strate their general knowledge on a demanding examination prior to entering the occupation. "These threshold requirements are designed to ensure that all new attorneys have learned how to find, understand, and apply legal rules." In addition, lawyers are screened at entry for "character and fitness" and sub-jected to a regime of peer discipline throughout their careers. The opinion concludes that the senior officials "were entitled to rely on the prosecutors' professional training and ethical obligations in the absence of a specific reason" to believe they were not qualified.[3]

Finally, Rachel Barkow has advanced a proposal for reorganizing prosecu-torial activity that focuses on the problem of bias. Barkow is worried about the kind of bias that arises from the design of professional roles. U.S. prosecutors are normally responsible both for investigating and referring for prosecution on the one hand, and for charging, determining what punishment to seek, and negotiating with the defendant on the other. Bias arises from the tendency of prosecutors to identify cognitively and emotionally with the understanding of the case that emerges in the investigation stage. This makes her resistant to revising this interpretation as new information emerges later. Barkow's solu-tion is to sub-divide functions, assigning separate lawyers to the tasks of investigation and "adjudication" (i.e., charging and plea bargaining).[4] The proposal departs from the traditional professional view in dividing the profes-sional decision in two and bringing in a second decision-maker. But each of the now separate decisions is made in the traditional manner – by indepen-dent individuals under unspecified criteria. Moreover, responding to bias in this manner carries a serious cost: the second decision-maker, by virtue of his separation from the investigation, may lack information that should be con-sidered in the "adjudication" decisions.

II RECENT TRENDS

This traditional view of decision-making is in strong tension with recent thinking in many fields about the nature of decision-making and its implica-tions for institutional design. In field after field, practices have been rede-signed on the basis of an opposed understanding.[5]

---

[3]   *Connick v. Thompson*, 131 S.Ct. 1350, 1361, 1363 (2010).
[4]   Rachel Barkow, *Institutional Design and the Policing of Prosecutors*, 61 *Stan. L. Rev.* 869 (2009).
[5]   See generally, Charles F. Sabel, "A Real Time Revolution in Routines," in *The Corporation as a Collaborative Community* (Paul Adler and Charles Hecksher, eds. 2006); Charles F. Sabel and William H. Simon, *Minimalism and Experimentalism in the Administrative State*, 100 *Georgetown L. J.* 58 (2011).

In the first place, this opposed understanding rejects any strong distinction between categorical and individualized decision-making. Psychologists demonstrate that thinking is always categorical.[6] People process decisions through implicit criteria derived both from idiosyncratic social experience and the surrounding culture. Social scientists observing individual decisions over many cases can infer the implicit criteria even though the subjects may be unaware of them. A mandate like Price's for individualized decisions does not result in unmediated contextuality, but rather decisions governed by tacit and perhaps unconscious criteria over more explicit and reflective ones.

Such a mandate has serious costs. To some extent, the implicit criteria that generate ostensibly individual decisions will vary across decision-makers, thus violating the value of horizontal equity. Such inconsistency is often invisible, but immigration asylum decisions provide an unusually salient and troubling example of it. The rates of asylum decisions in favor of applicants vary enormously and persistently among adjudicators.[7] Since cases are randomly assigned and each adjudicator decides many cases, it is hard to account for these variations other than as manifestations of idiosyncratic adjudicator views. Moreover, even where the tacit criteria influencing decisions reflect widely shared social dispositions, they may be illegitimate. For example, the pervasive unconscious influence of racial bias has been elaborately demonstrated in many other areas.[8]

In modern industrial organization, designers reject the tacit particularistic decision-making associated with traditional "craft"-style production (an industrial analogue to professionalism). They insist that tacit norms be made explicit. The craftsmen will rely on a learned, inarticulate sense of appositeness in deciding, say, how to apply stain to a table and what level of finish should be deemed adequate. Modern production insists these norms be made explicit and precise.[9] There are three reasons for this insistence. The process by which norms are articulated requires reflection that improves the quality of

---

[6] See, e.g., Steven Winter, *A Clearing in the Forest: Law, Life, and Mind* (2003).

[7] Jaya Ramji-Nogales, Andrew I. Schoenholtz, and Philip G. Schrag, *Refugee Roulette: Disparities in Asylum Adjudication*, 60 Stan. L. Rev. 295 (2007).

[8] See *Glossip v. Gross*, 576 U.S. (Breyer, J., dissenting) (2015), Slip Op. at 10–17 (discussing numerous statistical studies of the death penalty that conclude that its application does not correlate with plausible criteria of relative severity of offense and/or that it does correlate with factors that should not be considered, notably race). Note also Justice Thomas's reply in his concurrence that statistical results are unpersuasive in part because the analysts must abstract from the rich particularity observed by judges and juries at the trials. Slip Op. at 4–6. The reply misses the point of the analyses, which purport to show that the decisions are being driven by tacit criteria rather than ineffable particularity.

[9] E.g., Productivity Press Development Team, *Standard Work for the Shop Floor* (2002).

decisions. Explicit norms can be taught more quickly to newcomers. The learning model common to professionals and craft workers in which young workers learn from their seniors through a kind of informal osmosis has been discarded as inefficient. And most importantly, decisions under explicit norms are more transparent to observers, so they are more easily assessed and changed. The traditional model assumes a relatively stable body of specialized knowledge. But many fields face intensified pressure to adapt to changing circumstances.

Moreover, in the opposed understanding of judgment, the paradigmatic decision-maker is no longer an individual, but a group that draws, not on a single discipline, but on several. Group decisions tend to be more consistent than individual ones, and they can synthesize a broader range of knowledge. Moreover, individual participants in groups feel pressure to consciously consider and articulate matters they would take for granted in solitary or more homogeneous settings.

Group decision-making is in part a response to the problem of professional bias that Barkow addresses. Bias is addressed by forcing individuals to articulate their premises and lay them open to challenge. A diverse group will likely contain people who do not suffer from any particular bias (or who may have offsetting ones). This approach avoids the disadvantage of Barkow's suggested remedy of sub-dividing the decision among different individuals. The second decision-maker avoids the bias of the first only at the cost of less information about the case.

At the same time, decisions tend to be multidisciplinary. This tendency responds to two developments. One is the evolution of perceptions of social problems. Some pressing problems that were not salient when the modern professional disciplines were established implicate multiple disciplines. Mental health and substance abuse, for example, are viewed as simultaneously public health and law enforcement problems. At the same time, evolving understandings of organization suggest greater capacity to coordinate interventions across disciplines and across institutional separations. When complex judgment at the organizational frontline was the exclusive province of the individual professional, and the individual professional was nested in a predominantly bureaucratic organization, coordination across organizational boundaries was difficult. More flexible contemporary organizational forms open up greater possibilities.

Professionals often resist the move away from the traditional understanding of judgment because they assume such a move would entail bureaucratic organization. They resist bureaucracy because it threatens individual fairness by regimenting judgment. In addition, while bureaucracy is superficially more compatible with public accountability than professionalism, in practice, it can be equally opaque. Modern organizations that purport to operate in hierarchical, rule-governed manner described by Max Weber and Frederick Taylor in fact make room for a lot of frontline discretion. This discretion tends to be exercised informally on the basis of tacit peer cultures, and it tends to be substantially unobservable by supervisors and the public. Frontline agents ("street-level bureaucrats") can depart from the rules both for benign reasons (when the rules dictate patently unjust or inefficient decisions) and malign ones. Supervisors tolerate low-visibility rule departures either because the limits of their capacity to monitor leave them no choice, or because they favor the benign departures. But benign or malign, low-visibility discretion is unaccountable except perhaps through the kind of socialization and recruitment controls that the critics assert make professionalism an inadequate mode of organization for the tasks in question.[10]

In fact, bureaucracy is not the only alternative to loose, informal decentralization favored by traditional professionalism. Major trends in important sectors of both private and public organization have produced a post-bureaucratic model of organization. Post-bureaucratic organization responds to the demands for adaptive and individualizing capacities in a world where uniform answers are undesirable and tacit cultural understanding is indeterminate. It repudiates both inflexible rules and low-visibility discretion. Decision-making in these regimes tends to be group and multidisciplinary. Accountability does not depend either on monitoring compliance with fixed rules or socialization into an ineffable culture. The most distinctive mechanisms are (1) presumptive rules, (2) root cause analysis of unexpected events, (3) peer review, and (4) performance measurement.[11]

All these features can be observed in current prosecution practice. However, they seem less widespread and deep-rooted here than in other fields, and as Price, Thomas, and Barkow illustrate, they are often ignored or misunderstood. Indeed, where we find prosecutors involved in sophisticated post-bureaucratic regimes, they often seem to have been pulled in by leaders in fields other than law. Problem-Oriented Policing, which has reconceived crime control strategies, and the Juvenile Detention Alternatives Initiative, which has transformed pre-trial detention of juveniles, are

[10] Alvin Gouldner, *Patterns of Industrial Bureaucracy* (1954); Michael Lipsky, *Street-level Bureaucracy* (1980).

[11] For example, see Charles Kenney, *The Best Practice: How the New Quality Movement Is Transforming Medicine* (2010); Anthony Bryk et al., *Learning to Improve: How America's Schools Can Get Better at Getting Better* (2015). On the lagging position of the legal profession, see William H. Simon, *Where Is the Quality Movement in Law Practice?*, 2012 Wis. L. Rev. 387.

examples.[12] Prosecutors play important roles in both, but most of the pioneering work has been done, in the first, by police officers and criminal justice academics and, in the second, by probation officers and sociologists. The greater prestige and longer history of law as a professional discipline relative to these other fields may have been liabilities that have inhibited reconception of practice.

The most general contours of the move toward post-bureaucratic organization figure in what Catherine Coles describes as a trend away from "the felony case processing model" toward "the community prosecution model." The first model defines its goal as the maximization of convictions, weighted by seriousness of the crimes. Convictions are not ends in themselves, but the model assumes that they are the only relevant means of attaining the ultimate goals, so that there is no need for practitioners to refer directly to these goals in their decision-making. Decisions in this model are made by lawyers, often with frontline actors exercising substantial autonomy and "operat[ing]in relative isolation from other agencies" and stakeholders.[13]

In the Community Prosecution model, decision-makers are guided directly by the ultimate goals of public safety and quality of life. The model assumes that felony prosecution is not a uniformly effective intervention and that, even when it is effective, it is best combined with other strategies. The goal is to craft solutions tailored to specific problems. Lawyers work in offices with non-lawyer specialists and engage continuously with other agencies and stakeholders.

The term "community prosecution" connotes local initiatives, but the post-bureaucratic architecture Coles describes can be applied to initiatives on any scale. Ideally, local efforts are linked through central institutions that measure effectiveness and pool information on the relative success of different strategies. At the same time, national and international interventions can devolve operating initiatives to frontline actors while monitoring and analyzing their efficacy.

III ELEMENTS OF POST-BUREAUCRATIC ORGANIZATION

At any scale, the key features of post-bureaucratic organization are the presumptive rule, root cause analysis, peer review, and performance measurement. Note that each challenges the traditional dichotomy between

---

[12] See Herman Goldstein, *Problem-Oriented Policing* (1990); *Juvenile Detention Alternatives Initiative, Juvenile Detention Risk Assessment: A Practice Guide to Juvenile Detention Reform* (2006); Juvenile Detention Alternatives Initiative, *Two Decades of JDAI* (2009).

[13] Catherine Coles, "Evolving Strategies in 20th Century American Prosecution," in *The Changing Role of the American Prosecutor*, 177–209 (John L. Worrall and M. Elaine Nugent-Borakove eds. 2008).

bureaucratic and professional organization, and the associated premises that we must choose between rule-based and standards-based judgment and between centralized and decentralized organization.

A Presumptive Rule

A presumptive rule is neither a bureaucratic rule (a norm that dictates decision on the basis of a limited number of specified factors) nor a standard (a general value to be furthered by an all-things-considered judgment). A presumptive rule is more specific than a standard, but unlike a bureaucratic rule, those to whom it is addressed are expected to depart from it in circumstances where it would be counter-productive to follow it. The departure, however, must be signaled, and it triggers an immediate review of the departure. When the departure is sustained, the rule gets rewritten to reflect the new understanding achieved through review.

Practice under a regime of presumptive rules is more transparent because it conforms more tightly to the rules than in a conventional bureaucracy. Practice is also more self-conscious, since actors must justify decisions that would be taken for granted in a rule-governed regime. In a bureaucracy, following the rule is always an acceptable explanation, and rule departures are generally unobserved or ignored. But in a post-bureaucratic regime, following the rule is not appropriate where doing so would be counter-productive, and departures must be transparent. A key goal is to induce and facilitate learning. This occurs in two ways. The duty to depart when the rules are ineffective and to signal departure feeds back information from the front-line that facilitates revision. Second, as I will shortly emphasize, experimentalist regimes subject practices to testing, and only explicit practices can be tested with any rigor.

Constitutional doctrine on prosecution has shown little concern with internal administration. The courts insist that administrators respond to indications of frontline violations of rules they themselves have promulgated, but where those rules (and relevant statutes) leave prosecutors discretion, they seem indifferent to whether offices take initiative to structure that discretion.[14]

---

[14] See Charles F. Sabel and William H. Simon, *The Duty of Responsible Administration and the Problem of Police Accountability*, 34 *Yale J. on Reg.* 165 (2016). For example, *Connick v. Thompson* notes that some of the prosecutors in the case were uncertain whether they had a *Brady* duty to turn over or test blood evidence that *might* have turned out to be exculpatory if tested but had not been tested. The opinion assumes that, if *Brady* did not apply, there was no constitutional problem. No one suggested that the prosecutors had a duty to clarify this issue

Practice is thus free to vary, and it does widely. In some quarters, judgments are left to informal processes and minimally supervised individual decision-making. But we also find sophisticated policy manuals that make use of the presumptive rule. The Department of Justice U.S. Attorneys Manual is a notable example. It sets out some policies in detail and then says that local offices may depart from them "[i]n the interests of fair and effective law enforcement," but only with the approval of the appropriate Assistant Attorney General and the Deputy Attorney General.[15]

The Attorneys Manual deals mostly with trans-substantive rules that apply to practices that recur across various initiatives. They do not cover some important practices, and they do not deal in detail with decisions about the allocation of resources across initiatives or with the strategic configuration of particular initiatives. In a fully articulated presumptive rule regime, the rules form a plan that reflects a coherent but provisional understanding of the relevant mission. The plan is revised periodically both in both piecemeal and overall re-assessments. A comprehensive plan embraces sets of more specific plans.

Plans of this kind are most readily found in some self-consciously reformist initiatives, such as drug courts and problem-oriented policing. Problem-oriented policing was developed mostly in the policing field, but it necessarily involves prosecutors. At the frontline, it involves local plans focused on geographical sites associated with recurring criminal activity or individuals or groups engaged persistently in criminal activity. Multidisciplinary teams engage with stakeholders to craft interventions and then periodically re-assess their efficacy. The initial intervention is codified in an explicit plan that gets reconsidered in the light of experience. The plan is thus a set of presumptive rules.

The shift from informal standards associated with professionalism to the presumptive rule is salient in the Juvenile Detention Alternatives Initiative.[16] The initiative is a network of local criminal justice agencies supported by a foundation and responsive to a federal statutory mandate that the agencies produce and implement plans to reduce disparate racial impacts from their

---

internally with their own rule, though that is what basic norms of good management required once the issue was identified.

[15] US Attorneys Manual 9–27.140. In a fully developed post-bureaucratic regime, the rules would be periodically reconsidered and rewritten in the light of approved departures. There is no indication that this happens systematically in the Department of Justice.

[16] Annie E. Casey Foundation, *Two Decades of JDAI: From Demonstration Project to National Standard* (2009).

activities. A central reform that has emerged is the development of numerical Risk Assessment Instruments to govern pre-trial detention decisions.

The story parallels the one told about baseball recruiting in Michael Lewis' *Moneyball*. Traditionally, probation officers made detention decisions through minimally supervised individual all-things-considered judgments. Reformers believed that these judgments tended to be inconsistent, but there was no way to tell for sure because of limited review and the absence of articulated norms. Gradually, this process has been replaced by one in which a scorecard dictates decision on the basis of numerically scored indicators, such as prior offenses, school attendance, or substance abuse. The scorecard is a presumptive rule. The decisions it dictates can be over-ridden, but only with the approval of a supervisor. When the scoring norms are periodically reviewed, reviewers look at overrides to see if they suggest inadequacies in the rules. The reforms have led to more consistent judgments and have made it possible to investigate the predictive power of the indicators. They seem to have contributed to declines in detention in most jurisdictions that have adopted them and to have reduced racial disparities in some.

B Root Cause Analysis of Significant Operating Events

A significant operating event is an occurrence involving actual or potential harm that is unexpected or cannot be immediately explained. Examples include abnormal adverse health events in hospitals or "near misses" in aviation. Bureaucracy tends to treat such events as idiosyncratic. It tends to ignore the ones that do not involve tangible harm. It tends to respond to harm by sanctioning those responsible and/or compensating those who suffer the harm.

Post-bureaucratic organization requires more. Rather than viewing such events as idiosyncratic, it sees them as symptoms of potential systemic problems. Thus, it subjects them to root cause analysis. It traces the causal stage back through the system. The "5 Whys" slogan from the Toyota Production System suggests as a rule-of-thumb that the analysis goes back five stages. The goal is to use the event as a learning opportunity by exploiting its diagnostic significance.

For example, a *Brady* violation could signal a need for training of a particular prosecutor, or better information technology to track evidence and disclosure, or better communication between police and prosecutor, or clearer assignment of responsibilities for *Brady* compliance among those responsible for a case. Assigning blame to a particular prosecutor will not necessarily distinguish among these explanations, nor will sanctioning the prosecutor or compensating the defendant guarantee that the problem will be remedied. Root cause analysis insists on ambitious diagnosis and remediation.

Such practices, however, are little-developed in prosecution. The courts rely mainly on end-of-the-pipe punitive and compensatory remedies. A defendant who can show misconduct may get evidence suppressed, a case dismissed, or damages. However, such remedies are available only in the case of actual tangible harm, and they require proof that is often unavailable. Moreover, they have small deterrent effect, since the responsible officials virtually never bear the costs. Post-conviction exonerations have been numerous in recent years, often prompted by DNA analysis. The discovery of a wrongful conviction is an unexpected adverse event of the sort that would prompt root cause analysis in many fields. Hospitals, for example, conduct searing "mortality-morbidity" reviews in comparable circumstances. But no such practice is standard in prosecution.[17]

Disciplinary sanctions for prosecutor misconduct are rarely considered, much less applied. Justice Thomas in the *Connick* case did not even consider it relevant to ask whether the office in question had a functioning disciplinary process or what the likelihood was that the Louisiana bar would sanction an erring prosecutor. Judge Alex Kozinski of the Ninth Circuit recently expressed great frustration at this situation and took the extraordinary step of demanding that the California attorney general explain why her office had not filed criminal charges against a prosecutor who lied in an early stage of the case before him.[18]

It is important to sanction willful violations, but doing so is not adequate, and the focus on egregious cases can have perverse effects. Post-bureaucracy urges intervention, not just to induce compliance with clear obligations, but to promote learning. Many events that do not imply willful wrongdoing may yield diagnostic intervention. A search for causes can be informative and lead to valuable reforms. The "after action" reviews undertaken sometimes in high-profile cases can facilitate valuable inquiry of this sort.[19] If retrospective inquiry is predominantly associated with punishment or humiliation, it may have two unfortunate effects. Actors will hide or misreport information for fear it will used to inculpate them. And peers will be reluctant to express

---

[17] See, e.g., James Liebman, *The Overproduction of Death*, 100 *Columbia Law Review* 2030 (2000).

[18] *Johnny Baca v. Derral Adams*, youtube.com (Jan. 8, 2015), www.youtube.com/watch?v_2sC UrhgXjH4.; see also the critique of de facto immunity for prosecutorial misconduct in Alex Kozinski, *Preface: Criminal Law 2.0*, 44 *Geo. L. J. Ann. Rev. Crime. Proc.* xxxv–xli (2015).

[19] Erin Murphy and David Alan Sklansky, *Science, Suspects, and Systems: Lessons from the Anthrax Investigation*, 8 *Issues in Legal Scholarship* 1, 34–39 (2009).

reservations about each others' performance, since criticism implies incompetence or immorality.

C Peer Review

In the broadest sense, peer review refers to review of practice decisions by people working in the same field as those who made the decisions in question. As such, it overlaps the other elements of the post-bureaucratic approach. Here, however, I use the term more specifically to refer to relatively intense and qualitative review by peers of representative or exceptionally challenging decisions or practices. "Peer" is a capacious and somewhat ambiguous term in a world where decisions are typically multidisciplinary. The key desideraturm is that the review involve people working on comparable problems. Police officers or social workers might be appropriate members of a peer review team for a prosecutor or prosecutorial office. Reviewers could come from inside or outside the office.

Peer review is above all a learning process. The lawyer under review learns both by self-assessment and explanation of his decisions and by critical response from the reviewers. At the same time, peer review promotes the exchange of information across lawyers in the same office, and where the reviewers are outsiders, across offices. This means that lawyers can learn alternative approaches and benefit from others' experiences with them. It also tends to make practice decisions more consistent to the extent the peers develop a shared understanding that informs their decisions.

Peer review is most extensively developed in medicine. It takes various forms. In addition to "mortality-morbidity" reviews of adverse events, there is professional recertification review in which a particular practitioner's practice over a period of time is examined. And there is institutional certification review in which a hospital's operations and structures are assessed periodically. In addition, peer review can focus on particular practices; new treatments, where formal clinical trials are impracticable, are assessed through informal peer discussion.[20]

All these variations could be readily applied to law and to prosecution in particular. Perhaps the most ambitious involve the kind of intense qualitative discussion of particular cases of a sort exemplified in "morality-morbidity" reviews. The review need not be focused on cases with bad outcomes. It could draw random samples of cases, stratified to capture relevant categories where

---

[20] Robert J. Marder, *Effective Peer Review: The Complete Guide to Physician Performance Improvement* (3rd ed. 2013).

appropriate. Kathleen Noonan, Charles Sabel, and I have described such a procedure employed by social workers in some child welfare systems.[21] It is hard to find ambitious versions of such systems in law, and they are sometimes actively resisted. Gary Bellow once proposed and experimented with a version of such a system among civil legal aid programs. Observers were surprised both by the volume of errors or suggestions for improvement that reviewers found or made and by the amount of resistance by practitioners to the process, even when it was divorced from personnel or compensation decisions.[22]

Outside reviewers in law may create risks to preserving confidentiality. These concerns are less severe with prosecutors than in other areas. Since the client – the government – has a long-term interest in the quality of its lawyers' work, consent should be easier to get. And in any event, the concern is also present in medicine, but has been overcome there with the help of facilitative legislation.

Even when review is done by insiders, the bar has tended toward indifference, if not hostility. The American Bar Association flirted with the idea of prescribing that firms institute internal peer review procedures but quietly gave up the idea.[23] The bar has moved beyond the traditional idea that key professional learning takes place prior to certification by mandating "continuing legal education." But these programs, even when well-prepared, rarely focus on particular practice decisions in richly observed contexts.

D *Performance Measurement*

Performance is measured by translating the institution's goals into metrics and then periodically applying them. This was once a radical idea in the professions, and it is still controversial, but it has received increasing attention. Writing about a major federal gun-control initiative, Coles observes: "[I]t is likely the case that most U.S. Attorneys knew little about their cities' homicide rates. Project Safe Neighborhoods has changed that, prompting attention to the nature of decline (or increase) in [their] jurisdiction's homicide rate."[24]

---

[21] Kathleen G. Noonan, Charles F. Sabel, and William H. Simon, *Legal Accountability in the Service-based Welfare State: Lessons from Child Welfare Reform*, 34 *Law and Social Inquiry* 523 (2009).

[22] Gary Bellow, *Turning Solutions into Problems: The Legal Aid Experience*, 34 *NLADA Briefcase* (August 1977); available at www.garybellow.org/garywords/solutions.html.

[23] Susan Fortney, *Am I My Partner's Keeper: Peer Review in Law Firms*, 66 *U.Col. L. Rev.* 329 (1995).

[24] Coles, cited in note 13, at 154.

Performance metrics can measure process (such as charges filed) or outcome (such as convictions, or looking to ultimate outcomes, crime rates). Process metrics indicate whether plans are being implemented; outcome metrics indicate whether they are working. Without the process metrics, we don't know what practices are contributing to the outcomes; without the outcome metrics, we don't what the effects of the interventions are. A good set of metrics includes both types in a "balanced scorecard."[25]

Metrics can be used to induce compliance with instructions, or they can be used diagnostically to revise and adapt instructions. The two functions are not entirely complementary. In order to use metrics to reinforce incentives, one needs to be confident about what practices one wants to induce people to undertake, and one must be able to define them with reasonable precision and comprehensiveness. Metrics attached to rewards and sanctions can have well-known perverse effects, especially when the metrics are incomplete. They may drive behavior to goals captured by the metrics and away from ones not captured. "Teaching to the test" in education is the classic example. Maximizing convictions is the corresponding phenomenon in prosecution. Conviction rates alone do not tell us whether convictions were achieved ethically, how much resources were used to obtain them, the collateral social costs of the convictions, the relative priority of the crimes prosecuted, or the deterrent effect of the convictions.

In situations where there is uncertainty about the relevant practice and monitoring is designed to facilitate learning, the stakes for individuals have to be lowered. Metrics have to be provisional, and provisional metrics do not fit well with rewards and punishments because low scores are as likely to reflect the inadequacy of the measures as the quality of the performance.

From the learning perspective, metrics have three functions: first, the process of defining the metrics and interpreting their application structures and disciplines' ongoing assessment of the relevant practices. For example, discussion has recently arisen with respect to Compstat-style assertive policing regimes about whether the number of arrests should be treated as a measure of success or as a cost. Many departments have viewed it as a measure of success, but critics assert that this practice ignores the harm such arrests do in creating criminal records that impair the life chances of a broad segment of the community. Requiring that the program specify metrics may cause the issue to surface earlier and the discussion to become more precise.

---

[25] David Norton and Robert Kaplan, *The Balanced Scorecard* (1992).

Second, measurements produce information about the system that can guide reform. Pre-trial juvenile detention is an interesting case because there are only two permissible grounds for such detention – likely failure to appear for court proceedings or re-offense – and both are easily observable. Thus, once decision criteria are made explicit as they are in the scorecards, their predictive power can be readily studied. The Juvenile Detention Alternative Initiatives regime mandates that the criteria be validated initially and periodically thereafter in the light of experience. The validation studies are sometimes quite sophisticated, and the scorecards have often been revised.

Third, the metrics, when applied across comparable institutions or individuals, indicate relatively effective and ineffective actors. The relatively successful are studied for lessons about what produces success. The laggards are subject to intensified supervision and technical assistance. In the diagnostic perspective, failure is presumed until proven otherwise to result from incapacity rather than willfulness.

The most common use of metrics in prosecution appears to be in assessing the relative effectiveness of individual prosecutors for promotion purposes.[26] However, there are more ambitious efforts. Some offices monitor charging practices in order to ensure consistency and compliance with policies about evidence quality and prosecution priorities.[27]

The most sophisticated efforts combine aggregate metrics with ongoing rule revision, root cause analysis, and peer review. Examples can be found in initiatives inspired by the Vera Institute Project on Racial Justice. In the manner of the Juvenile Detention Alternatives Initiative, the program prescribes ongoing monitoring of racial disparities in the effects of prosecution practices, root cause analysis of disparities, and scanning for reforms that might mitigate the disparities. In Milwaukee, for example, sophisticated implementation that included revisions of charging practices and the development of diversion programs has significantly reduced disparities.[28]

Another example is the "focused deterrence" strategy that starts by identifying violence-prone actors through intensive surveillance and then offers them a package of moral exhortation, threats of prosecution for past offenses, and

---

[26] U.S. Government Accountability Office, GAO-04-422, *US Attorneys: Performance-Based Initiatives Are Evolving* (2004); see also M. Elaine Nugent-Borokove et al., *Exploring the Feasibility and Efficacy of Performance Measures in Prosecution and Their Application to Community Prosecution* (2009).

[27] Ronald F. Wright and Marc L. Miller, *The Worldwide Accountability Deficit for Prosecutors*, 67 *Washington & Lee Law Review* 1587, 1614–1618 (2010).

[28] Angela Davis discusses the Vera Initiative in her contribution to this volume. See also Vera Institute of Justice, *A Prosecutor's Guide for Advancing Racial Equity* (Nov. 2014).

offers of social services (for example, job training or substance abuse treatment). A distinctive component of the regime is the "call in" which invites (or in the case of probationers, requires) attendance at a meeting where prosecutors, community leaders, police, and social workers make presentation. In addition to creating tangible incentives for compliance, the intervention is designed to leverage peer relations by threatening or promising group punishments or benefits. Many focused deterrence regimes have been studied with rigor. An example from Cincinnati illustrates how measurement has been sufficiently fine-grained to yield information useful for reconfiguring the program to eliminate or revise specific ineffective elements.[29]

IV DEMOCRACY

We generally think of democratic accountability in terms of elections or the more diffuse pressures of public opinion. There is some ambiguity about the range of prosecutorial activity that should be controlled democratically. In some respects, prosecutors resemble judges. They make decisions of great consequence that should be made disinterestedly and reflectively on the basis of general, public, and prospective norms. Since public pressure can be infected by considerations that prosecutors are obliged to ignore in these decisions, it risks compromising fairness. At the same time, prosecutors are executive officials commanding resources and exercising discretion in ways that have broad impact on their communities. The public has a clear stake in the general efficiency and fairness of prosecutorial practice and in the ways prosecutors exercise discretion within the interstices of enacted law.

Public accountability seems most productive and least dangerous to fairness values when it focuses on general patterns of practice rather than individual decisions. Unfortunately, this has not been the traditional focus of discussion. Prosecution often has a low profile in elections and public debate. Incumbents running for re-election are often unchallenged and usually reelected. Moreover, where there is appraisal, it tends not to focus on general patterns. Discussion of practice tends to focus on a few high-profile cases. Otherwise, discussion is preoccupied with the background qualifications and character of the candidates.[30]

---

[29] See Robin S. Engel et al., *Reducing Gang Violence Using Focused Deterrence: Evaluating the Cincinnati Initiative to Reduce Violence (CIRV)*, Just.Q. 1, 28–32 (2011).

[30] Ronald F. Wright, *How Prosecutor Elections Fail Us*, 6 *Ohio State Journal of Criminal Law* 581 (2009).

This situation is in part a function of the traditional conception of prose-cutorial work that emphasizes individual, ineffable judgment. We have seen that the traditional conception puts great emphasis on character and qualifi-cations because it assumes that individual judgments are difficult to assess. In addition, the traditional conception assumes that judgment is necessarily idiosyncratic and ineffable, so it resists efforts to cabin discretion through explicit rules or to measure its effects. Practice under these assumptions is necessarily opaque.

The post-bureaucratic trends in the organization of prosecutorial discretion have two broad implications for democratic control of prosecutorial power. First, the basic tendency of post-bureaucratic reform is to make the broader system transparent in a way that increases control and adaptive capacity by insiders and outsiders alike. These reforms potentially enhance both fairness and accountability. Charles Sabel and I have argued that there is (or should be) a duty of responsible administration that requires administrators to adopt reforms to manage transparently so that courts and citizens can assess their compliance with substantive norms.[31] We find this duty in convergent themes of constitutional, statutory and common law, as they have been applied to a range of public institutions, including, prisons, police departments, and wel-fare programs. Courts have been reluctant to put such pressure on prosecution offices, in part because of the persistence of the traditional conception of prosecutorial judgment and the related assumption that accountability must take bureaucratic forms that would rigidify practice inappropriately. But initiatives from prosecutors themselves have demonstrated that there are ways of structuring discretion that enhance transparency without strait-jacket-ing practice. Courts could draw on these efforts to induce reforms by recalci-trant offices.

The "duty of responsible administration" idea runs directly counter to arguments like Price's that find the self-conscious structuring of prosecutorial discretion as an illegitimate assertion of law-making powers by executive officials. Price's argument implies that internal regulation enhances the power of senior administrators, rather than making it more accountable. This is wrong. A top administrator who wants to impose her will on the frontline has many tools for doing so without rule-making and transparent forms of review. She can, for example, make hiring, promotion, and compen-sation decisions on the basis of low-visibility signals of loyalty to her goals. Moreover, even where top officials leave broad autonomy to the frontline, there is no reason to assume that frontline decisions are benign. Without

---

[31]   Cited in note 14 above.

structure, frontline decisions may reflect the prejudices of the agents or may turn out to vary in arbitrary ways.

Second, the post-bureaucratic reforms often appeal to a conception of democracy somewhat different from the one that emphasizes elections. This alternative conception has attractive features, and it suggests the possibility of a thicker form of political legitimation.

The alternative conception is stakeholder democracy. Here, decisions should be made, where feasible, locally by the people most affected and knowledgeable about them. General elections are inadequate both because they bundle far too many issues for people to make and register informed decisions about, and because they weigh all votes equally on all issues without regard to intensity of knowledge or interest.[32] (Some account of intensity is taken in the design of jurisdictions and the assignment of issues to them, but within even local jurisdictions, there is a wide variation in knowledge and personal stake on many issues.)

Stakeholder democracy has to deal with the problem of who to admit to participation and how to reconcile differences when stakeholders disagree. But to the extent that representatives of diverse interests can come close to consensus on local interventions, they may confer a kind of democratic legitimacy that is unavailable in other processes. Even when stakeholders do not agree, their engagement may produce information that can influence official decision in ways that make it more acceptable.

The stakeholder conception resonates with various initiatives associated with "community prosecution." These initiatives are driven by the perceptions that, to the extent that the process is concerned with justice for victims, it should be more directly responsive to them; and to the extent it is concerned with deterrence, its efforts are most efficiently configured when coordinated with actions of other institutions and citizens and when they are configured in the light of information that can best be extracted through broad consultation.

In the stakeholder conception, the legislature's role is not to authorize specific decisions prospectively. Rather, the legislature sets basic parameters and provides resources for local deliberations and for central review of their efficacy. The legislature then retrospectively assesses the success of various interventions, perhaps mandating continuing experimentation where they are ineffective and perhaps codifying or promoting specific ones where success has been demonstrated.

---

[32] See the discussion of the "problem of intensity" in electoral democracy in Robert Dahl, *A Preface to Democratic Theory* (1956).

Stakeholder participation is not invariably beneficial. It can involve unproductive and expensive process costs and capture by unrepresentative sub-constituencies. But it has the potential to vindicate a different but complementary ideal of democracy from the one usually assumed in discussion of prosecutorial discretion.

7

Prosecutors, Democracy, and Race

Angela J. Davis

I INTRODUCTION

Prosecutors are the most powerful officials in the American criminal justice system. They make the most important decisions in the criminal process – whether an individual will be charged with a crime and whether he will be afforded the opportunity to plead guilty to reduced charges in order to reduce the length of a potential prison sentence. Prosecutors exercise almost boundless discretion in making these decisions with very little accountability to the people they serve.

The American criminal justice system is plagued with crises, including unwarranted racial disparities, the overuse of incarceration and police killings of unarmed people of color. Because of the dominant role that prosecutors play in the criminal process, their decisions have an impact on these crises and often drive them. Hence, they have a responsibility to correct the problems and should be held accountable if they do not.

Prosecutors on the state and federal levels are chosen through the democratic process. The vast majority of criminal cases are prosecuted on the state and local level, and most state prosecutors are elected officials. Federal prosecutors are nominated and approved by the United States Senate. Transparency and accountability are core tenets of a democracy, but the electoral system has not proven to be an effective mechanism of accountability for prosecutors, especially on the issue of racial fairness.

This chapter will discuss the role that prosecutors have played in perpetuating the racial injustices in the American criminal justice system and the failure of the democratic process to hold prosecutors accountable. An examination of how three elected prosecutors have managed the issue of racial fairness in their jurisdictions will demonstrate the complexities and difficulties of the electoral process as a means of achieving racial fairness in the criminal justice system.

The democratic process can work, but only with more transparency in the prosecution function and the election of prosecutors who are committed to racial justice.

II POWER, DISCRETION AND RACIAL DISPARITIES

A *Charging and Plea Bargaining*

The power and discretion of American prosecutors cannot be overstated. They essentially control the criminal justice system through their charging and plea bargaining decisions. These decisions are arguably the most important decisions by any criminal justice official, and prosecutors make them behind closed doors with very little accountability.[1] A police officer may arrest an individual if she has probable cause to believe that person has committed a crime,[2] but only prosecutors decide whether an individual will be charged with a crime. They may accept the recommendation of the police officer or reject it. Prosecutors may charge the individual with a more or less serious charge, or they may choose to forego charges altogether. They are not required to charge an individual even if they have probable cause to believe the person has committed a crime. The decision to charge is totally within the discretion of the prosecutor.

The charging decision has tremendous consequences for an individual accused of a crime. Because there is such a proliferation of criminal laws in both the federal and state criminal justice systems, prosecutors have a wide range of options when they are making the charging decision. For example, if a police officer arrests an individual who is in possession of ten bags of cocaine, the prosecutor has several choices. The officer may recommend that the prosecutor charge the individual with Possession with Intent to Distribute Cocaine – a felony that carries a mandatory minimum penalty of ten years in prison in many jurisdictions.[3] The prosecutor may accept the officer's recommendation, or she may decide to charge the individual with Possession of Cocaine – a misdemeanor with a maximum penalty of one year. The prosecutor may also decide not to charge the individual at all. The ramifications of this decision are far-reaching and permanent. If the prosecutor brings the

[1] See generally ANGELA J. DAVIS, ARBITRARY JUSTICE: THE POWER OF THE AMERICAN PROSECUTOR (2007).

[2] See *United States v. Watson*, 423 U.S. 411, 423 (1976).

[3] See 21 U.S.C. § 841 (2010) ("such person shall be sentenced to a term of imprisonment which may not be less than 10 years"); GA CODE ANN. § 16–13-31 (2015); N.Y. PENAL LAW § 70.00 (McKinney 2009).

felony charge, the defendant not only faces the possibility of a mandatory ten years in prison, but he will be saddled with a felony conviction and all of its associated collateral consequences, including difficulty securing employment after he is released,[4] possibly losing the right to vote[5] and losing eligibility for public housing and benefits,[6] among others. If the defendant is not a citizen, he may face deportation.[7] A misdemeanor conviction may have similar collateral consequences, although in most states they are not as severe.

Despite the importance of the charging decision and its life-changing consequences, prosecutors are not required to explain or justify their decisions to anyone (other than possibly their supervisors), nor are they required to follow rules or guidelines when making the decision. The charging decision is not made in open court, nor is there any public record of why or how the decision was made. These decisions are made behind closed doors, in the prosecutor's office, without any transparency.

Although there are no laws that govern the charging decision, the American Bar Association has established Standards for the Prosecution Function that serve as guidelines for prosecutors as they perform their various duties and responsibilities.[8] The Standards list a number of factors that prosecutors should consider when they are deciding whether to charge an individual with a crime. These factors include the seriousness of the offense, the interest of the victim in prosecution, the likelihood of conviction, and others.[9] However, prosecutors are not required to apply or even consider these factors or to follow the Standards at all.

There may be legitimate reasons for bringing different charges against two defendants who are alleged to have committed the same offense. The prosecutor may be justified in bringing felony charges against a defendant who has a prior criminal record while charging a first offender with a misdemeanor – even if they have committed the same offense. However, because prosecutors are not required to explain their decisions, they may make them arbitrarily or

---

[4] MICHELLE ALEXANDER, THE NEW JIM CROW: MASS INCARCERATION IN THE AGE OF COLORBLINDNESS 149–50 (2010).

[5] *Felony Disenfranchisement*, SENTENCING PROJECT, www.sentencingproject.org/template/pa ge.cfm?id=133 (last visited Dec. 21, 2015).

[6] *See* HUMAN RIGHTS WATCH, NO SECOND CHANCE: PEOPLE WITH CRIMINAL RECORDS DENIED ACCESS TO PUBLIC HOUSING 16 (2004).

[7] *See generally Ingrid v. Eagly, Criminal Justice for Noncitizens: An Analysis of Variation in Local Enforcement*, 88 N.Y.U. L. REV. 1126 (2013).

[8] AMERICAN BAR ASSOCIATION CRIMINAL JUSTICE STANDARDS COMMITTEE, *ABA STANDARDS FOR CRIMINAL JUSTICE: PROSECUTION FUNCTION AND DEFENSE FUNCTION* 4 (3rd ed. 1993).

[9] *Id.* at 70.

for the wrong reasons. The potential for unfairness is great, especially when these choices result in class or racial disparities.

The United States Constitution requires that charges in felony cases be brought by a grand jury in federal court.[10] Grand juries usually consist of a larger number of jurors than juries that decide guilt or innocence in criminal trials. The sole purpose of the grand jury is to decide whether criminal charges should be brought against a defendant. The formal charging document is called an indictment. A grand jury may return an indictment if it finds that there is probable cause to believe the defendant committed the crime or crimes.[11] Less than half of the states require grand juries in felony cases.[12]

Prosecutors entirely control the grand jury process. The defendant nor his lawyer have a right to be present, and although the grand jurors technically have the right to call witnesses, prosecutors usually decide which witnesses will testify in the grand jury. Prosecutors are not required to present evidence that would tend to exculpate the defendant.[13] Because grand juries usually hear only one side of the story and prosecutors only have to meet the low standard of probable cause, grand juries almost always return indictments.[14]

Prosecutors also control the plea bargaining process. Plea bargaining involves prosecutors making deals with defendants that permit them to plead guilty to a less serious charge in exchange for the prosecutor agreeing to dismiss the more serious charge or charges. In theory, plea bargains offer benefits to the prosecutor and the defendant. The prosecutor secures a conviction without the risk of a jury finding the defendant not guilty. She also saves the time and resources that would otherwise be devoted to a jury trial. Trials may last days or even weeks. Guilty pleas are usually over in minutes. Guilty pleas may also be beneficial to the defendant. If the defendant is charged with numerous offenses and is convicted of all charges after a trial, the judge may sentence him to time in prison for all of the charges. However, if the defendant pleads guilty to one offense and the rest of the charges are dismissed, the judge may only sentence him to time on that one charge. The

---

[10] *See* U.S. Const. amend. V; *see also Justice 101: Charging*, THE U.S. DEP'T OF JUST., www .justice.gov/usao/justice-101/charging (last visited Dec. 21, 2015).

[11] *See Justice 101: Charging*, THE U.S. DEP'T OF JUST., www.justice.gov/usao/justice-101/char ging (last visited Dec. 21, 2015).

[12] *Federal Grand Jury*, U. DAYTON SCH. L., www.campus.udayton.edu/~grandjur/stategj/abol ish.htm (last visited Dec. 21, 2015).

[13] *See United States v. Williams*, 504 U.S. 36, 51–52 (1992).

[14] OFFICE OF JUSTICE PROGRAMS, BUREAU OF JUSTICE STATISTICS, *Federal Justice Statistics 2010 – Statistical Tables*, www.bjs.gov/content/pub/pdf/fjs10st.pdf (Last updated Dec. 2013) (finding U.S. attorneys prosecuted 162,000 federal cases in 2010 and grand juries declined to return an indictment in 11 of them).

prosecutor gets fewer convictions and the defendant gives up the right to a trial, but both sides reap benefits as well.

In theory, plea bargaining may be beneficial to the defense, the prosecution and the entire court system. The reality is that it is frequently an unfair and one-sided process. Like the charging decision, plea bargaining is controlled entirely by the prosecutor. A prosecutor is not required to offer a plea bargain to a defendant, and as with the charging decision, he is not required to justify his decision to anyone. Judges may not compel prosecutors to offer a deal and in most jurisdictions are not involved with the plea bargaining process at all. The judge's role is limited to assuring that the defendant is pleading guilty voluntarily and that he understands that he is forgoing various constitutional rights, including the right to a trial.

Prosecutors need only meet the low standard of probable cause (more likely than not) to bring charges against the defendant. However, to convict the defendant of those charges, she must prove guilt beyond a reasonable doubt. The reasonable doubt standard is the highest standard in the criminal justice system. The defendant is presumed innocent unless and until the prosecutor meets that heavy burden, and the defendant has the constitutional right to demand a trial in which the prosecutor attempts to prove him guilty.

Despite these constitutional protections and the government's heavy burden, defendants plead guilty in 95% of all criminal cases[15] – primarily because of the prosecutor's tremendous power and discretion in the charging and plea bargaining process. Because they only have to meet the low probable cause standard to bring charges, prosecutors frequently bring charges they know they may not be able to prove beyond a reasonable doubt to give themselves an advantage in the plea bargaining process. When facing an overwhelming number of charges, each of which may carry long prison terms and/or mandatory minimum sentences, defendants often feel pressured to plead guilty. Going to trial is risky because the defendant doesn't know what a judge or jury may decide, regardless of the strength or weakness of the evidence.

In addition, most criminal defendants are indigent and represented by overworked court-appointed attorneys with few or no resources to investigate their cases.[16] They may plead guilty in cases where they may very well have prevailed at trial, simply because their lawyers do not have the time or resources to mount an investigation that might reveal weaknesses in the government's case and/or a

---

[15] *Plea and Charge Bargaining*, Res. Summary (Bureau of Just. Assistance U.S. Dep't of Just., Arlington, V.A.), Jan. 24, 2011, at 1.

[16] *Justice For a Few?*, Equal Just. Usa, www.ejusa.org/learn/indigent%2Bdefense (last visited Dec. 21, 2009).

defense to the crime. Prosecutors often increase the pressure by putting deadlines on plea bargains, requiring the defendant to accept or reject the plea by a
certain time or risk losing the deal. This puts defense attorneys in the unethical
position of advising their clients about whether to accept an offer before they
have had the opportunity to investigate the case and establish whether there is a
defense. Under these difficult circumstances, it is not surprising that so many
defendants plead guilty. The alternative is just too risky.

The risks are particularly high when the defendant is charged with crimes
that carry mandatory minimum sentences. Sentencing laws with mandatory
minimum sentences require the defendant to serve a certain minimum
number of years in prison. If a defendant is convicted of a crime that carries
a mandatory minimum sentence, the judge has no discretion to show
leniency; she is required to sentence the defendant to at least the mandatory
minimum. The defendant might be a first offender or may have played a
minor role in the crime, perhaps as an accomplice. Judges ordinarily take
these factors into account when deciding the appropriate sentence, but they
are not permitted to do so if the crime carries a mandatory minimum sentence.

During the 1980s and 1990s, the United States Congress passed a number of
harsh crime bills that included draconian mandatory minimum sentences for
drug offenses. The Anti-Drug Abuse Act of 1986 created five- and ten-year
mandatory minimum prison terms for first-time drug dealers,[17] and the Anti-
Drug Abuse Act of 1988 expanded the same mandatory minimum penalties to
include drug conspiracies and attempts.[18] The 1988 law made crack cocaine
the only drug with a mandatory minimum penalty for simple possession, even
for first-time offenders.[19] Most states also passed additional mandatory minimum sentencing laws, many with harsher sentences than the federal laws.[20]

In addition to passing harsh mandatory minimum sentencing laws, in 1984,
Congress established the United States Sentencing Commission and charged
it with the task of developing sentencing guidelines to establish uniformity in
sentencing.[21] Many members of Congress were concerned about disparities in

---

[17]   *Report on Cocaine and Federal Sentencing Policy*, U.S. SENT'G COMM'N, www.ussc.gov/rep
       ort-cocaine-and-federal-sentencing-policy-2 (last visited Dec. 21, 2015).
[18]   *Id.*   [19]   *Id.*
[20]   Kara Gotsch, *"After" the War on Drugs: The Fair Sentencing Act and the Unfinished Drug
       Policy Reform Agenda*, AM. CONST. SOC'Y FOR L. AND POL'Y (Dec. 2011), www.acslaw.org/
       sites/default/files/Gotsch_-_After_the_War_on_Drugs_0.pdf (noting that Missouri adopted a
       75-to-1 sentencing disparity between crack and powder cocaine, and Oklahoma set a 6-to-1
       quantity-based sentencing disparity that required a ten-year mandatory minimum sentence for
       possessing five grams of crack cocaine and twenty-eight grams of powder cocaine).
[21]   *An Overview of the United States Sentencing Commission*, www.ussc.gov/sites/default/files/pdf/
       about/overview/USSC_Overview.pdf (last visited Dec. 21, 2015).

sentencing among federal judges and believed that a system of determinate sentencing would resolve the problem. So in 1987, the federal sentencing guidelines were adopted and published in a complex 845-page manual. The guidelines established a narrow range of months within which judges were required to sentence defendants based solely on the offense and the defendant's criminal history.[22] Until the Supreme Court's decision in *United States v. Booker*,[23] the guidelines were mandatory – judges were required to sentence within the designated range, regardless of the facts and circumstances of the case. Even after the *Booker* decision, most judges continue to follow the guidelines, declining to depart from the established range of sentences.[24]

The combination of mandatory minimum sentences and mandatory sentencing guidelines gave prosecutors even more power and discretion at the charging and plea bargaining stages of the process. Congress did not eliminate discretion from the process; it was simply transferred from judges to prosecutors. If a prosecutor charges the defendant with one or more mandatory minimum offenses, the defendant faces the possibility of decades-long terms of imprisonment and sometimes even life in prison if convicted. Not surprisingly, the vast majority of defendants choose to accept plea bargains – even deals that result in long prison sentences.

Many states followed the lead of the federal government, passing tough mandatory minimum sentencing laws – some even harsher than the federal laws. Over half of the states also created sentencing commissions and established sentencing guidelines. Consequently, state prosecutors enjoyed a similar enhancement of their charging and plea bargaining power and discretion. Despite recent reforms on the federal and state levels,[25] there are still 2.2

---

[22] *See id.* [23] *United States v. Booker*, 543 U.S. 220 (2005).

[24] *See Report on the Continuing Impact of United States v. Booker on Federal Sentencing* (Dec. 2012), www.ussc.gov/sites/default/files/pdf/news/congressional-testimony-and-reports/booker-r eports/2012-booker/Part_A.pdf#page=55 (noting that the guidelines have continued to significantly influence sentences for most offenses).

[25] In 2010, Congress passed the Fair Sentencing Act, reducing the 100-to-1 disparity for crack offenses to 18-to-1. Subsequent amendments to the Act made the law partially retroactive, permitting some defendants to file motions requesting a reduction. More recently, there has been bipartisan support for reforms that would reverse more of the harsh sentencing laws passed during the 1980s. The Sentencing Reform and Corrections Act would permit federal judges to exempt a substantial number of non-violent drug offenders from mandatory minimum prison terms. Other parts of the Act would make the Fair Sentencing Act retroactive for many more prisoners. Between 2009 and 2013, forty states reduced the penalties for drug offenses. In addition, in 2014, the Justice Department announced a Clemency Initiative that would commute the sentences of federal prisoners who meet certain criteria. However, the initiative has been criticized because relatively few prisoners can meet the difficult criteria, and the office that handles the applications is not adequately funded. *See* Sentencing Reform and Corrections Act of 2015, S. 2123, 114th Cong. (2015); U.S. SENT'G COMM'N, REPORT TO

million people in America's prisons and jails,[26] largely because of the charging and plea bargaining decisions of federal and state prosecutors.[27]

B Racial Disparities

The criminal justice system is plagued with unwarranted racial disparities,[28] and prosecutors' charging and plea bargaining decisions often produce and perpetuate these disparities.[29] The earlier example of charging discretion involving the hypothetical drug case illustrates the point. Suppose a prosecutor is considering whether to charge two individuals with drug offenses. One of them is a white high school senior named Brian who is arrested for selling cocaine to his fellow classmates. The arresting officer recommends that he be charged with distribution of cocaine – a felony that carries a mandatory minimum sentence of five years in prison. This is the first time Brian has ever been arrested. Brian's parents hire a private attorney who informs the

THE CONGRESS: IMPACT OF THE FAIR SENTENCING ACT OF 2010 1,7 (2015); Drew Desilver, *Feds May Be Rethinking the Drug War, But States Have Been Leading the Way*, PEW RES. CTR. (Apr. 2, 2014), www.pewresearch.org/fact-tank/2014/04/02/feds-may-be-rethinking-the-dr ug-war-but-states-have-been-leading-the-way/.

[26] Nicole D. Porter, SENT'G PROJECT, THE STATE OF SENTENCING 2014: DEVELOPMENTS IN POLICY AND PRACTICE 1 (2015), www.sentencingproject.org/doc/publications/sen_State_of_ Sentencing_2014.pdf.

[27] Donald Trump was elected President of the United States on November 8, 2016. He nominated Jeff Sessions to be the Attorney General on November 18th and Sessions' nomination was confirmed on February 8, 2017. Soon after his confirmation, Sessions announced his intention to roll back the criminal justice reforms made during the Obama administration. On May 11, 2017, he directed federal prosecutors to charge defendants with the most serious provable crimes carrying the harshest penalties. Sara Horowitz and Matt Zapotosky, Sessions Issues Sweeping New Charging Policy (May 12, 2017), www.washingtonpost.com/world/nati onal-security/sessions-issues-sweeping-new-criminal-charging-policy/2017/05/11/4752bd42-369 7-11e7-b373-418f6849a004_story.html?utm_term=.54794c5b9609.

[28] See John Tyler Clemons, *Injustice: The Supreme Court, Implicit Racial Bias, and the Racial Disparity in the Criminal Justice System*, 51 AM. CRIM. L. REV. 689 (2014); see also Michael Tonry, *The Social, Psychological, and Political Causes of Racial Disparities in the American Criminal Justice System*, 39 CRIME & JUST. 273 (2010); Alfred Blumstein, *Racial Disproportionality of U.S. Prison Populations Revisited*, 64 U. COLO. L. REV. 743 (1993). See generally SENTENCING PROJECT, www.sentencingproject.org/issues/racial-disparity/ (last visited June 28, 2016).

[29] See Angela J. Davis, *In Search of Racial Justice: The Role of the Prosecutor*, 16 N.Y. U. J. LEGIS. & PUB. POL'Y 821, 833–35 (2013); see also Robert J. Smith & Justin D. Levinson, *The Impact of Implicit Racial Bias on the Exercise of Prosecutorial Discretion*, 35 SEATTLE U. L. REV. 795 (2012) (conducting an in-depth examination on how implicit bias affects prosecutorial discretion); Sonja Starr & Marit Rehavi, *Racial Disparity in the Criminal Justice Process: Prosecutors, Judges, and the Effects of United States v. Booker* (UNIV. OF MICH. LAW SCH., LAW & ECONS., Working Paper No. 53 2012) (finding that most unexplained sentencing racial disparities can be attributed by prosecutors' choices to bring mandatory minimum charges).

prosecutor that Brian is addicted to cocaine and that Brian's parents have enrolled him in a residential drug treatment program. The attorney also tells the prosecutor that Brian was admitted to a prestigious university and that a felony conviction and prison term would ruin his life. The prosecutor agrees to dismiss the case if Brian successfully completes the drug program.

The other defendant is an African American high school dropout named Marcus. Marcus was arrested for selling cocaine on a street corner in his neighborhood. The police officer recommends that Marcus be charged with the same mandatory minimum offense – Distribution of Cocaine. Marcus is represented by a public defender with a very high caseload. Marcus has no prior convictions, but has been arrested several times for misdemeanor offenses. His lawyer informs the prosecutor that he has a drug addiction and was selling cocaine to support his habit. Marcus's mother cannot afford to pay for a drug treatment program, and there are no free residential programs. The prosecutor charges Marcus with the felony drug offense. Because he has an arrest record, she decides not to make a plea offer. He is convicted after a trial and is sentenced to the mandatory five years in prison.

Brian and Marcus committed the same offense and both were first offenders, but the prosecutor agreed to dismiss Brian's case. Her decision created an unwarranted racial disparity, and she is not required to justify her decision to anyone. There are many possible reasons why the prosecutor might have made these charging decisions. She may have had an unconscious bias that favored Brian, believing that he had more to lose than Marcus because of his admission to a prestigious college. Or perhaps she considered the fact that Marcus had several prior arrests, although the prevalence of racial profiling by police officers might have explained Marcus's arrests, especially since he was never charged with a crime. The prosecutor may have wanted to offer the same deal to Marcus but didn't because he couldn't afford drug treatment. Thus the disparity in treatment may have been the result of either unconscious racial bias or race-neutral factors with unintended racial consequences. In either case, the racial disparity is unjustifiable.

Prosecutorial decisions may also produce racial disparities among crime victims. Suppose a prosecutor is considering how to proceed in two burglary cases. The first case involves an African American woman named Cynthia whose apartment was burglarized. Cynthia's television and several pieces of costume jewelry were stolen. The police make an arrest, and the prosecutor mails Cynthia a notice to appear at the prosecutor's office to prepare for trial. Cynthia gets the notice, but does not show up because she has to work that day. She doesn't have vacation time, so when she doesn't work, she doesn't get paid. The prosecutor tries to reach Cynthia by phone repeatedly and finally persuades her to come to the prosecutor's office for a meeting. Cynthia is a high school dropout, is not very articulate, and has a drug possession conviction that will be revealed to the jury when she testifies. The prosecutor decides that it's not worth taking the case to trial, so she offers a very favorable plea bargain to the defendant and he is placed on probation.

The second case involves a white woman named Amanda who was also a victim of burglary. Amanda's townhouse was burglarized, and her television set, computer and jewelry were stolen. Amanda shows up for the meeting with the prosecutor. She is educated, articulate and poised, and the prosecutor believes that she would do well on the witness stand. The prosecutor decides to take the case to trial. The defendant is convicted of all charges.

The prosecutor's decisions in these cases produced a racial disparity – similarly situated victims were treated differently. However, the decisions were not necessarily the result of racial bias. According to the ABA Standards for the Prosecution Function, the victim's interest in prosecution is one of the factors that prosecutors should take into account in deciding whether to proceed with a prosecution.[30] The prosecutor may very well have viewed Cynthia's failure to appear for meetings as demonstrating a lack of interest in prosecution. Another factor that prosecutors are urged to consider is "the probability of obtaining a conviction."[31] The prosecutor might reasonably believe that Cynthia's drug conviction and presentation on the witness stand may have hurt her chances of getting a conviction. Consideration of both of these factors would encourage the prosecutor to take the other case to trial. Amanda was a reliable, articulate witness, increasing the likelihood of a conviction in that case.

Even though the white victim appears to have received favorable treatment, the prosecutor's decisions do not necessarily reflect racial bias. The prosecutor may have been biased towards the white victim, but maybe she wasn't. The racial disparity may have been the result of the prosecutor's consideration of legitimate factors, again demonstrating that the application of race-neutral factors may produce racial disparities.

At any rate, victims of crime do not have standing to legally challenge the charging decisions of prosecutors. Some states have laws that require

---

[30] American Bar Association Criminal Justice Standards Committee, *ABA Standards for Criminal Justice: Prosecution Function and Defense Function* 54 (3rd ed. 1993). ("Where practical, the prosecutor should seek to insure that victims of serious crimes or their representatives are given an opportunity to consult with and to provide information to the prosecutor prior to the decision whether or not to prosecute, to pursue a disposition by plea, or to dismiss the charges.")

[31] American Bar Association Criminal Justice Standards Committee, *ABA Standards for Criminal Justice: Prosecutorial Investigations* 14–15 (3rd ed. 2014).

prosecutors to consult with victims and notify them of plea negotiations,[32] but victims have no remedy if prosecutors fail to follow the laws.[33] Even if the laws are followed, they only require prosecutors to confer with victims; the ultimate decision is left to the prosecutor.

If a prosecutor charges African Americans with crimes while declining to charge similarly-situated[34] whites, she may be engaging in race-based selective prosecution. Selective prosecution violates the Constitution,[35] but it is difficult to prove. The Supreme Court has consistently held that a defendant claiming race-based selective prosecution must show that the prosecutor intentionally discriminated against him.[36] However, racial disparity is not necessarily the result of intentional discrimination. To even get discovery in order to prove selective prosecution, the defendant must show that "similarly situated individuals of a different race [could have been prosecuted, but] were not"[37] – a difficult showing to make.

Prosecutors rarely intentionally discriminate against defendants based on race. If race does play a role, it is most likely implicit bias – subconscious views about others based on all kinds of characteristics, including race, ethnicity, gender and physical appearance.[38] These views are developed over a lifetime as a result of exposure to stereotypes that are prevalent in the media and in society in general. Implicit bias is difficult to detect, but even if it is discovered, there is no legal remedy for discrimination caused by implicit bias.

There have been a number of studies that have documented racial disparities in prosecutorial charging and plea bargaining decisions.[39] The Vera Institute's Prosecution and Racial Justice Program,[40] discussed in Part V,

---

[32] See Peggy M. Tobolowsky, *Victim Participation in the Criminal Justice Process: Fifteen Years after the President's Task Force on Victims of Crime*, 25 N. ENG. J. ON CRIM. AND CIV. CONFINEMENT (1999).

[33] See Davis, *supra* note 1, at 65 (citing H.R. 3396, 105th Cong. (1988)).

[34] Similarly-situated defendants are alleged to have committed the same or similar offenses, have the same criminal record, and have other relevant similar characteristics.

[35] See *Oyler v. Boles*, 368 U.S. 448, 456 (1962); see also *Yick Wo v. Hopkins*, 118 U.S. 356, 374 (1886).

[36] See *United States v. Armstrong*, 517 U.S. 456, 465 (1996); see also *McCleskey v. Kemp*, 481 U.S. 279, 297–98 (1987).

[37] *Armstrong*, 517 U.S. at 465.

[38] *Understanding Implicit Bias*, KIRWAN INST. FOR THE STUDY OF RACE AND ETHNICITY, www .kirwaninstitute.osu.edu/research/understanding-implicit-bias/ (last visited Dec. 23, 2015).

[39] See David C. Baldus, Charles Pulaski & George Woodworth, *Comparative Review of Death Sentences: An Empirical Study of the Georgia Experience*, 74 J. CRIM L. & CRIMINOLOGY 661 (1983); William J. Bowers, *The Pervasiveness of Arbitrariness and Discrimination under Post-Furman Capital Statutes*, 74 J. CRIM. L. & CRIMINOLOGY 1067 (1983).

[40] *Prosecution and Racial Justice Program*, VERA INST. OF JUST., www.vera.org/centers/prosecution-and-racial-justice-program (last visited Dec. 23, 2015).

206 Angela J. DavisAngela J. Davis

conducted studies in three prosecutors' offices and discovered racial bias in the charging decision in all of the offices.[41] These studies were conducted with the cooperation of the chief prosecutors in these offices, and they all voluntarily made changes in their charging practices to correct the disparities. There are no laws which require prosecutors to participate in such studies, and very few of them have done so.[42]

III PROSECUTORS AND THE ELECTORAL PROCESS

The American democracy functions through the three branches of government – the legislature, the judiciary, and the executive. Each branch serves a different function, and a system of checks and balances serves to ensure that no one branch exercises unlimited power.[43] The prosecution function falls within the executive branch of government, so in theory, the legislative and judicial branches should serve as a check on the power of the American prosecutor. In practice, neither has effectively done so. Although the Supreme Court has certainly required prosecutors to perform their functions in accordance with the Constitution,[44] it also has protected the power and discretion of prosecutors.[45] Neither the United States Congress nor state legislatures have restricted prosecutorial power. On the contrary, they have expanded that power through the passage of mandatory minimum sentencing laws that have served to amplify the significance of prosecutorial discretion in the criminal process.

Accountability is a core tenet of democracy. We demand accountability from those to whom we grant power. As the most powerful officials in our criminal justice system, prosecutors should certainly be accountable to the people they serve. However, prosecutors should also act independently as they perform their most important functions – the charging and plea bargaining

---

[41] *Prosecutor's Guide for Advancing Racial Equity*, VERA INST. OF JUST., www.vera.org/sites/default/files/resources/downloads/prosecutors-advancing-racial-equity.pdf (last visited Dec. 23, 2015).

[42] *See id.* The Vera Institute's Prosecution and Racial Justice Program no longer exists, but the program published a guide to assist prosecutors who wish to root out and correct racial bias in their offices.

[43] "[T]he colonists transmuted the British system of mixed government based on social classes to a government in which three branches, the legislative, executive, and judicial, would check each other, regardless of the social class from which the officials were drawn." Abner S. Greene, *Checks and Balances in an Era of Presidential Lawmaking*, 61 U. CHI. L. REV. 123, 139–40 (1994) (discussing the framers' overwhelming concern with either branch of government attaining power without sufficient checks).

[44] *See, e.g., Batson v. Kentucky*, 476 U.S. 79, 91 (1986); *Berger v. United States*, 295 U.S. 78, 88 (1935).

[45] *See Armstrong*, 517 U.S. at 464–65.

decisions. Prosecutors are professional criminal justice officials who must perform their duties in accordance with the law in a manner that is both fair and consistent with public safety. A prosecutor's constituents might demand that a particular individual be prosecuted and punished with the maximum penalty, but prosecutors should not bow to the whims of the majority in the name of accountability if their independent professional judgment demands a different outcome. Thus, there is an inherent conflict between accountability and independence. Prosecutors must perform their duties independently while also being accountable to the people they serve.

American prosecutors are held accountable through the electoral system. On the state and local level, where most crimes are prosecuted, most prosecutors are selected through public elections. This model emerged during the rise of Jacksonian democracy in the 1820s and was the country's first effort to hold prosecutors accountable to the people they serve.[46] By 1912, almost every state chose its prosecutors through public elections.[47] Currently, only Delaware, New Jersey, Rhode Island, Connecticut and the District of Columbia choose their chief prosecutors through an appointment process.[48]

Most states elect a state-wide prosecutor called the Attorney General. The Attorneys General in the forty-three states and the District of Columbia that hold elections for this position primarily focus on enforcing consumer protection and antitrust laws, housing regulations, and related matters.[49] They also serve as the chief legal advisors for state agencies and the legislature. State Attorneys General are rarely involved with the prosecution of ordinary street crimes.

The state prosecutors who handle criminal matters are called District Attorneys or State's Attorneys and most are elected on the county level. They are the chief prosecutors who determine the charging, plea bargaining and other policies of their offices. They also hire the prosecutors in their offices. These Assistant State's Attorneys or Assistant District Attorneys handle the criminal cases in their jurisdiction under the supervision of the State's Attorney or District Attorney.

In theory, the electoral process holds prosecutors accountable. If the electorate is not satisfied with how the State's Attorney does her job, it has the power to vote her out of office. In practice, elections are not very effective mechanisms of

---

[46] Davis, *supra* note 1, at 10 (citing JOAN E. JACOBY, THE AMERICAN PROSECUTOR: A SEARCH OF IDENTITY 8 (1980)).

[47] *Id.*

[48] Michael J. Ellis, *The Origins of the Elected Prosecutor*, 121 YALE L.J. 1528, 1530 (2012).

[49] *See About NAAG*, NAT'L ASS'N OF ATT'YS GEN., www.naag.org/naag/about_naag.php (last visited Dec. 23, 2015).

accountability for prosecutors. A prosecutor's constituents cannot hold her accountable if they don't know what she does. Since the prosecutor's most important duties – the charging and plea bargaining decisions – are performed behind closed doors, her constituents have no way of knowing whether she is performing these duties fairly and therefore no way of holding her accountable. When prosecutors run for office, they don't talk about their charging and plea bargaining policies. Historically, most have run on "tough on crime" platforms – pledging to keep their communities safe by prosecuting criminals and assuring that they are incarcerated.[50] Some discuss their own character traits, trial skills or outcomes in particular cases.[51] In recent years, some prosecutors have moved beyond the "tough on crime" rhetoric, pledging to implement community prosecution and diversion programs rather than focusing solely on prosecution and incarceration.[52] However, none explain their charging and plea bargaining policies, and it is doubtful if the public understands how these functions work or their importance.[53]

The selection process for federal prosecutors makes them even less accountable than state and local prosecutors. The President appoints the Attorney General of the United States and the United States Attorneys for each of the ninety-four federal judicial districts.[54] Each U.S. Attorney hires the Assistant United States Attorneys (AUSAs) for her office. All U.S. Attorneys serve at the pleasure of the President and newly elected Presidents often remove U.S. Attorneys from the previous administration.[55] Each appointment must be confirmed by a simple majority vote of the United States Senate.[56]

Since federal prosecutors are not elected officials, it is even more difficult for the public to hold them accountable. Members of the public may certainly

---

[50] Sanford C. Gordon & Gregory A. Huber, *Citizen Oversight and the Electoral Incentives of Criminal Prosecutions*, 46 AM. J. POL. SCI. 334, 335 (2002). *But see* Ronald F. Wright, *How Prosecutor Elections Fail Us*, 6 OHIO ST. J. CRIM. L. 581, 603–04 (2009) (research shows very little rhetoric about conviction rates).

[51] *See* Wright, *supra* note 43, at 600–03.

[52] *See, e.g., Brooklyn DA Ken Thompson*, THE BROOKLYN DIST. ATTORNEY'S OFFICE, www.br ooklynda.org/brooklyn-da-ken-thompson/ (last visited Dec. 23, 2015); Press Release, State of California Dep't of Just. Office of the Att'y Gen., Attorney General Kamala D. Harris Joins Manhattan District Attorney's Office and John Jay College of Criminal Justice to Launch New Institute for Innovation in Prosecution (Oct. 16, 2015).

[53] *Cf.* Wright, *supra* note 43 at 606–07. Campaign debate would better meet the needs of the public if the press would look into measures of quality in the work of prosecutor offices. The measures would focus on the dominant reality of plea negotiations instead of "conviction rates."

[54] *U.S. Attorneys' Manual*, THE U.S. DEP'T OF JUST., www.justice.gov/usam/usam-3-2000-uni ted-states-attorneys-ausas-special-assistants-and-agac (last visited Dec. 23, 2015).

[55] *See* 28 U.S.C. § 541(c) (2015).   [56] *See id.* at § 541(a).

contact their senators to express their views about whether a particular nominee should be confirmed, but as with elected prosecutors, they will rarely have information about how the nominee will perform his most important functions as U.S. Attorney. Even if the nominee previously served as either a state or federal prosecutor, members of the public will not have access to the internal policies of the nominee's prior office. After a U.S. Attorney has been appointed, any member of the public may contact her to express his views about how she is performing her duties, but U. S. Attorneys cannot be voted out of office. Only the President of the United States has the power to remove a U.S. Attorney.

Although the electoral process for state and local prosecutors has its flaws, it presents the best opportunity for holding prosecutors accountable. Although decisions of federal prosecutors carry tremendous ramifications due to the harsh mandatory minimum sentencing laws, the vast majority of criminal cases are prosecuted in state courts.[57] Thus, focusing on holding state and local prosecutors accountable through the electoral process might result in improvements in the overall administration of justice, including a more racially just criminal justice system.

One of the inherent challenges in relying on the prosecutorial elections is that State's Attorneys frequently run unopposed.[58] Some serve for decades without being challenged, and when they are challenged, they have all of the advantages of incumbency. Unless longstanding district attorneys are marred by a scandals or allegations of misconduct,[59] they are difficult to unseat.[60]

The democratic process cannot hold prosecutors accountable unless members of the public become more involved in prosecutorial elections. The public should be more informed about the duties and responsibilities of prosecutors so that they are equipped with the information to ask questions and demand responses. The lack of transparency in the prosecution function keeps the public largely in the dark and totally dependent on the prosecutor's

---

[57] Giovanna Shay & Christopher Lasch, *Initiating a New Constitutional Dialogue: The Increased Importance under AEDPA of Seeking Certiorari from Judgments of State Courts*, 50 WM. & MARY L. REV. 211, 243 (2008). ("Because the vast majority of criminal cases in the U.S. are prosecuted in state courts, certain kinds of important federal constitutional issues may arise more frequently-or nearly exclusively-in state court criminal proceedings.")

[58] *See* Wright, *supra* note 43, at 593 (noting that in general election campaigns, prosecutor incumbents ran unopposed in 85% of the races they entered).

[59] *See, e.g.*, Rich Calder & Josh Saul, *Hynes Ousted as Brooklyn DA*, N.Y. POST, Sept. 11, 2013, www.nypost.com/2013/09/11/hynes-ousted-as-brooklyn-da/; *see also* Fran Spielman, *Alvarez Accused of Deliberately Filing Wrong Charge against Police Detective*, CHICAGO SUN TIMES (Apr. 22, 2015), www.chicago.suntimes.com/politics/alvarez-accused-of-deliberately-filing-wrong-charge-against-police-detective/.

[60] *See* Wright, *supra* note 43, at 592–94.

willingness to share information. Public information campaigns that serve to educate the public about the prosecution function would be a helpful first step towards promoting prosecutorial accountability.[61]

IV THE ROLE OF THE PROSECUTOR IN ACHIEVING RACIAL JUSTICE

Prosecutors have played a significant role in causing and enhancing the racial disparities in the criminal justice system. However, they have the power and discretion to take steps to eliminate, or at least reduce, these disparities. The election of prosecutors who prioritize racial fairness and pledge to take steps to achieve it is essential to eliminating racial disparities in the criminal justice system.

Although the general public rarely pays attention to prosecutorial elections, that phenomenon may change as a result of the response to a number of high-profile police killings of unarmed black men in recent years. Although police killings of black men are not recent phenomena,[62] these killings have received much attention during the past several years and have renewed the ongoing national discussion about racial justice in the American criminal justice system. The failure of prosecutors to charge the police officers involved in a number of these killings has sparked widespread protests and has caused members of the public to pay closer attention to prosecutors and the important role they play in determining whether people of color are treated fairly in the criminal justice system.

One of the first killings of an unarmed black male that focused attention on the prosecutor was the February 26, 2012, killing of Trayvon Martin – a seventeen-year-old who was killed while walking to his father's home in Sanford, Florida, after going to a convenience store to buy snacks. The person who shot and killed him – George Zimmerman – was not a police officer, but was patrolling the neighborhood in his role as a member of a neighborhood watch group. Zimmerman was taken into custody, questioned and released after he told police officers he had acted in self-defense when he killed the unarmed teen.[63] Zimmerman's release and the failure of the local prosecutor to charge him with

---

[61]   See Angela J. Davis, *The American Prosecutor: Independence, Power, and the Threat of Tyranny*, 86 IOWA L. REV. 393, 462 (2001).

[62]   See Rich Juzwiak & Aleksander Chan, *Unarmed People of Color Killed by Police, 1999–2014*, GAWKER (Dec. 8, 2014), www.gawker.com/unarmed-people-of-color-killed-by-police-1999-20 14-1666672349 (detailing numerous accounts where men and women of color were killed by police custody).

[63]   See generally Fla. Stat. Ann. § 776.0013 (West 2014); see also *"Stand Your Ground" Policy Summary*, Law Ctr. to Prevent Gun Violence (July 18, 2013), www.smartgunlaws.org/stand-your-ground-policy-summary/ (explaining that Zimmerman invoked the Florida "stand your

homicide sparked protests and marches across the country, online petitions and a renewed national conversation about racial profiling. The governor ultimately appointed a special prosecutor who charged Zimmerman with second-degree murder six weeks after Martin's death. Zimmerman went to trial and was acquitted on July 13, 2013. The prosecutor who tried the case was criticized and even accused of intentionally losing the case.[64]

Many unarmed people of color were killed by police officers in the years after Trayvon Martin's death.[65] Although some of the police officers were prosecuted,[66] most were not,[67] even when the killings were videotaped. Eric Garner's death was videotaped by a bystander who filmed Staten Island police officers choking Garner to death as he repeatedly gasped, "I can't breathe."[68] Twelve-year-old Tamir Rice was gunned down by a police officer in Cleveland, Ohio.[69] His killing also was videotaped.

ground" law, which allows a person to use deadly force in a public place in self-defense, even if the force could have been avoided by retreating the area).

[64] *E.g.*, David G. Savage & Michael Muskal, *Zimmerman Verdict: Legal Experts Say Prosecutors Overreached*, L.A. TIMES (July 14, 2013), www.articles.latimes.com/2013/jul/14/nation/la-na-z immerman-legal-20130715; *see also* Robert Kolker, *5 Ways the Prosecution Messed up the Zimmerman Case*, NEW YORK (July 15, 2013), www.nymag.com/daily/intelligencer/2013/07/5-ways-the-prosecution-blew-the-zimmerman-case.html.

[65] *See* Juzwiak & Chan, *supra* note 55; *see also* Josh Sanburn, *From Trayvon Martin to Walter Scott: Cases in the Spotlight*, TIME (Apr. 10, 2015), www.time.com/3815606/police-violence-timeline/.

[66] *See generally* Taylor Kate Brown, *The Case Where US Police Have Faced Killing Charges*, BBC (Apr. 8, 2015), www.bbc.com/news/world-us-canada-30339943; *see also* Jon Swaine, *Former Police Officer Who Shot Walter Scott Indicted for Murder*, GUARDIAN (June 8, 2015), www.theguardian.com/us-news/2015/jun/08/walter-scott-shooting-michael-slager-charged-m urder (stating that if convicted, Slager could get up to thirty years to life in prison without the possibility of parole); *see also* Ben Feuerherd & Bob Fredericks, *Cops Arrested for Murder, Manslaughter in Freddie Gray's Death*, NEW YORK POST (May 1, 2015), www.nypost.com/20 15/05/01/cops-to-be-charged-in-freddie-gray-homicide/ (charging six Baltimore cops with murder and five others for manslaughter and assault).

[67] *See* Jake Halpern, *The Cop*, NEW YORKER (Aug. 20, 2015), www.newyorker.com/magazine/2015/08/10/the-cop (showing how Wilson was exonerated twice of criminal wrongdoing, once by the grand jury and once by the Department of Justice); *see also* AJ Vicens, *No Indictments for New Jersey Officers Who Shot Black Man with Hands Up*, MOTHER JONES (Aug. 20, 2015), www.motherjones.com/politics/2015/08/officer-who-killed-jerame-reid-not-indicted; Andrew Siff et al., *Grand Jury Declines to Indict NYPD Officer in Eric Garner Chokehold Death*, NBC NEW YORK (Dec. 3, 2014), www.nbcnewyork.com/news/local/Grand-Jury-Decision-Er ic-Garner-Staten-Island-Chokehold-Death-NYPD-284595921.html.

[68] *See generally 'I Can't Breathe': Eric Garner Put in Chokehold by NYPD Officer-Video*, GUARDIAN (Dec. 4, 2014), www.theguardian.com/us-news/video/2014/dec/04/i-cant-breathe-e ric-garner-chokehold-death-video.

[69] *See generally Tamir Rice: Police Release Video of 12-Year-Old's Fatal Shooting-Video*, GUARDIAN (Nov. 26, 2014), www.theguardian.com/us-news/video/2014/nov/26/cleveland-vide o-tamir-rice-shooting-police.

Two of the cases that focused the most attention on the actions of the prosecutor were the police killings of Michael Brown in Ferguson, Missouri, and Freddie Gray in Baltimore, Maryland. The prosecutors in Ferguson and Baltimore handled these cases very differently. An examination and comparison of these two prosecutors and the decisions they made in these cases sheds light on the importance of prosecutorial elections in the pursuit of racial fairness in the criminal justice system.

A Robert McCulloch and the Michael Brown Case

Michael Brown was an eighteen-year-old African American teenager who was killed by police officer Darren Wilson on August 9, 2014. The circumstances of his death were disputed, but witnesses claimed that the conflict that led to Brown's death started when Officer Wilson saw Michael Brown and another young man walking in the middle of the street. Wilson believed that Brown fit the description of a suspect in a convenience store theft. He confronted Brown and there was an altercation between the two of them in or near Wilson's vehicle that resulted in Wilson firing his gun twice. One bullet grazed Brown's hand. Brown then ran and Wilson pursued him on foot. At one point, Brown stopped and turned around. Some witnesses say that Brown started to move towards Wilson just before Wilson fired his gun a total of ten times. Six of the bullets hit Brown, killing him. Initial accounts of the shooting reported that Brown's hands were up in a surrender position at the time he was shot. Some witnesses who later testified in the grand jury claimed that his hands were down. Everyone, including Wilson, reported that Brown was unarmed.

There were massive protests in Ferguson for many weeks following Michael Brown's death. Although most of the protestors were peaceful, some were not. Some protestors threw bottles at the police, and the police responded with extreme force in armored cars, using rubber bullets, teargas, and flash grenades against the protestors, including the peaceful ones. After widespread condemnation of the police tactics, the governor announced that the Missouri Highway State Patrol would take over the policing function during the protests. Although the protests were more peaceful for a while, the unrest continued with some looting and criminal behavior by a few protestors.

There were marches and protests across the country after Michael Brown's death.[70] The phrase "Black Lives Matter," which trended on social media after Trayvon Martin was killed, was revived and evolved into a social justice

[70] *See The 2014 Ferguson Protests over the Michael Brown Shooting, Explained*, Vox, www.vox .com/cards/mike-brown-protests-ferguson-missour (last visited Dec. 22, 2015); *see also* Ray

movement and organization.[71] The phrase re-emerged on social media and was the most common sign in marches and protests nationwide. Many protestors held their hand in the air as they believed Michael Brown had done and chanted "Hands Up! Don't Shoot!"

The protestors also demanded that Officer Darren Wilson be charged with homicide. Wilson claimed that he was justified in using deadly force, and he was not arrested. However, prosecutors may charge an individual in the absence of an arrest, and there was much pressure for the prosecutor to proceed against Wilson.

The chief prosecutor in Ferguson was Robert McCulloch – a white elected prosecutor who had been in office since 1991. There were concerns about McCulloch's ability to conduct a fair investigation long before the grand jury reached its decision. Whenever prosecutors are tasked with investigating criminal allegations against police officers, there is a possibility of a conflict of interest, especially if the prosecutor is investigating a police officer in his jurisdiction. Police officers work closely with prosecutors, investigating their cases and testifying as witnesses. Prosecutors cannot bring cases without the work and cooperation of police officers. It certainly would appear that prosecutors might have a bias towards police officers.

The evidence of bias towards police officers seemed particularly strong in McCulloch's case. His father, brother, nephew and cousin were all police officers with the St. Louis Police Department. When McCulloch was a child, his father was killed in the line of duty. He wanted to become a police officer himself, but was not able to do so because he lost a leg to cancer when he was a teenager. So McCulloch decided to become a prosecutor, serving as an Assistant Prosecuting Attorney from 1978 to 1985. McCulloch left the office for private practice until 1991 when he decided to run for the Prosecuting Attorney for St. Louis County. He was elected, and has been consistently re-elected, now serving for over two decades.

There was broad support for the appointment of a special prosecutor – a prosecutor from another jurisdiction with no ties to Ferguson – before McCulloch began the grand jury process. Missouri law permits the governor to appoint a special prosecutor in appropriate cases,[72] but Governor Jay Nixon

Sanchez, *Michael Brown Shooting, Protests Highlight Racial Divide*, CNN (Aug. 15, 2015), www.cnn.com/2014/08/14/justice/ferguson-missouri-police-community/.

[71] Shannon Luibrand, *How a Death in Ferguson Sparked a Movement in America*, CBS NEWS (Aug. 7, 2015), www.cbsnews.com/news/how-the-black-lives-matter-movement-changed-america-one-year-later/.

[72] *See Special Prosecutors: Investigations and Prosecutions of Police Use of Deadly Force*, LEGAL SIDEBAR (Dec. 12, 2014), www.fas.org/sgp/crs/misc/specpro.pdf; *see also* William Freivogel, *What's a Grand Jury? How Will It Work in the Ferguson Case?*, St. Louis Pub. Radio (Aug. 20, 2014), www.news.stlpublicradio.org/post/whats-grand-jury-how-will-it-work-ferguson-case.

refused.[73] Missouri State Senator Jamilah Nasheed submitted a petition with 70,000 signatures asking McCulloch to recuse himself from the case, but McCulloch made it quite clear that he would not step down.[74]

McCulloch decided to present the case to a grand jury, but he used the grand jury process very differently from the way criminal cases are usually handled. Prosecutors usually go to the grand jury to seek an indictment, and they almost always get one. They call witnesses that will testify against the suspect and they rarely call witnesses that might provide exculpatory evidence. However, McCulloch turned the ordinary grand jury process on its head. Not only did McCulloch and two of the Assistant Prosecuting Attorneys from his office call numerous witnesses who supported Wilson's claim that he used reasonable, lawful force, but they permitted Darren Wilson to testify in the grand jury. Even though Wilson was the target of the grand jury investigation, the prosecutors presented Wilson's testimony as if he was a witness for the state. They never challenged or questioned any of his assertions.[75] This treatment was in stark contrast to how witnesses who testified against Wilson were treated. They were questioned and challenged constantly. One witness was repeatedly asked whether Brown ran towards the officer. When the witness repeatedly stated that he did not, the prosecutor asked the witness about his criminal record and suggested that the grand jurors take his record into account in determining his credibility.[76]

The prosecutors also provided inaccurate and misleading information to the grand jury about the circumstances under which police officers are permitted to use deadly force. One of the prosecutors informed the grand jurors that a police officer may use deadly force if he reasonably believes that the person he is attempting to arrest has committed or attempted to commit a felony.[77] This was a misstatement of the law and in direct conflict with the Supreme Court's holding in *Tennessee v. Garner*,[78] which only permits police

---

[73] *See* Alex Stuckey, *Nixon: No Special Prosecutor in Darren Wilson Case*, St. Louis Today (Nov. 26, 2014), www.stltoday.com/news/local/crime-and-courts/nixon-no-special-prosecutor-in-darren-wilson-case/article_e07403a6-0b8d-539e-b236-16c487a55685.html.

[74] Andrew Romano, *Why Ferguson Is So Mad at Prosecutor Bob McCulloch*, Yahoo News (Nov. 25, 2014), www.news.yahoo.com/how-prosecutor-bob-mcculloch-s-controversial-past-is-making-matters-worse-in-ferguson-212622087.html.

[75] Letter from Sherrilyn A. Ifill, Dir.-Counsel, NAACP Legal Defense and Educational Fund, to Judge Maura McShane, Presiding Judge, 21st Judicial Circuit Missouri (Jan. 5, 2015) (on file with the NAACP Legal Defense and Educational).

[76] *Id.*

[77] *Id.* (explaining that prosecutor Kathi Alizadeh gave inaccurate and confusing legal instructions to the grand jurors when distributing copies of the Missouri Statute § 563.046, which does not comply with federal law).

[78] 471 U.S. 1 (1985).

officers to use deadly force to stop a fleeing felon if he has "probable cause to believe that the suspect poses a significant threat of death or serious physical injury to the officer or others."[79] The prosecutor provided the incorrect information to the grand jurors on the day Wilson testified and only attempted to correct her mistake weeks later. It is clear from the transcript that the prosecutor's explanation of the law left the grand jurors confused. At least one grand juror asked several questions indicating confusion, and the prosecutor never presented an accurate explanation of the law, at one point stating, "We don't want to get into a law class."[80]

Not surprisingly, the grand jury did not indict Officer Wilson. McCulloch didn't ask the grand jury to indict Wilson and presented the evidence in a way that assured he would not be indicted. On November 24, 2014, McCulloch held a press conference announcing the grand jury's decision and took the unusual step of releasing the entire transcript of the grand jury proceedings. The protests and riots continued, along with calls for a federal investigation. Then-Attorney General Eric Holder ordered an investigation. Although there was not sufficient evidence to bring federal civil rights charges against Wilson,[81] the Justice Department's investigation of the Ferguson Police Department revealed a pattern or practice of police officers violating the constitutional rights of the residents of Ferguson.[82] Specifically, the report issued by the Department found that the Ferguson Police Department had a pattern or practice of stopping individuals without reasonable suspicion, arresting them without probable cause, and using excessive force. The report also found a pattern or practice of racial bias in the police department and the municipal court.[83]

B Marilyn Mosby and the Freddie Gray Case

On April 12, 2015, four police officers on bicycles decided to pursue Freddie Gray and another young man on the streets of Baltimore. Gray and his

[79] *Id.* at 11.

[80] *See* William Freivogel, *Grand Jury Wrangled with Confusing Instructions*, St. Louis Public Radio (Nov. 26, 2014), www.news.stlpublicradio.org/post/grand-jury-wrangled-confusing-instructions.

[81] 18 U.S.C. § 242 (2009) (deadly force by law enforcement officers); *see also* Ryan J. Reilly et al., *Darren Wilson Will Not Face Civil Rights Charges in Michael Brown's Death*, HUFFINGTON POST (Mar. 3, 2015), www.huffingtonpost.com/2015/03/04/darren-wilson-not-charged_n_6800404.html.

[82] *See generally Justice Department Announces Findings of Two Civil Rights Investigations in Ferguson, Missouri*, DOJ (Mar. 4, 2015), www.justice.gov/opa/pr/justice-department-announces-findings-two-civil-rights-investigations-ferguson-missouri.

[83] *Id.*

companion ran when they saw the police, but they were quickly subdued. Gray was arrested for carrying a knife. A bystander videotaped Gray's arrest. In the videotape, Gray appears to be crying out in pain and struggling to stand up. Some witnesses claimed that the officers used excessive force while arresting him – a claim the officers denied.[84]

At about 8:42 a.m., the officers called for a van to transport Gray to the police station. Before the van arrived, Gray requested an inhaler but his request was denied. When the van arrived, Gray was placed in the back of the van without a seatbelt. At one point, the driver of the van stopped and several officers placed Gray in leg irons before returning him to the back of the van. The van stopped a second time to pick up another prisoner and a third time at a grocery store before arriving at the police station at 9:24 a.m. At that point, paramedics began treating Gray, and at 9:45 he was taken to the University of Maryland Shock Trauma Center in a coma. He had three fractured vertebrae, injuries to his voice box, and a severed spine.[85] Gray died on April 19th.

On April 24th, then-Police Commissioner Anthony Batts admitted that the police officers who transported Gray to the police station failed to get medical attention for Gray in a timely fashion. He also admitted that the officers failed to strap him into the van with a seatbelt, in violation of police department policy.[86] Gray's injuries occurred as a result of him being thrown around in the back of the police van.

The public reaction to Gray's death was very similar to the response to Michael Brown's death. The day before Gray died, there was a protest outside the Baltimore Police Department, and after he died, there were numerous protests in Baltimore – some peaceful and some violent. Some protesters set fires and looted stores. Numerous people, including police officers, were injured. Governor Larry Hogan declared a state of emergency and activated the Maryland National Guard. Many protesters were arrested. On April 28th, Mayor Stephanie Rawlings-Blake announced a curfew from 10 p.m. to 5 a.m. that remained in effect until May 3rd. As with Michael Brown's death, there were

---

[84] See Oliver Laughland, 'Freddie Gray Was Me': Frustration with Police Simmers after Death in Baltimore, GUARDIAN (Apr. 25, 2015), www.theguardian.com/us-news/2015/apr/25/freddie-gra y-death-triggers-frustration-baltimore-police.

[85] See generally Timeline: Freddie Gray's Arrest, Death and the Aftermath, BALTIMORE SUN, data. baltimoresun.com/news/freddie-gray/ (last visited Dec. 22, 2015).

[86] See Liz Fields, Baltimore Police Confirm Freddie Gray Was Not in Seat Belt During Arrest, VICE NEWS (Apr. 24, 2015), www.news.vice.com/article/baltimore-police-confirm-freddie-gr ay-was-not-in-seat-belt-during-arrest.

massive protests nationwide – in New York, Washington, D.C., Philadelphia, Seattle and many other cities.[87]

Marilyn Mosby was the State's Attorney for Baltimore City. Mosby, who is African American, started her prosecutorial career as an Assistant State's Attorney in Baltimore in 2005, and left the office in 2012 to work for an insurance company. In 2013, Mosby announced that she would run for State's Attorney, and in 2014, she defeated her predecessor, Gregg Bernstein. She was sworn into office in January 2015 at the age of thirty-four, becoming the nation's youngest chief prosecutor of a major city. Like McCulloch, Mosby has longstanding ties to the law enforcement community. Both of her parents were police officers in Boston, as were her grandfather and uncle.

Mosby's response to Freddie Gray's death stands in stark contrast to Bob McCulloch's actions after Michael Brown was killed. On May 1st, less than two weeks after Gray's death, Mosby held a press conference during which she announced charges against all six police officers involved in Gray's arrest and transport to the police station. Caesar Goodson, Jr., the officer who drove the police van, was charged with second-degree depraved-heart murder – the most serious of all of the charges. Goodson, Lieutenant Brian Rice, Sergeant Alicia White, and Officer William Porter were charged with involuntary manslaughter. Rice and Officers Edward Nero and Garrett Miller were charged with false imprisonment for their arrest of Freddie Gray. All six officers were charged with second-degree assault and misconduct in office.[88]

Mosby's press conference contrasted with McCulloch's, not only because of the message she delivered, but in the way it was delivered. She stated that her office had begun its own independent investigation of Freddie Gray's death the day after he died, and she took the extraordinary step of providing a detailed account of the evidence in support of the charges. According to Mosby, the officers did not have probable cause to arrest Gray because it was not against the law to carry the knife that was in his possession. She then described numerous occasions in which the officers ignored Gray's pleas for medical attention. Mosby also noted that the officers placed Gray in the back of the van in a manner that caused his injuries, which were exacerbated by their failure to secure him with a seatbelt.

Mosby also made other statements during the press conference that separated her office from the police department. Although she referenced her

---

[87] See *Baltimore Death Sparks Protests in New York, Boston*, LEX 18 (Apr. 30, 2015), www.lex18 .com/story/28938879/baltimore-death-sparks-protests-in-new-york-boston.

[88] See David A. Graham, *The 'Depraved-heart Murder' of Freddie Gray*, ATLANTIC (May 1, 2015), www.theatlantic.com/national/archive/2015/05/the-depraved-heart-murder-of-freddie-gray/39 2132/.

family ties to law enforcement and praised the police officers who had been working to keep the city safe during the protests, Mosby repeatedly stressed her independence from the Baltimore Police Department. At one point, she paraphrased the familiar protest chant "No Justice. No Peace," stating "To the people of Baltimore and the demonstrators across America, I heard your call for no justice, no peace . . . .Your peace is sincerely needed as I work to deliver justice on behalf of this young man."[89] After Mosby's announcement, instead of protests, hundreds celebrated in the streets, waving flags and carrying signs thanking Mosby. All six officers were processed at the Central Booking and Intake Center and released after posting bail.

There were calls for the appointment of a special prosecutor, but those requests came from the Baltimore police union. Union officials claimed that Mosby had a conflict of interest because of a personal and professional relationship with the attorney for the Gray family. They also claimed that her decisions would be influenced by how they might affect the political career of her husband, Baltimore City Councilman Nick Mosby.[90] Like McCulloch, Mosby refused to recuse herself from the case, citing her responsibility to her constituents.

Mosby also presented the evidence to a grand jury and indictments were returned against all six officers on May 21st. The charges largely mirrored those announced by Mosby at her May 1st press conference. The false imprisonment charges were removed, but reckless endangerment charges were added against all six officers. Unlike McCulloch, Mosby did not release the transcript of the grand jury proceedings, so there is no way to know how the evidence was presented.[91]

The cases were assigned to Judge Barry Williams, who decided that the defendants would have separate trials. None of the police officers were convicted. Goodson, Nero and Rice chose to have bench trials, and Judge Williams acquitted all three of them. Mosby dropped the charges against Porter, Miller and White, acknowledging the likelihood that they also would be acquitted by Judge Williams.[92]

---

[89] *Id.*

[90] Letter from the Gene Ryan, President Fraternal Order of Police, Baltimore City Lodge No. 3, to Marilyn Mosby, State Attorney (on file with author).

[91] *See* Jess Bidgood & Sheryl Gay Stolberg, *Acquittal in Freddie Gray Case Casts Doubts about Future Trials*, New York Times (June 23, 2016), www.nytimes.com/2016/06/24/us/verdict-fre ddie-gray-caesar-goodson-baltimore.html.

[92] *See* Kevin Rector, *Charges Dropped, Freddie Gray Case Concludes with Zero Convictions against Officers*, Baltimore Sun (July 27, 2016), www.baltimoresun.com/news/maryland/fre ddie-gray/bs-md-ci-miller-pretrial-motions-20160727-story.html; *see also Transcript: State's Attorney Marilyn Mosby on the Dropped Charges*, Baltimore Sun (July 27, 2016), www.balt imoresun.com/news/maryland/freddie-gray/bal-transcript-state-s-attorney-marilyn-mosby-on-t he-dropped-charges-20160727-story.html.

C McCulloch, Mosby and the Electoral Process

Many of the residents of Ferguson, including members of the African American community, believe that McCulloch failed to achieve justice in the Darren Wilson case. And this was not the first time that he failed to charge police officers involved in the shooting of unarmed black men. One of the most controversial was a 2000 case in which police officers shot and killed an alleged drug dealer and his companion while they were in a car. A federal investigation revealed that the officers had lied about the circumstances of the shooting, falsely claiming that the car was moving towards them at the time they shot the driver and passenger.[93] McCulloch lied to the public about witness accounts of the shooting, and spent a substantial amount of time presenting the grand jury with evidence of the victims' arrests in an attempt to smear their character. His entire presentation to the grand jurors steered them away from an indictment. McCulloch even referred to the victims as "bums" at a press conference.[94] There were other police shootings of unarmed citizens in St. Louis County during McCulloch's tenure as prosecutor, and he has never charged any of them with a crime.[95]

The Justice Department's investigation of the Ferguson Police Department revealed a pattern and practice of unlawful behavior by Ferguson police officers. In addition to the racially discriminatory stops and arrests of African Americans, the investigation found a pattern of the excessive use of force against African Americans in violation of the Fourth Amendment.[96] The report documents cases in which officers used extreme force against African Americans, including the use of canines and Tasers. The report refers to the officers' retaliatory and punitive use of excessive force as "criminal."[97]

As the chief prosecutor for St. Louis County, McCulloch has the responsibility to enforce the laws fairly and equitably. Police officers are not immune

---

[93] *See* Alan Pyke, *If You Want to Understand the Ferguson Prosecution, You Should Know about the Jack in the Box Case*, THINK PROGRESS (Jan. 10, 2015), www.thinkprogress.org/justice/2015/01/10/3610288/that-other-time-ferguson-prosecutor-mcculloch-whitewashed-police-killing/; *see also* Pema Levy, *Ferguson Prosecutor Robert P. McCulloch's Long History of Siding with the Police*, NEWSWEEK (Aug. 29, 2014), www.newsweek.com/2014/09/12/ferguson-prosecutor-robert-p-mccullochs-long-history-siding-police-267357.html.

[94] *See* Pyke, *supra* note 87.

[95] *See* Nicole Colson, *The Obstruction-of-Justice System in Ferguson*, SOCIALIST WORKER (Sept. 17, 2014), www.socialistworker.org/2014/09/17/obstruction-of-justice-in-ferguson (finding that in McCulloch's twenty-three years as a prosecutor, there have been at least a dozen fatal shootings by police, but his office had not prosecuted a single shooting in those years).

[96] *See generally Investigation of the Ferguson Police Department*, DOJ, 1–105 (Mar. 4, 2015), www.justice.gov/sites/default/files/opa/press-releases/attachments/2015/03/04/ferguson_police_department_report.pdf.

[97] *Id.* at 105.

from prosecution if they commit criminal offenses. Police officers who use excessive force should be charged with assault. The Justice Department investigation revealed that these officers routinely and disproportionately assaulted African Americans. McCulloch's failure to prosecute them implicates him in the ongoing racial disparities in St. Louis' criminal justice system.

Bob McCulloch is one of the chief prosecutors who has served for decades and frequently ran unopposed. Because St. Louis County is heavily democratic, the primary race is more important than the general election. The Democrat who wins the primary race wins the election. McCulloch was most recently elected in 2014, and that election is instructive on the complexities of prosecutorial elections.

The 2014 primary election was on August 5th, just days before Michael Brown was killed. Even before Michael Brown's death, McCulloch was criticized in the African American community. He had a history of failing to investigate complaints against the police,[98] and in 2014, he threw his support behind a white candidate who ran against the first African American County Executive for St. Louis County.[99] The white candidate won. An African American municipal judge ran against McCulloch in the primary, and he defeated her soundly.[100]

McCulloch did not have a Republican challenger in the November 2014 election, but the number of votes he received is telling. 10,645 voters turned out for the November 4th general election, and almost all of them cast votes for county executive and county assessor. 4,000 of these voters did not vote for McCulloch, even though he ran unopposed. 1,000 voters wrote in a name for Prosecuting Attorney and 3,000 didn't vote for Prosecuting Attorney at all.[101]

African Americans almost always vote for Democratic candidates, but because McCulloch helped to unseat the African American candidate for County Executive in the primary election, many African American Democrats decided to vote for the Republican candidate in the general election, solely because McCulloch supported the Democrat.[102] The Republican candidate for County Executive campaigned in the black community, criticized McCulloch's handling of the Brown investigation and

---

[98]   *See* John Nichols, *An Inconvenient Political Truth: That St. Louis Prosecutor Is a Democrat*, NATION (Nov. 26, 2014), www.thenation.com/article/inconvenient-political-truth-st-louis-prosecutor-democrat/.

[99]   *Id.*

[100] *See* John Gaskin III, *Race in St. Louis: Hands up, Let's Vote*, ST. LOUIS (Oct. 17, 2014), www.stlmag.com/news/race-in-st.-louis-hands-up-lets-vote/.

[101] *See* Nichols, *supra* note 98.

[102] *Id.* (finding that the Republican nominee lost by just one percent of the vote).

pledged to support a proposal to appoint a special prosecutor in all cases involving police shootings.[103] He lost by only one percent of the vote. McCulloch is not up for re-election until 2018. African Americans comprise only about twenty-four percent of the population of St. Louis County.[104]

Marilyn Mosby is serving her first term as the State's Attorney for Baltimore City. She defeated the incumbent Gregg Bernstein, a white man who only served one term. Although many believed Mosby won the election because Baltimore is a majority black city, that analysis may not be accurate. Bernstein defeated an African American woman who had served as the State's Attorney for Baltimore City for sixteen years, demonstrating that Baltimore voters don't necessarily vote along racial lines. In addition, post-election census and precinct data showed that Mosby defeated Bernstein in majority white precincts.[105] Ironically, during the campaign, she criticized the way Bernstein handled the investigation of the death of a black man named Tony West who died while in police custody.[106] Little did she know at the time that she would be front and center on the national stage dealing with the very same issue just three months after being sworn into office.

Although Mosby has received much praise from the African American community for her swift prosecution of the officers involved in Freddie Gray's death, her actions in this one case do not prove that she is committed to racial justice and fairness in Baltimore's criminal justice system. Baltimore's incarceration rate is three times that of the State of Maryland,[107] and African Americans are over 5.6 times more likely to be arrested for marijuana possession than whites, even though marijuana use among the races is similar.[108] African Americans comprise 92 percent of all marijuana possession arrests in Baltimore – one of the highest racial disparities in the country.[109]

---

[103] *Id.*

[104] *See generally Quick Facts United States: St. Louis County, Missouri*, UNITED STATES CENSUS BUREAU, www.quickfacts.census.gov/qfd/states/29/29189.html (last modified Dec. 2, 2015) (citing 23.9% in 2014).

[105] *See* Luke Broadwater & Ian Duncan, *Mosby Cut into Bernstein's Support in White Neighborhoods, Data Suggest*, BALTIMORE SUN (July 12, 2014), www.articles.baltimoresun.com/2014-07-12/news/bs-md-ci-mosby-race-20140712_1_marilyn-mosby-neighborhoods-attorney-gregg-bernstein.

[106] *Id.*

[107] *See The Right Investment?: Corrections Spending in Baltimore City*, Prison Policy Initiative (Feb. 2015), www.prisonpolicy.org/origin/md/report.html.

[108] *See* Bill Quigley, *The "Shocking" Statistics of Racial Disparity in Baltimore*, COMMON DREAMS (Apr. 28, 2015), www.commondreams.org/views/2015/04/28/shocking-statistics-racial-disparity-baltimore.

[109] *Id.*

When Mosby ran for State's Attorney, she did not mention the racial disparities in Baltimore's criminal justice system, much less announce plans to address them. She has implemented a pilot diversion program called Aim to B'More for first-time nonviolent drug offenders which offers participants a chance to get a job and expungement of their criminal record.[110] This program is very similar to the diversion programs that have been offered in many prosecutor offices for decades and will not have an impact on the stark racial disparities in Baltimore's criminal justice system.[111]

It is difficult to draw conclusions from an examination and comparison of elected prosecutors McCulloch and Mosby. McCulloch fits the model of the longstanding incumbent who runs unopposed and serves for decades. His tenure demonstrates the difficulty of unseating an incumbent, even an unpopular one. Mosby's election and even the election of her predecessor demonstrate that incumbents can be unseated with a well-run campaign. Mosby's election also demonstrates that although the race of the candidate may be relevant,[112] it is not determinative of the outcome. Their starkly different approaches to very similar cases show that prosecutorial elections do matter and can make a difference. However, neither a prosecutor's race nor handling of a high-profile case with racial significance determines her commitment to racial justice. A prosecutor's handling of a single high-profile case will not have an impact on the unwarranted racial disparities that plague the entire system as a result of the prosecution of the ordinary criminal cases that prosecutors handle every day. A prosecutor's commitment to racial justice can only be demonstrated by a pledge to take affirmative steps to remedy the problem.

V JOHN CHISHOLM'S COMMITMENT TO RACIAL JUSTICE

One elected prosecutor who made a commitment to racial justice and took steps to achieve it is John Chisholm, the white District Attorney for Milwaukee County, Wisconsin. Chisholm demonstrated his commitment through his

---

[110] *See* Alison Knezevhich, *Mosby: New Program Gives Nonviolent Offenders a Second Chance*, BALTIMORE SUN (May 14, 2015), www.baltimoresun.com/news/maryland/baltimore-city/bs-md-ci-mosby-new-program-20150514-story.html.

[111] The Justice Department conducted an investigation of the Baltimore Police Department ("BPD") similar to the investigation in Ferguson. The Justice Department concluded that the BPD engaged in a pattern and practice of unconstitutional behavior, including racially discriminatory law enforcement practices. *See* U.S. Department of Justice, Civil Rights Division, *Investigation of the Baltimore City Police Department* (August 10, 2016), www.justice.gov/crt/file/883296/download.

[112] *See* David A. Graham, *Most States Elect No Black Prosecutors*, ATLANTIC (July 7, 2015), www.theatlantic.com/politics/archive/2015/07/american-prosecutors-are-incredible-whitedoes-it-matter/397847/ (finding that three in five states have no black elected prosecutors).

participation in a program called the Prosecution and Racial Justice Program (PRJ). PRJ was a pilot program established by the Vera Institute of Justice – a New York-based nonprofit organization. The program involved the collection and analysis of data in prosecution offices to determine the impact of discretionary decisions. According to the Program's website:

> Vera's Prosecution and Racial Justice Program (PRJ) enhances prosecutorial accountability and performance through partnerships with prosecutors' offices nationwide. PRJ works collaboratively with its partners to analyze data about the exercise and impacts of prosecutorial discretion; assists in developing routine policies and practices that promote fairness, efficiency and professionalism in prosecution; and provides technical assistance to help prosecutors implement those measures. By collaborating with prosecutors, analyzing data, and devising solutions, PRJ works alongside prosecutors to improve their performance and related criminal justice outcomes.[113]

The PRJ staff developed a series of performance indicators that focused on four important stages of the prosecutorial process that involve the exercise of discretion: initial case screening, charging, plea offers and final disposition. The program's analysis revealed whether similarly situated defendants were being treated differently based on race at each of these steps. The goal of the program was to help prosecutors exercise discretion in a way that reduced the risk of racial disparity in the decision-making process.

The program started in 2005 and continued for ten years.[114] During that ten-year period, PRJ formed partnerships with a number of chief prosecutors in three jurisdictions, but by all accounts, John Chisholm put the most time and energy into implementing the program and was the most successful in addressing the racial disparity problems in his jurisdiction.

The partnership with Milwaukee County began with Chisholm's predecessor, Michael McCann, who resigned shortly after the work began after serving as District Attorney for almost forty years. Chisholm, who was an Assistant District Attorney in McCann's office, ran for District Attorney and was elected in 2007. Chisholm immediately continued the work with PRJ, giving its staff full access to the data necessary to conduct the study. The results of the staff's work revealed

---

[113] *See generally A Prosecutor's Guide for Advancing Racial Equity*, VERA INSTITUTE OF JUSTICE (Nov. 2014), www.vera.org/sites/default/files/resources/downloads/prosecutors-advancing-racial-equity.pdf [hereinafter *A Prosecutor's Guide*].

[114] *See Prosecution and Racial Justice Program*, VERA INSTITUTE OF JUSTICE www.vera.org/centers/prosecution-and-racial-justice-program (last modified 2015) (about program). But *see A Prosecutor's Guide*, *supra* note 113 (finding that the Vera Institute ended the Prosecution and Racial Justice Program in 2015, but published this guide for prosecutors interested in implementing the program).

stark racial disparities in the prosecution of four offenses: possession of drug paraphernalia, prostitution, resisting or obstructing an officer and domestic violence.[115]

Chisholm immediately took action to address the disparities. He implemented an early intervention program that results in either dismissal or reduction of charges for those who successfully comply with the program's conditions. Chisholm does not limit participation in the program to low-level offenders. Defendants charged with a wide range of felonies are eligible to participate. Individuals charged with very serious violent offenses are not eligible, but according to Chisholm, these individuals only constitute ten to fifteen percent of offenders in Milwaukee County.[116] Eligibility is determined by a detailed assessment of each defendant involving the completion of one or more questionnaires that explore the defendant's criminal history, background, lifestyle and other relevant factors. Instead of focusing on the charge recommended by the arresting police officer, Chisholm's program focuses on the individual. Individuals admitted to the program are closely supervised and participate in programs that address their needs, including drug treatment and education.

Chisholm is making progress. He prosecutes many fewer low-level drug offenses and does not prosecute possession of drug paraphernalia at all. Chisholm drastically reduced the number of misdemeanor prosecutions – down from nine thousand to fifty-two hundred.[117] The number of African Americans sent to prison for drug offenses has been cut in half since 2006.[118]

VI CONCLUSION

Prosecutors play a significant role in causing and maintaining the unwarranted racial disparities in our criminal justice system. The democratic process should hold them accountable, but unfortunately it has been inefficient and ineffective on both the federal and state levels. Many elected state prosecutors serve for decades, often running unopposed. Nonetheless, the electoral system provides an opportunity to tackle the racial disparities in our criminal justice system through the election of prosecutors who are committed to racial justice. Although the public has not paid much attention to prosecutorial elections in the past, the high-profile, tragic killings of unarmed black men in recent years

---

[115] See *District Attorneys Discuss Vera Institute Findings on Racial Disparity in Criminal Cases*, HARVARD LAW TODAY (Dec. 8, 2014), www.today.law.harvard.edu/district-attorneys-discuss-vera-institute-findings-racial-disparity-criminal-cases-video/.

[116] See Jeffrey Toobin, *The Milwaukee Experiment*, NEW YORKER (May 11, 2015), www.newyorker.com/magazine/2015/05/11/the-milwaukee-experiment.

[117] *Id.*   [118] *Id.*

have shined the spotlight on prosecutors and provide an opportunity to inform the public about the importance of holding prosecutors accountable through the electoral process.

There is some evidence to suggest that the electoral process, despite its flaws, can work. A number of incumbent prosecutors were defeated by challengers in November 2016.[119] Two incumbents were defeated by challengers who criticized their handling of police killings of unarmed black males. Anita Alvarez was the State's Attorney for Cook County when unarmed, 17-year-old Laquan McDonald was shot sixteen times by a police officer. She waited thirteen months before indicting him, and then only after a judge ordered the release of a videotape of the shooting. Alvarez was the target of young activists in the Black Lives Matter movement who protested her decisions, and ultimately she was soundly defeated by Kim Foxx, a former prosecutor who previously worked for her. Foxx strongly condemned Alvarez throughout her campaign, not only for the way she handled the McDonald case, but for her practices and policies that perpetuated racial disparities and the overuse of incarceration.[120] Tim McGinty, the District Attorney for Cuyahoga County who failed to indict the police officer who killed 12-year-old Tamir Rice, also was defeated. His challenger, Michael O'Malley, criticized McGinty's handling of the Rice case during his campaign.[121]

The newly-elected prosecutors may be anomalies or the beginning of a sea change in prosecutorial elections. The electoral process has not changed. Running for office is an expensive endeavor, and incumbents are difficult to unseat. Foxx and O'Malley were successful, at least in part, because of how their predecessors handled high-profile cases. It is not clear that they would have won without the national spotlight on these troubling cases.

There is reason to believe that the electoral process may become a more effective means of holding prosecutors accountable. Elected officials, including prosecutors, have begun to support criminal justice reform.[122] Prosecutors

---

[119]   C. J. Ciaramella, *Problem Prosecutors Lost Big on Election Night* (Nov. 10, 2016), www.reason .com/blog/2016/11/10/problem-prosecutors-lost-big-on-election.

[120]   *See* Brandon Ellington Patterson, *Black Lives Matter Notches Wins in Chicago*, MOTHER JONES (Mar. 15, 2016), www.motherjones.com/politics/2016/03/chicago-primary-black-lives-matter.

[121]   *See* Cory Shaffer, *Michael O'Malley Formally Launches Campaign for Cuyahoga County Prosecutor*, CLEVELAND.COM (Jan. 21, 2016), www.cleveland.com/metro/index.ssf/2016/01/mi chael_omalley_formally_launc.html.

[122]   *See* St. John Barned-Smith & Mike Ward, *Police Leaders Call on Reform in Criminal Justice System*, HOUSTON CHRONICLE (Oct. 21, 2015), www.houstonchronicle.com/news/houston-texas/ houston/article/Police-leaders-call-on-reform-in-criminal-justice-6583048.php (stating that the newly formed group, Law Enforcement Leaders to Reduce Crime and Incarceration, a nation-wide organization of police chiefs, sheriffs, prosecutors and attorneys general, met with President Obama to discuss prison reform policies).

like John Chisholm, Ken Thompson and Kim Foxx successfully campaigned on themes of racial justice and less incarceration and won their elections. Their successes may inspire others who are committed to racial fairness in the criminal justice system to run for office. The tragic killings of unarmed black men and boys sparked a renewed political activism in support of criminal justice reform and a focus on the power and discretion of prosecutors. Time will tell whether this combination of events has created the perfect conditions for an effective democratic process that will hold prosecutors accountable to the people they serve.

8

Prosecuting Immigrants in a Democracy

Ingrid V. Eagly[*]

INTRODUCTION

Over the past few decades, the criminal justice system has played an increasingly central role in American immigration enforcement. In federal courts, immigration crime now constitutes almost half of all criminal convictions.[1] In state courts, the tightening connection between immigration and criminal enforcement means that a mere arrest or minor conviction can result in swift deportation.[2] Leading political figures, such as President Donald Trump, have advocated for even greater criminalization of immigrants, including by growing funding for immigration enforcement and defunding so-called "sanctuary cities" that protect immigrants caught up in the criminal justice system from deportation.[3]

[*] Professor of Law, UCLA School of Law. The author thanks Angela Davis, Máximo Langer, David Sklansky, and other workshop participants for their comments on this chapter.

[1] In the fiscal year ending September 30, 2016, immigration crimes constituted forty-three percent of criminal offenses disposed of by federal district and magistrate judges. THOMAS F. HOGAN, JUDICIAL BUSINESS OF THE UNITED STATES COURTS, ADMIN. OFFICE OF THE U.S. COURTS tbl.D-4 & tbl.M-2 (2016) (reporting that immigration crime constituted 47,962 out of 79,969 criminal cases disposed of by federal magistrate courts and 20,352 out of 77,318 criminal cases disposed of by federal district courts). Despite these record-high levels of immigration crime prosecutions, in 2017 the Department of Justice announced a "renewed commitment" to immigration crime prosecution and mandated that all federal prosecutors make "immigration offenses higher priorities." Memorandum from Attorney General Jeff Sessions to All Federal Prosecutors, Renewed Commitment to Criminal Immigration Enforcement (Apr. 11, 2017), www.justice.gov/opa/press-release/file/956841/download.

[2] A Homeland Security Advisory Council reviewing the federal government's jail-based deportation screening program known as Secure Communities concluded that the program "resulted in the arrest and deportation of minor offenders and non-criminals." HOMELAND SECURITY ADVISORY COUNCIL TASK FORCE ON SECURE COMMUNITIES, FINDINGS AND RECOMMENDATIONS 16–17 (Sept. 2011), www.dhs.gov/xlibrary/assets/hsac-task-force-on-secur e-communities-findings-and-recommendations-report.pdf.

[3] See generally Executive Order, Enhancing Public Safety in the Interior of the United States, Jan. 25, 2017, www.whitehouse.gov/the-press-office/2017/01/25/presidential-executive-order-en hancing-public-safety-interior-united.

This state of affairs raises the important normative question of how the criminal law in a democratic society ought to treat noncitizens. As a threshold matter, therefore, it is necessary to clarify the set of democratic values that should be fostered by a criminal justice system. On this point, I borrow from the foundational work of Sharon Dolovich, who has convincingly argued that a liberal democracy must, at a minimum, require "a commitment to what we can think of as the 'baseline' liberal democratic values," including "individual liberty, dignity, and bodily integrity," "the primacy and sovereignty of the individual," and "equal consideration and respect."[4] Legal scholar Nicola Lacey's work on punishment and democracy is also informative on this point; she sketches a "broad definition of democracy as a set of values relating to ideal governance structures," which are in turn informed by concern about matters such as "respect for human rights" and "accountability of officials for proper conduct and efficient delivery of policies in the public interest."[5]

The project of crafting a criminal justice system for noncitizens is complicated by the reality that democracies themselves are inherently exclusionary. The rights and privileges of a democracy are presumptively universal for members of the society.[6] However, by many accounts, immigrants are not full-fledged members.[7] For example, noncitizens cannot serve on a jury.[8] Nor

---

[4]   Sharon Dolovich, *Legitimate Punishment in Liberal Democracy*, 7 Buff. Crim. L. Rev. 307, 314, 441 (2004).
[5]   Nicola Lacey, The Prisoner's Dilemma: Political Economy and Punishment in Contemporary Democracies 9 (2008).
[6]   As Hiroshi Motomura has put it, "there's a special problem in immigration law with regard to equality." Hiroshi Motomura, Brown v. Board of Education, *Immigrants, and the Meaning of Equality*, 49 N.Y.L. Sch. L. Rev. 1145, 1145 (2005). According to Motomura, "[t]he source of this problem is the premise – though not entirely uncontested – in immigration and citizenship that it is permissible to draw some distinctions between people who are citizens and people who are not." *Id.*
[7]   As Juliet Stumpf has convincingly shown in her work on the "crimmigration" convergence, the immigration system is fundamentally about membership – it functions to define and segregate society and to "determine whether and how to include individuals as members of society." Juliet Stumpf, *The Crimmigration Crisis: Immigrants, Crime, and Sovereign Power*, 56 Am. U. L. Rev. 367, 397 (2007).
[8]   Radical participatory approaches to social transformation, like jury nullification, are less viable when members of the affected immigrant community themselves cannot cast their vote on a jury. *See* Paul Butler, Essay, *Racially Based Jury Nullification: Black Power in the Criminal Justice System*, 105 Yale L.J. 677 (1995) (arguing that race can be an appropriate consideration for jurors when choosing to exercise the power of jury nullification). Daniel Morales has argued, however, that the citizen jury could be convinced through the democratic jury process that "migrants are also members of society deserving citizens' moral and political concern." Daniel I. Morales, *Immigration Reform and the Democratic Will*, 16 U. Pa. J. L. & Soc. Change 49, 52 (2013) (proposing that immigration cases be decided by citizen juries rather than immigration judges). For a compelling argument that at least lawful permanent residents

can they vote in democratic elections or hold elected office.[9] Immigrants without lawful status are also unable to obtain certain forms of paid work or qualify for a driver's license in many states.[10]

Should the values of a liberal democracy nonetheless extend to noncitizens charged with crimes? Antony Duff has argued for development of a "positive account of the proper aims of the criminal law" as "a law that citizens impose on themselves."[11] In this approach, equal protection of the laws applies regardless of the citizen's status as "law-abiding, or victims or perpetrators of crime," yet those who are not formally designated as citizens are excluded from participating in shaping the criminal law.[12] Lucia Zedner, in contrast, has critiqued such a citizen-centered ideal. As she explains, "predicating the obligations of criminal law upon citizenship" will result in "intractable problems for those whose citizenship status is absent, in doubt, or irregular."[13]

This chapter takes as an entry point the principle that the core democratic values that guide the criminal law must apply equally to the citizens and noncitizens subject to its power. Because, as this chapter reveals, this approach does not reflect the current reality of American criminal justice,[14] implementation requires criminal justice actors to move beyond the immigration system's formal

---

ought to be allowed to serve on American juries, see Amy R. Motomura, *The American Jury: Can Noncitizens Still Be Excluded?*, 64 STAN. L. REV. 1503 (2012).

[9]   The limitation of voting to citizens means that noncitizens cannot participate in the political process to reform law enforcement or choose their public prosecutor. *See generally* Tracey L. Meares & Dan M. Kahan, *The Wages of Antiquated Procedural Thinking: A Critique of Chicago v. Morales*, 1988 U. CHI. LEGAL F. 197, 208 (arguing that minority communities should use their "political power" and "work with their elected officials" to shape the criminal justice system); Ron Wright, *How Prosecutor Elections Fail Us*, 6 OHIO ST. J. CRIM. LAW 581, 581, 590 (2009) (arguing that a "system of voter accountability" can help to guard "against abusive prosecutors through direct democratic control").

[10] For a timely discussion of how some states and localities have incorporated immigrants into their citizenry, including by granting them access to public programs and benefits such as driver's licenses and state identification cards, see Peter L. Markowitz, *Undocumented No More: The Power of State Citizenship*, 67 STAN. L. REV. 869 (2015).

[11] R. A. Duff, *A Criminal Law for Citizens*, 14 THEORETICAL CRIM. 293, 293 (2010).

[12] *Id.* at 301. In so arguing, Professor Duff does acknowledge that citizenship is not "an unproblematic foundation for criminal law," in part because of the danger that "a citizens' law will be in various ways exclusionary rather than inclusionary." *Id.* at 301–02.

[13] Lucia Zedner, *Is the Criminal Law Only for Citizens? A Problem at the Borders of Punishment* in THE BORDERS OF PUNISHMENT 40, 41–42 (Katja Frank Aas & Mary Bosworth eds., 2013).

[14] Although this chapter focuses on prosecutors in the United States, its contribution may have broader application given that criminal prosecutors in other countries have similarly seen their institutional function expand into immigration enforcement, with few systemic controls in place to limit these powers. For discussion of these issues outside the United States, see Ana Aliverti, *Exploring the Function of Criminal Law in the Policing of Foreigners: The Decision to Prosecute Immigration-Related Offenses*, 21 SOC. & LEGAL STUDIES 511 (2012); Mary Bosworth & Mhairi Guild, *Governing Through Migration Control: Security and Citizenship in Britain,*

citizenship rules for rights distribution and toward what Linda Bosniak has termed a "universalist ethic."[15] Put differently, all persons subject to the criminal justice system should be granted membership rights, including equal protection from prosecutorial abuses and similar treatment for similar crimes.[16]

   This chapter proceeds in two parts. Part I reveals how American prosecutorial power has been deployed in ways that threaten basic democratic values.[17] For example, the rise of punitive treatment of immigrants has incentivized some prosecutors to bring cases based on the deportation consequence of the prosecution – rather than to focus on the most serious crimes deserving of prosecutorial attention. In addition, prosecutors may draw on civil immigration enforcement tools, such as immigration detention and the threat of deportation, in ways that distort and undermine the protections normally afforded by criminal procedure rules. Prosecutorial control over immigration outcomes is also tied to more severe punishment of noncitizens in the form of longer sentences, under more punitive conditions, buttressed by harsh civil collateral consequences. The end result is a criminal justice regime for immigrants that extends beyond the institutional role granted to prosecutors by legislatures drafting the criminal law and by courts constructing procedural rules. Furthermore, this citizenship inequality disproportionately affects racial and ethnic minorities, who become easy targets for immigration policing.[18]

---

   48 BRITISH J. OF CRIMINOLOGY 703 (2008); Alessandro De Giorgi, *Immigration Control, Post-Fordism, and Less Eligibility: A Materialist Critique of the Criminalization of Immigration Across Europe*, 12 PUNISHMENT & SOC. 147 (2010); Maartje A. J. van der Woude et al., *Crimmigration in the Netherlands*, 39 LAW & SOC. INQUIRY 560 (2014).

[15] LINDA BOSNIAK, THE CITIZEN AND THE ALIEN: DILEMMAS OF CONTEMPORARY MEMBERSHIP 2 (2006).

[16] As Jerry López forcefully advocates, "pursuit of radical democracy" means achieving a world in which "equal citizenship is a concrete everyday reality and not just a vague promise." Gerald P. López, *Changing Systems, Changing Ourselves*, 12 HARV. LATINO L. REV. 15, 31 (2009).

[17] For background on the powerful role of prosecutors in the United States criminal justice system, see ANGELA J. DAVIS, ARBITRARY JUSTICE: THE POWER OF THE AMERICAN PROSECUTOR (2007) (contending that most forms of prosecutorial discretion will generate gross injustice in the criminal law system); Rachel E. Barkow, *Separation of Powers and the Criminal Law*, 58 STAN. L. REV. 989 (2006) (arguing that the criminal law operates like an administrate state with almost no institutional checks); Máximo Langer, *Rethinking Plea Bargaining: The Practice and Reform of Prosecutorial Adjudication in American Criminal Procedure*, 34 AM. J. CRIM. L. 223 (2006) (concluding that prosecutors in the United States are the primary adjudicators of criminal procedure in coercive plea bargaining).

[18] *See generally* Devon W. Carbado & Cheryl I. Harris, *Undocumented Criminal Procedure*, 58 UCLA L. REV. 1543 (2011) (demonstrating how immigration enforcement has imported into the Fourth Amendment law a lower standard of protection that legitimates racial profiling in policing); Adam B. Cox & Thomas J. Miles, *Policing Immigration*, 87 U. CHI. L. REV. 87 (2013) (concluding that federally supported immigration policing programs target counties

Part II explores possible institutional reforms to constrain prosecutorial power over immigrants and make the system more equal, less punitive, and more consistent with democratic ideals. This discussion centers on three possible systemic reforms. First, prosecutor offices could adopt written guidelines that allow prosecutors to take the adverse consequence of deportation into account when arriving at a just plea offer. Second, criminal court sentencing judges could be given the authority to assess the merits of individual cases and recommend against deportation in appropriate cases. Third, more institutional resources could be dedicated to ensuring that public defender offices are able to provide quality and comprehensive representation for noncitizen clients.

Before proceeding, a few clarifications regarding the scope of this chapter are in order. The reforms featured in this chapter are by no means the only route to achieving greater citizenship equality in criminal justice. As a series of democratically adopted reforms in California and other states make clear, many other aspects of state and local criminal justice systems could be changed to address some of the ways that the immigration system distorts criminal case outcomes for noncitizen defendants.[19] Likewise, complementary redesign of the immigration law to decouple deportation from criminal convictions could be pursued.[20]

It is also crucial to acknowledge that this chapter's focus on unbalanced treatment along formal citizenship lines is part of a broader structure of intersecting forms of discrimination and oppression experienced by the poor and people of color in the American criminal justice system. As Armada Armenta and other scholars have noted, the system that polices and prosecutes immigrant communities "is not colorblind but rather is a system of structural racism that creates

---

with large Hispanic populations); Kevin R. Johnson, *Racial Profiling in the 'War on Drugs' Meets the Immigration Removal Process: The Case of* Moncrieffe v. Holder, 48 U. MICH. J.L. REFORM 967 (2015) (arguing that racial profiling in the "war on drugs" has been aggravated by the federal government's immigration removal system).

[19] *See generally* Ingrid V. Eagly, *Criminal Justice in an Era of Mass Deportation: Reforms from California*, 20 NEW CRIM. L. REV. 12 (2017) (discussing recent criminal justice reforms from the state of California that address some of the inequality concerns facing noncitizen criminal defendants).

[20] Numerous immigration scholars have called for a fundamental rethinking of crime-based deportation rules in the United States. *See, e.g.,* Jason A. Cade, *Enforcing Immigration Equity*, 84 FORDHAM L. REV. 661, 716–17 (2015) (proposing that Congress "reallocate broad power to immigration judges to balance the equitable fairness of deportation in individual cases"); Allegra M. McLeod, *The U.S. Criminal-Immigration Convergence and Its Possible Undoing*, 49 AM. CRIM. L. REV. 105 (2012) (arguing in favor of legal reforms that would reduce reliance on crime-based removal); Nancy Morawetz, *Rethinking Drug Inadmissibility*, 50 WM. & MARY L. REV. 163, 167 (2008). ("It is time for policymakers to review the standards for barring immigrants based on past violations of drug law.")

racial inequality and reinforces ideas about racial difference."[21] Devon Carbado's influential work has revealed that formal citizenship rules do not fully account for the ways in which criminal justice institutions function in practice to treat minorities – even those who are citizens – as nonmember outsiders.[22] Recent ethnographic research by Amy Lerman and Vesla Weaver has powerfully documented how the "lived experience of American citizenship" is distorted by routine encounters with criminal justice practices that "have broken with the democratic norms that govern most American institutions."[23] Existing protective procedures within the criminal justice system have failed to remedy these inequalities.[24] The reforms discussed in this chapter are thus a necessary part of restructuring the systems that result in these institutionalized forms of intersecting inequalities. However, achieving a criminal justice system informed by liberal democratic values requires that these proposed reforms be considered together with other systemic remedies that address the fear and vulnerability experienced "in everyday life" by policed communities of color in America.[25]

[21] Amada Armenta, *Racializing Crimmigration: Structural Racism, Colorblindness and the Institutional Production of Immigrant Criminality*, Soc. of Race & Ethinicity, online first (2016) (documenting how police as "frontline" immigration enforcers "amplify racialized outcomes through their interactions" with noncitizens). *See also* Naomi Murakawa & Katherine Beckett, *The Penology of Racial Innocence: The Erasure of Racism in the Study and Practice of Punishment*, 695 Law & Soc'y Rev. 695, 706 (2010) (arguing that the role of race in the "construction of particular issues as crime problems" and the "propensity to rely on coercive control mechanisms to solve these problems" has been obscured).

[22] Devon W. Carbado, *Racial Naturalization*, 57 Am. Q. 633, 637–39 (2005) (questioning whether inclusion in citizenship necessarily delivers social equality due to the process of "national identity displacement or racial extraterritorialization").

[23] Amy E. Lerman & Vesla M. Weaver, Arresting Citizenship: The Democratic Consequences of American Crime Control 7 (2014).

[24] The example of money bail serving as a barrier to pretrial release for the poor, immigrants, and people of color is but one powerful example of how the criminal justice system writ large has failed to live up to its democratic ideals. *See* Equal Justice Under Law, Ending the American Money Bail System (2014), equaljusticeunderlaw.org/wp/current-cases/ending-the-american-money-bail-system/ (discussing litigation efforts to reform state practices that rely on secured money bail for new arrestees); Human Rights Watch, The Price of Freedom: Bail and Pretrial Detention of Low Income Nonfelony Defendants in New York City (2010), www.hrw.org/sites/default/files/reports/us1210webwcover_0.pdf (revealing that in eighty-seven percent of cases, defendants were unable to post bails set at $1,000 or less and remained incarcerated pending trial).

[25] Nicolas P. De Genova, *Migrant "Illegality" and Deportability in Everyday Life*, 43 Ann. Rev. of Anthropology 419 (2002). *See also* Susan Bibler Coutin, *The Rights of Noncitizens in the United States*, 7 Ann. Rev. of Law and Social Sci. 289, 290–91 (2011). (explaining that "both legal status and immigration enforcement" can be understood as part of a broader regime that excludes "society's 'others'"); Murakawa & Beckett, *supra* note 21, at 696 ("[I]n the lives of many people of color, criminal justice is expanding, commonplace, and located in systemwide penal policies and practices[.]").

I IMMIGRATION ENFORCEMENT'S THREAT TO THE PROSECUTORIAL FUNCTION

This Part discusses three important ways in which the blurring of immigration and criminal enforcement has distorted the prosecutorial function. First, the prosecutor's ability to trigger deportation raises concerns about prosecutorial motivation. Specifically, prosecutors may pursue criminal charges pretextually in order to incapacitate immigrant defendants through deportation. Second, the merging of criminal and immigration enforcement can distort core procedural safeguards. That is, prosecutors may use their immigration powers in ways that bypass the protections that are normally part of the criminal process, thereby fostering unequal treatment based on citizenship status. Third, immigrants are often exposed to an enhanced set of criminal punishments, including by being deemed ineligible for alternative, less punitive sentencing arrangements.

A Pretextual Prosecution

Pretextual prosecution generally refers to the practice of suspecting someone of a greater crime, but instead prosecuting the person with a different, lesser crime.[26] Routine in both federal and state courts, such prosecutions are a tool by which prosecutors target elusive defendants with lower-level criminal behavior that can be more readily proven.[27] As Bill Stuntz succinctly put it, pretextual prosecution occurs when prosecutors "go after not *crimes* but *criminals*."[28] Normative critiques of pretextual prosecution have focused on how their lack of transparency undermines the public prosecutor's legitimacy.[29]

---

[26] Daniel C. Richman & William J. Stuntz, *Al Capone's Revenge: An Essay on the Political Economy of Pretextual Prosecution*, 105 COLUM. L. REV. 583, 583 (2005).

[27] *See, e.g.*, Erin Murphy, *Manufacturing Crime: Process, Pretext, and Criminal Justice*, 97 GEO. L.J. 1435, 1442 (2009) (showing how process crimes – such as perjury or failure to appear – can be used in lieu of pursuing the "real" criminal behavior); Richman & Stuntz, *supra* note 26, at 608 (explaining that pretextual prosecution may occur in state court drug cases, particularly when someone believed to be a drug dealer is charged with possession of small amounts of drugs).

[28] William J. Stuntz, *Unequal Justice*, 121 HARV. L. REV. 1969, 1998 (2008) (emphasis in the original).

[29] *See, e.g.*, Richman & Stuntz, *supra* note 26, at 586 (arguing that pretextual prosecution is a concern because it lacks transparency and undermines prosecutorial credibility); Lisa Kern Griffin, *Criminal Lying, Prosecutorial Power, and Social Meaning*, 97 CALIF. L. REV. 1515 (2009) (arguing that pretextual federal prosecutions reduce the transparency of the criminal system); Harry Litman, *Pretextual Prosecution*, 92 GEO. L.J. 1135, 1149 (2004) (pretextual prosecutions raise a number of concerns, including the "appearance of impropriety" and inappropriate "institutional roles"); Murphy, *supra* note 27, at 1497 (explaining that pretextual prosecutions raise "familiar concerns about transparency, state legitimacy, and self-dealing").

The movement of immigration enforcement into criminal courts has heightened the problem of pretextual prosecution. In Los Angeles, for example, county and federal prosecutors collaborated in an effort to target suspected gang members with illegal reentry prosecutions.[30] The then-District Attorney Steve Cooley described the cooperative program as "an initiative [he] decided to undertake and encourage because a good chunk of our gang problem in Los Angeles County is committed by individuals who have been previously deported and then re-entered the country."[31] In other words, prosecutors wanted to pursue suspected gang members for higher-order crimes, but realized that they could instead use the illegal reentry statute to more easily incapacitate this population.

Illegal reentry cases are notoriously easy to prove and result in astonishingly high guilty plea rates.[32] As federal prosecutors in Los Angeles told reporters, "reentry cases . . . rarely go to trial and don't require much time."[33] Rather than proving the drug distribution conspiracy or violent acts proliferated by urban gangs, prosecutors simply have to demonstrate that the individual was previously deported and lacked permission to return to the United States.[34] As a result, over the past two decades, the number of illegal reentry crimes has skyrocketed.[35]

Prosecutors can also target immigrant populations deemed criminal by using low-level state crimes as pretext. In this approach, deportation is not just a collateral consequence, but rather the prosecutorial goal.[36] As legal scholar Eisha Jain explains, prosecutors who believe that deportation is a

---

[30] Ingrid V. Eagly, *Criminal Justice for Noncitizens: An Analysis of Variation in Local Enforcement*, 88 N.Y.U. L. Rev. 1126, 1194 (2013). *See also* Jennifer Chacón, *Whose Community Shield?: Examining the Removal of the "Criminal Street Gang Member,"* 2007 U. Chi. L. F. 317 (examining the unintended consequences of efforts to deport immigrant gang members).

[31] Troy Anderson, *Prosecutors Join Anti-Gang Effort; D.A., City Attorney to Focus on Deportation of Illegals*, Daily News of L.A., Apr. 6, 2007, at N4 (quoting Los Angeles County District Attorney Steve Cooley).

[32] Ingrid V. Eagly, *Prosecuting Immigration*, 104 Nw. U. L. Rev. 1281, 1329 (2010).

[33] Anna Gorman & Scott Glover, *Illegal Reentry into the U. S. Increasingly Leads to Prison*, L.A. Times, Mar. 16, 2008, www.articles.latimes.com/2008/mar/16/local/me-crackdown16 (quoting Thom Mrozek, spokesperson for the United States Attorney's Office in Los Angeles).

[34] *See* 8 U.S.C. § 1326 (2016) (making entering the country without permission after deportation a felony).

[35] Jennifer M. Chacón, *Overcriminalizing Immigration*, 102 J. Crim. L. & Criminology 613, 634 (2012); David Alan Sklansky, *Crime, Immigration, and Ad Hoc Instrumentalism*, 15 New Crim. L. Rev. 157, 169 (2012).

[36] Eagly, *supra* note 30, at 1181 (discussing an "immigration enforcement model" for criminal adjudication in which prosecutors intentionally seek out collateral consequence of deportation as a desirable aim of the criminal process).

"desirable end" may "structure pleas to maximize the likelihood of deportation."[37]

There are a number of ways that local prosecutors can use criminal state laws to target immigrants – a practice that Annie Lai has termed "criminalization by proxy."[38] For example, in most states, driving without a license can subject a driver to criminal prosecution.[39] In an era of vigorous immigration enforcement, criminalization of driving without a license intersects with state laws that prohibit the undocumented from obtaining a driver's license.[40] Local discretion over the enforcement of license laws during routine traffic stops thus has a profound effect on the undocumented population.[41]

Identity-related crimes, such as document fraud, provide another tool that local prosecutors can use in ways that target immigrants.[42] From the state vantage point, these types of low-level crimes can serve as pretext for the greater objective, which is incapacitation of the immigrant by way of deportation from the United States. Even the most minor conviction can result in the immigrant being transferred into immigration detention and deported.

Pretextual prosecutions against immigrants also have unintended consequences. In the federal system, filling prosecutorial dockets with immigration crimes diverts prosecutorial resources from the crimes most in need of prosecution and thereby undermines the moral authority of the criminal law.[43]

---

[37] Eisha Jain, *Prosecuting Collateral Consequences*, 104 GEO. L.J. 1197, 1221 (2016).

[38] Annie Lai, *Confronting Proxy Criminalization*, 92 DENV. U. L. REV. 879, 881 (2015) (arguing that criminalization "by proxy" is "no less a perversion of state criminal justice systems" than making undocumented status a crime).

[39] *See, e.g.*, CAL. VEH. CODE § 12500 (2017) (driving without a license); ARIZ. REV. STAT. ANN. § 28-3380 (2017) (operating a motor vehicle in violation of a driver license restriction); TEX. TRANSPORT. CODE § 521.457 (2017) (driving while license invalid).

[40] All but a few states require proof of lawful presence in the United States in order to obtain a driver's license. Since the passage of the federal REAL ID Act in 2005, the number of states that offer licenses to undocumented residents has dwindled. REAL ID Act of 2005, Pub. L. No. 109-13, Div. B, 119 Stat. 231, 302–23 (giving states the option to issue a driver's license to undocumented residents, but requiring a unique design or color, and words stating that the license will not be accepted by the federal government).

[41] *See generally* Devon W. Carbado *(E)racing the Fourth Amendment*, 100 MICH. L. REV. 946, 1031 (2002). ("Any discussion of race and policing that excludes an examination of traffic stops is necessarily incomplete.")

[42] For example, state criminal codes punish possession of false or misleading identity documents or providing false information regarding one's identity to law enforcement. *See, e.g.*, ARIZ. REV. STAT. ANN. § 13-2002(A) (possession or presentment of a false document); TEX. PENAL CODE ANN. § 38.02(b) (2017) (giving false information to a peace officer).

[43] *See generally* Ana Aliverti, *The Wrongs of Unlawful Immigration*, CRIM. L. & PHIL., online first (2015) (arguing that immigration crimes "are peculiarly objectionable" because "they fall short in fulfilling the harm principle and, given that criminal punishment as used against immigration offenders is often a secondary, ancillary sanction to deportation, they license

In the state system, the pursuit of low-level charges against immigrants to achieve the collateral sanction of deportation effectively transfers federal immigration enforcement decisions to county-level law enforcement who are not accountable to the Executive and lack any formal authority to enforce the immigration law.[44] Finally, studies have found that the incentive to fuel deportation through the criminal process is associated with the targeting of racial and ethnic minorities for low-level crimes, such as traffic offenses.[45] This type of profiling is objectionable on its own,[46] but when the targets are immigrants, such discriminatory enforcement can also trigger the harsh sanction of immigration enforcement.

B Disparities in Procedural Protections

Up to this point, this chapter has argued that the availability of immigration-related crimes and the collateral sanction of deportation can result in pretextual prosecution. A second aspect of this dynamic is the dilution of procedural protections that apply to noncitizens.

One way that procedural distortions occur is when prosecutors rely on the tools of the immigration system – such as detention and deportation – to buttress the criminal prosecution in ways that would not be available for citizen defendants. Consider, for example, the situation that occurs when immigrants seek pretrial release in their criminal case. Frequently, they will be transferred into federal immigration custody instead of being released on bail.[47] These transfers occur because of what is referred to as an immigration detainer, which essentially is a request by federal authorities to be notified if an immigrant is to be released from criminal custody.[48] Thus, while eligible

---

excessive imposition of pain"); Zedner, *supra* note 13, at 51–52 (contending that "core principles of the criminal law are imperiled by many immigration offences").

[44] *See generally* Arizona v. United States, 132 S. Ct. 2492, 2498 (2012). ("The federal power to determine immigration policy is well settled.") Eisha Jain has persuasively shown how even arrests without conviction can be used in practice as a strategic tool to trigger a range of consequences, such as deportation, eviction, license suspension, or custody disruption. Eisha Jain, *Arrests as Regulation,* 67 Stan. L. Rev. 809 (2015).

[45] *See, e.g.,* Trevor Gardiner II & Aarti Kohli, The C.A.P. Effect: Racial Profiling in the ICE Criminal Alien Program (Sept. 2009), www.law.berkeley.edu/files/policybrief_ir ving_0909_v9.pdf (finding that Latinos comprise ninety-three percent of individuals taken into custody after local arrests associated with an immigration enforcement program, despite the fact that they only comprise seventy-seven percent of the undocumented population).

[46] *See generally* Angela J. Davis, *In Search of Racial Justice: The Role of the Prosecutor,* 16 N.Y.U. J. Legis. & Pub. Policy 821, 829 (2013) (discussing the serious problem of racial profiling of African Americans and Latinos).

[47] Eagly, *supra* note 32, at 1302, 1307–08.   [48] 8 C.F.R. § 287.7 (2017).

citizens granted pretrial release can immediately rejoin their families and participate in their defense from the outside, similarly situated noncitizens often languish in immigration detention.[49] Remaining detained prior to trial is correlated with higher rates of conviction and more severe sentences.[50]

The ready availability of deportation as a consequence of a criminal conviction can also incentivize prosecutors to avoid other procedural protections. Paul Crane has argued that an immigration enforcement approach can motivate prosecutors to avoid the standard rules of criminal procedure.[51] By engaging in what Crane calls "strategic undercharging," prosecutors bring misdemeanors rather than felonies, knowing that misdemeanors can yield the same potent deportation penalty as the harder-to-prove felony. Yet, misdemeanors also allow prosecutors to bypass the procedural entitlements that attach to felonies, such as rights to grand jury, a preliminary hearing, expanded pretrial discovery, and jury trial. According to Crane, prosecutors choose this easier path because they "can still achieve the penalty they desire without having to endure the greater costs generated by felony prosecutions."[52] Eisha Jain has likewise warned that civil immigration enforcement can serve as a flexible tool that criminal prosecutors call on to "supplement or to replace criminal consequences."[53] Even when the "evidence needed in criminal court" is weak or insufficient, criminal prosecutors can rely on immigration courts and "their relatively lax procedural standards" to ensure swift deportation.[54]

C Unequal Punishment Practices

Current prosecutorial practices have also resulted in systematically greater punishments for immigrants than for their citizen counterparts. An insightful study by sociologist Michael Light documents such disparities, with noncitizens receiving

---

[49] For analysis of the immigration court process for setting terms of release from immigration custody, see Emily Ryo, *Detained: A Study of Immigration Bond Hearings*, 50 LAW & SOC'Y REV. 117 (2016).

[50] *See, e.g.*, Charles E. Ares et al., *The Manhattan Bail Project: An Interim Report on the Use of Pretrial Parole*, 37 N.Y.U. L. REV. 67, 84–86 (1963) (establishing that defendants who are incarcerated pending trial are more likely to be convicted than those at liberty to prepare for trial).

[51] Paul T. Crane, *Charging on the Margin*, 57 WM. & MARY L. REV. 775 (2016).

[52] *Id.* at 780.   [53] Jain, *supra* note 44, at 815.

[54] *Id.* at 846–47. *See also* Alexandra Natapoff, *Misdemeanor Decriminalization*, 68 VAND. L. REV. 1055, 1055 (2015) (pointing out that the downward trend in charging severity has a "dark side," in that "it preserves many of the punitive features and collateral consequences" while at the same time stripping defendants of procedural protections and "making it easier" to supervise and punish "an ever-widening population").

harsher criminal sentences than citizens in federal courts.[55] For instance, his data reveal that ninety-six percent of convicted noncitizens received a prison sentence, compared to only eighty-five percent of United States citizens.[56] This noncitizen sentencing penalty was not explained by factors normally associated with sentencing severity, such as the seriousness of the offense or criminal history.[57] Nor could these differences be statistically explained by other characteristics of the defendants, such as race or gender.[58] Future research should explore the racialized effects that these citizenship penalties produce.

In some criminal justice systems, immigrants may be deemed ineligible for sanctions that are less punitive than incarceration. For example, prosecutors may bar suspected undocumented immigrants from participating in a beneficial drug treatment program or receiving a plea bargain for a less punitive form of punishment, such as probation or a halfway house.[59] A related issue is that even if immigrants remain eligible for alternative disposition programs, they are often structured to require a guilty plea that would render the noncitizen deportable prior to accessing the beneficial programming. Given the choice, immigrants may forego participation in these otherwise beneficial programs and instead opt for a custodial sentence that does not carry the deportation penalty.[60]

Also demanding attention are the conditions under which noncitizens must serve their sentences. Emma Kaufman's probing investigation documents that the United States Bureau of Prisons has created a separate carceral system – known as Criminal Alien Requirement ("CAR") prisons – to punish immigrants.[61] These "all-foreign prisons" house exclusively noncitizens, are run by for-profit companies, and reserve ten percent of their bed space for extreme isolation.[62] Compared to other Bureau of Prisons facilities, all-foreign prisons provide less programming, such as education and work opportunities.[63] Additionally, federal prison rules

---

[55]   Michael T. Light, *The New Face of Legal Inequality: Noncitizens and the Long–Term Trends in Sentencing Disparities Across U.S. District Courts, 1992–2009*, 48 LAW & SOC'Y REV. 447 (2014) (documenting a noncitizen "penalty" at sentencing).

[56]   *Id.* at 457 (citing data from 2008).   [57]   *Id.* at 451.   [58]   *Id.* at 454.

[59]   Eagly, *supra* note 30, at 1177 (describing a plea bargaining policy in Harris County, Texas, that requires undocumented immigrants to be sentenced to jail time rather than probation).

[60]   Alina Das, *Immigrants and Problem-Solving Courts*, 33 CRIM. JUST. REV. 308, 310–11 (2008) (documenting the increasing reliance by problem-solving courts on requirements that adversely affect immigrant defendants seeking to participate these alternative disposition programs).

[61]   Emma Kaufmann, *The Rise of the All-Foreign Prison* (draft on file with author). For an essential introduction to the American prison system, see Sharon Dolovich, *Incarceration American-Style*, 3 HARV. L. & POL'Y REV. 237 (2009).

[62]   Kaufmann, *supra* note 61.

[63]   *See generally* AMERICAN CIVIL LIBERTIES UNION, WAREHOUSED AND FORGOTTEN: IMMIGRANTS TRAPPED IN OUR SHADOW PRIVATE PRISON SYSTEM 4 (June 2014), www.aclu .org/sites/default/files/assets/060614-aclu-car-reportonline.pdf.

render noncitizens ineligible for a range of rehabilitative programs that offer significant benefits, including by shortening prison sentences as a reward for successfully completing a drug treatment program.[64]

This unequal and punitive treatment of immigrants is particularly misplaced in view of the lack of any empirical evidence showing that immigrants are more criminally inclined than citizens. To the contrary, research has consistently found that the foreign-born have a lower crime rate than native-born citizens.[65] Immigrant communities also boast lower crime rates,[66] in part because structural features of immigrant families (such as intact, two-parent households) are associated with neighborhood crime rate stabilization.[67]

In sum, American prosecutors have expansive control not only over their criminal cases, but also over immigration outcomes for noncitizen defendants. Compounding these problems, prosecutors can use these de facto immigration powers to engage in pretextual prosecutions and borrow from the immigration enforcement regime in ways that can distort the normal set of procedural protections. Within this system, immigrants are subject to punishments that are harsher than those of their citizen counterparts.

II REFORMING THE TREATMENT OF NONCITIZENS IN THE CRIMINAL JUSTICE SYSTEM

As Part I has shown, the growing convergence of criminal and immigration law has expanded the power of criminal prosecutors. Yet, these immigration powers

---

[64] *See* Nora V. Demleitner, *Terms of Imprisonment: Treating the Noncitizen Offender Equally*, 21 FED. SENT. R. 174 (2008–09).

[65] *See, e.g.*, RUBÉN G. RUMBAUT ET AL., DEBUNKING THE MYTH OF IMMIGRANT CRIMINALITY: IMPRISONMENT AMONG FIRST- AND SECOND-GENERATION YOUNG MEN, MIGRATION INFORMATION SOURCE (June 1, 2006), www.migrationpolicy.org/article/debunking-myth-im migrant-criminality-imprisonment-among-first-and-second-generation-young; WALTER EWING ET AL., THE CRIMINALIZATION OF IMMIGRATION IN THE UNITED STATES, AMERICAN IMMIGRATION COUNCIL (July 13, 2015), www.americanimmigrationcouncil.org/s ites/default/files/research/the_criminalization_of_immigration_in_the_united_states.pdf.

[66] *See, e.g.*, Garth Davies & Jeffrey Fagan, *Crime and Enforcement in Immigrant Neighborhoods: Evidence from New York City*, 641 ANNALS AM. ACAD. POL. & SOC. SCI. 99, 116–17 (2012) (concluding that immigrant neighborhoods have less crime than native-born neighborhoods); Tim Wadsworth, *Is Immigration Responsible for the Crime Drop? An Assessment of the Influence of Immigration on Changes in Violent Crime Between 1990 and 2000*, 91 SOC. SCI. Q. 534, 546 (2010) (concluding that cities with the largest increases in immigration in the 1990s experienced the largest decreases in violent crime).

[67] Graham C. Ousey & Charis E. Kubrin, *Exploring the Connection Between Immigration and Violent Crime Rates in U.S. Cities, 1980–2000*, 56 SOC. PROBS. 447, 463–64 (2009) (arguing that immigration lowers violent crime rates because it is correlated with the stabilizing effect of two-parent family structures).

are often applied behind the scenes and out of view. As research by Marc Miller and Ronald Wright has demonstrated, peering inside the "black box" of internal prosecutorial regulation is rare, particularly given that "the absence of controlling statutes or case law makes it possible for prosecutors to do their daily work without explaining their choices to the public."[68] Similarly, there is no transparent system of checks and balances for the treatment of noncitizens within the criminal justice system, such as explicit constitutional constraints or independent oversight.

Nonetheless, there are several strategies that could be pursued to boost the checks on prosecutorial power over immigrants in ways that would promote democratic values, such as equality and transparency. This Part introduces three possible criminal justice reforms, each of which serves as an institutional counterweight to prosecutorial control. These proposed reforms include (1) adopting written prosecutorial policies for weighing the collateral consequence of deportation in the plea bargaining process, (2) allowing judicial oversight by sentencing judges over deportation decisions, and (3) increasing public defender resources dedicated to effective representation of noncitizens.

A *Requiring Prosecutors to Consider Collateral Consequences in Reaching Just Plea Bargains*

At least ninety-five percent of today's criminal cases are resolved by plea, rather than trial.[69] Within this plea bargained system, prosecutors hold the power not only to make charging decisions, but also to dictate the terms of a plea agreement and determine the sentence. From this powerful position, prosecutors may have the incentive to use their "vast and unreviewable discretion" to "shape civil outcomes" – a dynamic that Eisha Jain has aptly called "prosecuting" collateral consequences.[70] This power held by prosecutors over immigration outcomes in the plea bargaining context is particularly potent today given that deporting immigrants with certain types of criminal convictions is now an explicit institutional priority of the immigration system.[71]

[68] Marc L. Miller & Ronald F. Wright, *The Black Box*, 94 Iowa L. Rev. 125, 129 (2008).
[69] Lafler v. Cooper, 132 S. Ct. 1376, 1388 (2012).   [70] Jain, *supra* note 37, at 1197.
[71] *See* Memorandum from John Morton to All ICE Employees, Civil Immigration Enforcement: Priorities for the Apprehension, Detention, and Removal of Aliens (March 2, 2011), www.ice.gov/doclib/news/releases/2011/110302washingtondc.pdf (prioritizing the removal of criminal aliens based on the type of criminal conviction). Angélica Cházaro has argued that these kind of prosecutorial discretion programs that prioritize removal of so-called "criminal aliens" are a troubling "form of net widening" that functions to justify using "the full force of the detention and deportation apparatus" against immigrants. Angélica Cházaro, *Challenging the "Criminal Alien" Paradigm*, 63 UCLA L. Rev. 594, 645 (2016).

A watershed decision by the United States Supreme Court in 2010 signaled a possible counterweight to the growing prosecutorial power over immigration outcomes. In *Padilla v. Kentucky*, the Court announced that noncitizen defendants have a Sixth Amendment right to counsel on the potential immigration consequences of a guilty plea.[72] The Court characterized deportation as a "drastic measure" that is an "integral part – indeed, sometimes the most important part – of the penalty that may be imposed on noncitizen defendants who plead guilty to specific crimes."[73] In so ruling, the *Padilla* majority stressed that taking deportation into account in the plea bargaining process could encourage pleas that "better satisfy the interests of both parties."[74] Defense counsel may be able to "craft a conviction and sentence that reduce the likelihood of deportation, as by avoiding a conviction for an offense that automatically triggers the removal consequence."[75] Prosecutors can also benefit because "the threat of deportation may provide the defendant with a powerful incentive to plead guilty to an offense that does not mandate that penalty in exchange for a dismissal of a charge that does."[76]

One way to implement *Padilla* is by requiring prosecutors to consider immigration status in plea bargaining. Office-wide guidelines that define parameters for considering when punishment is disproportionate to the crime can make clear to line prosecutors that immigration status is something that they should consider in arriving at a just case outcome. As Norman Abrams has argued, internal guidelines for prosecutor offices are a recognized tool for achieving "tolerable consistency" and efficiency in the exercise of prosecutorial discretion.[77] Professor Angela Davis has also expressed optimism about the potential for prosecutors to use their "power and discretion to help" improve the criminal justice system by implementing internal policies that constrain potential bad actors.[78] Davis has shown how the problem of racial discrimination in drug prosecutions can be addressed by creating an office-wide policy to refer arrestees to drug treatment programs in lieu of pursuing criminal charges against them.[79]

With expanded awareness of immigration consequences, some prosecutor offices have begun to address the issue of deportation in their office policies on

---

[72] Padilla v. Kentucky, 130 S. Ct. 1473 (2010) (holding that a defense attorney's failure to advise his client of the immigration consequence of a guilty plea falls below the minimum standard for effective counsel).

[73] *Id.* at 1480. [74] *Id.* at 1486. [75] *Id.* [76] *Id.*

[77] Norman Abrams, *Internal Policy: Guiding the Exercise of Prosecutorial Discretion*, 19 UCLA L. REV. 1, 7 (1970).

[78] Davis, *supra* note 46, at 823. [79] *Id.* at 840.

plea bargaining.[80] For example, the Los Angeles District Attorney's Office allows prosecutors to consider collateral consequences, including deportation, when plea bargaining on low-level felonies and misdemeanors. Under the written policy, deviation from standard settlement rules is considered to be "in the interest of justice" when "indirect or collateral consequences to the defendant in addition to the direct consequences of the conviction" constitute "unusual or extraordinary circumstances."[81] Negotiating a collateral consequence under the policy could involve a "lateral move," meaning a plea to an equally serious crime as initially charged that does not carry an adverse immigration consequence. Alternatively, it could involve bargaining over the sentence imposed. For instance, something as small as a sentence of 364 days instead of 365 days can mean the difference between deportation and saving one's lawful immigrant status.[82]

In conclusion, collateral consequences policies help to foster plea bargaining that incorporates an awareness of immigration consequences. As Heidi Altman has argued, such programs "normalize" the practice of crafting "alternative plea offers" for noncitizens that will "preserve noncitizen defendants' immigration status."[83] Their expansion to a growing number of prosecutor offices is a notable step forward in promoting transparency in criminal justice decisionmaking and fair treatment of immigrants in plea bargaining.

B *Empowering Criminal Court Judges to Adjudicate Immigration Outcomes*

Internal prosecutorial policies requiring line deputies to consider collateral sanctions in plea bargaining offer considerable promise for curbing prosecutorial overzealousness in the immigration arena. However, such a solution is necessarily incomplete. It would be unrealistic to expect self-regulation to eliminate the pervasive problem of prosecutorial overreaching. Additional checks and balances are needed to promote democratic values. One such solution, as Bill Stuntz argued, is to enhance judicial oversight of

---

[80] *See* Ingrid V. Eagly, *Immigrant Protective Policies in Criminal Justice*, 95 Tex. L. Rev. 245, 264–71 (2016) (discussing four California prosecutor offices that have adopted model collateral consequences policies).

[81] Special Directive 03-04 from Steve Cooley, Dist. Attorney, L.A. Cnty., to All Deputy Dist. Attorneys (Sept. 25, 2003), libguides.law.ucla.edu/ld.php?content_id=13655226.

[82] For example, a misdemeanor crime of violence is an "aggravated felony" under the immigration law (and thus a bar to most all forms of immigration relief) so long as the judge sentences the defendant to a term of imprisonment of at least a year. INA § 101(a)(43)(F), 8 U.S.C. § 1101 (a)(43)(F).

[83] Heidi Altman, *Prosecuting Post-*Padilla: *State Interests and the Pursuit of Justice for Noncitizen Defendants*, 101 Geo. L.J. 1, 9 (2012).

prosecutors to ensure that punishment is "fair and proportionate given the defendant's criminal conduct."[84]

Until 1990, sentencing judges were empowered to ameliorate the often harsh immigration consequence of a conviction. Under the procedure, known as a Judicial Recommendations Against Deportation ("JRAD"), immigrants could petition the criminal court judge to issue an order precluding the immigration agency from using the conviction as a basis for deportability. When such an order was granted, it was binding on the immigration agency, and the immigrant could not be deported.[85]

Judicial authority to adjudicate immigration outcomes through the JRAD process was never fully implemented because most criminal defense lawyers did not know that the provision existed.[86] However, Congress abandoned the JRAD program in 1990,[87] leaving the sole authority over relief from crime-based deportation with immigration judges. At the same time, the forms of relief from deportation available to immigration judges have been drastically narrowed by other legislative amendments. Over the years, the number of criminal deportations has increased: 139,950 immigrants with criminal convictions were removed in 2015, compared to 92,380 in 2004.[88]

Judith Resnik has argued that modern courts, and the judges presiding over them, are core democratic institutions.[89] However, this democratic function is possible only when judges are given the authority to act independently in deciding their cases. Without a JRAD-type procedure, criminal court judges can only rule on the criminal aspect of punishment, yet lack any direct authority to mitigate the resulting deportation outcome.

Reviving the JRAD program is one possible policy change that could help restore the independence of sentencing judges to mitigate disproportionate

---

[84] William J. Stuntz, *The Rise of Plea Bargaining and the Decline of the Rule of Law* in CRIMINAL PROCEDURE STORIES 351 (Carol S. Steiker & Pamela S. Karlan eds., 2006).

[85] DAN KESSELBRENNER & LORY D. ROSENBERG, IMMIGRATION LAW AND CRIMES (2015), Appendix A1, Judicial Recommendations Against Deportation Prior to November 29, 1990 (citing Velez-Lozano v. INS, 463 F.2d 1305 (D.C. Cir. 1972)).

[86] Margaret H. Taylor & Ronald F. Wright, *The Sentencing Judge as Immigration Judge*, 51 EMORY L.J. 1131, 1148 (2002) (explaining that the JRAD procedure was not widely understood by practicing attorneys and courts).

[87] Immigration Act of 1990, Pub. L. No. 101–649, § 505, 104 Stat. 4978 (1990).

[88] U.S. DEP'T OF HOMELAND SEC., 2015 YEARBOOK OF IMMIGRATION STATISTICS tbl.41 (2015), www.dhs.gov/immigration-statistics/yearbook/2015#* (reporting that the number of criminal deportations reached as high as 200,143 in 2012).

[89] Judith Resnick, *Reinventing Courts as Democratic Institutions*, 143 DÆDALUS 9 (2014) (arguing "that courts have themselves become sites of democracy because the particular and peculiar practices of adjudication produce, redistribute, and curb power among disputants who disagree in public about the import of legal rights").

punishment of noncitizens charged with crimes. Margaret Taylor and Ronald Wright have set forth a compelling case for the JRAD's resurrection, arguing that judges presiding over criminal cases are well situated to make case-specific decisions regarding whether deportation ought to flow from the conviction.[90] Immigration scholar Stephen Lee has praised JRADs as "an intriguing alternative to the current prosecutor-centered" system of control over immigration.[91] Even the United States Supreme Court has spoken glowingly of the JRAD program. As Justice Stevens wrote for the majority in *Padilla*, JRADs provided a "critically important procedural protection to minimize the risk of unjust deportation."[92]

When deportation is allowed to proceed without consideration of the merits of the immigrant's case, what Angela Banks calls "disproportionate deportation" may occur.[93] Allowing sentencing judges to ameliorate deportation consequences by considering factors such as length of residence, community ties, and the seriousness of the criminal offense is therefore a critical step in tempering the immigration powers of public prosecutors. In addition, empowering sentencing judges to grant immigration relief in worthy cases might reduce prosecutorial incentives to use the criminal court as a venue for securing deportation.

C Expanding Access to Defense Counsel for Noncitizens

As the previous discussion demonstrated, the availability of judicial override may restrain some of practices described in Part I of this chapter. Yet, the criminal justice system in the United States is built on an adversarial ideal, within which defense lawyers play a pivotal role.[94] As Máximo Langer points out, defense attorneys have "the burden of persuading the prosecutor" that an alternative case disposition is just and equitable.[95] Ensuring that this burden is

---

[90] Taylor & Wright, *supra* note 86, at 1184. More recently, Jason Cade has renewed the call for a JRAD procedure, pointing out that a sentencing judge's recommendation against deportation "could serve as a disproportionality rule of thumb, tempering and refining the role that criminal history plays" in deportation decisions. Jason A. Cade, *Return of the JRAD*, 90 N.Y.U. L. REV. ONLINE 36, 39 (2015).

[91] Stephen Lee, *De Facto Immigration Courts*, 101 CALIF. L. REV. 553, 598 (2013).

[92] Padilla, 130 S. Ct. at 1479.

[93] Angela M. Banks, *The Normative and Historical Cases for Proportional Deportation*, 62 EMORY L.J. 1243, 1298 (2013). *See also* Juliet Stumpf, *Fitting Punishment*, 66 WASH. & LEE L. REV. 1683, 1722–25 (2009); Michael J. Wishnie, *Immigration Law and the Proportionality Requirement*, 2 U.C. IRVINE L. REV. 415 (2012).

[94] As Professor Langer argues, in practice, the United States criminal justice system is more of a "unique hybrid between both adversarial and inquisitorial conceptions of the criminal process[.]" Langer, *supra* note 17, at 226.

[95] *Id.* at 261.

taken on competently and zealously – particularly in the case of noncitizen clients – requires public investment in training and support for defense services.

Criminal defendants unable to afford their own attorney have long enjoyed the constitutional right to the appointment of counsel in felony cases.[96] As recently as 2002, the Supreme Court affirmed that even petty offense cases require counsel if they expose the defendant to possible incarceration.[97] However, the quality of criminal defense in the United States is notoriously inadequate.[98] For example, in Florida, every public defender carries an astonishing 500 felonies and 2,225 misdemeanors per year.[99] A 2009 study conducted by the National Association of Criminal Defense Lawyers found each public defender in New Orleans handled almost 19,000 cases a year, which meant that, on average, attorneys only spent seven minutes on each case.[100] These enormous caseloads far exceed the maximum yearly number accepted in national guidelines for public defenders of 150 felonies or 400 misdemeanors per attorney.[101]

Given the funding crisis that has plagued public defender offices, it is little wonder that many offices have been unsuccessful in fully integrating *Padilla*'s mandate into their daily work. The complexity of immigration law has contributed to this challenge of providing accurate and timely advice to noncitizen clients. Yet, without adequate public defense, courts cannot function properly as open and democratic institutions that provide access for all that come before them.

In searching for a way forward, policymakers can look to model defender programs that have already developed effective programs for assisting their

---

[96] Gideon v. Wainwright, 372 U.S. 335 (1963). [97] Alabama v. Shelton, 535 U.S. 654 (2002).

[98] *See generally* Stephen B. Bright & Sia M. Sanneh, *Fifty Years of Defiance and Resistance After Gideon v. Wainright*, 122 YALE L. J. 2150 (2013).

[99] LAURENCE A. BENNER, WHEN EXCESSIVE PUBLIC DEFENDER WORKLOADS VIOLATE THE SIXTH AMENDMENT RIGHT TO COUNSEL WITHOUT A SHOWING OF PREJUDICE (Mar. 2011), www.acslaw.org/files/BennerIB_ExcessivePD_Workloads.pdf.

[100] ROBERT C. BORUCHOWITZ ET AL., MINOR CRIMES, MASSIVE WASTE: THE TERRIBLE TOLL OF AMERICA'S BROKEN MISDEMEANOR COURTS 21 (2009), www.nacdl.org/public.nsf/defen seupdates/misdemeanor/$FILE/Report.pdf. Given that funding for public defense often comes from local government revenues, the quality of public defender offices within states can also be quite uneven. Beth A. Colgan & Lisa R. Pruitt, *Justice Deserts: Spatial Inequality and Local Funding of Indigent Defense*, 52 ARIZ. L. REV. 219 (2010).

[101] These guidelines were introduced in a 1973 report by the National Advisory Commission on Criminal Justice Standards and Goals. *See* NAT'L RIGHT TO COUNSEL COMM., CONSTITUTION PROJECT, JUSTICE DENIED: AMERICA'S CONTINUING NEGLECT OF OUR CONSTITUTIONAL RIGHT TO COUNSEL (2009), www.constitutionproject.org/wp-content/up loads/2012/10/139.pdf.

noncitizen clients to achieve immigration-safe case results. Thea Johnson's empirical study of public defenders in four states reveals the myriad of ways that public defenders representing noncitizens must engage in "creative plea bargaining" to "piece together" a plea that addresses the priorities of their immigrant clients.[102] Some of these public defender offices have immigration experts working within the defender office. With this embedded-expert approach, the immigration specialist is "physically present" in the office and available to conduct training and work directly with clients.[103] Andrés Kwon argues that this kind of holistic in-house representation "foster[s] a culture and practice of seamless integration of criminal and civil immigration defense."[104]

Even without additional funding, public defender offices may be able to improve their immigrant representation by devoting a greater proportion of their scarce resources to misdemeanor cases.[105] As Irene Joe's insightful analysis reveals, public defender offices have traditionally invested the majority of their resources in handling felony cases, not low-level misdemeanors.[106] However, misdemeanors are massive in number and carry significant collateral penalties that wreak havoc on clients' lives.[107] Joe advocates that public

---

[102] Thea Johnson, *Measuring the Creative Plea Bargain*, 92 IND. L. J. 901 (2017).

[103] *See* PETER L. MARKOWITZ, PROTOCOL FOR THE DEVELOPMENT OF A PUBLIC DEFENDER IMMIGRATION SERVICE PLAN, IMMIGRANT DEF. PROJECT & N.Y. ST. DEF. ASS'N 1, 5 (2009), www.immdefense.org/wp-content/uploads/2011/03/Protocol.pdf. *See also* Ronald F. Wright, *Padilla and the Delivery of Integrated Criminal Defense*, 58 UCLA L. REV. 1515 (2011).

[104] Andrés Dae Keun Kwon, *Defending Criminal(ized) "Aliens" After Padilla: Toward a More Holistic Public Immigration Defense in the Era of Crimmigration*, 63 UCLA L. REV. 1035 (2016).

[105] A misdemeanor is generally defined as an offense for which the punishment may not exceed one year. Misdemeanors often result in sanctions other than incarceration, such as fines, community service, or supervision by a probation officer. *See generally* Beth A. Colgan, *Reviving the Excessive Fines Clause*, 102 CALIF. L. REV. 277 (2014) (documenting the harmful consequences of fines for those unable to afford them, including incarceration, exclusion from public benefits, and persistent poverty); Issa Kohler-Hausmann, *Misdemeanor Justice: Control without Conviction*, 119 AM. J. SOC. 351, 352 (2013) (arguing that misdemeanors and lower-level infractions or code violations represent the "modal criminal justice encounter" and reveal how the criminal justice system "operates as a mode of social control").

[106] Irene Oritseweyinmi Joe, *Rethinking Misdemeanor Neglect*, 64 UCLA L. REV. 738 (2017). *See also* Alexandra Natapoff, *Misdemeanors*, 85 S. CAL. L. REV. 1313, 1315 (2012) (explaining that while "serious felonies get closer to the gold standard of due process," misdemeanors suffer from underfunding and either no counsel or attorneys who can only provide "scant attention" to their clients).

[107] For immigrants, even these minor cases can result in lifetime banishment. *See generally* Jason A. Cade, *The Plea-Bargain Crisis for Noncitizens in Misdemeanor Court*, 34 CARDOZO L. REV. 1751 (2013); Jordan Cunnings, *Nonserious Marijuana Offenses and Noncitizens: Uncounseled Pleas and Disproportionate Consequences*, 62 UCLA L. REV. 510 (2015);

defender offices respond by "emphasizing misdemeanor representation even at the expense of felonies."[108]

A few visionary public defender offices have taken the extra step of continuing their representation beyond the criminal court to provide representation on immigration matters in immigration court. For example, attorneys at The Bronx Defenders provide comprehensive immigration legal representation for their clients charged with crimes, including by representing them on petitions for relief from deportation in immigration court.[109] Such immigration services are vitally needed. Nationally, only fourteen percent of detained immigrants are represented by counsel,[110] and a mere two percent of immigrants obtain free legal services from a nonprofit or pro bono attorney.[111] For those detained immigrants who do not obtain counsel, removal is virtually guaranteed: ninety-eight percent are ordered removed.[112]

Without representation, poor immigrants facing removal based on criminal convictions may be advised by their public defender that they are technically eligible for relief, but remain unable to secure such relief due to the lack of counsel. A pioneering new program known as the New York Immigrant Family Unity Project has taken on this problem. With funding from the City Council of New York City, public defenders now provide universal representation to noncitizens who are detained and facing removal.[113] This kind of initiative will be closely studied and serve as a model for other public defender offices seeking to expand services for immigrants.[114]

Jenny Roberts, *Why Misdemeanors Matter: Defining Effective Advocacy in the Lower Criminal Courts*, 45 U.C. DAVIS L. REV. 277 (2011).

[108] Joe, *supra* note 106.

[109] Kwon, *supra* note 104, at 1042. *See also* Robin Steinberg, *Heeding* Gideon's *Call in the Twenty-First Century: Holistic Defense and the New Public Defense Paradigm*, 70 WASH. & LEE L. REV. 961 (2013) (describing the practice of holistic defense at The Bronx Defenders).

[110] Ingrid V. Eagly & Steven Shafer, *A National Study of Access to Counsel in Immigration Court*, 164 U. PA. L. REV. 1, 32 (2015).

[111] *Id.* at 27–28 & fig. 5.

[112] *Id.* at 49–50 & fig. 14. Even after controlling for other factors that could affect case outcome, immigrants with attorneys fare far better; among similarly situated removal respondents, the odds are fifteen times greater that immigrants with representation, as compared to those without, seek relief from removal, and five-and-a-half times greater that they obtain such relief. *Id.* at 9.

[113] NEW YORK IMMIGRANT FAMILY UNITY PROJECT, GOOD FOR FAMILIES, GOOD FOR EMPLOYERS, AND GOOD FOR ALL NEW YORKERS, www.populardemocracy.org/sites/default/fi les/immgrant_family_unity_project_print_layout.pdf (last visited May 8, 2017) (explaining that public defender offices – The Bronx Defenders, Brooklyn Defender Services, and the Legal Aid Society of New York – were selected to provide universal representation to immigrants).

[114] *See* Robert A. Katzmann, *When Legal Representation Is Deficient: The Challenge of Immigration Cases for the Courts*, 143 DÆDALUS 37, 45 (2014) (noting that "organizations across the country" have expressed interest in implementing the New York model).

Finally, some public defender offices have found that they are better able to meet the needs of their immigrant clients by embracing a new defense model known as participatory defense.[115] This organizing model involves families and communities affected by the criminal justice system in seeking fundamental change. In the words of community organizer Raj Jayadev, participatory defense seeks to challenge the "unspoken belief" that "when a case hits the judicial process," community members cannot "effect change."[116] One example of an activity taken on by participatory defense organizers is creating "social biography videos" that document the life history of the person facing criminal charges. Assisted by these community-produced videos, public defenders can advocate more effectively – they have secured release for their clients pending trial, convinced prosecutors to offer immigration-safe pleas, and persuaded judges that more lenient sentences are warranted.[117] Cutting-edge public defenders in Alabama, California, Pennsylvania, Missouri, Kentucky, and Washington have embraced participatory defense,[118] helping to make the criminal justice system more responsive to what is happening on the ground and, ultimately, more democratic.[119]

CONCLUSION

This chapter has argued that the criminal justice system should be grounded in core democratic principles, including equal treatment, accountability, and transparency. Moreover, these democratic principles should be applied to all

---

[115] See Janet Moore et al., *Make Them Hear You: Participatory Defense and the Struggle for Criminal Justice Reform*, 78 ALB. L. REV. 1281 (2015). On the imperative of training future public defenders to work directly with subordinated communities, see Gerald P. López, *Training Future Lawyers to Work with the Politically and Socially Subordinated: Anti-Generic Legal Education*, 91 W. VA. L. REV. 305 (1989).

[116] Raj Jayadev, *The Story of Participatory Defense*, SILICON VALLEY DE-BUG, May 22, 2015, www.siliconvalleydebug.org/articles/2015/05/22/story-participatory-defense.

[117] Moore et al., *supra* note 115, at 1286.

[118] David Bornstein, *Guiding Families to a Fair Day in Court*, N.Y. TIMES, May 29, 2015, www .opinionator.blogs.nytimes.com/2015/05/29/guiding-poor-families-to-a-fair-day-in-court/?_r=0.

[119] A substantial body of research has shown that communities that feel a public institution, such as a public defender office, is working for them are more likely to perceive the system as legitimate. See, e.g., E. ALLAN LIND & TOM R. TYLER, THE SOCIAL PSYCHOLOGY OF PROCEDURAL JUSTICE 106 (1988) ("The perception that one has had an opportunity to express oneself and to have one's views considered by someone in power plays a critical role in fairness judgments."); Jonathan D. Casper et al., *Procedural Justice in Felony Cases*, 22 LAW & SOC'Y REV. 483, 503 (1988) (finding that defendants' evaluations of their treatment in court "do not appear to depend exclusively upon the favorability of their sentences," but are also "substantially influenced" by "their sense of fairness – in terms of both procedural and distributive justice").

defendants, according to universal membership rules that do not delineate between citizens and noncitizens. Achieving this result requires a multipronged approach to decouple criminal prosecution from punitive reliance on the membership rules of the immigration system. Guidelines for prosecutors are a start, but it is also necessary to enhance the supervisory authority of judges and to adequately fund and train public defenders to do their vital work. Other complementary reforms beyond those discussed in this chapter could also be pursued, such as amending the immigration law to make lawful immigrant status easier to gain and harder to lose. Ultimately, changes in both the criminal and immigration systems are necessary to foster a criminal law that rejects formal rules of citizenship as a legitimate starting point for allocating the substantive law and procedural protections of the criminal justice system.

9

Beyond Tough on Crime: Towards a Better Politics of Prosecution

Jonathan Simon[1]

I DEMOCRACY, PENAL POLICY AND AMERICAN PROSECUTORS

Criminal justice reform has emerged as one of the defining issues of this decade, headlined by the festering overcrowding and poor health in our prisons and the casual sacrifice of young Black lives by our police. Historically, "policy windows" opened because of a conjuncture of developments in different places within the established order, problems in existing institutions, new ways of representing a problem of solving it, as well as political alignments (Kingdon 1984). With this new wave of interest, the first in decades to be concerned with downsizing and rebalancing our distended carceral state,[2] a host of new alliances have emerged, pairing forces once considered solidly supportive of "tough on crime" policies with grassroots and NGO opponents of mass incarceration (Aviram 2015; Gottschalk 2015). What Ian Loader and Richard Sparks called for in their important 2010 monograph, *Public Criminology?*, "a better politics of crime and punishment", seems to be emerging. But with some exceptions, prosecutors, the most important actors in the criminal justice system, and the most politically successful, have been notably absent from the visible leadership of the reform camp.[3]

---

[1] Adrian A. Kragen Professor of Law, Faculty Director, Center for the Study of Law & Society.

[2] This concept helpfully encompasses both penal and police institutions and much else; see Fortner 2013.

[3] Consider one example; the recent *Leaders in Law Enforcement* alliance, launched in conjunction with the liberal reform-oriented Brennan Center at NYU Law School, bills itself as an alliance of police, sheriffs and prosecutors, but few of the "leaders" identified on its website are currently serving prosecutors. Only one, Cyrus Vance, the Manhattan District Attorney, is listed among the steering committee.

Perhaps this should not be surprising. Few actors in the criminal justice system benefitted more from mass incarceration in increased power in both the criminal justice system and beyond than prosecutors (Stuntz 2013; Simon 2007; Lacey & Soskice 2015). "Tough on crime" became a successful posture for prosecutors in the era of rising violent crime and increasing voter concern, leading other politicians to compete for aligning themselves with the same values and capacities. Not enough has changed, at least at the voting booth, to fundamentally alter that. Indeed, few electorally sensitive actors in the system are as exposed to the risk of blame for acts of leniency than prosecutors. Furthermore, while considerable criticism and direct challenges to legitimacy have been raised with regard to the police and to mass imprisonment, few prosecutors have so far come under similar challenge. For the most part, prosecutors escape blame for the excesses of police and prisons, even though they are among the most responsible for them. Yet prosecutors are also at risk of losing their authority through law with defendants and juries if they ignore growing popular discontent with the supersized and aggressive version of the carceral state that has accumulated. Prosecutorial power is legal power through and through, and if the growing anger at police violence and correctional abuses turns into a larger crisis of legitimacy of the criminal law, prosecutors may find themselves reaping the whirlwind (to borrow the biblical metaphor, Hosea 8:7 Metzger and Murphy 1991, 1156).

Nationally, individual elected prosecutors in some large cities and two recent US Attorney Generals have become identified with the cause of criminal justice reform. In a number of major cities on the east and west coast particularly, self-described reform prosecutors have won elections, including the late Ken Thompson in Brooklyn (Feuer 2016), Marilyn Mosby in Baltimore (2016) and Craig Watkins in Dallas (Crain 2009), and are among the most widely discussed national figures. In San Francisco, the state's most liberal city, which has long had liberal prosecutors relatively parsimonious in their use of prison and generally abolitionist on the death penalty, two recent incumbents, Kamala Harris (Bazelon 2016) (then Attorney General of California and now its Senator) and her successor, George Gascón (Ho 2016), have taken a more visible role as criminal justice reform leaders. Just to the South, in equally liberal, but also traditionally suburban and crime-sensitive, Santa Clara County, District Attorney Jeffrey Rosen is another reformer (Herhold 2016). Gascón and Rosen were notably the only two DAs in California to publically endorse Proposition 47, the landmark ballot initiative approved by the voters in 2014 which led to thousands of prisoner releases and the elimination of felony charges for important low-level drug possession and property-related crimes. At the federal level, the second term of the

Obama Administration saw the Department of Justice (DOJ) become a significant champion of reform both under Eric Holder, and now his successor Loretta Lynch. In directives to US Attorneys, in testimony to Congress and in "Dear Colleague Letters" to court administrators in the states (DOJ 2016), both Holder and Lynch urged initiatives to reduce the use of incarceration for non-violent offenses and to change the government's relationship with formerly incarcerated Americans.

This is too small a sample of even reform-oriented DAs to make generalizations, but it is noteworthy that all but one of the prosecutors just named are from minority backgrounds (mostly Black). All are significantly younger than the DAs they replaced, mostly members of Obama's generation (trailing edge baby-boomers or Gen-Xers) and are appealing to still younger voters who are less obsessed with fear of crime than older voters. Many were elected after scandals weakened incumbents who faced little direct danger to their tough on crime policies. All face or faced real danger of losing because of opposition from police.

The minority (and particularly Black) experience of the carceral state in recent decades is an essential component of a potential reform prosecutorial model and I will return to it (Butler 2010). The primary focus of this paper, however, is on the values that reform prosecutors can use to become leaders in the next phase of criminal justice reform. A slogan that has been invoked by most of these prosecutors is the title of Kamala Harris's 2009 book, *Smart on Crime*. Rhetorically, it is an obvious rebuke to "tough on crime" and both a telling and potentially effective political slogan. As an alternative, it remains to be seen whether it can teach the public to think differently about crime and their political world in ways that reaffirm the old normative expectations or create new ones. Its main elements, thus far, are a focus on "recidivism," along with better empirical evidence to track it, a greater emphasis on re-entry as opposed to prison time and alternatives to incarceration for non-serious and non-violent crime, and providing social services such as providing poor families with training in parenting. It also suggests a broader intellectual strategy for aligning reform with prosecutorial authority and leadership.

A second program has only recently begun to emerge and has thus far gone unnamed, but might be called a dignity politics of prosecution, that emphasizes both social justice (especially racial inequality) and the humanity of those being prosecuted. One intellectual major source of this is the growing empirical research showing that procedural justice enhances the legitimacy of even the most coercive state institutions (Tyler and Huo 2002). Another is the increasing strength of dignity as a constitutional value in US Supreme Court case law (*Brown v. Plata* 2011).

The tough on crime approach to prosecutorial politics, whatever its short-comings, was well-grounded in the crisis of legitimacy faced by penal welfar-ism during the crime wave years of the 1960s through the 1980s. Whether a better prosecutorial politics of crime is likely to emerge may depend in part on how far prosecutorial reform leaders are able to go in confronting the crisis of legitimacy that has emerged for the carceral state since the beginning of this decade.

In this chapter, I develop an account of prosecutorial values from the tough on crime era and consider the challenges that account is facing at present, as well as how more recent prosecutorial values like "smart on crime" and dignity may fare in addressing a growing legitimacy deficit at the centre of crim-inal law.

II VALUES, PROSECUTORS, AND LEGITIMACY IN THE US CARCERAL STATE

In the US, stark changes in penal policies and practices are generally driven by democratic processes. This means that however technical and insular these practices and policies may seem in normal times, transformations are inevi-tably political and rooted in crises of legitimacy. Forty years ago, when "penal welfarism" underwent a legitimacy crisis, democratic processes were very much part of it, including legislation (and voter initiatives where those were available) to abolish parole and lengthen prison sentences, judicial recalls, and constitutional amendments to restore the death penalty. The high degree of democracy in US penal transformations has gone along with penal severity as a competitive penal populism swept the political field (Simon 2007; see also Garland 2001; Stuntz 2011). The "tough on crime" version of crime policy that emerged in the 1980s in response to this crisis produced mass incarceration and the punitive style of policing that has become dominant in many US cities. It went along with a newly resonant value that prosecutors became the major symbol of: public safety. Today, while public safety remains a central public value, the "tough on crime" version of the carceral state is experiencing what looks very much like its own legitimacy crisis (Simon draft). Once again, democratic processes seem very much in evidence, including reform proposi-tions and legislation, demonstrations and competitive electoral politics of reform (Gottshalk 2015).

Prosecutors in the US model sit at the centre of this surfeit of electoral democracy. Accountable to a rarely roused local electorate, prosecutors enjoy the most untrammelled discretion available in modern government (with the possible exception of immigration policy, an increasingly parallel enterprise).

While other modern democracies tie the legitimacy of prosecution power to systemic legal controls (whether internally through rigorous administrative guidelines, or through transnational human rights norms), it comes down to politics (Brown 2016). Although perhaps rarely tested electorally (Wright 2012), the legitimacy of prosecution in the US is more political than it is legal. Even if reformers were to drive an ambitious program of legally constraining the prosecution function in the future, contemporary prosecutors are likely to remain far more sensitive to politics than to law into the foreseeable future.

Whatever might be possible in more legally constrained penal systems, such as the European Community and its structure of human rights norms, substantial reform of the US carceral state will require democratic success. Prosecutors are likely to remain central to shaping those politics, as they were during the last crisis of penal legitimacy. In that case, those of us hoping for substantial reform must hope for what Ian Loader and Richard Sparks have called a "better politics" of crime and in this case a better prosecutorial politics.

Ian Loader (2014) has argued that the political influence of police consists largely in their ability to "teach citizens about the political world they inhabit." This is even more true of prosecutors in the US who tend to enjoy the leading role in the media's presentation of crime and its consequences. The politics of prosecution then consists not mostly of running for office, but in influencing how citizens and other actors in the carceral state imagine crime and the penal system and further in promoting a specific set of normative expectations about what political institutions can do about crime and how they should be judged.

The paradox that US prosecutors are globally unique in facing competitive elections, but almost never do (until recently), may be resolved in part by observing that the politics of prosecution are largely those of normative expectations. Election competition in most offices happens routinely, whether or not a crisis has arisen around that office. Voting an incumbent out of office does not necessarily or even usually suggest that the incumbent is seen as illegitimate, but rather that the competitor is preferred along a number of policy or personality dimensions. Recent campaigns aside, voting an incumbent prosecutor out of office has been exceptional and generally linked to a breach of broadly held normative expectations, such as by bungling a high-publicity prosecution or being exposed as unethical.

The study of normative expectations (Beetham 2013a,b) falls between the subjective feelings of a citizen or public actor about the exercise of the power to punish, and the philosophical principles that might follow logically from our commitments to democracy and rationality. Empirical social scientists study the former, while philosophers generally study the latter. Normative expectations are a hybrid, treating people as both having subjective feelings about the legitimacy of actors in the carceral state, but also reasons for those feelings that are brought into being or sustained by real historical and discursive conditions that produce both experiences (like fear of crime) and understandings. These feelings have substantive normative content also shaped by those conditions, values as lofty as human dignity or as indefensible as white supremacy.

III NORMATIVE EXPECTATIONS OF TOUGH ON CRIME

Beginning in the 1970s, the US carceral state's turn towards "tough on crime" was led at the local level by prosecutors who helped to promote through local and state politics a way of using criminal law to address the growing crisis of confidence in modern welfarist governance generally, and in the criminal justice realm in particular (Garland 2001). The penal welfarist penology of the 1970s was premised on an effort to classify prisoners correctly according to their criminogenic deviances and find the right treatment approach, or at least gauge their relative dangerousness. This promise came under pressure as rising crime, and a broader crisis of confidence in the ability of expert-based government to reform people convicted of serious crimes, brought penal welfarism and its key institutions, such as probation, parole boards and juvenile justice under attack.

Since most of these modern institutions were encroachments on the power of prosecutors to attain harsher punishment, the growing legitimacy crisis was an opportunity for prosecutors to redefine themselves as governing leaders in the drive to replace it. Tough on crime prosecutors, who emerged in California and across the country during the 1970s, framed their approach to respond to the scepticism about penal welfarism (Gilmore 2007; Campbell 2014). The latter had been particularly ambitious and dependent on external forms of knowledge and expertise. In place of psychological expertise about criminal dangerousness, prosecutors offered their own expertise and in alliance with the police, as judges of character and criminal record. In place of the administrative autonomy of parole boards, prosecutors offered their closeness to both crime victims and voters. In place of methods of identifying individual causes and solutions to criminal conduct, prosecutors offered their commitment to using the law to produce the maximum punishment and make incapacitation possible. The theme that came to summarize this whole package of policies was "public safety."

The political world that this prosecutorial politics communicates is one where citizens are endangered in their basic ability to move in the public or enjoy the fruits of their private success by high levels of serious and violent crimes, and in which the judicial and sentencing processes of penal welfarism have failed to do what is necessary to reduce that crime, namely incapacitate repeat criminals. This is a political world where part of the state – the judicial and parole authorities – have betrayed both the public and the other parts of the state – police, prosecutors and prison guards.[4] This is a political world narrowed by fear of violence to a battle line between friend and enemy drawn on the overlapping basis of class and race defined as criminal dangerousness.

The political lessons of this portrait of the world are ones that have greatly rewarded prosecutorial power. The first is the "presumption of dangerousness" towards the criminalized population. Any criminal conduct, no matter how minor, at least if carried out by a high-risk person, is too minor to negate the potential for violence. Fear of the next Charles Manson makes it plausible, at least in good times, to lock up even people convicted of minor crimes. The second is the presumption of competence on the part of law enforcement, and especially prosecutors. Even as the political power of tough on crime wanes, these presumptions remain powerful restraints on the radicalness of reform.

Against the insecurities of this world, tough on crime prosecutorial politics offered two essential promises to deliver public safety. First, to bond with police officers in a crime fighting alliance on behalf of crime victims against criminal defendants, their lawyers and the judges who sometimes rule in their favour (Van Cleve 2016). This alliance has meant that, despite their supervisory responsibilities over the police under codes of legal ethics, prosecutors almost uniformly act to validate police decisions and rarely investigate or question police tactics. The second was to promote incapacitation through incarceration as broadly as possible across the criminal population and for as long as possible, especially with serious, violent, or repeated crime. The success of this project was soon covered up by the even more florid political discourse about crime coming from politicians, but it helped to produce lasting parts of the contemporary intellectual context of crime reform that continue to operate as constraints on reform.

In addition to their commitment to public safety, prosecutors in the tough on crime era also aligned themselves with an emerging political and legal consensus in favour of a colour-blind conception of racial equality, one in which intentional discrimination against individuals on the basis of race or nationality was illegal, but structural forms of racial hierarchy maintenance

---

4 I am drawing here on my extended 2007 account of these developments.

are often acceptable (Haney Lopez 2010). This colour-blind version of equality has been so well-suited to mass incarceration with its astounding concentration of policing and punishment on people of colour (Alexander 2010) that it is easy to overlook that anti-discrimination, albeit in this narrowed form, remains a significant normative expectation that tough on crime prosecution politics promoted even while turning a blind eye to the racial profiling going on in policing (Van Cleve 2016). This allowed prosecutors throughout the period of growing incarceration to fend off most constitutional challenges to their enormous discretion. Tough on crime prosecution politics could both benefit from its close alignment with the police, and paradoxically from the perception that prosecutors were guardians of civil rights compared to police officers (who had a reputation for racial animus against Blacks and Latinos in the 1970s).

The distinctive features of the American prosecutor were well-adapted to rise in influence and autonomy within a penal environment created by the normative expectations of public safety with equality through an alliance of police and prosecutors to maximize imprisonment, and to the protection of civil rights through the oversight and discretion of prosecutors. As these expectations became hegemonic, prosecutors became the dominant actors, not only in the carceral, but as a model of executive authority in many, if not most, sectors of government and sometimes private organizations as well – during the social and political conjuncture opened up by the period of high crime rates and high incarceration rates. But there were to be consequences for sustainability of government, consequences that would only be largely masked until the crisis inside mass incarceration prisons made it visible since the turn of the century (Simon 2014). When that crisis finally crashed through the strong habits of the judiciary and mainstream journalism against noticing the conditions of imprisonment, it exposed major deficits in the legitimacy of prosecutors; specifically, on the grounds that they over-punished people who posed less serious risk to public safety and did so on the basis of race[5]. At the beginning of this decade, a wave of criticism and calls for reform of the carceral state emerged, but prosecutors were largely out of the direct line of fire. Instead, it was correctional officers and managers who were blamed for overcrowding, poor medical care and mental health treatment, and for using violence or extreme discipline to maintain order (*Brown v. Plata*, 2011; Simon 2014). It was police officers and their managers who were blamed for killing unarmed people. More recently, courts and their

---

[5] It is true that the Supreme Court gave prosecutors near-immunity for racial patterns of excessive punishment in *McCleskey v. Kemp* (1987) 481 US 279.

practices of financing themselves through the exaction of legal fines and fees from the same largely poor, regularly criminalized population have come to public notice and withering criticism for a logic that is both predatory and plainly unrelated to crime reduction objectives (Civil Rights Division 2015; Gupta 2016).

While prosecutors as a class have thus far escaped much blame for any of these,[6] the crisis of legitimacy in policing, courts and corrections cannot long escape them; indeed, they sit at the very centre. Even more importantly, retaining the current version of tough on crime politics risks positioning prosecutors badly against a new historical experience of crime and the carceral state, and an attendant revaluing of normative expectations comparable in scope to the one that swept away penal welfarism in the 1970s (Hall et al. 1979; Garland 2001). If so, the normative expectations which prosecutors helped create a generation ago may now undermine them in two ways. First, as the signalling about the nature of crime and the polity that tough on crime prosecutors perfected in the 1990s comes increasingly out of alignment with the experiences and competing fears of the rising generations, the very normative expectations that prosecutors created in the past – their close alliance with the police and their total commitment to maximize imprisonment – may become major vulnerabilities, while their commitment to colour-blind equality, long compromised by public fear of crime, may become a central charge against individual prosecutors (who may find themselves facing suddenly competitive races) and the broader profession. Second, if new normative expectations emerge from the present moment of crime politics, the natural features of the American prosecutor, the autonomy and discretion that comes with being a locally elected executive, may play far less well than was the case during the past several decades.

Nationally, reform prosecutors have emphasized a number of policy changes that distinguish them from the tough on crime version of prosecutorial politics. Roughly, these break down into two categories. One is concerned with racial justice and dignity, reflected in new units to investigate wrongful convictions (Feuer 2016) and the prosecution of police for unjustified killings of Black citizens (Hylton 2016). The other is concerned with greater efficiency and diminishing the severity of punishment (Harris 2009; Bazelon 2016).

---

[6] As John Pfaff (2012) has argued, even academic critics of mass incarceration tended to overlook prosecutors.

VI THE PROSECUTORIAL POLITICS OF SMART ON CRIME

Smart on crime (Harris 2009) is more than a good slogan. Like community policing, it contains a whole complex of ways of talking about and acting on crime and the carceral state, along with new or refined normative commitments. At the heart of these is the promise to better manage the carceral state and reduce its size and cost without jeopardizing public safety. Each might be thought of as elements of a potential politics for the present era, rather than the politics of tough on crime.

Return on Investment

There has been a major emphasis across the reform movement on economic rationality (Aviram 2015; Gottschalk 2015). Being smart on crime, like being smart with money, generally means maximizing "return on investment." In a Neoliberal age, no concept is more powerful than that government should seek the same kind of return on investment that private businesses seek from their expenditures. Mass incarceration and punitive policing, from this perspective, along with measures like the death penalty, can be attacked as failing to deliver in public safety relative to their cost. Smart on crime prosecutors promise to act as managers of the criminal justice system, using their discretion to assure that costly measures like prisons are reserved for those persons who pose a sufficient enough risk of public safety, as in this quote from California Attorney General and former San Francisco DA Kamala Harris' contribution to a collection of high-profile political voices on reform (Harris 2015, 38).

> Instead of a one-size-fits-all justice system that responds to all crime as equal, we need a "Smart on Crime" approach – one that applies innovative, data-driven methods to make our system more efficient and effective.

The language of return on investment, like "efficient and effective," is also a way of signalling about the nature of crime and the nature of the political community. If crime investments, especially those on policing, prosecuting and incarcerating, are just like every other public and private investment, we are already in a different political world than that signalled by tough on crime prosecutors since the 1970s. Then, crime victims, and those who could credibly speak for them to law-makers, were perceived as privileged subjects of democratic government, not to be thrown in with the bargaining politics of welfare, education, highways and the thousands of other ways modern administrations govern.[7]

The end of the era of budgetary exceptionalism for many law and order expenses, much-heralded across the political spectrum, may mark a longer term shift in the politics of crime and punishment. If nothing else, it invites the subjects of this discourse to develop normative expectations more in line with the objectives framed by other aspects of government, rather than the largely faith-based premise that mass incarceration keeps crime contained.

While the language of return on investment may help produce a better politics of prosecution, it is not clear how much of a break it represents with the tradition of tough on crime prosecution politics, normatively speaking. Tough on crime prosecutors never doubted that their exercise of discretion was producing a sound return on investment, especially when the values imputed a high risk of potential violence and a high estimate of the economic cost of violence. More importantly, just where the arguments about return on investment might have the most consequence for reducing incarceration costs (both human and financial), i.e., in reconsidering the incapacitative value of long prison sentences for violent crime, virtually all of the smart on crime prosecutors stop short. Harris, for example, defines as one of the pillars of her strategy "maintain[ing] a relentless focus on reducing violence and prosecuting violent criminals" even while seeking early intervention and rehabilitation for others (2015, 38).

Evidence-based Empiricism (Recidivism)

One of the most intriguing aspects of the smart on crime vision of prosecution is its emphasis on data and "evidence-based" policies (Gottschalk 2015). The tough on crime era was characterized by a negative approach towards empirical data and social scientific expertise. Prosecutors (and other law enforcement and correctional actors) claimed the superiority of their own experiential knowledge of the criminal class (as well as that of frontline police officers), and saw little added value in testing those "findings" through social science. At the beginnings of the last major paradigm crisis of the carceral state, penal welfarism was badly undercut by the perception (often misleading) that empirical research showed that "nothing works in prison rehabilitative programming and parole supervision, that could drive down stubbornly persistent

---

[7]   Of course, this privileged crime victims only in their demands for more punitive justice and generally more prison, a feedback loop that further strengthened the legitimacy of tough on crime prosecutors who were the only government actors who could directly deliver that.

'recidivism rates'" (Simon 1993). In rejecting evidence-based empiricism, and largely ignoring the issue of recidivism, tough on crime prosecutors successfully insulated themselves from any real accountability. The only statistic that the public might even possibly know about the local prosecutors was their conviction rate (Sklansky 2016).

It is thus quite significant that "smart on crime" prosecutors have made the embrace of empirical research such a signature part of their prosecutorial politics. The focus on recidivism has gone along with efforts to channel many of those convicted of non-violent offenses away from prison or even jail, a strategy that can then be tested by studies of recidivism, an approach that Kamala Harris introduced to much fanfare in San Francisco (Bazelon 2016).

It is clear that this concession is one that responds implicitly to the crisis of mass incarceration. Smart on crime prosecutors concede that the tough on crime era involved irrational and unjustifiable uses of penal severity. San Francisco District Attorney George Gascón, for example, writing in an editorial in favour of Proposition 47, speaks collectively for prosecutors in the era of tough on crime and implicitly for the overwhelming majority of elected prosecutors who refused to join him in supporting the proposition. "We have lost our ability to distinguish the dangerous from the nuisance. We can no longer afford – either economically or socially – to be merely the tough guys. It's time to start also being the smart guys."[8]

The greater concern is whether social science can provide the answers necessary to produce consensus on the proper degree of downsizing the carceral state ought to undergo through reform. The proper scale of imprisonment or any other component of the carceral state (arrests, probations, fines), is ultimately as much a normative and political judgment as it is a matter of empirics. Consider recidivism, which California's highest-profile smart on crime prosecutor, Attorney General Kamala Harris, made her signature issue as AG; not reducing, but defining it (Harris 2015). Harris created a new Division of Recidivism Reduction and Reentry (DR3). In October 2014, she created a new state-wide scientific definition of recidivism to standardize the use of the term throughout the state. The term has been loosely used to include quite different outcomes for people on parole or probation-type community service, from violating a condition that becomes known only through the monitoring of the supervising agent (technical violations), arrests for new suspected crimes (even insufficient evidence is available to go forward on new charges that may support a violation of one or more of the general conditions of supervision), convictions for a new crime (by a court) or being

---

[8] www.sacbee.com/opinion/op-ed/article2617783.html#storylink=cpy.

re-incarcerated as a result of that conviction or on the basis of an administrative decision to revoke parole or probation. AG Harris' solution, one likely to be embraced by social scientists, is to count it all.

While more knowledge may be helpful to making the normative decision about how to scale the level of the carceral state, it is even more likely to be a product of those decisions (or prior ones). Whether decision-makers in either the administrative system (parole and probation agents and administrators) or the courts (prosecutors and trial judges) decide to use technical conditions to "violate" and re-incarcerate a person to seek incarceration as a sentence for a new criminal conviction, is the most significant factor in whether "recidivism" rates go up or down.[9]

Then the readiness of both parole authorities and courts to send large numbers of people to prison was largely baked into the common sense about how to bring down persistently high crime rates. Today, much of that common sense has been discredited and elements of a new common sense (Garland 2001; Simon 2014) are evident in many places, including in the discourse of smart on crime prosecutors. It remains to be seen how much this new common sense can change routines. It has been helpful that many of those routines have been disrupted (for example, the shift of most California prisoners from state parole supervision upon release to county-level probation supervision), but no one should underestimate the potential for pro-incarceration routines to re-establish themselves (perhaps now jail rather than prison). The main point, however, is that it is far from clear how counting recidivism better can shape the outcome of that struggle one way or the other.

The empirical prosecutor is an improvement over the "know nothing" mentality that was worn with pride by some tough on crime prosecutors. However, there is a strong tendency in the history of the liberal state for social science to substitute for real engagement with the multiple publics to whom prosecution is addressed, and there is a risk of that here as well. Evidence-based or intelligence-based prosecution is an effort to leverage social science techniques to address the legitimacy deficit that has opened up under the extraordinary discretion of prosecutors. Shoring up the legitimacy of criminal law is a perfectly sensible, indeed critical, thing for smart on crime prosecution

---

[9]   When I undertook a qualitative (and small quantitative) study of California's parole division in the late 1980s (Simon 1993), parole agents (and middle-level managers) were ready to send parolees back to the state's already overcrowded prisons for technical violations (not the first usually), something that was especially true for those without jobs and stable housing (most of those in the high-poverty areas I studied).

politics to take on, but it will be largely superficial (as CompStat programs are in many police departments) if it does not come along with normative expectations that can gain acceptance by both frontline prosecutors and the public audience of prosecution. Reducing recidivism is almost completely focused on the back end of the criminal process, re-entry and the possibility of new crimes. The focus on recidivism maintains the primary emphasis of tough on crime prosecution politics on the dangerous classes of criminals and the ability of prosecutors and police to pick the right ones. It so far says little about the front end where prosecutorial decisions to seek and obtain convictions produce the scale of the carceral state. New normative expectations for prosecutors and their publics would be more consequential. It is hard to credit Harris as Attorney General, or any other well-known public prosecutor, with making much progress on this front. California prosecutors have been involved in numerous scandals involving tampering with witnesses, failure to turn over exculpatory evidence, and abetting police misconduct. So entrenched is such behaviour that Judge Alex Kosinski, of the Ninth Circuit Court of Appeals, which takes federal habeas claims arising from California convictions, described the state as having a "culture of misconduct" in prosecution. Harris as Attorney General remained conspicuously silent on this. If instead she had taken an aggressive stand towards not defending convictions obtained by improper methods, the knowledge produced by "DR3" might make more of a difference to frontline prosecutors.

Transparency

Another normative expectation cultivated by some smart on crime prosecutors is that of transparency about prosecution priorities, an objective with a long history of academic advocacy (Sklansky 2016, 37). Perhaps the best example was the Obama administration's immigration program to limit the most severe consequences, incarceration and deportation, for whole categories of either criminal suspects or candidates for deportation.[10] In the immigration program, transparency combined with broad categorical exercises of discretion to create a modicum of order and security to people facing possible deportation. In a recent compilation of essays on criminal justice reform from political and law enforcement "leaders," Former Secretary Janet Napolitano pointed to this as a possible model in a recent volume devoted to ideas for reform.

---

[10] The immigration policy has now been ruled unconstitutional by virtue of a tie vote in *United States v. Texas*, 597 U.S. _____ (2016).

Early on at my time at DHS we issued a series of memos to Immigration and Customs (ICE) agents in the field, instructing them to focus their efforts on the "bad actors" – individuals who presented risks to national security, or who had committed felonies, or who had joined gangs, and so on. As for military veterans; long-time, law-abiding residents; nursing mothers; people with certain family ties; the severely ill; and Dreamers – policy memos issued by the ICE director made clear that these no longer fit the priorities (Napolitano 2015).[11]

The Department of Justice under former Attorney General Eric Holder issued directives on mandatory minimums intended to protect categories of non-violent drug defendants from the mandatory prison sentences built into the guidelines.[12] Implementation of the immigration program has been permanently suspended by the Supreme Court decision and it is not clear whether Holder's directives actually influence US Attorneys in the districts who retain considerable autonomy in current practice. Yet this kind of categorical and transparent exercise discretion is a significant departure from the logic of tough on crime prosecutors who demanded a kind of individualized discretion that could brook no structure of explanation and limitation, as in California's extreme Three Strikes law. Our common-law cousins, the English, have for some time had guidelines published by the Crown Prosecution Service, outlining how the Crown will use its discretion to charge serious crimes (Richman, this volume).

It is noteworthy that these initiatives have come in the waning years of a second-term presidential administration. So far, there is little evidence that this model is being taken up by local elected prosecutors or state Attorney Generals, but it offers a path towards a better politics of prosecution in so far as it invites a democratic political process around the enforcement priorities of the office, as well as a check on racial profiling in the exercise of discretion.

Smart on Crime

Smart on crime offers new kind of signal to the communities both in and outside the carceral state about the kind of political world we are living in than was communicated by tough on crime. This is a world with a considerably

---

[11] Whether this kind of structured discretion is actually discretion or simply law-making by administrative fiat is precisely what is at issue in the federal court battle over the Administration's effort to suspend deportation for whole categories of people subject to possible deportation action. See [add district and 5th Cir. Opinions].

[12] For AG Holder's directives on mandatory minimums and concern that it was being overridden by US Attorneys, see www.salon.com/2015/12/03/the_government_is_abusing_mandatory_mi nimums_how_law_enforcement_is_ruining_a_generation_of_americans/.

cooler climate, to use Loader and Spark's metaphor of penal heating. It is a world where the use of prison can be reduced for some crimes and where better reentry work can prevent costly future crimes and incarcerations. However, rather than telling a completely different story about crime, smart on crime prosecution draws a line between non-violent and unserious crime on the one hand, and violent and serious crime on the other. Smart techniques, apparently, can only be applied to the former. Meanwhile, the normative commitments remain largely intact. Prosecutors are expected to protect civil rights, but they remain in a close alliance with law enforcement machinery (at both state and federal levels) whose racial discrimination is increasingly visible. They promote a model of public safety less uniformly focused on incarceration for all crimes, but equally committed to the prison as tough on crime was for violent and serious crimes.

Even in California however, few prosecutors have been willing to support sentencing reform consistent with the smart on crime perspective. Especially notable was Proposition 47, a 2014 California ballot initiative that not only reclassified six "wobbler" crimes (chargeable as misdemeanours or felonies) as solely misdemeanours, but resulted in thousands of releases from prison or jail for people serving time under previous felony convictions for these offenses. This move, no matter how modest, was a clear assault on the tough on crime paradigm and a test of the political viability of the "smart on crime" model (which the ballot proponents emphasized). Only two of the reform-oriented prosecutors, George Gascón of San Francisco and Jeffrey Rosen of Santa Clara, supported the initiative. In breaking with the dominant law enforcement position on 47, both showed a willingness to test the success of an alternative politics of prosecution. The third, Kamala Harris, who had by then moved into the Attorney General's office, remained neutral on the measure, a move which she attributed to appropriate impartiality since the AG has a role in writing the precise ballot language used for referenda,[13] but which also avoided any conflict with law enforcement ahead of her senate run in 2016.

VI THE PROSECUTORIAL POLITICS OF DIGNITY

There seems to be a second cluster of prosecutorial politics emerging in response to the legitimacy crisis of the tough on crime carceral state. This cluster includes racial justice and "procedural justice" reforms, efforts to

---

[13] A position at least one of her predecessors described to a reporter (I cannot attribute either name) as "bullshit."

increase prosecutorial accountability for police racism and prison overcrowding, and efforts to humanize those who are being prosecuted and punished. It is not nearly as well-defined as "smart on crime," nor as easy to name and market, but it may pose a more radical departure from the politics of "tough on crime." I use the term "prosecutorial politics of dignity" because this cluster points to respect for human dignity and a deeper concern for equality than is reflected in colour-blind jurisprudence, as emergent legal values of our time. Dignity in this sense means taking steps to protect the humanity of all of those affected by the carceral state including: victims, people prosecuted and their communities. At the centre of this, one imagines a prosecutor who asserts leadership as the official most responsible for assuring this respect for dignity for victims and those accused and convicted across the system from arrest through incarceration and reentry.

Procedural Justice

Procedural justice proffers the simple idea that when legal authorities treat people in the legal process with more respect for their human dignity, those people feel more positively inclined to obey the law (as well as more positive about their experience with the law) (Tyler and Huo 2002). Delivering procedural justice in this sense can involve things as simple as giving people a hearing, treating them with personal respect, providing reasons for your decisions and appearing impartial. President Obama's Taskforce for 21st Century Policing and many of the nation's police chiefs have embraced procedural justice as basis for rethinking how police conduct citizen interactions, but few prosecutors have followed suit. This is surprising both because it is one of the most law-oriented approaches to reforming the carceral state (law has always promoted its virtues through procedures), as well as one of the most empirically supported approaches towards improving the perception of legitimacy. Perhaps prosecutors already rate highly in delivery of procedural justice, at least compared to the police, but there is little empirical study of this. In states like California with serious patterns of prosecutorial misconduct, it would seem respect for procedural justice values is low and could be, but has not been, a major focus for new prosecutorial leadership

Taking Responsibility for the Excesses of the Carceral State

Another current in prosecutorial politics is a revitalized sense of prosecutors as quasi-judicial overseers of the criminal process, and guarantors of its integrity against the potential excesses of policing and punishment. This was arguably always one of the normative commitments of prosecutors and is canonized in legal ethics where prosecutors are characterized as "ministers of justice" (Richman, this volume). During the tough on crime era, however, prosecutors played this down in favour of their special alliance with police and their commitment to mass imprisonment. The new moves seem intended both to put space between prosecutors and these other more disreputable parts of the carceral state and to use that distance to force institutional changes in those organs. While power grabs by prosecutors are not news, power grabs aimed at protecting the dignity of those criminalized and punished are.

Here, it is noteworthy that so many of the reform prosecutors are people of colour who identify with and openly cite the over-policing and punishment of communities of colour as a priority for reform. This is not the first wave of elected prosecutors of colour (although in some cities, they have been), but it is the first to make racial justice an explicit value for their offices.

One of the most visible arenas for this has been the reactivated use of investigatory powers over state and local police held by the Department of Justice under Attorney General Eric Holder. This power goes back to federal crime legislation in 1994 that in many ways fit the tough on crime prosecution politics model, but spurred by the Rodney King beating scandal and subsequent riot earlier in that decade, Congress gave new powers to the DOJ to investigate and, if necessary, sue police departments (Rushin 2014). In practice, these powers often lead to institutional reforms through the vehicle of a consent decree with enforceable powers. Already in use somewhat during the Clinton Administration, and less so under that of George W. Bush, Attorney General Holder embraced wider use of these investigatory powers to address a growing tide of complaints about police violence and racism.

These intensive investigations, usually prompted by patterns of lethal police shootings of people of colour, constitute an empiricism of a quite different sort than the "smart on crime" focus on recidivism statistics. In DOJ investigations, statistics are collected, but other means of audit and observation are also used to create a far more comprehensive portrait of police conduct. The resulting institutional reforms bypass the lengthy process of litigation over civil rights violations and can result in significant changes in training, internal investigations and deployments. The effectiveness of these reforms is highly complex to assess. But whatever their effects on police, DOJ investigations represent a strikingly different politics of prosecution, one in which the prosecutor is providing signals that help define the "political world we're in," to quote Loader again, but this time not just about crime, but about the carceral state itself.

More recently, and using a different mechanism of civil rights law, Vanita
Gupta, head of the Office of Civil Rights in DOJ, sent a "dear colleague" letter
(Gupta 2016) to court administrators across the country, calling their attention
to the grave potential for constitutional violations in the way people are held
without bail pre-trial because of their inability to afford money bail and urging
them to take immediate steps towards reducing such custody. Dear colleague
letters are a form of soft law, providing guidance as to the proximity of a
potential legal violation with the aim producing voluntary reforms.

Perhaps the most innovative local District Attorney in the US (and certainly
California) with similar institutional investigation and reform ambitions is
San Francisco District Attorney George Gascón, who has turned his long
experience as a police officer in LA, and later a police chief in San Francisco,
into a reflexive narrative of insight and redemption about the war on crime. In
2016, Gascón launched a blue ribbon task force made up of retired judges,
which in July of 2016 published a highly critical report about the San
Francisco Police Department's failures to respond adequately to citizen complaints about police misconduct. His efforts to reform SFPD from the DA's
office are ongoing.

Perhaps even more striking has been Gascón's interest in helping to reduce
the prison population, a radical departure from tough on crime prosecutorial
politics. In 2014, Gascón was the leading voice in the state campaigning for
that cycle's Proposition 47, which, as noted above, reduced potential felonies
to simple misdemeanours. In an editorial in support of Proposition 47, a
headline which advertised the "return on investment" line of thinking,
Gascón placed tough on crime under a different and historical context.

> The beginning of my career coincided with the start of the "tough on crime"
> generation. Thirty years ago, I joined the Los Angeles Police Department.
>   Three decades later, having served as a beat cop in some of L.A.'s roughest
> neighborhoods, as chief of the San Francisco Police Department and as the
> elected district attorney, I can assure you that the politically popular "tough
> on crime" era has not made us safer. It has, however, nearly bankrupted the
> state. And it has certainly torn the fabric of those communities hit hardest by
> drug abuse. (Gascón 2014)

In the campaign and in the recriminations that have circulated since from law
enforcement complaining of the impact of Prop 47 on crime, Gascón has not
hesitated to use this historical framing to put his opponents on the defensive.

> The extraordinary level of discontent with Proposition 47 from a majority of
> law enforcement officials is not surprising. Virtually everyone working in law
> enforcement today – myself included – cut our teeth during the war-on-drugs

era. We've never experienced another approach, and after decades of jailing people for simple drug possession, it's difficult to embrace alternatives. (Gascón 2015)

Answering police criticism in a newspaper article summarizing the controversy, Gascón highlighted the way the tough on crime era has left its mark on police values and organization, in ways that may diverge from public safety goals.

"Police culture, by and large, places a great deal of value on felony arrests," he said. "If you're a hunter, that is the elephant-hunting world. Now all of a sudden we are asking you to do pigeon hunting." (Ho 2015)

Not only did Gascón become the public face of a lenience campaign deeply disliked by local police, sheriffs and prosecutors – and thereby broken with the powerful political solidarity and power derived from that strong alliance – he has done so in terms that advance the debate over sentencing reform and shrinking the carceral state more generally by challenging the presumed normative construction of insecurity first laid in place in the 1960s and 1970s by tough on crime prosecutorial politics, and preserved largely unchanged within some law enforcement organizations.

Humanizing the Punished

Related to procedural justice, but perhaps aimed at an audience beyond just the specific person being engaged by the carceral state, some prosecutors are emphasizing the importance of treating those being prosecuted and those who have been punished by the carceral state with respect for their human dignity including in the aftermath of prison. In 2016, the Office of Justice Programs of DOJ announced a program to stop using disparaging terms like "offenders" or "felons" when describing people convicted of crimes out of concern that this unduly stigmatized them, especially after the completion of their sentence. Similar nomenclature changes have been announced by state correctional chiefs and county sheriffs. The goal is one of de-stigmatization and placing the prosecuted and punished back into the human family, where their crime and punishment is just one facet.

Prosecutorial Politics of Dignity Summary

If there is a meaningful coherence at all to this inchoate cluster of practices and discourses, it involves a marked shift in both signalling about the political community and normative expectations of the carceral state, compared to the prosecutorial politics of tough on crime. The signalling here is about the carceral state itself. If it helps the public imagine the nature of their political world, it does so in a way that centres on the performance of the state itself, and, in this context, its faults. That is a distinct change from the populist punitiveness and scapegoating of those prosecuted and punished. While the downwardly focused populist punitiveness often leaves citizens even more alienated from the common political community by emphasizing the threat posed by others, this state-centred focus might conceivably motivate more engagement in the democratic process necessary to drive any sustained reform of the carceral state.

Public safety as a normative expectation has not been so much displaced as embedded in a responsibility to the whole community, including those policed aggressively or punished excessively. In this respect, the biggest change is in the relationship to both police and prisons. Police, which tough on crime prosecutorial politics made into a special ally, become a subject of scrutiny and influence. When prosecutors directly take on police as criminal defendants, this may create significant tensions with the cooperation generally necessary between police and prosecutors for the latter to succeed at the main task of prosecuting cases. In Baltimore, where Marilyn Mosby's office prose-cuted six police officers following the death of Freddie Gray in police custody, the DA has faced withering criticism from police and may leave office after losing the cases (Hylton 2016). However, examples including both DOJ and San Francisco DA George Gascón suggest that another less conflict-ridden path is possible. If equal focus is placed on reforming the basic police mission to deemphasize aggressive confrontation through pretextual stops, we will avoid many of the predictable failures of holding individual police officers responsible for particular instances of misconduct. What police officers rightly resist is being told to racially profile and aggressively use force and then being made into the scapegoat for it when the images become public.

VII CONCLUSION

The US carceral state is facing its biggest legitimacy crisis since the 1970s. Then, a tough on crime prosecutorial politics helped lead a sea change in beliefs about crime and punishment and normative expectations about the carceral state. The result was forty years of mass imprisonment and punitive policing of communities of colour. Those two outcomes have themselves become a major challenge to the legitimacy of the carceral state today. Aided no doubt by historically low recorded levels of the kinds of serious property and violent crimes that have mobilized public concern in the past, and by the maturation of a generation that knew little about the crime waves of the 1960s through the 1980s, many Americans are joining what has long been a skepticism in the Black and Latino communities about the legitimacy of the carceral state.

So far, prosecutors have been less a focus than more visible police deaths and prison excesses. The vast majority of prosecutors appear to be banking on this lasting and reform subsiding without any significant limitations on prosecutorial power, let alone new or revised normative expectations. They could well be right. The relative invisibility of the prosecution operation combined with their potential hyper visibility as a media opinion-maker and the short time open typically for reforms before legitimacy crisis fatigue sets in could limit both short-term political risk and long-term risk of a change in prosecutorial power.

Despite that, a different set of prosecutorial politics is emerging with two distinct discursive formations. One prefers to talk the language of dollars and results (Aviram 2015). The other is willing to invoke the language of dignity and empathy. One would leave the major presumptions of criminal dangerousness and prosecutorial and law enforcement expertise largely unchanged. The other would very much challenge both. Should the legitimacy crisis now facing the carceral state deepen, and in particular more directly engage the court apparatus that lies between policing and mass incarceration, all of these and undoubtedly others unobserved may begin to combine and coalesce. In addition to their current powers within the political and penal fields, prosecutors have natural advantages in driving the politics of crime. Should a better successor to tough on crime emerge and help shape the normative sensibilities of the next political settlement about crime, reform of mass incarceration and policing are likely to be far more profound than otherwise.

To critics of excessive democracy in the US carceral state, even the most optimistic vision offered here leaves prosecutors largely political and unregulated by law. Without prejudice to whether greater legalization is itself desirable, it is possible that revised beliefs about our political world and new normative expectations for prosecutors within the carceral state can themselves change the degree to which the prosecution can be made more regulated. After all, given the most pessimistic assessments about the political community and the most desperate normative expectations, even robust forms of legal regulation, as criminal procedure law might be for police, have proven ineffectual. The 1970s, with its desperate sense that only prison could contain rampant violent crime, came very close that. Given more optimistic projections of the political world, and normative expectations that emphasize prudence and dignity, the small amount of prosecutor law we do have may produce a lot more work.

REFERENCES

Alexander, Michelle. *The New Jim Crow: Mass Incarceration in the Age of Color-Blindness, Rev. Ed.* New York: New Press, 2010.

Aviram, Hadar. *Cheap on Crime: Recession Era Politics and the Transformation of American Punishment.* University of California Press, 2015.

Bazelon, Emily. Walking the Line [Profile of Kamala Harris], *The New York Times Magazine*, May 29, 2016.

Beetham, David. *The Legitimation of Power*, 2nd Edition London: Palgrave, 2013b

Beetham, David. "Revisiting Legitimacy: Twenty Years On," in Justice Tankebe and Alison Liebling eds. *Legitimacy and Criminal Justice: An International Exploration.* OUP Oxford, 2013b.

Brown, Darryl K. *Free Market Criminal Justice: How Democracy and Laissez Faire Undermine the Rule of Law.* New York: Oxford University Press, 2016.

Butler, Paul. *Let's Get Free: A Hip-Hop Theory of Justice.* The New Press, 2010.

Campbell, Michael. "The Emergence of Penal Extremism in California: A Dynamic View of Institutional Structures and Political Processes," *Law & Society Review*, 48, no. 2, 377–409. 2014.

Civil Rights Division, U.S. Department of Justice, *Investigation of the Ferguson Police Department*, Mar. 4, 2015, www.justice.gov/crt/about/spl/documents/ferguson_findings_3-4-15.pdf.

Crain, Zac. "The Last Temptation of Craig Watkins," *D Magazine*, March 2009, www.dmagazine.com/publications/d-magazine/2009/march/the-last-temptation-of-craig-watkins/.

Feuer, Alan. "Ken Thompson, Brooklyn District Attorney, Dies after Disclosing Cancer," *The New York Times*, October 9, 2016, www.nytimes.com/2016/10/10/nyregion/ken-thompson-brooklyns-first-black-district-attorney-dies-at-50.html?_r=0.

Fortner, Michael. *Black Silent Majority: The Rockefeller Drug Laws and the Politics of Punishment.* Cambridge: Harvard University Press, 2015.

Garland, David. *The Culture of Control: Crime and Social Order in Contemporary Society.* Chicago: University of Chicago Press.

Gascón, George. "View Point: Prop 47 Would Reduce Crime and Save Money," *Sacramento Bee*, October 3, 2014, www.sacbee.com/opinion/op-ed/article2617783.html#storylink=cpy.

Gascón, George. "Op-ed: California's Prop 47 Revolution: Give Reform a Chance to Work," *Los Angeles Times*, October 23, 2015, www.latimes.com/opinion/op-ed/la-oe-1026-gascon-prop-47-pro-20151026-story.html.

Gilmore, Ruth. *Golden Gulag: Prison, Surplus, Crisis and Opposition in Globalizing California.* Berkeley, California: University of California Press, 2007.

Gottschalk, Marie, *Caught: The Prison State and the Lockdown of American Politics*, Princeton University Press, 2015.

Gupta, Vanita. *Dear Colleague Letter on Court Fees and Fines*, Civil Rights Division, U.S. Department of Justice, March 14, 2016, www.justice.gov/opa/file/832541/download

Haney-López, Ian F. "Post-racial Racism: Racial Stratification and Mass Incarceration in the Age of Obama." *California Law Review*, 98, no. 3 (2010): 1023–1074.

Harris, Kamala. *Smart on Crime.* San Francisco: Chronicle Books, 2009.

Harris, Kamala. "End the Revolving Door from Prison," 37–42 in *Solutions: American Leaders Speak out on Criminal Justice*, Inimai Chettiar and Michael Waldman eds. New York: Brennan Center, New York University, 2015, www.brennancenter.org/publication/solutions-american-leaders-speak-out-criminal-justice.

Herhold, Scott. "Herhold: Could Jeff Rosen Be a Candidate for Attorney General?" *San Jose Mercury News*, August 12, 2016, www.mercurynews.com/2015/01/28/herhold-could-jeff-rosen-be-a-candidate-for-attorney-general/.

Ho, Vivien. "Prop 47: Deep Split over Law Reducing 6 Felonies to Misdemeanor," *San Francisco Chronicle*, November 5, 2015, www.sfgate.com/crime/article/S-F-district-attorney-defends-Prop-47-which-6614091.php.

Ho, Vivien. "SF D.A. Gascón's Divide with Law Enforcement Deepens," *San Francisco Chronicle*, March 9, 2016, www.sfchronicle.com/bayarea/article/D-A-Gasc-n-s-divide-with-law-enforcement-6880747.php.

Hylton, Wil S. "Baltimore v. Marilyn Mosby," *The New York Times Magazine*, September 28, 2016, www.nytimes.com/2016/10/02/magazine/marilyn-mosby-freddie-gray-baltimore.html.

Justice, Benjamin and Tracey Meares, "How the Criminal Justice System Educates Citizens, *Annals of the American Academy of Political and Social Science*, 651, no. 1 (2014): 159–177.

Kingdon, John. *Agendas, Alternatives and Public Policies*, Boston: Little, Brown 1984.

Lacey, Nicola and David Soskice. "Crime, Punishment and Segregation in the United States: The Paradox of Local Democracy." *Punishment & Society*, 17, no. 4 (2015): 454–481.

Loader, Ian and Richard Sparks. *Public Criminology?* London: Routledge. 2010.

Loader, Ian. "In Search of Civic Policing: Recasting the 'Peelian' Principles." *Criminal Law and Philosophy*, 10, no. 3 (2014): 1–14.

Lerman, Amy and Vesla M. Weaver. *Arresting Citizenship: The Democratic Consequences of American Crime Control.* Chicago: University of Chicago Press, 2014.

Metzger, Bruce M. and Roland E. Murphy. *The New Oxford Annotated Bible with Apocryphal/Deuteronical Books.* New York: Oxford University Press, 1991.

Napolitano, Janet. "Prosecutorial Prioritization," 73–78. In *Solutions: American Leaders Speak out on Criminal Justice.* Edited by Inimai Chettiar and Michael Waldman. New York: Brennan Center, New York University, 2015.

Pfaff, John. The Micro and Macro Causes of Prison Growth. *Georgia State University Law Review*, 28, no. 4 (2012): 1.

Richman, Daniel. "Accounting for Prosecutors," *Prosecutors and Democracy (This Volume)*, __-___. Edited by Máximo Langer and David Sklansky. (2016 draft).

Rushin, Stephen. "Federal Enforcement of Police Reform." *Fordham Law Review*, 82, no. 6 (2014): 3189–3248; Illinois Public Law Research Paper No. 14–38. Available at SSRN: www.ssrn.com/abstract=2414682.

Simon, Jonathan. *Poor Discipline: Parole and the Social Control of the Underclass 1890–1990.* University of Chicago Press, 1993.

Simon, Jonathan. *Governing through Crime: How the War on Crime Transformed American Democracy and Created a Culture of Fear.* New York: Oxford University Press, 2007.

Simon, Jonathan. *Mass Incarceration on Trial: A Remarkable Court Decision and the Future of Prisons in America.* New York: New Press, 2014.

Lacey, N. and D. Soskice. Crime, Punishment and Segregation in the United States: The Paradox of Local Democracy. *Punishment & Society*, 17 no. 4, pp. 454–481. 2015.

Sklansky, David Alan. "The Nature and Function of Prosecutorial Power," *Journal of Criminal Law and Criminology*, 106, no. 3 (2016): 473–520.

Stuntz, William. *Collapse of American Criminal Justice.* Cambridge: Harvard Belknap Press 2011.

Travis, Jeremy, Bruce Western, and Steve Redburn. *The Growth of Incarceration in the United States.* National Academy Press, 2014, www.download.nap.edu/login.php?record_id=18613&page=http%3A%2F%2Fwww.nap.edu%2Fdownload.php%3Frecord_id%3D18613.

Tyler, Tom and Yuen J. Huo. *Trust in the Law: Encouraging Public Cooperation with the Police and Courts.* New York: Russell Sage Foundation, 2002.

Van Cleve, Nicole. *Crook County: Racism and Injustice in America's Largest Criminal Court.* Stanford Books, 2016.

Weaver, Vesla M. and Amy Lerman. Political Consequences of the Carceral State, *American Political Science Review*, 104, no. 4 (November 2010): 817–833.

Wright, Ronald F. "How Prosecutor Elections Fail Us, *Ohio State Journal of Criminal Law*, 6. no. 2 (2009): 581–610.

CASES

Brown v. Plata, 563 U.S. 493 (2011).
McCleskey v. Kemp, 481 U.S. 279 (1987).

10

Unpacking the Relationship between Prosecutors and Democracy in the United States

David Alan Sklansky*

The relationship between prosecutors and democracy is shrouded in confusion, far more so than the relationship between police and democracy. A good deal of ambiguity, to be sure, surrounds the ideal of democratic policing, but there is widespread agreement that this *is* an ideal, that it is meaningful and important for democratic commitments to inform police practices. In fact, there is a broad and longstanding consensus, sometimes tacit but often quite explicit, that reconciling the police with democracy is the central task for police reform, the central problem that the police present.[1] Almost everyone favors "democratic policing," even if they disagree about what it means. There is no similar consensus about the desirability of "democratic prosecution." There are plenty of calls for prosecutors to be more democratic in one way or another – more "accountable," "responsive," or "transparent." If anything, those calls have grown more common over the past decade or two. At the same time, though, there are repeated suggestions that American prosecutors, in particular, are pathologically democratic – that the involvement of prosecutors in politics, along with the involvement of politics in prosecution, has played a large role in making criminal punishment in the United States excessively harsh, scandalously discriminatory, and profoundly unjust. These suggestions, too, have proliferated in recent years.

My goals in this chapter are to explore why there is so little agreement about the relationship between prosecutors and democracy and to suggest some new ways to think about the question. My arguments here will build on a claim I defend in a recent article,[2] that the key to understanding prosecutors,

* I am grateful to the participants in the UCLA roundtable conference for helpful feedback.
[1] See DAVID ALAN SKLANSKY, POLICE AND DEMOCRACY (2007).
[2] David Alan Sklansky, *The Nature and Function of Prosecutorial Power*, 106 J. CRIM. L. & CRIMINOLOGY 473 (2016).

especially at least in the United States and probably also elsewhere, is that they are first and foremost mediating figures, bridging key conceptual and organizational divides in criminal justice. Prosecutors blur the boundaries between adversarial and inquisitorial forms of procedure, between law and discretion, and between the police and the courts. The boundary-blurring provided by prosecutors makes criminal justice more flexible, but it also can make the system harder to pin down, less transparent and less principled. The mediating functions of prosecutors, I will suggest here, also help to explain why there is so little agreement about the implications of democracy for prosecutors, and vice versa – and why those implications may deserve more attention than they have received.

David Nelken rightly stresses the need for close attention to context in assessing the meaning and desirability of prosecutorial "independence."[3] Accordingly, I will focus here on the relationship between prosecutors and democracy in the United States, although I hope what I say will be of broader relevance.

I DIVERGENT PERSPECTIVES

The range of views about the proper relationship between prosecutors and democracy is strikingly broad. For present purposes, we can limit ourselves to the four most common positions.

A *Politics as the Enemy of Justice*

The last thing we should want from prosecutors is "democratic accountability," Michael Tonry suggests, "since it seems self-evident that external considerations should be irrelevant to decisions in individual cases."[4] This is a widely shared view. It is why Tonry, along with many others, thinks it unfortunate and embarrassing that most prosecutors in the United States work in offices headed by elected officials – an arrangement no other legal system has seen fit to copy. Tonry envies civil-law societies for the "neutrality, objectivity, and independence" of their career prosecutors.[5] The political nature of prosecution in the United States, along with the culture of "adversariness" it has

---

[3] David Nelken, *Can Prosecutors Be Too Independent? An Italian Case Study*, in European Penology? 249 (Tom Daems, Dirk van Zyl Smit, & Sonja Snacken eds., 2013). See also Jacqueline Hodgson's chapter in this volume.

[4] Michael Tonry, *Prosecutors and Politics in Comparative Perspective*, in Prosecutors and Politics: A Comparative Perspective 1, 12 (Michael Tonry ed., 2012).

[5] *Id.* at 7.

fostered within prosecutors' offices, makes the United States, in Tonry's view, "the last place in the developed world where an informed, rational, and self-interested person would choose to be prosecuted."[6]

All of this is consistent with a longstanding critique of American prosecutors as overly political and, as a consequence, overly aggressive in pursuing criminal convictions and seeking to impose harsh punishment – except when law enforcement officials engage in wrongdoing, when prosecutors, fearful of losing critical endorsements at election time, are insufficiently aggressive.[7] That critique has gained momentum over the past two decades as concern has mounted that the United States imprisons far too many people for far too long: that too many defendants, guilty or not, are railroaded into guilty pleas or convicted – and sometimes sentenced to death – in trials marred by prosecutorial misconduct; that police officers, in contrast, are too rarely held accountable for misconduct; and that the logic of criminalization permeates our politics and our modes of governance. All of these pathologies are often blamed, at least in part, on the involvement of prosecutors in politics. Politics drives prosecutors to excessive zeal (except when fellow law enforcement personnel are accused of crimes), and prosecutors drive politics to paranoia and a "culture of control."[8] Far better if prosecutors were career, quasi-judicial civil servants who stayed out of politics and who felt, as a consequence, little pressure to secure convictions and long sentences.

B Politics as a Substitute for Bureaucratic Professionalism

Complaints about the political nature of United States prosecutors, and unfavorable comparisons with European prosecutors, are such longstanding themes of American criminal procedure scholarship that there is also well-established response. The response goes like this: The United States and Europe have different systems, and what works in one is not necessarily required, or even helpful, in the other. Europe puts more faith in governmental bureaucracies than we do, and has a stronger tradition of a muscular, professionalized civil service. So Europe relies on hierarchical oversight to guide prosecutors and to keep them in check. Americans prize local democratic control, so we do with

---

[6] *Id.* at 17, 19.

[7] *See, e.g.,* Mary Ann Georgantopoulos, *Chicago State's Attorney Takes Heat Following Officer's Acquittal,* BuzzFeed News, May 8. 2015.

[8] David Garland, The Culture of Control: Crime and Social Order in Contemporary Society (2001); *see also* Jonathan Simon, Governing Through Crime: How the War on Crime Transformed American Democracy and Created a Culture of Fear (2006).

elections what Europeans do with multi-tiered bureaucracy. And we have an adversarial rather than an inquisitorial system, so we use the clash between opposing lawyers to accomplish some of what Europe seeks to achieve through a prosecutorial culture of detached objectivity. Politics might be a bug in European systems of prosecution, but it is a feature in ours.[9]

Each of these first two views about the relationship between politics and prosecutors in the United States can – and often does – coexist with a deep concern about prosecutorial power. Some scholars who think prosecutors too powerful view politics as a valuable check, but others do not – they may worry, in fact, that the broad power and wide discretion exercised by prosecutors makes it particularly undesirable for prosecutors to have their eye on the electorate.

Part of the explanation is that these first two views about the relationship between politics and prosecution draw on two different intuitions about prosecutorial elections. The first view, politics as the enemy of justice, generally assumes that prosecutors will campaign by promising to be harsh and aggressive; incumbents will trumpet their conviction rates, and any sign of lenience is likely to cost a candidate votes. Elections therefore will push prosecutors to be "tough on crime," and over time will ratchet up the severity of criminal justice.[10] The second view, politics as a substitute for bureaucratic oversight, is more sanguine about the electorate. The assumption here is that voters can and should be trusted, at least when elections function properly. The electorate isn't just out for blood. People draw distinctions, or at least they do sometimes. Marilyn Mosby, an African-American who won election as Baltimore State's Attorney in 2014, defeated a White incumbent in part by promising aggressive prosecution of police misconduct, and she made good on that promise just months after her election, when she secured swift indictments against four police officers implicated in the death of a Black arrestee named Freddie Gray.[11] Scott Colom, an African-American reform candidate, defeated a tough-on-crime, long-serving incumbent District Attorney in Mississippi in November 2015 after promising, in part, to send fewer young

---

[9] *See, e.g.*, William T. Pizzi, *Understanding Prosecutorial Discretion in the United States: The Limits of Comparative Criminal Procedure as an Instrument of Reform*, 54 OHIO ST. L. REV. 1325 (1993).

[10] There is some evidence, for example, that the percentage of cases taken to trial rather than plea-bargained increases before a prosecutorial election. *See* Siddhartha Bandyopadhyay & Bryan C. McCannon, *The Effect of the Election of Prosecutors on Criminal Trials*, 161 PUB. CHOICE 141 (2013). One way to read this result is that elections "distort [the] decision making" of prosecutors and make them more "hawkish." Bryan C. McCannon, *Prosecutor Elections, Mistakes, and Appeals*, 10 J. EMPIRICAL LEGAL STUD. 696, 697 (2013).

[11] *See* John Woodrow Cox, Keith L. Alexander, & Ovetta Wiggins, *Who Is Baltimore State's Attorney Marilyn Mosby?*, WASH. POST, May 1, 2015.

offenders to prison.[12] That same month, James Stewart became the first African-American District Attorney in the history of Caddo Parish, Louisiana, with a campaign emphasizing professionalism and ethics rather than convictions; he succeeded Dale Cox, an outspoken champion of the death penalty and long prison sentences, who had attracted growing criticism both for his aggressiveness and for his office's pattern of removing Black jurors.[13] In March 2016, voters in Cook County, Illinois, and Cuyahoga County, Ohio, unseated incumbent prosecutors widely criticized for their lethargy in pursuing charges against police officers who shot and killed unarmed African-Americans.[14] If winning a race for District Attorney by promising less incarceration would have been "unthinkable in an earlier era,"[15] it is not unthinkable today.[16]

C Improving Politics with Transparency

Even today, though, it may be the exception rather than the rule for prosecutors to win elections by promising more moderation in punishment, or to be turned out of office for being too friendly with the police. Colum, Stewart, and Kim Foxx – who defeated the incumbent State's Attorney in Cook County, Illinois – all won with heavy, out-of-district support from the same deep-pocketed contributor.[17] In the usual case, prosecutorial elections may neither drive prosecutorial practices toward across-the-board severity, nor make prosecutors responsive to nuanced community concerns. In the usual case, prosecutorial elections may be just a distraction, with little impact on the choices prosecutors make. Prosecutors who seek reelection rarely lose, and campaigns focus heavily on

---

[12] *See* Jimmie E. Gates, *Scott Colom Ousts Longtime DA Forrest Allgood*, JACKSON CLARION-LEDGER, Nov. 6, 2015; Leon Neyfakh, *How to Run against a Tough-on-Crime DA — and Win*, SLATE, Nov. 12, 2015.

[13] *See* Alexandria Burris, *Stewart Wins Caddo DA Race*, SHREVEPORT TIMES, Nov. 22, 2015; *Darth Vader's Lament*, ECONOMIST, Nov. 21, 2015.

[14] *See* Jon Swaine, *Black Lives Matter Movement Sees Series of Victories in Midwest Elections*, GUARDIAN, Mar. 16, 2016.

[15] Neyfakh, *supra* note 12.

[16] Colum suggested his election should be "a big signal to district attorneys and assistant DAs and judges, if they're paying attention, that there's been a shift in public opinion." *Id.* For further evidence of that shift, see David Alan Sklansky, *The Changing Political Landscape for Elected Prosecutors*, 14 OHIO ST. J. CRIM. L. 647 (2017).

[17] George Soros, "a New York financier and longtime supporter of the Democratic Party, gave almost $400,000 to a new Mississippi political action committee, and the money went to support Colom's campaign as well as the re-election campaign of Hinds County District Attorney Robert Shuler Smith." Gates, *supra* note 12. Soros spent more than $850,000 on Stewart's campaign, *see Darth Vader's Lament, supra* note 13, and gave $333,000 to a political action committee that supported Foxx, *see* John Byrne & Hal Dardick, *Foxx: Cook County State's Attorney Win about "Turning the Page,"* CHICAGO TRIBUNE, Mar. 16, 2016.

character, not policies.[18] Moreover, "[w]hen the campaign rhetoric does turn to office performance, the claims relate to quantity of cases processed rather than the quality of results" or "overarching values."[19] So a third, increasingly common perspective on prosecutors and democracy is that local elections *could* be a valuable mechanism for making criminal justice more responsive to community concerns and more reflective of community values, but that elections don't serve that function today, and we should try to fix that. The remedy most often suggested is greater transparency: routine collection and reporting of data about how prosecutors' offices operate, the decisions they make, and the results they achieve.[20]

Exactly what *kind* of data should be collected and disseminated is another question; there is little if any agreement about that, even among champions of greater prosecutorial transparency.[21] What they do agree about, though, is that the best way to improve prosecution in the United States is to harness the power of democratic oversight, rather than relying on courts or on internal bureaucratic controls to bring prosecutors into line. Recent scholarship on prosecutors in the United States is both continuous with and a departure from the scholarship of the late twentieth century. It is continuous with that earlier work in that it finds prosecutors troubling, largely because of the vast discretion they exercise, and because it argues for a fairly uniform set of reforms: modest restraints on discretion imposed through bureaucratic guidelines, supervisory oversight, and standardized procedures providing defendants with some minimal opportunities to be heard and to appeal adverse decisions. Where the current scholarship differs from the scholarship of a half-century ago is that the older generation called for courts to force these changes,[22] whereas the newer scholarship tends to pin its hopes on the electorate.[23]

---

[18] *See, e.g.,* Ronald F. Wright, *How Prosecutor Elections Fail Us,* 6 OHIO ST. J. CRIM. L. 581, 591–606 (2009).

[19] *Id.* at 591, 606. There are signs, though, that this may be changing. *See* Sklansky, *supra* note 16.

[20] *See Id.* at 606–08; Stephanos Bibas, *Prosecutorial Regulation versus Prosecutorial Accountability,* 157 U. PA. L. REV. 959, 960–61 (2009); Russell Gold, *Promoting Democracy in Prosecution,* 86 WASH. L. REV. 69 (2011); Marc L. Miller & Ronald F. Wright, *Reporting for Duty: The Universal Prosecutorial Accountability Puzzle and an Experimental Transparency Alternative, in* THE PROSECUTOR IN TRANSNATIONAL PERSPECTIVE 392 (Erik Luna & Marianne L. Wade eds., 2012).

[21] *See* Sklansky, *supra* note 2, at 37.

[22] *See, e.g.,* Norman Abrams, *Internal Policy: Guiding the Exercise of Prosecutorial Discretion,* 19 U.C.L.A. L. REV. 1 (1971); Leland E. Beck, *The Administrative Law of Criminal Prosecution: The Development of Prosecutorial Policy,* 27 AM. U. L. REV. 310 (1978); James Vorenberg, *Decent Restraint of Prosecutorial Power,* 94 HARV. L. REV. 1521 (1981).

[23] See, for example, the chapter by Angela J. Davis in this volume. *See also* Bibas, *supra* note 20; Gold, *supra* note 20.

D Prosecution as Community Empowerment

A separate strain in recent discussions of prosecutors – both by scholars and by prosecutors themselves – also pins its hopes on democracy, but in a different way. Instead of arguing for greater transparency as a means of making electoral oversight of prosecutors more meaningful, it celebrates "community prosecution," or sometimes "neighborhood prosecution." Those terms are poorly defined, but the general idea is that large, metropolitan prosecutors' offices set up smaller, satellite offices, embedded within neighborhoods troubled by crime, and the prosecutors in those offices then work with residents to use prosecutorial power to solve the neighborhood's problems. The idea of community prosecution, or neighborhood prosecution, thus draws on ideas associated with community policing and problem-oriented policing; it calls for prosecutorial power to be decentralized, proactive, and exercised in consultation with community members.[24]

Community prosecution often figures in campaign rhetoric, but it is far from clear that it ever represents a significant change in how prosecutors' offices actually operate. Community prosecution programs appear in most instances to be largely symbolic – an exercise in public relations. Still, it is worth noting what they symbolize: decentralized efforts at using prosecution proactively, to solve community problems. They therefore represent an ideal very different from controlling prosecution discretion through office-wide guidelines, internal supervision, and standardized procedures – regardless whether those controls are adopted in response to electoral direction or judicial prodding.

It is worth noting in passing that the ideas associated with community prosecution are also in tension with another set of ideas often put forward today by prosecutors thought to be forward-looking – "intelligence-led prosecution." The core of intelligence-led prosecution (sometimes called "predictive prosecution"[25]) is the notion that prosecutors should identify individuals responsible for a disproportionate share of crime in a community and then concentrate on building cases against them and securing lengthy sentences of incarceration. The program operates top-down, much like intelligence-led policing, from which it draws inspiration.[26] Prosecutors associated with intelligence-led prosecution are often also associated with community prosecution;

---

[24] See, e.g., Anthony V. Alfieri, *Community Prosecutors*, 90 CAL. L. REV. 1465 (2002); Anthony C. Thompson, *It Takes a Community to Prosecute*, 77 NOTRE DAME L. REV. 321 (2002); Ronald F. Wright, *Community Prosecution, Comparative Prosecution*, 47 WAKE FOREST L. REV. 361 (2012).

[25] See Andrew Guthrie Ferguson, *Predictive Prosecution*, WAKE FOREST L. REV. (forthcoming), available at www.ssrn.com/abstract=2777611.

[26] See, e.g., Jennifer Gonnerman, *A Daughter's Death*, NEW YORKER, Oct. 5, 2015.

this is true, for example, of George Gascon in San Francisco and Cyrus Vance Jr. in Manhattan.[27] But that just demonstrates how shallow the commitment to community prosecution really is – or maybe how shallow the commitment to intelligence-led policing is, or maybe both. Because the ideas are in conflict, unless one assumes – contrary to available evidence[28] – that what "community members" want, generally, is intelligence-led prosecution.

II WHAT KIND OF DEMOCRACY?

What explains the wide variation in common views about the proper relationship between prosecutors and democracy? Part of the explanation is divergent ideas about democracy. Democracy is a famously protean term. Every country on earth now claims to be "democratic." But democracy isn't an empty idea; it is better understood as an "essentially contested concept," a multifaceted ideal that can't be defined without making normative judgments.[29] In the United States, there are at least two competing conceptions of democracy – or, more precisely, a longstanding, coherent, and controversial conception of democracy, opposed by a looser set of ideas. The coherent ideal is democratic pluralism, an understanding of American democracy that in the 1950s and early 1960s was thoroughly dominant both in academic and popular writings and that even today remains influential.[30] The looser set of ideas includes participatory democracy, deliberative democracy, and a range of other viewpoints defined in large part in opposition to democratic pluralism. The most important of these, for present purposes, is participatory democracy.

---

[27] *See* Chip Brown, *Cy Vance Jr.'s 'Moneyball' Approach to Crime,* N.Y. TIMES, Dec. 3, 2014; Heather Mac Donald, *First Came Data-driven Policing; Now Comes Data-driven Prosecution,* L.A. TIMES, Aug. 10, 2014.

[28] *See, e.g.,* David Alan Sklansky, The Persistent Pull of Professional Policing 3–4 (National Inst. of Justice, 2011)

[29] W. B. Gallie, *Essentially Contested Concepts,* 56 PROC. ARISTOTELIAN SOC'Y 167 (1955–56), *reprinted in* THE IMPORTANCE OF LANGUAGE 121, 135 (Max Black ed., 1962).

[30] The key texts include ANGUS CAMPBELL ET AL., THE AMERICAN VOTER (1960); ROBERT A. DAHL, A PREFACE TO DEMOCRATIC THEORY (1956); ROBERT A. DAHL, WHO GOVERNS? DEMOCRACY AND POWER IN AN AMERICAN CITY (1961); V. O. KEY, JR., POLITICS, PARTIES, AND PRESSURE GROUPS (1942); SEYMOUR MARTIN LIPSET, POLITICAL MAN: THE SOCIAL BASES OF POLITICS (1960); DAVID B. TRUMAN, THE GOVERNMENTAL PROCESS: PUBLIC INTERESTS AND PUBLIC OPINION (2nd ed. 1971) (1951). For illustrative critiques of democratic pluralism, see THE BIAS OF PLURALISM (William E. Connolly ed., 1969); PETER BACHARACH, THE THEORY OF DEMOCRATIC ELITISM: A CRITIQUE (1967); KENNETH PREWITT & ALAN STONE, THE RULING ELITES: ELITE THEORY, POWER, AND AMERICAN DEMOCRACY (1973); Daryl Baskin, *American Pluralism: Theory, Practice, and Ideology,* 32 J. POL. 71 (1970).

Simplifying somewhat, the key themes of democratic pluralism include *elites, elections,* and *end results.*[31] Pluralism was in a part a reaction against the idea that American democracy could or should operate mainly through grass-roots participation – the kind of thing celebrated by de Tocqueville and by admirers of New England town meetings. The pluralists thought democracy worked through elites, who mediated conflicts between groups. For this reason, the pluralists also deemphasized constitutional checks and balances. They thought the key constitutional mechanisms of American democracy were elections – not because elections put ordinary people in charge, but precisely because it allowed them to delegate the task of governance.[32] It is true that this left ordinary people only peripherally involved in the large questions of public policy that often wound up shaping their lives, but the pluralists thought that was for the best, because most people knew little about public affairs and had neither the time nor the inclination to learn more, and because the purpose of democracy was to generate sound policies, so what mattered were end results, not the collective experience of self-government.

In contrast, the key theme of participatory democracy is *engagement* – engagement that is widespread, continuous, and intrinsically valued. Participatory democracy is anti-elitist; it places its trust in the good judgment and dispersed intelligence of ordinary people, not in leaders or experts. It therefore calls for broad participation in the work of self-government, and participation that is not limited to the arid act of voting; it embraces the Toquevillian tumult rejected as a wishful fantasy by the democratic pluralists. It sees widespread, continuous engagement in self-government not only as the best way to ensure that government promotes the common good, but also as something valuable in and of itself, part of a life well-led and a community well-constituted.

I used the past tense in describing democratic pluralism because its heyday was half a century ago, and it bears the stamp of its time. Pluralism was the collective creation of scholars who had lived through World War II and were living through the Cold War. They had seen the rise of totalitarianism on two continents, they knew the compatibility of mass politics with demagoguery, and they had witnessed the finest hours of American military know-how. They wanted a theory of democracy that responded to the dangers of fascism, Stalinism, and McCarthyism, and they believed in leadership and expertise.

---

[31] For a fuller account, see SKLANSKY, *supra* note 1, at 14–32.

[32] This was the idea, more or less, to which Mayor Rahm Emanuel appealed in late 2015 when he refused to step down in the face of criticism over his handling of a police shooting. "We have a process," he explained, "it's called the election ... The voters spoke. I'll be held accountable and responsible for my actions and decisions I make." Monica Davey, *Rahm Emanuel Says He Won't Resign over Police Shooting and Video,* N.Y. TIMES, Dec. 2, 2015.

Participatory democracy emerged in the 1960s as a response to and rejection of democratic pluralism. It, too, bears the stamp of its time: the torpor of the 1950s, the alienation of the post-war generation, and the disastrous performance of "the best and the brightest" in Vietnam. The past tense seems less appropriate here, because participatory democracy never really lost its attraction, at least as rhetoric. In the space of a decade – from the mid-1960s to the mid-1970s – participatory democracy went from a language of critique to something approaching mainstream common-sense, so much so that it became, at times, a vehicle of apology and cooptation, a way of justifying and "legitimizing" the system. The rhetoric of participatory democracy continues to play both roles today. It functions both as utopian aspiration and a pragmatic strategy of "building trust."[33]

It should be clear how these divergent understandings of democracy are reflected in divergent ideas about the relationship between prosecutors and democracy. Community prosecution, for example, draws heavily on the ideas underlying participatory democracy, and it reflects the twofold nature of participatory democracy, as idealism and expedience. Community prosecution appeals in part to an unreachable ideal, an imagined arrangement where prosecutors completely mirror the instincts, concerns, and priorities of the "community," itself conceived as well-defined and homogeneous. At the same time, community prosecution is a pragmatic strategy of statecraft, a tool to build popular acceptance and support for prosecutors and the law – a form, in short, of public relations.

The relationship seems equally clear between democratic pluralism and the agenda of empowerment through transparency. The advocates of transparency place heavy weight on elections as a tool of oversight, and they also place heavy weight on groups and elites – just as the pluralists did. Ordinary voters are unlikely to pore over statistics released by prosecutors' offices, but reformers hope that "a small number of sophisticated or committed users of good data,"[34] housed in "intermediary institutions" – advocacy groups and media organizations – will do the work for us, "watching closely . . . and competing with one another" as "data interpreter[s]" and "to receive credit for offering the service."[35] Voters would play essentially the same role in regulating prosecutors that consumers play in regulating the marketplace – again, matching the role that the pluralists allocated to voters.[36]

---

[33] *See* SKLANSKY, *supra* note 1, at 61–73.

[34] Marc L. Miller & Ronald F. Wright, *The Black Box*, 94 IOWA L. REV. 125, 186–87 (2008).

[35] Ronald F. Wright, *Beyond Prosecutor Elections*, 67 S.M.U. L. REV. 593, 610 (2014); *see also* Gold, *supra* note 20, at 91, 101–04 & n.137.

[36] *See* SKLANSKY, *supra* note 1, at 21–23.

There may be contestable ideas about democracy lurking as well behind the two other positions sketched above about the relationship between prosecutors and democracy. The first view – politics as the enemy of justice – can draw strength from the pluralists' pessimism about mass politics, but doesn't seem to share its optimism about the possibilities of groups and elites to sand off the rough edges of populism. The second view – politics as a substitute for bureaucratic professionalism – is compatible with either a pluralist or a participatory understanding of democracy, because what drives this position is less any particular faith in American democracy than a rejection of what seems to be its alternative, European-style bureaucracy. Most people, though, want more from prosecutors' offices than an absence of bureaucracy, and the view that American prosecutors are performing just fine, thank you, seems increasingly unconvincing. That leaves us with the options of trying to improve prosecutors' offices through some version of democracy, or through something else – and the choice among those options will depend, inevitably, on our views about democracy.

III WHAT KIND OF PROSECUTORS?

It will depend as well on our understanding of the prosecutor's role. Prosecutors mediate fundamental divides in criminal justice: between adversarial and inquisitorial forms of adjudication, between the courts and the police, between law and discretion, and between vengeance and mercy. This is, in fact, the key characteristic of prosecutors; first and foremost, they are boundary-blurrers.[37] We have conflicting expectations of prosecutors. We want them to be zealous crime fighters and dispassionate ministers of justice, crusading avengers and agents of mercy, and – as we have seen – responsive public officials and apolitical servants of the law. We place inconsistent demands on judges and police officers, too, but not to the same extent. Prosecutors are the lubricants of criminal process; they serve as emissaries between the world of the police to the world of the courts, and they reconcile – or submerge – our divergent aspirations for and understandings of the criminal justice system.

Prosecutors cross the theoretical and organizational divides of criminal justice pervasively and systematically, and they do so not because they refuse to stick to their assigned role, but because intermediation *is* their assigned role. Nonetheless, it is possible to imagine prosecutors as being more at home on particular sides of some of these divides. Most people who spend any time thinking about prosecutors probably do this. For example, they may think of prosecutors – either descriptively or aspirationally – as predominantly adversarial (even if they

---

[37] *See* Sklansky, *supra* note 2.

sometimes act inquisitorial), as essentially part of law enforcement (even if they have a foot in the courtroom), and as exercising power that is largely discretionary (even if there are rule-bound aspects of their work). Or they may think that prosecutors are, or should be, mainly but not entirely inquisitorial, allied more with judges than with police officers, and creatures more of law than of discretion.

The various boundaries that prosecutors cross do not neatly coincide, so thinking of prosecutors as predominantly inquisitorial, say, is consistent with thinking of them as, say, essentially judicial or as essentially allied with the police. And any of these understandings is consistent with the recognition that prosecutors regularly intermediate across these boundaries. So there is complex array of possible understandings of the prosecutor's role, each of which can be layered on top of a view of prosecutors as, first and foremost, boundary-crossers. This complicates the task of assessing the proper relationship between prosecutors and democracy, and would do so even if with broad agreement about the meaning of democracy.

To see the point, let us simplify, for purposes of discussion, the crosscutting variations in possible understandings of the prosecutor's role. We can imagine two ideal types. The first sees the prosecutor as (a) more of an advocate and adversary than a dispassionate adjudicator, (b) working more closely with the police than with the courts, and (c) operating more in the realm of discretion than of law. The second is the opposite; it sees the prosecutor as (a) more of an inquisitor, or adjudicator, than an adversary, (b) more of an officer of the court than a part of law enforcement, and (c) more of an agent of the law than a wielder of discretion. The first ideal type probably approximates how many people think of the traditional American prosecutor; the second is, more or less, the classic picture of the European prosecutor. Neither comes close to fully capturing current reality in all of its complexity, but they will serve our purposes, allowing us to explore how different conceptions of prosecutors can interact with different conceptions of democracy.

We can construct a two-by-two grid, crossing these two idea types of prosecutors with the two accounts of democracy we surveyed earlier:

	Adversarial Prosecutor	Inquisitorial Prosecutor
Democratic Pluralism	I	III
Participatory Democracy	II	IV

Box I, in the upper left-hand corner of the grid, corresponds to a traditional, American-style adversarial prosecutor, seen from the vantage point of democratic pluralism. If prosecutors are seen primarily as advocates, exercising discretion rather than themselves applying legal standards, and if the strength of American democracy is thought to lie largely in elites who are held accountable through elections, then the transparency agenda makes a good deal of sense. Prosecutorial decision-making resembles lots of other categories of executive-branch decision-making; it is policy, not law. It is *constrained* by law, just as other executive-branch actions are constrained by law; but interpreting and applying the law is the job of the courts, not the Executive Branch. What is wanted from prosecutors under this view, like what is wanted from other officers of the political branches, is faithful pursuit of the public interest. And under demo-cratic pluralism, that is a matter that, on a day-to-day basis, is left to be worked out by elected officials in consultation with other elites. Ordinary citizens oversee these decisions only by their periodic choices at the ballot box. From this perspective, therefore, it makes complete sense that prosecutors should be elected, and we should want those elections to benefit from reasonably broad dissemination of pertinent information about what the prosecutors are actually doing. It isn't necessary that the average voter be in a position to assess a prosecutor's performance, but opinion leaders – the media, advocacy groups, etc. – should be able to do so. Once that is made possible, the system should work. Since the "adversarial prosecutor" is an ideal-type corresponding to the traditional image of the American district attorney – think Thomas Dewey, or Hamilton Burger – and since democratic pluralism was the consensus under-standing of American democracy in the middle decades of the twentieth century, it is unsurprising that the elected District Attorney seemed a sensible, relatively uncontroversial institution well into the 1960s and 1970s.

Box II, in the lower left-hand corner, corresponds to a traditional, American-style adversarial prosecutor, but seen from the vantage point not of democratic pluralism, but of participatory democracy. If prosecutors are understood as discretion-wielders rather than rule appliers, but elites seem untrustworthy and elections seem insufficient as avenues for popular involvement in collec-tive self-government, then community prosecution begins to seem a perfectly sensible, even an obvious, idea.

Moving from the left-hand column to the right-hand column of the grid corresponds to a shift from seeing prosecutors as adversarial wielders of discretion to seeing them as inquisitorial officers of the law – roughly from the traditional ideal of the American prosecutor to the traditional ideal of the European prosecutor. And once this shift is made, any form of democratic oversight begins to seem problematic – just as democratic control of judges seems problematic. If anything, participatory democracy seems even more troubling here than democratic pluralism – which may be why, although many state judges in the United States are elected, there has been little call for judges to respond to grassroots expressions of community sentiment. Calls for "community courts" or "neighborhood courts" are calls for courts that are *located* in communities and neighborhoods and that *address* the problems of communities and neighborhoods – not for courts that are *accountable* to communities and neighborhoods. "Community prosecution" and "neighborhood prosecution" often wind up being largely similar – efforts to decentralize the *location* and *focus* of prosecutors, but not to decentralize political oversight.

Part of the reason is that, in practice, the expectations placed on American prosecutors do not stay neatly in the left-hand column. We think a prosecutor should be something more than "a mere advocate."[38] We want prosecutors to "maintain a healthy distance from the police,"[39] acting as "gatekeepers" of the criminal justice system and assessing the legality and propriety of police activities.[40] And although we want "the rigors of the penal system" to be "mitigated by prosecutorial discretion,"[41] we also expect prosecutors to "follow the law,"[42] and prosecutors themselves regularly legitimize their activities by claiming to be doing exactly that.[43]

IV PROSECUTORS AS BOUNDARY-BLURRERS

So far we have explored the ways in which the relationship between prosecutors and democracy will vary according to what we mean by democracy and what we expect of prosecutors. But the expectations that any particular individual has for prosecutors are typically inconsistent – so much so that it makes sense to view boundary-blurring and intermediation as central rather

---

[38] NDAA NATIONAL PROSECUTION STANDARDS, pt. 1, commentary at 3 (3rd ed. 2009); *see also, e.g.*, Miller & Wright, *supra* note 34, at 178 (describing the prosecutor as "something more than a litigant who operates 'in the shadow of the law'"); Vorenberg, *supra* note 22, at 1557 (noting that a prosecutor is "expected to be more (or is it less?) than an adversary").

[39] Chip Brown, *Cy Vance Jr.'s 'Moneyball' Approach to Crime*, N.Y. TIMES, Dec. 3, 2014 (quoting Steve Zeidman).

[40] *Id.*; Daniel Richman, *Prosecutors and Their Agents, Agents and Their Prosecutors*, 103 COLUM. L. REV. 749, 758 (2003); *see also, e.g.*, JEROME H. SKOLNICK, JUSTICE WITHOUT TRIAL: LAW ENFORCEMENT IN DEMOCRATIC SOCIETY 196, 228 (3rd ed. 1994); Russell M. Gold, *Beyond the Judicial Fourth Amendment: The Prosecutor's Role*, 47 U.C. DAVIS L. REV. 1591, 1596, 1641 (2014); Jennifer Laurin, *Quasi-Inquisitorialism*, 90 NOTRE DAME L. REV. 783, 818 (2014).

[41] *Cheney v. United States District Court*, 542 U.S. 367, 386 (2004).

[42] Ronald F. Wright & Kay L. Levine, *The Cure for Young Prosecutors' Syndrome*, 56 ARIZ. L. REV. 1065, 1071 (2014).

[43] *See, e.g.*, Terry Frieden, *"No One is above the Law," Holder Says of Torture Inquiry*, CNN. COM, Apr. 22, 2009.

than incidental to the prosecutor's role.[44] And the boundary-blurring nature of the prosecutor's role has important implications for the relationship between prosecutors and democracy, first and foremost because it complicates the most familiar strategies of accountability.

In theory, the boundary blurring by prosecutors could increase rather than decrease the available levers of accountability. And in fact, prosecutors in the United States are often described as answering to "a complex set of constraints."[45] Because they "straddle the line that separates courts from politics,"[46] they are answerable both to the law and to the public.[47] Because they mediate between courts and the police, they have to justify their activities both to judges[48] and to law enforcement officers.[49] Because they are both advocates and government officials, they are subject, on the one hand, to rules of professional responsibility and the discipline of the adversary process,[50] and on the other hand to special obligations and expectations not imposed on defense counsel.

In practice, however, border hopping by prosecutors winds up frustrating rather than enhancing accountability. Too often, prosecutors seem answerable neither to politics nor to the law. Political selection gives them an aura of democratic legitimacy that makes courts hesitate to regulate them, but in practice, voters almost never turn a sitting district attorney out of office,[51] and a strong convention bars Presidents from firing U.S. Attorneys mid-term for "political" reasons.[52] Stories like Forrest Allgood – the tough-on-crime Mississippi prosecutor defeated at the polls by Scott Colum[53] – remain unusual (although they have recently become somewhat less so[54]), in part because the technical nature of prosecutors' jobs makes it difficult for the electorate to assess their performance; the same factor makes it hard for the President, despite his own electoral mandate, to replace United States Attorneys except when he first comes into office. In other words, the political side of the prosecutor's role makes judicial control more difficult, while the jurisprudential side of the prosecutor's role frustrates political control.

[44] See Sklansky, *supra* note 2.
[45] JOAN E. JACOBY, THE AMERICAN PROSECUTOR: A SEARCH FOR IDENTITY xx (1980).
[46] John L. Worrall, *Prosecution in America: A Historical and Comparative Account, in* THE CHANGING ROLE OF THE AMERICAN PROSECUTOR 3, 4 (John L. Worrall & M. Elaine Nugent-Borakove eds., 2008).
[47] See, e.g., Miller & Wright, *supra* note 20, at 392.
[48] See, e.g., SKOLNICK, *supra* note 40, at 196, 228.   [49] See, e.g., Richman, *supra* note 40.
[50] See, e.g., Pizzi, *supra* note 9, at 1349–51.   [51] See *supra* note 18 and accompanying text.
[52] See Adrian Vermeule, *Conventions of Agency Independence,* 113 COLUM. L. REV. 1163, 1201–03 (2013).
[53] See supra notes 13–17 and accompanying text.   [54] See Sklansky, *supra* note 16.

Prosecutors need the cooperation of law enforcement agents to build their cases,[55] but pressure from police departments and other investigatory agencies more often than not pushes prosecutors toward harsher treatment of defendants – except, perhaps, when the defendants are themselves law enforcement officers. And the fact that prosecutors mediate between law enforcement agencies and the courts probably makes it even harder for judges to regulate them; not only do prosecutors have a mantle of democratic legitimacy, but they are allied – however loosely – with law enforcement organizations that judges, too, fear alienating, because most judges in the United States also run for reelection.

Prosecutors' ambiguous relationship with the professional bar also tends to frustrate accountability. Prosecutors are advocates, but they are also "more than mere advocates."[56] Courts sometimes hesitate to regulate prosecutors precisely because, judges note, "a prosecutor stands perhaps unique, among officials whose acts could deprive persons of constitutional rights, in his amenability to professional discipline by an association of his peers."[57] At the same time, prosecutors escape serious regulation by bar associations precisely because they are "fundamentally different from ... lawyers who represent clients."[58]

American constitutional law is often said to keep government in check not through accountability, per se, but rather through separation of powers – relying, in Madison's famous formulation, on "[a]mbition ... to counteract ambition."[59] But border crossing by prosecutors can interfere with these kinds of checks and balances, too. Commentators have noted that prosecutors exercise "both executive and judicial power – posing the very danger the Framers tried to avoid."[60] In fact, it is sometimes said that prosecutors do not just have authority both to "*execute* the law" and to "*adjudicate* matters"; prosecutorial discretion also allows them to "*legislate* criminal law, setting the penal code's effective scope."[61]

Prosecutors escape accountability by blurring boundaries. Unsurprisingly, then, many of the most common suggestions for reforming prosecutors' offices

---

[55] *See* Richman, *supra* note 40.   [56] *See* supra note 38 and accompanying text.

[57] *Imbler v. Pachtman*, 424 U.S. 409, 429 (1976).

[58] Angela J. Davis, Arbitrary Justice: The Power of the American Prosecutor 145 (2007); *see also* Bruce A. Green, *Prosecutors and Professional Regulation*, 25 Geo. J. Legal Ethics 873, 873 (2012); Sklansky, *supra* note 2, at 24 n.144; David Alan Sklansky, *Starr, Singleton, and the Prosecutor's Role*, 26 Fordham Urb. L.J. 509, 533–36 (1999).

[59] The Federalist No. 51, at 252 (James Madison) (Cambridge 2003); *see also, e.g.,* Jon D. Michaels, *An Enduring, Evolving Separation of Powers*, 115 Colum. L. Rev. 515 (2015).

[60] Rachel E. Barkow, *Separation of Powers and the Criminal Law*, 58 Stan. L. Rev. 989, 1048 (2006).

[61] Erik Luna, *Prosecutor King*, 1 Stan. J. Crim. L. & Policy 48, 57 (2014).

amount to efforts to corral them within the categories they routinely transcend, imposing on them the same obligations of impartiality and evenhandedness we have for judges, or treating wrongdoing by prosecutors the same way we treat wrongdoing by police officers,[62] or treating and regulating them as advocates. Other reform proposals attempt to segregate functions within prosecutors' offices, so that, for example, some prosecutors will be expected to act like judges, while others act as advocates.[63]

There is a broad consensus that none of these proposals have gained much traction. Prosecutors have not become more accountable; instead, their power and their discretion seem to keep increasing.[64] At least part of the explanation is that all of these reform proposals swim against the current. The boundary blurring by prosecutors puts them at the vanguard of a broad trend in legal consciousness: the mounting enthusiasm for institutional flexibility, and the downplaying of formal rules and rigid categories.[65] "New Governance"[66] and "ad hoc instrumentalism"[67] are both parts of this broad trend. So is the growing power and importance of prosecutors. Increasingly, in fact, prosecutors are put forward as the model for bringing flexibility to other areas of governance. For example, the Obama Administration defended its proposed overhaul of immigration rules with an explicit analogy to prosecutorial discretion. Critics called the analogy flawed, but virtually no one on either side of the debate suggested that prosecutorial discretion is a bad thing, something that should be avoided rather than emulated.[68]

When you want government to be nimble and adaptable, prosecutors are natural role models – and efforts to make prosecutors themselves more constrained, to take discretion away from them and to conform their activities to rules and rigid legal categories, face great difficulties. The problem of reconciling prosecutors with democracy is harder, and deeper, than is typically recognized. It is, in part, the problem of reconciling democracy with the broad movement toward greater flexibility in government.

---

[62] *See, e.g.*, Brandon Buskey, *Prosecuting the Prosecutors*, N.Y. Times, Nov. 27, 2015, at A29.

[63] *See* Rachel E. Barkow, *Institutional Design and the Policing of Prosecutors: Lessons from Administrative Law*, 61 Stan. L. Rev. 869 (2009).

[64] *See, e.g., Id.* at 921; Bibas, *supra* note 20, at 978; Gold, *supra* note 20, at 99; Wright, *supra* note 35, at 595.

[65] *See* Sklansky, *supra* note 2.

[66] *See, e.g.*, Jason M. Solomon, *New Governance, Preemptive Self-regulation, and the Blurring of Boundaries in Regulatory Theory and Practice*, 2010 Wisc. L. Rev. 591.

[67] David Alan Sklansky, *Crime, Immigration, and Ad Hoc Instrumentalism*, 15 New Crim. L. Rev. 157 (2012).

[68] *See, e.g.*, Adam B. Cox & Cristina M. Rodríguez, *The President and Immigration Law*, 125 Yale L.J. 1 (2015).

V IMPLICATIONS

Where does this leave us? How should a concern for democracy affect our thinking about prosecutors? I have tried to show that the answer is complicated, for three different reasons. First, it will depend on our ideas about democracy, and these vary widely. In the United States, there at least two very different clusters of ideas about democracy – democratic pluralism and participatory democracy – and they have different implications for how we should think about prosecutors. Second, the implications of any understanding of democracy for prosecutors will depend on what we want from prosecutors, and those desiderata themselves vary widely. Reconciling democracy with prosecutors is one kind of task if we have our expectations for prosecutors are, loosely speaking, "adversarial," and a different kind of task if our expectations are instead, loosely speaking, "inquisitorial." Third, expectations for prosecutors do not just vary widely from person to person; most of us, as individuals, want conflicting things from prosecutors, because we have come to depend on prosecutors to mediate between conflicting expectations for the legal system as a whole. As a result, prosecutors blur key boundaries that structure our thinking about criminal justice, a fact that itself makes it more difficult to hold prosecutors accountable in any customary way.

Despite these three layers of complication, I do think there are practical, noncontroversial implications for reforming prosecutors' offices – at least in the United States, and perhaps elsewhere as well. These imperatives are "noncontroversial" in that they do not rely, or at least do not rely strongly, on any particular understanding of democracy or any particular understanding of the prosecutor's role. The imperatives do assume that prosecutors, at least in the United States, perform – and are expected to perform – an "adversarial" and not just an "inquisitorial" function, exercising broad discretion and not just applying legal standards. Without that assumption, as we have seen, the case is weak for any kind of democratic oversight of prosecutors. Beyond that, though, the suggestions I am about to make do not rely on any particular set of ideas about how prosecutors should combine their various roles – when and to precisely what extent they should be adversaries or inquisitors, discretion-wielders or law-appliers, quasi-judicial figures or law enforcement leaders.

The first imperative, in fact, flows more or less directly from the very ambiguity that surrounds the prosecutor's role. Government flexibility has become something of a new orthodoxy; there are regular calls for government to be nimbler, more entrepreneurial, more adaptive, and more data-responsive. This is perhaps especially true in criminal justice, where many of the most celebrated crime-control initiatives of recent years fall within a category sometimes

described as "pulling levers"; the idea is to have local officials pool their
resources and their "tools" – i.e., the legal procedures they can initiate – and
then deploy those resources and tools strategically and selectively against the
worst offenders.[69] Prosecutors have always been engaged in "pulling levers"; in
some sense that is what prosecutorial discretion is all about. "Intelligence-led
prosecution" usually boils down to prosecutors using their traditional tools more
strategically and also employing new tools – legal proceedings other than
criminal prosecution – in conjunction with other agencies (immigration enforcement, public housing administration, parole agencies, etc.). There is much to
be said for all of this, but it raises serious problems of accountability. And if, as I
have suggested, the rise of prosecutorial power is linked to the growing emphasis
on flexibility in law and governance, then thinking seriously about prosecutors
and democracy will require thinking seriously about the turn toward flexibility
and the challenges it poses for accountability.

The second imperative pertains to the demographic diversity of prosecutors. The demographics of prosecutors in the United States are very different
from the demographics of the nation as a whole; racial minorities are
significantly underrepresented among prosecutors.[70] This appears to be
true both among elected prosecutors and among the rank-and-file lawyers
who staff prosecutors' offices. (I say "appears" because statistics on the
demographics of rank-and-file prosecutors are surprisingly limited – a matter
to which I will return below.) In California, for example, Latinos comprise
almost 39% of the state population but only 9% of prosecutors; Whites are
slightly more than 38% of all Californians, but nearly 70% of state's prosecutors.[71] At the federal level, 8% of Assistant United States Attorneys nationwide are Black and 5% are Latino, compared with a national population that
is 13% Black and 17% Latino.[72]

Reducing disparities of this kind is important from the standpoint of just
about any set of ideas about the relationship between democracy and prosecutors. Recall the two-by-two grid we constructed earlier, with its four ideal-
type combinations of ideas about democracy and ideas about prosecutors.
Consider each of these combinations in turn, starting in the upper left-hand

---

[69] *See, e.g.,* David M. Kennedy, *Old Wine in New Bottles: Policing and the Lessons of Pulling
Levers, in* POLICE INNOVATION: CONTRASTING PERSPECTIVES 155 (David Weisburd &
Anthony A. Braga eds., 2006); Sklansky, *supra* note 67, at 101, 203 & 208 n.168.

[70] *See, e.g.,* Nicholas Fando, *A Study Documents the Paucity of Black Elected Prosecutors: Zero in
Most States,* N.Y. TIMES, July 7, 2015.

[71] *See* KATHERINE J. BIES ET AL., STANFORD CRIMINAL JUSTICE CENTER, STUCK IN THE '70S:
THE DEMOGRAPHICS OF CALIFORNIA PROSECUTORS 6 (2015).

[72] *See id.* at 8–9.

corner with the traditional American-style, discretion-wielding, adversarial prosecutor, combined with democratic pluralism, which relies on elections and elites to mediate group differences. Dramatic underrepresentation of any group among the ranks of elected prosecutors or their subordinates suggests that elections may not be functioning properly; the interests of minority groups not be receiving full recognition. When an adversarial understanding of prosecutors is combined with participatory democracy – the lower left-hand corner of our two-by-two grid – the significance of demographic diversity becomes even clearer. If discretion-wielding prosecutors derive their democratic legitimacy by serving as a vehicle for popular participation in governance, if we count on prosecutors to move the criminal justice system in directions consonant with community concerns by involving the community in the formulation of enforcement priorities, then having prosecutorial workforces that are broadly representative of the communities they serve becomes even more important. If prosecutors are understood more as adjudicators and rule-appliers than as advocates and discretion-wielders – if we are on the right-hand side of the grid – then the race of prosecutors might be expected to make less of a difference, but only if one believes that the rules leave no room for interpretation or judgment, and that prosecutors can leave their identities at the office door. If racial diversity among judges matters – and it surely does – then racial diversity among prosecutors matters, too, even if prosecutors are thought of as quasi-judicial.

In the heyday of democratic pluralism, the 1950s and 1960s, when democratic pluralism heavily dominated virtually all discussions of American democracy, underrepresentation of minorities in government workforces was more often than not viewed as relatively unimportant; elites were trusted to mediate the concerns of all Americans. But this reflected not so much the underlying logic of democratic pluralism as a degree of myopia about the salience of race in the United States as a social marker and constructor of identity. Despite the emphasis they placed on groups as an engine of democracy, the pluralists were oddly dismissive of the importance of racial categories.[73] And the limited quantitative evidence available suggests that racial diversity in a prosecutor's office does make a difference. Researchers have found, for example, that "[b]lack defendants are more likely to be sentenced to prison than their white counterparts, even after controlling for legally relevant variables, but when black defendants are sentenced in districts with increased representation of black prosecutors, they have a decreased likelihood of being

---

[73] *See* SKLANSKY, *supra* note 1.

imprisoned, resulting in more racially equitable sentences."[74] And several decades of research on police departments – organizations for which we have much better demographic data than for prosecutors – similarly suggests that diversity matters, not so much because minority officers are less prone to bias (the evidence on that point is conflicting), but because they bring their experiences and perspectives in the office, altering attitudes, assumptions, and behaviors throughout the organization, and because they help the organization build bridges to minorities in the communities they serve.[75]

The third imperative pertains to transparency. The available statistics on the demographics of American prosecutors are paltry compared to those that are available on the police – and that have been available for decades. And this just one piece of a larger pattern of secrecy; the policies and practices of prosecutors' offices are, if anything, more opaque than their personnel.[76] Prosecutor's offices are instinctively secretive and insular, the way that police departments were half a century ago. The lack of transparency makes it difficult to evaluate prosecutors' offices; this is one of the reasons that prosecutors' election campaigns are so superficial and that the elections themselves have generally proven a weak tool of accountability. The opacity of prosecutors' offices thus poses a significant problem for democratic pluralism, with the emphasis that theory places on the check provided by the ballot box. The pluralists of the 1950s and 1960s thought voters in most elections were poorly informed, so elections ordinarily served only a loose check.[77] But the check was nonetheless valuable, partly because it allowed the populace to set the general direction of government while leaving the day-to-day details to the elites.[78] Prosecutorial elections, though, generally do not facilitate even this very loose kind of popular oversight, in part because the public knows so little about how prosecutors' offices operate. That is a matter of concern from the standpoint of participatory democracy, as well – perhaps even a greater

---

[74] Amy Farrell, Geoff Ward, & Danielle Rousseau, *Race Effects of Representation among Federal Court Workers: Does Black Workforce Representation Reduce Sentencing Disparities?*, 623 ANNALS AM. ACAD. POL. & SOC. SCI. 121, 131 (2009); *see also* Ryan D. King, Kecia R. Johnson, & Kelly McGeever, *Demography of the Legal Profession and Racial Disparities in Sentencing*, 44 L. & SOC'Y REV. 1, 23, 26 (2010).

[75] *See* David Alan Sklansky, *Not Your Father's Police Department: Making Sense of the New Demographics of Law Enforcement*, 96 J. CRIM. L. & CRIMINOLOGY 1209 (2006).

[76] *See, e.g.*, John F. Pfaff, *The War on Drugs and Prison Growth: Limited Importance, Limited Legislative Options*, 52 HARV. J. LEGIS. 173, 177 (2015).

[77] *See, e.g.*, ANGUS CAMPBELL ET AL., UNIV. OF MICH. SURVEY RES. CENTER, THE AMERICAN VOTER (1960).

[78] *See, e.g.*, SKLANSKY, *supra* note 1, at 18–21.

concern. It is difficult for the public to participate in or partner with institutions it cannot understand.

The boundary-blurring nature of the prosecutor's role may make transparency still more important. Because prosecutors move back and forth across so many of the key divides in criminal justice – acting sometimes as advocates, sometimes as inquisitors, sometimes as law enforcement officers, and sometimes as quasi-judicial figures – they are able more often than not to evade the formal mechanisms of accountability tailored to the categories that they transcend. Courts hesitate to regulate prosecutors the way police are regulated, for example, in part because prosecutors are subject to professional discipline[79]; the organized bar, meanwhile, exempts them from serious regulation, because a prosecutor is "expected to be more (or is it less?) than an adversary."[80] One advantage of transparency as a strategy for prosecutorial reform is that it can be largely agnostic as to essential nature of the prosecutor's role and the particular legal mechanisms through which prosecutors are best held accountable.

The great weakness, so far, of the strategy of transparency is that the near-total lack of consensus regarding what should count in assessing the performance of a prosecutor's office. Pretty much everyone agrees that conviction rates are a very poor measure of how well prosecutors are doing their jobs, but that is where agreement ends. There is no consensus whatsoever regarding the indicia that should be added to, or supplemented for, conviction rates. The suggestions include crime and recidivism rates[81] and total criminal justice expenditures,[82] to the rate at which criminal defendants are convicted as charged,[83] changes in the rate at which convicted defendants are diverted from prison,[84] the percentage of prosecutions devoted to "violent" and "serious" offenses,[85] ratings of head prosecutors by their staff and by other stakeholders,[86] and measures of transparency itself, like whether the office releases information about the cases it declines to prosecute.[87] Unless they are co-authors, no two scholars or sets of reformers ever propose the same metric for prosecutorial effectiveness. This lack of consensus is the result of our varied and conflicting expectations for prosecutors.

---

[79] *See supra* note 57 and accompanying text.

[80] James Vorenberg, *Decent Restraint of Prosecutorial Power*, 94 HARV. L. REV. 1521, 1557 (1981).

[81] *See* LAUREN BROOKE-EISEN ET AL., BRENNAN CENTER FOR JUSTICE, FEDERAL PROSECUTION FOR THE 21ST CENTURY 4 (2014).

[82] *See* Gold, *supra* note 20, at 108.

[83] *See* Ronald Wright & Marc Miller, *The Screening/Bargaining Tradeoff*, 55 STAN. L. REV. 29, 33 (2002).

[84] BROOKE-EISEN ET AL., *supra* note 81, at 4.   [85] *Id.*   [86] *See* Bibas, *supra* note 20, at 989.

[87] *See* Wright, *supra* note 35, at 612–13.

One way to bolster the power of transparency as a driver of prosecutorial reform would be to create a ranking system or "report card" based on an eclectic set of performance measures, added together in the simplest possible manner, sidestepping disputes about which measures are best or how they ideally should be weighted and combined. This is an approach that has been used to assess governmental performance – and empower democratic oversight – in a range of other contexts, ranging from environmental protection to electoral fairness.[88] Rankings and scorecards have drawbacks, of course; chief among these are their potential to create a false sense of objectivity and to divert attention from things that aren't easily measured and quantified. Precisely for this reason, the use of rankings and ratings in education, for example, is highly controversial.[89] Rankings and scorecards as drivers of education reform have plenty of champions, though, and any ranking or rating system itself needs to be evaluated against a baseline. The "crucial question" is "As opposed to what?"[90] And the current system (if you can call it that) for regulating for prosecutors' offices in the United States has very few defenders.

There are other reasons to think that prosecutors are a particularly promising subject for a data-driven system of rankings or ratings. First, unlike other governmental functions for which rankings or scorecards have been implemented or proposed, prosecution is the responsibility, in general, of a highly visible, publicly elected official – the district attorney. If the prosecutors in a particular jurisdiction are doing a bad job, there is an obvious person to blame.[91] More to the point, the district attorney is very likely to *fear* being blamed, and is in a position to change things. In this respect, prosecution is a much more promising area for rankings or ratings than, say, environmental protection, voting procedures, or even education. Second, criminal justice is a field that is rich in statistics and that lends itself in many ways to quantitative assessment, even if prosecutors to date have been less interested in collecting, sharing, and learning from data than courts and the police. Third, despite our conflicting expectations for prosecutors and the wide range of possibilities

[88] *See, e.g.,* HEATHER GERKEN, THE DEMOCRACY INDEX: HOW OUR ELECTION SYSTEM IS FAILING AND HOW TO FIX IT (2009); FREEDOM HOUSE, FREEDOM IN THE WORLD 2015 (2015); ANGEL HSU ET AL., YALE CENTER FOR ENVIRONMENTAL LAW & POLICY, 2014 ENVIRONMENTAL PERFORMANCE INDEX: FULL REPORT AND ANALYSIS (2014); Pew Elections Performance Index, at www.pewtrusts.org/en/multimedia/data-visualizations/2014/elections-performance-index.

[89] *See, e.g.,* Emmarie Huetteman, *Senate Approves Overhaul of No Child Left behind Law,* N.Y. TIMES, Dec. 10, 2015.

[90] GERKEN, *supra* note 88, at 102.

[91] This is true for federal prosecutions as well, although to a somewhat lesser extent. *See, e.g.,* Sklansky, *supra* note 67, at 215–16.

about the proper relationship between prosecutors and democracy, there is broad agreement about some of what we should want from prosecutors – energy, legal skill, evenhandedness, proportionality, respectful treatment of victims, and constitutional compliance – and some of what we don't want – vindictiveness, incompetence, partiality, and deception.

The opacity surrounding the operation of most public prosecutors' offices suggests that there are likely to be offices that would score low on virtually any plausible composite measure of performance. Even if we cannot reliably and uncontroversially identify the very best prosecutors' offices, we may be about to flag the worst, and that itself could be productive. The trick will be to find quantifiable performance measures for prosecutors that are reasonable proxies for widely agreed-upon desiderata. That may prove too much of a challenge, but we will not know until we try.

Epilogue
Prosecutors and Democracy – Themes and Counterthemes

By Máximo Langer & David Alan Sklansky*

The essays in this collection have analyzed the relationship between prosecutors and democracy in various countries, using various methodologies, and drawing on various theoretical perspectives. They have amply demonstrated, we think, how complex it can be to tease out what democracy means for prosecutors, and what prosecutors mean for democracy. They have shown, too, how dependent that task can be on the particular social and legal contexts in which prosecutors operate. Many of the contributors have been understandably, and perhaps admirably, hesitant to generalize beyond the national settings they know best.

In this Epilogue, though, we want to take a step back and to trace some very broad patterns in the discussions that have made up this volume by articulating four competing ways to think about the relationship between prosecutors and democracy, including some that our chapters did not explore or did not analyze as such. We want to identify four competing themes, each theme corresponding to a different way in which prosecutors might be thought to be "democratic" – or, maybe more precisely, to a different kind of "democracy" that criminal prosecution can help to constitute. Prosecutors can promote *representative democracy*, by serving as an agent of the people. Prosecutors can be key figures in what can be called *legal democracy*, by serving as neutral and independent ministers of justice, advancing the rule of law. Prosecutors can be democratic by advancing the

* We would like to thank Charles Anderson, Stuart Banner, Beth Colgan, Julie Cramer, Ingrid Eagly, Matthew Fox, Jack Katz, Ricardo Lillo Lobos, Emily Murphy, Jyoti Nanda, Richard Re, and Joanna Schwartz for comments on an earlier draft at the UCLA Criminal Justice Faculty Workshop. We would also like to thank Ernesto Matías Díaz, John Haley, Jacqueline Hodgson, Astrid Liliana Sánchez Mejía, Máximo Sozzo, and María Luisa Villamarín López for their feedback on aspects of Colombian, French, and Spanish law and their help on some of the sources we use.

values that embody a given conception of democracy, such as *liberal democracy* and its values of liberty, dignity, and equality. Finally, systems of criminal prosecution can be configured to promote various conceptions of *participatory democracy*, by securing roles for the victims of crime and for members of the community more generally; the extreme version of this approach is to allow private individuals themselves to bring criminal prosecutions.

The first three of these themes – representative democracy, legal democracy, and liberal democracy – have all figured prominently and repeatedly in the chapters of this book – though without all of them being conceptualized as such. The fourth theme, participatory democracy, has been noticeable more for its absence, although it has surfaced occasionally – for example, in the discussions of the "community prosecution" movement in the United States. One thing we want to highlight in this Epilogue is how discussions drawing on these four different themes can sometimes seem like ships passing in the night. As guides for thinking about prosecutors, the four themes can be understood as rooted in different "strands" of democracy, but they also can be seen as following alternative, mutually inconsistent lodestars. They can be understood, that is to say, as themes and counterthemes.

The four themes we have identified, and the four kinds of democracy to which they correspond, are not full-fledged theories of democracy; they are not comparable to, say, democratic pluralism, or to deliberative democracy, or to the account of democratic federalism developed in *The Federalist*. They are themes and counterthemes; clusters of ideas that march under the banner of "democracy" and that, in various ways at various times, shaped political and institutional aspirations in societies around the world.

By mapping these four possible relationships between prosecutors and democracy, we hope both to highlight the ways in which the chapters of this book have been in conversation with each other and to bring out certain aspects of that conversation that have remained largely below the surface. We also will try to use our mapping to draw a particular prescriptive lesson. We think that discussions of the relationship between prosecutors and democracy have been excessively dominated by a narrow understanding of democracy as a principal-agent relationship in which prosecutors, as representatives of the people, are responsive to their wishes. A richer understanding of the sources of legitimation of prosecutors and of the relationship between prosecution and democracy, we will suggest, may help deepen our understanding of what it is distinctive about prosecutors in the United States and open possible avenues for discussion and reform in the United States and elsewhere.

I REPRESENTATIVE DEMOCRACY: PROSECUTORS AS AGENTS OF THE POPULAR WILL

Leaving aside federal prosecutors, a distinctive, if not unique, feature of prosecutors in the United States is that they are elected by the people.[1] Most heads of the local prosecution offices, typically known as district attorneys, and most state attorneys general have been selected in this manner since the nineteenth century.[2] This gives prosecutors in the United States a mantle of democratic legitimacy that prosecutors do not have in other countries. It enables prosecutors in the United States to speak for "the people," as the very names given to cases – i.e., *People v. Joe Doe* – suggest.[3]

The legitimacy conferred by popular election is rooted in a particular kind of democracy: representative democracy. If the prosecutorial function is an aspect of self-government, the election of prosecutors enables the people to rule themselves through their representatives. As representatives of the people, prosecutors are entitled to prosecute crime and, since the head of the prosecutor office has limited terms, the people may hold them accountable in periodic elections. In this sense, local prosecutors in the United States are political figures who get at least part of their legitimacy from the same sources than other local political officials. These figures include not only the major and local council representatives, but other figures who also play a role in the criminal justice system, such as judges and police chiefs.

Despite the increasing role of prosecutors in criminal justice around the world, no other political system we are aware of has established the popular election of prosecutors in recent years. In Western Europe, Central and Eastern Europe, Latin America, and Asia, there have been changes in the way prosecutors are appointed and other reforms on the prosecutor's office.[4]

---

[1] In at least one canton in Switzerland, citizens participate in the election of the head of the prosecutor's office, but in the great majority of cantons, she is elected by parliament. *See* GWLADYS GILLIÉRON, PUBLIC PROSECUTORS IN THE UNITED STATES AND EUROPE: A COMPARATIVE ANALYSIS WITH SPECIAL FOCUS ON SWITZERLAND, FRANCE, AND GERMANY 179–181 (2014) (explaining that one of the systems for electing and nominating the head of the prosecutor's office is election or nomination directly by citizens, but without clearly stating all the cantons in which citizens participate in the election and nomination of prosecutors).

[2] JOAN E. JACOBY, THE AMERICAN PROSECUTOR: A SEARCH OF IDENTITY 19–28 (1980); Michael J. Ellis, *The Origins of the Elected Prosecutor*, 121 YALE L.J. 1528 (2012).

[3] *See, e.g.*, William T. Pizzi, *Understanding Prosecutorial Discretion in the United States: The Limits of Comparative Criminal Procedure as an Instrument of Reform*, 54 OHIO ST. L. REV. 1325 (1993).

[4] *See, e.g.*, LUNA & WADE, *infra* note 136; Máximo Langer, *Revolution in Latin American Criminal Procedure: Diffusion of Legal Ideas from the Periphery*, 55 AM. J. COMP. L. 617 (2007) [hereinafter *Revolution*]; Public Prosecutors Office Japan, *Prosecution Reform Initiatives in the Past Three Years* (2015), available at www.kensatsu.go.jp/content/001142803.pdf (last visited on November 22, 2016).

But none of them have included the introduction of popular elections to appoint prosecutors. That is a striking fact and one worth pondering, given the tight connection between popular election and the perceived legitimacy of prosecutors in the United States.

Part of the explanation, no doubt, is that Americans themselves – or at least American legal academics – have repeatedly expressed reservations about the practice of electing prosecutors. Commentators have picked up on this distinctive United States feature to explain other features – largely unattractive – of the American criminal justice system. In the last four decades, for example, the United States more than quadrupled its incarceration rate, becoming more punitive in this respect than any other major nation.[5] This trend originated in the context of increasing crime levels between the 1960s and the 1980s and a politicization of crime that became an important issue in the public agenda and public discourse – including in electoral contests.[6] In response to constructed or perceived public demands for higher punitiveness, legislators and popular ballots hardened criminal laws and prosecutors charged more serious statutes and offenses.[7] In fact, some empirical assessments suggest that prosecutorial charging decisions were the most important implementing mechanism of the increasing levels of incarceration rates.[8] The conventional view of prosecutorial politics in the United States over the past several decades is that there was a constructed or perceived wish by the people to harden criminal justice responses to crime, and prosecutors as representatives of the people responded to political incentives and followed this command.[9]

---

[5] *See, e.g.*, www.prisonpolicy.org/reports/overtime.html (last visited on November 29, 2016); www.prisonstudies.org/highest-to-lowest/prison_population_rate?field_region_taxonomy_ti d=All (last visited on October 21, 2016).

[6] *See*, e.g., DAVID GARLAND, THE CULTURE OF CONTROL: CRIME AND SOCIAL ORDER IN CONTEMPORARY SOCIETY (2001); JONATHAN SIMON, GOVERNING THROUGH CRIME: HOW THE WAR ON CRIME TRANSFORMED AMERICAN DEMOCRACY AND CREATED A CULTURE OF FEAR (2007) [hereinafter GOVERNING THROUGH CRIME].

[7] *See, e.g.*, MICHELLE ALEXANDER, THE NEW JIM CROSS: MASS INCARCERATION IN THE AGE OF COLOR-BLINDNESS (2010); GARLAND, *supra* note 6; SIMON, GOVERNING THROUGH CRIME *supra* note 6; WILLIAM STUNTZ, COLLAPSE OF AMERICAN CRIMINAL JUSTICE (2013) [hereinafter COLLAPSE]; Sanford C. Gordon & Gregory A. Huber, *Citizen Oversight and the Electoral Incentives of Criminal Prosecutions*, 46 AM. J. POL. SCI. 334, 335 (2002); Nicola Lacey and David Soskice, *Crime, Punishment and Segregation in the United States: The Paradox of Local Democracy*, 17 PUNISHMENT AND SOCIETY 454 (2015); William J. Stuntz, *The Pathological Politics of Criminal Justice*, 100 MICH. L. REV. 505 (2001)[hereinafter *Pathological Politics*].

[8] John Pfaff, *The Micro and Macro Causes of Prison Growth*, 28 GEORGIA STATE UNIVERSITY LAW REVIEW 1 (2012).

[9] See, e.g., Michael Tonry, *Prosecutors and Politics in Comparative Perspective, in* PROSECUTORS AND POLITICS: A COMPARATIVE PERSPECTIVE 1 (Michael Tonry ed., 2012).

But political winds can shift. After the great recession of 2007, a political consensus started to arise on the need to reduce or slow down incarceration levels. For part of the political right, mass incarceration – especially as applied to nonviolent offenders – began to be seen as an unjustifiable tax on public budgets. For the political left, incarceration was not only too costly, but also inhumane and racially disproportionate in the burdens it imposed.[10] There are signs that, once again, the criminal justice system has been responsive to these demands, with legislatures and popular ballots reducing the harshness of criminal laws and a number of prosecutor offices calling for and implementing less draconian enforcement practices.[11] Also, in some counties, people voted out of office prosecutors who were considered "tough on crime" and elected prosecutors who promised a less punitive approach.[12]

At a positive/descriptive level, if prosecutors are understood and understand themselves as representatives of the people who are supposed to follow people's commands, one would expect prosecutors becoming softer on crime once perceived people's wishes have changed. At a normative level, it could be argued that this is how democracy should work. If the public demands harsher or softer criminal justice policies at different points in time, prosecutors as agents of the people should implement people's wishes. If people's wishes were unwise, this would not be the responsibility of prosecutors, but of the people who can always learn and change over time.

One could question these descriptive and normative views even within the framework of representative democracy. As Newton Minow said in a different context, one should not equate the public interest with what interests the public.[13] Under alternative views of representative democracy, even if elected by the people, prosecutors should pursue the public interest rather than simply implementing people's wishes. This would be consistent with the view of

---

[10] *See, e.g.,* Hadar Aviram, Cheap on Crime: Recession Era Politics and the Transformation of American Punishment (2015); Marie Gottschalk, Caught: The Prison State and the Lockdown of American Politics (2015); Jonathan Simon, *Beyond Tough on Crime: Towards a Better Politics of Prosecution,* in this volume [hereinafter *Better Politics of Prosecution*].

[11] *See, e.g., Brooklyn DA Ken Thompson,* The Brooklyn Dist. Attorney's Office, www.br ooklynda.org/brooklyn-da-ken-thompson/ (last visited September 15, 2016); *District Attorney Vance and John Jay College President Travis Announce Partnership to Launch New Institute for Innovation in Prosecution,* available at www.jjay.cuny.edu/news/district-attorney-vance-and-j ohn-jay-college-president-travis-announce-partnership-launch-new (last visited September 15, 2016).

[12] *See* David Alan Sklansky, *The Changing Political Landscape for Elected Prosecutors,* 14 Ohio St. J. Crim. L. 647 (2017) [hereinafter *Elected Prosecutors*].

[13] Newton N. Minow, Television and the Public Interest, Address to the Nat'l Ass'n of Broadcasters, May 9, 1961.

representative democracy animating *The Federalist Papers*, and with the understandings of the democratic pluralists. Even if the people elect prosecutors, people would not have the information or the knowledge to make decisions on individual criminal cases. Rather, it would be prosecutors, as experts, public officials, and members of responsible elites, who would make these decisions.[14]

This type of alternative account of representative democracy and prosecutors can explain, to some extent, prosecutorial practice in the United States. After all, at a descriptive level, prosecutors do not even know what the people want in many cases and prosecutors have to make their own decisions based on their own understanding of the public interest. This type of alternative account may also be normatively appealing. There is a broad consensus in the United States, as well as elsewhere, that the treatment of individual defendants should be decided apolitically – through the application of neutral standards, not based on public opinion. As William Simon notes in his contribution to this volume, the case for making prosecutors publicly accountable seems strongest with regard to policies and general practices, rather than with regard to particular cases.[15] Even at the level of policy and practices, though, there are advantages to having prosecutors exercise independent, professional judgment, rather than seeing themselves as agents of the popular will. The lesson of the past several decades may be, precisely, that public opinion regarding criminal justice is subject to excessive and irrational swings, and that it is easy, in particular, for politicized criminal justice to become overly draconian criminal justice.[16] Experts may be better situated to balance concerns of crime control and public safety against considerations of fairness and restraint.[17] In fact, professional standards on prosecutors may reflect this view.[18]

However, in the United States, the understanding of prosecutors as agents of the popular will has been durable and powerful. If anything, it has grown

---

[14] *See* David Alan Sklansky, *Unpacking the Relationship between Prosecutors and Democracy in the United States*, in this volume [hereinafter *Unpacking*].

[15] William H. Simon, *The Organization of Prosecutorial Discretion*, in this volume [hereinafter *Organization*].

[16] *See, e.g.,* FRANKLIN E. ZIMRING, GORDON HAWKINS & SAM KAMIN, PUNISHMENT AND DEMOCRACY: THREE STRIKES AND YOU'RE OUT IN CALIFORNIA (2001).

[17] *See, e.g.,* Angela J. Davis, *Prosecutors, Democracy and Race*, in this volume [hereinafter *Prosecutors*] (prosecutors should not bow to the whims of the majority in the name of accountability if their independent professional judgment demands a different outcome).

[18] *See, e.g.,* AMERICAN BAR ASSOCIATION CRIMINAL JUSTICE STANDARDS COMMITTEE, ABA STANDARDS FOR CRIMINAL JUSTICE: PROSECUTION FUNCTION AND DEFENSE FUNCTION, STANDARD 3–1.2(b) (4th ed. 2015): "The prosecutor serves the public interest and should act with integrity and balanced judgement to increase public safety . . ."

stronger in recent decades, as democratic pluralism has waned in appeal[19] and as a growing number of criminal justice reformers have turned to elections, rather than judicial or legislative oversight, as the most promising tool for improving how prosecutors exercise their authority.[20] If the criminal justice system is too punitive and unequal and does not prosecute enough police brutality – just to mention some of the possible ills of criminal justice in the United States – the perceived solution, increasingly, is persuading or educating the people about the right criminal justice policies or improving the system of election of prosecutors. One can interpret a whole set of diagnoses, proposals, and initiatives from commentators, activists, and other reformers as fitting within this framework. This is the position ultimately adopted, for example, by Angela Davis in her contribution to this volume.

The "community prosecution" movement, reviewed approvingly by William Simon in his contribution to this volume, can be understood at least in part as a way to make prosecutors more faithful agents of the popular will and more responsive to public views on how the power of the criminal justice system should be deployed.[21] But it is far from clear how significant "community prosecution" is in the day-to-day operation of district attorneys' offices, as opposed to the level of symbolism.[22] The most powerful mechanisms for making prosecutors agents of the popular will in the United States are the elections in which district attorneys are selected and then either retained or removed from office. Much attention has been paid in recent years to the possibility of making those elections more meaningful. For instance, commentators and activists have concluded that the problems of this system include that the election of prosecutors is often not *contested* and that the incumbent is typically reelected.[23] In addition, the public often lacks information about the district attorney's work.[24] Proposed solutions to these problems include higher transparency and accountability so that the people may make more informed decisions when electing prosecutors.[25] There have also been proposals to educate the public

---

[19] On the retreat of democratic pluralism and how it affected ideas about police, see DAVID ALAN SKLANSKY, POLICE AND DEMOCRACY (2008) [hereinafter POLICE AND DEMOCRACY].

[20] *See, e.g,* Simon, *Better Politics of Prosecution, supra* note 10 (the legitimacy of prosecution in the U.S. is more political than it is legal and, as a consequence, the substantial reform of the U.S. carceral state will require democratic success).

[21] *See* Simon, *Organization, supra* note 15.   [22] *See* Sklansky, *Unpacking, supra* note 14.

[23] Ronald F. Wright, *How Prosecutor Elections Fail Us,* 6 OHIO ST. J. CRIM. L. 581 (2009); David Alan Sklansky, *Elected Prosecutors, supra* note 12.

[24] *See* Davis, *Prosecutors, supra* note 17 (a prosecutor's constituents cannot hold her accountable if they don't know what she does).

[25] *See* Davis, *Prosecutors, supra* note 17 (the democratic process can work, but only with more transparency in the prosecution function and the election of prosecutors who are committed

about the duties and responsibilities of prosecutors and to get the public more involved in prosecutorial elections.[26] The recent interest by people and media on police unnecessary killings of black men and women, together with social justice movements like Black Lives Matter, may be helping to mobilize people who have traditionally been uninterested in prosecutorial elections.[27] Progressive donors have supported these efforts by donating to district attorney candidates who promise to reduce punitiveness levels and advance equality.[28]

In a few recent district attorney elections and prosecutorial initiatives, the new political climate on criminal justice, social mobilization, and renewed electoral strategies have delivered some promising results from reformers' perspectives.[29] However, critics have cautioned about the true promise of at least some of these trends. For instance, in her chapter for this collection, Angela Davis argues that even if elections present the best opportunity to hold prosecutors accountable, the handling of a single high-profile case will not have an impact on systemic unwarranted racial disparities. To eliminate or reduce these disparities, it is necessary that a prosecutor take affirmative and more systematic steps to remedy the problem, such as empirically identifying the office's handling of which cases produce the most important disparities and then implement policies to address them.[30]

In his chapter, Jonathan Simon notices that prosecutors have been mostly absent from the leadership of the reform camp and warns about the power of prosecutors to resist change if they do not support it.[31] Prosecutors do not only follow, but also importantly shape criminal justice politics.[32] Simon analyzes "smart on crime" policies advanced by some prosecutors that include maximizing return on criminal justice investment, evidence-based-empiricism to deal with recidivism, and transparency about prosecutorial priorities. While

to racial justice). In a similar direction, see Stephanos Bibas, *Prosecutorial Regulation Versus Prosecutorial Accountability*, 157 U. PA. L. REV. 959, 960–61 (2009); Russell Gold, *Promoting Democracy in Prosecution*, 86 WASH. L. REV. 69 (2011); Marc L. Miller & Ronald F. Wright, *Reporting for Duty: The Universal Prosecutorial Accountability Puzzle and an Experimental Transparency Alternative, in* THE PROSECUTOR IN TRANSNATIONAL PERSPECTIVE 392 (Erik Luna & Marianne L. Wade eds., 2012); Wright, *supra* note 23.

[26] *See* Davis, *Prosecutors, supra* note 17.   [27] *See* Davis, *Prosecutors, supra* note 17.
[28] George Soros is an example. *See, e.g.*, Sklansky, *Unpacking, supra* note 14.
[29] *See, e.g.*, Davis, *Prosecutors, supra* note 17 (describing the work of John Chisholm and the electoral victories of Kim Foxx over Anita Alvarez and Michael O'Malley over Tim McGinty); Sklansky, *Unpacking, supra* note 14; Sklansky, *Elected Prosecutors, supra* note 12.
[30] *See* Davis, *Prosecutors, supra* note 17 (comparing the work done by district attorneys Marylin Mosby and John Chisholm).
[31] Simon, *Better Politics of Prosecution*, supra note 10.
[32] *See also* SIMON, GOVERNING THROUGH CRIME, *supra* note 6.

he considers "smart on crime" as an improvement over "tough on crime," he also discusses the limits of these policies to generate a substantially better politics of prosecution. These limits would include still trusting the exercise of prosecutorial discretion to produce a sound return on the funds invested in criminal justice, not reconsidering the incapacitative value of long prison sentences for violent crime and applying smart techniques only to nonviolent crimes and unserious crimes, assuming that empirical work may replace normative choices and not be determined by them, not articulating a new set of normative expectations for prosecutors and their publics, and keeping a close alliance between prosecutors and the federal and state law enforcement machinery and its racial discrimination.[33]

Simon contrasts "smart on crime" with "the prosecutorial politics of dignity" that would include "procedural justice" reforms, efforts to increase prosecutorial accountability for police racism and prison overcrowding, and efforts to humanize those who are being prosecuted and punished. Though not as easy to name and market, "the prosecutorial politics of dignity" may present a more radical departure from the politics of "tough on crime."[34] So it seems especially noteworthy that some recent district attorney races have been won by candidates campaigning on platforms that drew on some of the themes Simon includes within the politics of dignity.[35]

Despite all of this, grave doubts linger about the reform strategy of making United States prosecutors more politically accountable, and not just because, as Jonathan Simon warns, "tough on crime" politics have never really gone away and could well stage a resurgence. (Donald Trump's successful presidential campaign in 2016 represented a fullthroated return to "law and order" rhetoric not just as appeal for stricter criminal justice policies, but as the foundation of an entire political agenda, what Simon has called "governing through crime."[36]) More fundamentally, as we noted earlier, there is a striking dearth of interest in other Western democracies in emulating the American practice of electing head prosecutors – even as prosecutorial power and concerns about prosecutorial power continue to grow in many of these other democracies. Part of the reason is that there are rival ideas about what "democracy" requires of prosecutors.

---

[33]　Simon, *Better Politics of Prosecution*, supra note 10.
[34]　Simon, *Better Politics of Prosecution*, supra note 10.
[35]　*See* Sklansky, *Elected Prosecutors*, *supra* note 12.
[36]　*See, e.g.,* Yamiche Alcindor, *Trump Rally in Wisconsin Finds Support for the Police*, N.Y. Times, August 17, 2016, at A9.

II LEGAL DEMOCRACY: PROSECUTORS AS INDEPENDENT AND NEUTRAL MINISTERS OF JUSTICE

If one way prosecutors can be considered "democratic" is by representing the popular will, another quite different way is by faithfully implementing the rule of law. A few of this book's chapters discussed this conception of prosecutors, though generally not referring to it as a democratic conception. However, when we ask whether a country is a "democracy," or a "constitutional democracy," often what we are asking, at least in part, is whether it honors the rule of law.[37] And so sometimes what democracy is thought to require of prosecutors is that they act as independent and neutral ministers of justice, applying the law evenhandedly across cases. It is consistent with this role that the prosecutor also have responsibility to design and implement criminal justice policy and to consider the public interest in the handling of cases, so long as they give content to criminal justice policy and the public interest neutrally and independently, rather than based on their own political calculations and self-preservation. As public officials of a democracy, prosecutors may still speak as representatives of the polis and be subjected to accountability.[38] But if they are seen as independent and neutral ministers of justice – if their principal allegiance is understood to be to the rule of law – then those accountability mechanisms are unlikely to include popular balloting.

This understanding of the relationship between prosecutors and democracy is stronger in Europe than in the United States, which is a large part of the reason that the American method of selecting head prosecutors has never caught on in Europe. But one finds this ideal – the ideal of the prosecutor as an agent of *legal* democracy – embraced and implemented in different degrees not only in Europe, but also in Latin America and elsewhere – including, as we will discuss later, in the United States.[39] This ideal includes three different

---

[37] *See, e.g.*, Aharon Barak, *Foreword: A Judge on Judging: The Role of a Supreme Court in a Democracy*, 116 Harv. L. Rev. 16 (2002); Michel Rosenfeld, *The Rule of Law and the Legitimacy of Constitutional Democracy*, 74 S. Cal. L. Rev. 1307 (2001); Sandra Day O'Connor, *Remarks at the Inaugural Sandra Day O'Connor Distinguished Lecture Series*, 41 Tex. Tech. L. Rev. 1169 (2007).

[38] Antony Duff, *Discretion and Accountability in a Democratic Criminal Law*, at 16–17, in this volume.

[39] David Held, Models of Democracy 201–209 (3rd ed., 2006) uses the term "legal democracy" to refer to Friedrich Hayek's conception of democracy that would include not only rule of law as one of its key features, but also features such as minimal state intervention in civil society and private life and a free-market society given fullest possible scope. We use the term "legal democracy" in a broader and looser way to encompass various conceptions of democracy that include rule of law as one of its components.

interrelated elements that it is analytically important to distinguish: independence, neutrality, and faithful application of the law by prosecutors.

In terms of independence, the institutional location of the office of the
prosecutor is one of the ways to protect prosecutors from political interference.
In order to advance this ideal, there are countries that have located the office of
the prosecutor within the judiciary or as an extra branch of government
different from the three traditional branches. For instance, Colombia, Costa
Rica, and Italy locate the office of the prosecutor within the judiciary, while
Argentina and Brazil consider it an extra branch of government.[40] In either
case, the institutional location is intended to protect the independence of
prosecutors from political actors. The extent to which this independence exists
in practice depends on, among other factors, the strength of the country's
institutional system.[41] However, at least in some countries, the institutional
location of the office of the prosecutors as an extra branch of government or
within the judiciary seems to have contributed to the ability of prosecutors to
investigate government officials and other powerful figures.[42]

---

[40]   See, e.g., Colombian Constitution, Article 249; Argentine Constitution, Article 120; Brazilian
       Constitution, Article 127.
[41]   See, e.g., Anne van Aaken et al., *Do Independent Prosecutors Deter Political Corruption? An
       Empirical Evaluation across Seventy-eight Countries*, 12 Am. L. & Econ. Rev. 204, 218 (2010)
       (measuring *de facto* or actual independence on variables such as whether prosecutors are
       forced to retire or removed from office against their will, frequent changes in the legal
       foundations for the prosecution of crimes committed by members of government, and
       adequate paid for prosecutors).
[42]   See, e.g., Carlo Rossetti, *The Prosecution of Political Corruption: France, Italy and the USA – A
       Comparative View*, 13 Innovation 169 (2000). For a debate on whether Italian prosecutors are too
       independent, see Giuseppe Di Federico, *Prosecutorial Independence and the Democratic
       Requirement of Accountability in Italy*, 38 British Journal of Criminology 373 (1998);
       Carlo Guarnieri, *Prosecution in Two Civil Law Countries: France and Italy*, in Comparing
       Legal Cultures 183 (David Nelken, 1997), 183–93; David Nelken, *Can Prosecutors Be Too
       Independent? An Italian Case Study*, in European Penology 249 (Tom Daems, Dirk van Zyl
       Smit, & Sonja Snacken eds., 2013). In Colombia, despite the institutional location of the office of
       the prosecutor within the judiciary, there have been criticisms about lack of independence of the
       office of the prosecutor whose head is appointed for six years with central participation by the
       president of the country. See, e.g., *Politización de la Fiscalía*, El Tiempo, October 28, 2001,
       available at www.eltiempo.com/archivo/documento/MAM-678576 (last visited on November 23,
       2016); Omar Flórez, *No a la politización de la Fiscalía*, Semana, April 25, 2004, available at www
       .semana.com/opinion/articulo/no-politizacion-fiscalia/65055-3 (last visited on November 23,
       2016); *Sin importar quién lo puso en la Fiscalía, Iguarán fue tibio con la parapolítica*, La Silla
       Vacía, February 28, 2011, available at www.lasillavacia.com/historia/sin-importar-quien-lo-puso-
       en-la-fiscalia-iguaran-fue-tibio-con-la-parapolitica-22187 (last visited on November 23, 2016). It is
       also important to notice that *de jure* or formal independence (such as the institutional position of
       the office of the prosecutor) and *de facto* or actual independence may not correlate with each other
       because strong *de jure* mechanisms of independence may be a response to a history of low *de facto*
       independence and high levels of corruption. See van Aaken et al., *supra* note 41, 223–25, 229.

   In other jurisdictions, prosecutors are members of a ministry of justice that is headed by a political appointee to whom prosecutors are accountable. This institutional structure can be interpreted as trying to strike a balance between prosecutorial independence and prosecutorial accountability to democratically elected leaders.[43] Varying from country to country, the independence of prosecutors from political influence is protected through limits on the instructions they may receive, the way they are appointed and removed, their professional status, and other constitutional, institutional, legal, political, and professional formal and informal norms. However, as our chapters on England, France, and Germany suggest, the degree to which independence from political incentives – including from improper protection of politically powerful or connected defendants – is achieved varies from place to place.[44]

   For instance, in France, prosecutors work in a hierarchical structure within the ministry of justice. As Jacqueline Hodgson and Mathilde Cohen note in their respective contributions to this volume, this structure confers legitimacy on French prosecutors by virtue of the French political tradition, which considers that the state represents the will of the people, and in which the executive "is supposed to protect citizens from excesses of unelected judges rather than judges protecting citizens from the executive, as in the Anglo-American tradition."[45] French prosecutors are considered magistrates and are initially recruited through the same process as judges; they have civil servant status and share their offices, budgets, and staff with judges.[46] However, they do not have the same independence as judges, and they are supposed to implement governmental policies and work collectively within the internal hierarchy of prosecutors.[47] There have been many indications – including public scandals – of pressure exercised on French prosecutors by the executive branch, including the President, to protect its own patrons and supporters.[48] Consequently, reforms have been introduced

---

[43] *See, e.g.*, Di Federico, *supra* note 42.

[44] *See also, e.g.*, John O. Haley, *Public Prosecution in Japan*, in OXFORD HANDBOOKS ONLINE 6 (2015) (stating that though the procuracy in Japan is formally subject to the direction of the minister of justice, the independence of the procuracy from external influences, especially political intervention, is among its distinguishing attributes and that no political supervision is permitted over the prosecutors responsible for a particular case).

[45] Mathilde Cohen, *The French Prosecutor as Judge. The Carpenter's Mistake?*, at 117 in this volume. *See also* Jacqueline S. Hodgson, *The Democratic Accountability of Prosecutors in England and Wales and France: Independence, Discretion and Managerialism*, in this volume [hereinafter *Democratic Accountability of Prosecutors*].

[46] Cohen, *supra* note 45.   [47] Cohen, *supra* note 45.

[48] *See* JACQUELINE S. HODGSON, FRENCH CRIMINAL JUSTICE: A COMPARATIVE ACCOUNT OF THE INVESTIGATION AND PROSECUTION OF CRIME IN FRANCE 80–85 (2005) [hereinafter FRENCH CRIMINAL JUSTICE]; Hodgson, *Democratic Accountability of Prosecutors, supra* note

to try to limit undue political influence, such as not allowing prosecutors to receive instructions in individual cases.[49] Unions of magistrates have also been pushing for greater individual and collective prosecutorial independence from the executive.[50] In her chapter for this collection and against the background of proposals to separate French prosecutors and judges in two distinct and separate corps, Mathilde Cohen argues that the preservation of the prosecutors' self-image as magistrates and their belonging to the judiciary with the judges may be key to preserving their independence.[51]

In Germany, prosecutors are located in the ministries of justice of the federal and state governments and may receive orders from their superiors.[52] However, German prosecutors are supposed to be apolitical figures, independent from judges and the police, with a duty to objectivity and beholden only to the law. German prosecutors have life tenure, and, for the most part, superiors give general instructions to prosecutors rather than instructions about how to handle individual cases.[53] Though at periods in German history, prosecutors equated the public interest with political ends, in recent decades, they have developed a quasi-judicial identity.[54] As Shawn Boyne explains in her contribution to this volume, the role of a German prosecutor is to be a "guardian of the law" and a pillar of the *Rechtsstaat*, according to which not only the power of the state is constrained by law, but the state must act in a lawful way.[55] Elections may change the political leadership of ministries of justice, but the leadership within the prosecution service is largely insensitive to electoral results.[56] Nevertheless, though efforts to exert political influence are not widespread, prosecutors are not immune from it through formal and informal mechanisms. Since in Germany's parliamentary system, the minister of justice responds to the legislature, parliamentary investigations, often started by an opposition party, are the main political check

---

45; Jacqueline S. Hodgson, *The French Prosecutor in Question*, 67 WASH. & LEE L. REV. 1361 (2010).

[49] C. PR. PÉN. Article 30 (France).   [50] Cohen, *supra* note 45.   [51] Cohen, *supra* note 45.

[52] Some commentators have considered the prosecution service as its own separate institution within the criminal justice system or as in between the executive and the judicial branches due to their duty to objectivity and other protections. But most commentators consider it located within the executive. *See* Shawn Boyne, *German Prosecutors and the Rechtsstaat*, in this volume [hereinafter *German Prosecutors*] (citing Ekaternia Trendafilova and Werner Róth, *Report on the public prosecution service in Germany*, in PROMOTING PROSECUTORIAL ACCOUNTABILITY, INDEPENDENCE AND EFFECTIVENESS. COMPARATIVE RESEARCH 237 (2008)).

[53] Boyne, *German Prosecutors*, *supra* note 52.   [54] *Id.*

[55] *Id. See also* SHAWN MARIE BOYNE, THE GERMAN PROSECUTION SERVICE. GUARDIANS OF THE LAW? (2013)[hereinafter THE GERMAN PROSECUTION SERVICE].

[56] Boyne, *German Prosecutors*, *supra* note 52.

over improper political influence. However, reformers have considered them insufficient and that it is necessary to introduce changes to make prosecutors not more accountable, but rather more independent such as giving regional prosecutors autonomy from their justice ministries and making government's instructions to prosecutors on individual cases more transparent.[57]

In England and Wales, where the public interest is regarded as an interest separate from that of the state, a hierarchical supervisory structure under the direction of state ministers, as in France, would be considered unacceptable political interference.[58] Even if both the Attorney General and the Director of Public Prosecutions in England and Wales are politically appointed, prosecutors, as Jacqueline Hodgson notes in her contribution to this volume, have a high degree of professional autonomy.[59] The Director of Public Prosecutions "is appointed by and responsible to, the Attorney General, whose office advises the government and represents the public interest in a range of capacities. This creates a less direct line of political accountability and one which, by convention, is 'exercised very sparingly, and not used to further the narrow political interests of the government and its supporters.'"[60]

Besides the institutional location of the office of the prosecutor, the prosecutors' status and the way prosecutors are recruited and removed may also advance the ideal of prosecutors as independent ministers of justice. In several countries in Europe, Latin America, and elsewhere, prosecutors are considered magistrates or civil servants who are, at least to some extent, peers of judges; are recruited right after law school, and together with judges; and are appointed, promoted, and removed by judicial councils composed by prosecutors and judges.[61]

---

[57] Id.

[58] Hodgson, *Democratic Accountability of Prosecutors, supra* note 45 (quoting Vera Langer, *Public Interest in Civil Law, Socialist Law, and Common Law Systems: The Role of the Public Prosecutor*, 36 AM. J. COMP. L. 279–280 (1988)).

[59] Hodgson, *Democratic Accountability of Prosecutors, supra* note 45.

[60] Id. (quoting Antoinette Perrodet, "The Public Prosecutor," in *European Criminal Procedures*, ed. Mireille Delmas-Marty and John Spencer (Cambridge: Cambridge University Press, 2002), 422).

[61] *See, e.g.,* CONSTITUTION DE LA RÉPUBLIQUE FRANÇAISE, Article 65 (France); EUROPEAN COMMISSION FOR THE EFFICIENCY OF JUSTICE, EUROPEAN JUDICIAL SYSTEMS. EFFICIENCY AND QUALITY OF JUSTICE (2014); Antoinette Perrodet, *The Public Prosecutor, in* EUROPEAN CRIMINAL PROCEDURES 415, 422–23, 427, 430–32 (Mireille Delmas-Marty and J. R. Spencer eds., 2002); European Commission of Democracy Through Law (Venice Commission), Report on European Standards as Regards the Independence of the Judicial System: Part II – The Prosecution Service, Study No. 494/2008 (Adopted 2010), at 34. www.coe.int/t/dghl/cooperation/capacitybuilding/Source/judic_reform/europeanStandards_en.pdf; CONSTITUCIÓN DE LA CIUDAD DE BUENOS AIRES, Articles 115–16 and 126. On Japan, see, e.g., Haley, *supra* note, at 5–6 (explaining the career path of Japanese prosecutors); United Nations Asia and Far East Institute for the Prevention of Crime and the Treatment of Offenders, *The Criminal Justice System in Japan: Prosecution* 3, Resource Material Series No. 53 (1997) (stating that public

However, the level of independence protection that these mechanisms provide also varies from place to place. For instance, in France, prosecutors are magistrates who are recruited and trained with judges, but prosecutors belong to a different branch of the judiciary than judges, they can be transferred to another post without their agreement, and the President and the Minister of Justice have a key role in their selection and promotion.[62] In fact, while the high council of the judiciary – an independent commission composed by judges, lawyers, and outside political appointees – has final decision-making on judges' promotions and removals, the council "has a much more limited role when it comes to prosecutors as the Ministry of Justice largely determines their career, including promotion, transfer, discipline and removal from office."[63] In addition, "those determining promotions are explicitly instructed to reward loyalty and conformity and to penalize independence."[64]

In Germany, the Federal Prosecutor General is "nominated by the Minister of Justice, appointed by the President, and then confirmed by the Federal Legislature."[65] State prosecutors report to the ministry of justice at the Land-level and the minister of justice is chosen by the Minister-President of the Land. In "most states, the state level Minister appoints the state's regional prosecutors," while in "other states, the State Ministry of Justice works with a judicial selection committee to recommend candidates for consideration."[66] "Up until recently, the Minister of Justice could remove the General Prosecutor in four states for political reasons. However, during the past fifteen years, all of Germany's Federal States have now abolished that possibility."[67] The "Ministry of Justice sets overall prosecution priorities, allocates budget dollars, and makes the key promotion decisions within the prosecution

---

prosecutors in Japan have a status equivalent to that of judges, receive equal salaries according to the length of the term in office, and their independence and impartiality are also protected by law), available at www.unafei.or.jp/english/pdf/RS_No53/No53_10FP.pdf (last visited on November 22, 2016).

[62] *See, e.g.,* Hodgson, *Democratic Accountability of Prosecutors, supra* note 45; Mathilde Cohen, *supra* note 45. The European Court of Human Rights has held that French prosecutors are not judicial officers for the purposes of Article 5.3 of the European Convention on Human Rights — that establishes the right by anyone arrested for the commission of an offense to be promptly brought before a judge or other officer authorized by law to exercise judicial power — because French prosecutors are not independent from the executive. *See, e.g., Case of Medvedyev and others v. France,* European Court of Human Rights (Grand Chamber), no. 3394/03, March 29, 2010, §§123–125; *Affaire Moulin c. France,* European Court of Human Rights, no. 37104/06, November 23, 2010, §§53–60. Seminal cases in this line of cases include *Schiesser v. Switzerland,* European Court of Human Rights, no. 7710/76, December 4, 1979, and *Huber v. Switzerland,* European Court of Human Rights (Plenary), no. 12794/97, October 23, 1990.

[63] Cohen, *supra* note 45, at 114.   [64] *Id.* at 118.

[65] Boyne, *German Prosecutors, supra* note 52, at 144.   [66] *Id.* at 144.   [67] *Id.* at 144.

offices."[68] Prosecutors have life-tenure and over the course of their careers, most prosecutors are not promoted to a supervisory level.[69] However, when they prosecute powerful figures and do not follow formal or informal suggestions to dismiss this type of case, their career may be side-tracked or they may be "promoted" to unappealing positions.[70] Prosecutors are particularly vulnerable in those state systems in which prosecutors are rotated frequently between the office of the prosecutor and the judiciary.[71]

Jurisdictions also express and implement in multiple ways neutrality and faithful application of the law by prosecutors, the other two elements of the ideal of prosecutors as ministers of justice. Conceptions of the criminal process may express and affect whether and to what extent prosecutors are considered and considered themselves as neutral ministers of justice. In this sense, while adversarial systems tend to consider the prosecutor as a party that is opposed to the defense, inquisitorial systems tend to consider the prosecutor as an impartial official.[72] Several countries in Europe, Latin America, and elsewhere consider prosecutors as impartial officials who have to look equally for inculpatory and exculpatory elements of proof;[73] have to document all their procedural activity and do not consider the elements of proof that they gather as elements of the prosecutor, but rather of the state's impartial investigation;[74] do not consider that they lose if the defendant is acquitted;[75] and may even appeal a conviction in favor of the defendant.[76] Scholars have debated to what extent these conceptions of the criminal process and legal and institutional rules actually shape prosecutors' self-perception and performance as impartial or neutral officials,[77] and more qualitative empirical studies are

---

[68] *Id.* at 144.   [69] *Id.*   [70] *Id.*   [71] *Id.*

[72] *See, e.g.*, Máximo Langer, *From Legal Transplants to Legal Translations: The Globalization of Plea Bargaining and the Americanization Thesis in Criminal Procedure*, 45 HARV. INT'L L.J. 1 (2004) [hereinafter *Globalization of Plea Bargaining*].

[73] *See, e.g.*, C. PR. PÉN. Articles 31 and 39-3 (France); StPO §160.2 (Germany); CÓDIGO PROCESAL PENAL DE LA REPÚBLICA DOMINICANA, Article 260 (Dominican Republic); CÓDIGO NACIONAL DE PROCEDIMIENTOS PENALES Article 129 (Mexico); CÓDIGO PROCESAL PENAL DE LA PROVINCIA DE BUENOS AIRES, Article 56 (Province of Buenos Aires, Argentina).

[74] *See* Máximo Langer & Kent Roach, *Rights in the Criminal Process: A Case Study of Convergence and Disclosure Rights*, in HANDBOOK ON CONSTITUTIONAL LAW 273 (Mark Tushnet et al. ed., 2013).

[75] *See, e.g.*, Boyne, *German Prosecutors*, *supra* note 52.

[76] *See, e.g.*, StPO §296.2; CÓDIGO PROCESAL PENAL DE LA REPÚBLICA DOMINICANA, Article 395 (Dominican Republic); CÓDIGO PROCESAL PENAL DE LA PROVINCIA DE BUENOS AIRES, Article 422 (Province of Buenos Aires, Argentina).

[77] *See, e.g.*, John H. Langbein & Lloyd L. Weinreb, *Comparative Criminal Procedure: "Myth" and Reality*, 87 YALE L.J. 1549 (1978).

necessary on different jurisdictions. However, even critical ethnographic studies suggest that, to some extent, they do.[78]

In addition, as a way to manifest and implement the ideal that prosecutors have to apply the law faithfully and evenhandedly across cases, many countries have adopted a pure legality principle or a version of the opportunity principle that formally eliminates or reduces the discretion that prosecutors have to dismiss cases, and have created also other mechanisms to make prosecutors accountable for their charging decisions.[79]

Italy still formally applies the principle of mandatory prosecution without any statutory exceptions and gives to it constitutional status.[80] In Germany, the legality principle or principle of mandatory prosecution requires that the prosecutor file charges whenever there is sufficient evidence to do so, but in recent decades, the opportunity principle was introduced to deal with an increasing docket and allows the prosecutor to dismiss non-serious cases and other specific cases in situations defined by the law.[81] Prosecutors "in most departments believe that they enjoy significant decision-making freedom."[82] However, the requirement that prosecutors document all their procedural

---

[78]　See, e.g., BOYNE, THE GERMAN PROSECUTION SERVICE, *supra* note 55 (arguing that even if the ideal of "objectivity" of German prosecutors has been recently undermined and does not rest on the law, there is reason for cautious optimism about it to the degree that it is embedded in prosecutorial organizational culture); HODGSON, FRENCH CRIMINAL JUSTICE, *supra* note 48 (stating that the inquisitorial roots of French criminal procedure are significant for our understanding of the present day roles of legal actors, as well as the different ways in which investigations are undertaken and the rights of the accused protected, even if in practice criminal procedures are played out rather differently than in the procedural models). *See also* Máximo Langer, *Strength, Weakness or Both? On the Endurance of the Adversarial and Inquisitorial Systems in Comparative Criminal Procedure, in* HANDBOOK ON COMPARATIVE CRIMINAL PROCEDURE 519, 524–25 (Jacqueline E. Ross & Stephen C. Thaman eds., 2016). Relatedly, on the ethos of Japanese prosecutors towards accuracy and consistency, see DAVID T. JOHNSON, THE JAPANESE WAY OF JUSTICE (2002).

[79]　For a brief analysis of the historical origins of the legality principle, see, e.g., Mirjan Damaška, *The Reality of Prosecutorial Discretion: Comments on a German Monograph*, 29 AM. J. COMP. L. 119, 125–126 (1981). For an argument within this paradigm in favor of the opportunity principle over the legality principle, see Duff, *supra* note 38, at 19–32. It is important to notice that different regulations about the degree of prosecutorial discretion not only are a way to advance in different degrees the ideal of the prosecutor as a neutral minister of justice, but may also help to strike different balances between this ideal and local demands and accountability. For instance, in France, in recent years, prosecutors have become more immersed in and intertwined with local officials and communities. The goal has been to make prosecution more sensitive to local needs, and prosecutorial discretion has been one of the ways to allow for local input. *See* Hodgson, *Democratic Accountability of Prosecutors, supra* note 45. *See also* Cohen, *supra* note 45. This same process has helped prosecutors gain more independence from the executive. *See Id.*

[80]　COSTITUZIONE ITALIANA (Italian Constitution) Article 112.　　[81]　StPO §§ 152–54.

[82]　Boyne, *German Prosecutors, supra* note 52, at 152.

activity in a file that will go to the court and an organizational culture of informal collegial controls place limits on and shape decision-making.[83] In addition, the alleged victim may lodge a complaint against a prosecutor's decision to dismiss a case; the complaint triggers review within the office of the prosecutor and may be taken to the courts.[84]

In Latin America, as part of the wave of adversarial reforms in the region, most countries have replaced or complemented the principle of mandatory prosecution with an opportunity principle that gives prosecutors the power not to file charges even if there is evidence that an offense has been committed, if situations defined by the law are present.[85] The arguments for the introduction of the opportunity principle have included enabling the criminal justice system to concentrate on the most serious cases and providing non-punitive responses to the less serious offenses.[86] But at least in theory (there are no empirical studies on the issue), the opportunity principle still cabins prosecutorial discretion and calls for an equal application of the law by prosecutors in serious cases.

In France, prosecutors have broad discretion on the initial charging decision, protecting individual prosecutorial decisions from review.[87] However, prosecutors are under legal duty to give reasons when they decide not to prosecute.[88] In addition, if the prosecutor decides not to prosecute, the complainant may ask that the decision be reviewed by a superior within the office of the prosecutor.[89] Furthermore, if the victim of crime or another entity initiates a criminal process by presenting a civil suit before the investigating judge, the prosecutor does not have discretion to dismiss the case.[90] Also, even in cases without a civil party, if a prosecutor decides to formally initiate a criminal process before an investigating judge, the courts have the final say on whether the case should be dismissed based on the available elements of proof.

In England and Wales, the Director of Public Prosecutions has issued guidance to structure prosecutorial decisions on dispositions and charging,

---

[83] *Id.*   [84] STPO § 172.

[85] *See, e.g,* CÓDIGO PROCESAL PENAL DE LA REPÚBLICA DOMINICANA, Articles 30 and 34 (Dominican Republic); CÓDIGO NACIONAL DE PROCEDIMIENTOS PENALES Article 256 (Mexico); CÓDIGO PROCESAL PENAL DE LA PROVINCIA DE BUENOS AIRES, Article 56bis (Province of Buenos Aires, Argentina).

[86] Langer, *Revolution, supra* note 4.

[87] C. PR. PÉN. Articles 40–1 (France); Hodgson, *Democratic Accountability of Prosecutors, supra* note 45.

[88] C. PR. PÉN. Articles 40–2 (France). One potential problem with prosecutors publishing their reasons for dismissal is that it can expose those about whom decisions are made to public prejudice. *See* Duff, *supra* note 38.

[89] C. PR. PÉN. Articles 40–3 (France).   [90] C. PR. PÉN. Articles 80 and 86 (France).

investigations, and about case law and how to deal with specific offenses.[91] Many of these guidelines are preceded by public consultation (which creates prosecutorial accountability to the public) and the guidelines are to be implemented uniformly through local Crown Prosecution offices.[92] Legal guidance has also implied that prosecutors "are required to justify their decisions and their application of specific criteria through detailed record keeping that is subject to later review."[93] Except in serious, complex, and sensitive cases, no single Crown Prosecutor is responsible for a case that passes through numerous sets of hands.[94] In the case of the charging decision, the *Code for Crown Prosecutors* establishes a full code test that includes an evidential test that requires that "there is sufficient evidence to provide a realistic prospect of conviction against each suspect on each charge" (para. 4.4) and a public interest test for whose application the *Code for Crown Prosecutors* lists considerations that prosecutors should take into account (para. 4.12).[95] In addition, the victim may ask for a review of the decision not to prosecute.[96]

Also in terms of procedural regulations, there has been a global trend towards the adoption of plea bargaining and other consensual mechanisms. This is relevant in this context because commentators in the United States have considered that plea bargaining may enhance prosecutorial discretion and may undermine the ideal of a faithful application of the law by creating incentives for prosecutors to overcharge, not to disclose exculpatory evidence to the defense, and to have an instrumental relationship with the law more generally, in order to obtain guilty pleas.[97] However, in many jurisdictions, these mechanisms still present substantial differences with plea bargaining in the United States because they do not apply to the most serious crimes, they are not used for investigatory purposes, the defendant has a right to access the prosecutor's file or judicial dossier before pleading guilty or otherwise agreeing with the application of the consensual mechanism, only sentencing bargaining is allowed, there is a fixed sentencing reduction for the use of consensual mechanisms, or penalty enhancements against the defendant for going to trial

---

[91] *See* Hodgson, *Democratic Accountability of Prosecutors, supra* note 45.   [92] *Id.*
[93] *Id.* at 21.   [94] *Id.*
[95] For an analysis of these two tests and mechanisms to make prosecutors accountable for their decisions, see Duff, *supra* note 38.
[96] *See, e.g.,* CROWN PROSECUTION SERVICE, VICTIMS' RIGHT TO REVIEW GUIDANCE, www .cps.gov.uk/publications/docs/vrr_guidance_2016.pdf; *R v. Christopher Killick* [2011] EWCA Crim 1608.
[97] *See, e.g.,* BROWN, *infra* note 106; Albert Alschuler, *The Prosecutor's Role in Plea Bargaining*, 36 U. CHI. L. REV. 50 (1968).

are not as substantial or are not under prosecutors' control like in the United States.[98]

The ideal of the prosecutor as a neutral and independent minister of justice can be undermined not only from political incentives and influence, but also from efficiency and managerial pressures. In many places, these pressures have not only increased the power of prosecutors to deal with criminal cases with a wide range of diversionary and adjudicatory tools, but also redefined the role of the prosecutor as an administrator and manager of the caseload. These managerial pressures may lead prosecutors to prioritize keeping the criminal docket under control and to standardize their decisions, rather than to ensure that justice is done in each individual case, to use efficiency and managerial instead of justice criteria to make decisions over cases, and may lead to less accountable and transparent ways to dispose of criminal cases.[99]

It should also be noticed that though efficiency pressures to dispose of criminal cases faster and out of court have increased the power of prosecutors and affected their role in many jurisdictions, not all jurisdictions have reacted equally, even within the same country.[100] For instance, while in some jurisdictions, these pressures may lead to a dismissal of cases that would have been prosecuted, in other places, they may lead to a processing of cases that would have been dismissed, thus creating a net-widening effect of the criminal justice system.[101]

---

[98] *See generally* Langer, *Globalization of Plea Bargaining, supra* note 72. It is also important to notice that in some countries, the introduction of broader prosecutorial discretion and consensual mechanisms related to plea bargaining have not given prosecutors more power to obtain criminal convictions. For instance, in Germany, efficiency pressures and a less punitive criminal justice system seem to have resulted in prosecutors dismissing many cases, rather than using the potential trial punishment as leverage to obtain convictions through consensual mechanisms. Boyne, *German Prosecutors, supra* note 52.

[99] *See, e.g.,* ANTOINE GARAPON ET AL., LA PRUDENCE ET L'AUTORITÉ: L'OFFICE DU JUGE AU XXIE SIÈCLE (2013); Malcolm M. Feeley and Jonathan Simon, *The New Penology: Notes on the Emerging Strategy of Corrections and Its Implications*, 30 CRIMINOLOGY 449 (1992). Among our chapters on these trends, see Hodgson, *Democratic Accountability of Prosecutors, supra* note 45 (describing the comparison between two French court regions by Laura Aubert, *Systématisme pénale et alternatives aux poursuites en France: una politique pénale en trompe-L'œil,"* 74 DROIT ET SOCIÉTÉ 17 (2010)).

[100] On these efficiency pressures, see, e.g., Hodgson, *Democratic Accountability of Prosecutors, supra* note 45.

[101] Boyne, *German Prosecutors, supra* note 52 (describing criticisms of German prosecutors for their proclivity to dismiss charges or defer prosecution and under-prosecute certain type of cases and describing high variation in dismissal rates in minor crime cases in different German states); Hodgson, *Democratic Accountability of Prosecutors, supra* note 45.

The ideal of the prosecutor as an apolitical and impartial agent of the law is weaker in the United States than in other countries. At the local level, as we have seen, the head of the office of the prosecutor is generally elected by the people. Even if, as we will see, there are elements in the United States that reflect a conception of prosecutors as apolitical and neutral agents of the law, the very system of popular election of prosecutors reflects, in itself, a competing, and at times predominant, normative ideal on prosecutors that is in tension with the ideal of prosecutors as neutral agents of the law and that seems to have actual effects in criminal justice practices – as we discussed in the prior section.

At the federal level, the Department of Justice is part of the executive branch and the Attorney General, and the 93 U.S. Attorneys are appointed by the President with consent by the Senate and they can be removed by the President.[102] Assistant U.S. Attorneys are appointed and may be removed by the Attorney General.[103] In this sense, the formal protections of federal prosecutors' independence are substantially weaker than in many other countries.[104] However, it is important to note that institutional and political checks and traditions, among other factors, seem to provide more independence to federal prosecutors in the United States than in many other countries.[105]

The ideal of the prosecutor as a minister of justice is weaker regarding its two other elements of prosecutors as neutral and faithful agents of the law. Both at the federal and state/local levels, prosecutors are not considered magistrates or judges, do not have life tenure, often see themselves as an opponent to the defense in an adversarial criminal process, and do not have a duty to look for both inculpatory and exculpatory evidence.[106] Also at the federal and state/local levels, prosecutors have broad discretion at the charging decision. They are not required to articulate their grounds to dismiss charges

---

[102] 28 U.S. Code § 541. U.S. Attorneys are appointed for a period of four years.

[103] 28 U.S. Code § 542.

[104] *See, e.g.,* Van Aaken et al., *supra* note 41, at 220 and 237–38 (the United States ranks 64 out of 78 countries in terms of *de jure* independence).

[105] Van Aaken et al., *supra* note 41, at 220 and 237–38 (the United Kingdom and the United States jointly rank 18 out of 76 countries in *de facto* independence). For analysis on the independence of federal prosecutors in the United States, see, e.g., Sanford C. Gordon, *Assessing Partisan Bias in Federal Public Corruption Prosecutions,* 103 AMERICAN POLITICAL SCIENCE REVIEW 534 (2009); Daniel Richman, *Political Control of Federal Prosecutions: Looking Back and Looking Forward,* 58 DUKE L.J. 2087 (2009) [hereinafter *Political Control*].

[106] *See, e.g.,* DARRYL K. BROWN, FREE MARKET CRIMINAL JUSTICE: HOW DEMOCRACY AND LAISSEZ FAIRE UNDERMINE THE RULE OF LAW (2016) [HEREINAFTER FREE MARKET CRIMINAL JUSTICE].

and their decision may not be circumvented by victims and is unreviewable by the courts.[107] Many offices of the prosecutor have guidelines, but these guidelines are not always made available to the public, are not preceded by public consultation, and are not generally enforceable before the courts.[108] And the extensive practice of plea bargaining creates incentives for local, state, and federal prosecutors to overcharge and undercharge, withhold evidence to the defense, and have an instrumental relationship to the law more generally.[109] The United States legal system prides itself as being "adversarial" rather than "inquisitorial," and "anti-inquisitorialism" – the use of the Continental legal system as a kind of negative polestar against which the American system is defined – is a pervasive and persistent theme in the constitutional law of American criminal procedure.[110] And the neutral minister of justice, working within a hierarchical bureaucracy, is often understood as epitomizing the kind of "inquisitorial" process that the American legal system rejects.[111] Though we need many more single-jurisdiction and comparative studies on how these regulations and adversarial legal identity actually affect the self-perception and work by prosecutors, the available scholarship suggests that they not only express or signify a normative ideal that is

---

[107]   See, e.g., Linda R.S. v. Richard D. and Texas et al., 410 U.S. 714 (1973); Leeke v. Timmerman, 454 U.S. 83 (1981); United States v. Armstrong, 517 U.S. 456 (1996).

[108]   Norman Abrams, Internal Policy: Guiding the Exercise of Prosecutorial Discretion, 19 UCLA L.R. 1 (1971); Ellen Podgor, Department of Justice Guidelines: Balancing "Discretionary Justice," 13 CORNELL J. L. & PUB. POL'Y 167, 177 (2004) (courts will not use their supervisory powers to enforce a DOJ guideline if the sole basis for the argument is that a federal prosecutor violated internal policy); Jane Patrick Hanlon & Eric Reilley Lewis, The Federal Criminal Investigation Process, in JAMES T. O'REILLEY ET AL, PUNISHING CORPORATE CRIME 67, 78–84 (2009).

[109]   See, e.g., BROWN, supra note 106; Alschuler, supra note 97. The extensive practice of guilty pleas and plea agreements also substantially reduces the importance of the trial by jury as a mechanism of democratic accountability of prosecutors to the people.

[110]   David Alan Sklansky, Anti-Inquisitorialism, 122 HARV. L. REV. 1634 (2009).

[111]   Nonetheless, there are also persistent elements of what looks like "inquisitorial" process in the American criminal justice system, and the most pronounced of those elements involve prosecutors. The broad deference granted to prosecutors and the vast discretion they exercise, particularly in negotiating plea bargains, can be understood as a stripped-down, American version of inquisitorialism—or, as Jennifer Laurin describes, "quasi-inquisitorialism." See Jennifer E. Laurin, Quasi-Inquisitorialism: Accounting for Deference in Pretrial Criminal Procedure, 90 NOTRE DAME L. REV. 783 (2014). See also Máximo Langer, Rethinking Plea Bargaining: The Practice and Reform of Prosecutorial Adjudication in American Criminal Procedure, 33 AM. J. CRIM. L. 223, 248–56 (2006) [hereinafter Rethinking Plea Bargaining] (characterizing this system of prosecutorial de facto adjudication as a specific hybrid between adversarial and inquisitorial conceptions of the criminal process and other elements that do not fit into either of these conceptions). It is stripped down, in large part, by eliminating many of the bureaucratic and professional controls that European countries have placed on prosecutorial power. Id. at 256–66.

in tension with the prosecutor as a neutral minister of justice, but also have an effect on how prosecutors see themselves and operate.[112]

There is a long tradition of academic commentary in the United States of criticizing broad prosecutorial discretion and the extensive use of plea bargaining as dangers to the rule of law.[113] These criticisms have often relied on comparative examples of legal systems like France, Germany, and Italy.[114] Criticisms of prosecutorial discretion in the Unites States started in the 1960s, at a time in which there was widespread criticism of police discretion, later followed by criticism of judges' sentencing discretion, both inspired in rule of law concerns.[115] However, the relative small impact of these criticisms in the decisions by the courts and the work by Congress and other legislatures is another indication that the ideal of prosecutors as neutral or impartial agents of the law is weaker in the United States than in other places.

Starting with the Warren Court, courts tried to cabin police discretion through constitutional rules. Congress and state legislatures tried to cabin judges' sentencing discretion through sentencing guidelines, mandatory minima, and other sentencing restrictions. Regardless of how one evaluates the outcomes of these reforms to cabin police and judges' discretion, there is no question that these were serious and encompassing reforms.

In contrast, there have been no serious attempts to cabin prosecutorial discretion and plea bargaining or to otherwise restrain prosecutorial power.[116]

---

[112] *See, e.g.*, BROWN, *supra* note 106; WILLIAM T. PIZZI, TRIALS WITHOUT TRUTH (1999).

[113] *See* e.g., ANGELA J. DAVIS, ARBITRARY JUSTICE: THE POWER OF THE AMERICAN PROSECUTOR (2007); KENNETH CULP DAVIS, DISCRETIONARY JUSTICE: A PRELIMINARY INQUIRY (1969) [HEREINAFTER DISCRETIONARY JUSTICE]; PIZZI, *supra* note 112; Abrams, *supra* note 108; James Vorenberg, *Decent Restraint of Prosecutorial Power*, 94 HARV. L. REV. 1521 (1981).

[114] *See, e.g., See, e.g.*, BROWN, *supra* note 106; DAVIS, DISCRETIONARY JUSTICE, *supra* note 113; Wayne R. LaFave, *The Prosecutor's Discretion in the United States*, 18 AM. J. COMP. L. 643 (1970); John H. Langbein, *Land without Plea Bargaining: How the Germans Do It*, 78 MICH. L. REV. 204 (1979); Langbein & Weinreb, *supra* note 77.

[115] *See, e.g.*, DAVIS, DISCRETIONARY JUSTICE, *supra* note 113; MARVIN E. FRANKEL, CRIMINAL SENTENCES: LAW WITHOUT ORDER (1973); U.S. NAT'L ADVISORY COMM'N ON CRIMINAL JUSTICE STANDARDS AND GOALS, COURTS (1973).

[116] An exception was the ban of plea bargaining adopted in Alaska in 1975 that was formally in place until 1993. For a history and evaluation of this ban, see Teresa White Carns & Dr. John Kruse, *A Re-Evaluation of Alaska's Plea Bargaining Ban*, 8 ALASKA L. REV. 27 (1991). Also, some restrictions were applied to plea bargaining as part of the victims' rights movement such as the adoption of Proposition 8 in 1982 that prohibited plea bargaining in "serious felony" cases in California. For an early evaluation of the effects of this proposition, see California Department of Justice, Candace McCoy & Robert Tillman, *Controlling Felony Plea Bargaining in California: The Impact of the "Victims' Bill of Rights"* (1986), *California Agencies*, Paper 232, available at www.digitalcommons.law.ggu.edu/cgi/viewcontent.cgi?article=1229&context=caldocs_agencies (last visited on November 23, 2016).

In the case of the police, there were concerns in the 1940s, 1950s and 1960s from the perspective of democratic pluralism as the then-prevailing theory of democracy in the United States about the police's "authoritarian mentality" and being a discrete and unified group, alienated from mainstream society.[117] There were no similar concerns regarding prosecutors as a group, given that prosecutors were educated and part of the local, state, and national elites that democratic pluralism celebrated as leaders of American democracy.[118] In addition, while the police acted before adversary checks started, prosecutors acted after adversary proceedings had been put in motion.[119]

Thus, while the Warren Court set a wide range of constitutional limits on police arrests, searches, seizures, and interrogations, it set few direct constitutional limits on prosecutorial power.[120] There were Warren Court cases that strengthened the right to counsel, the right to trial by jury, and other features associated with adversary process that could be interpreted as indirectly setting checks on prosecutorial power,[121] but these decisions did not strongly embrace or advance the ideal of prosecutors as neutral agents of the law. The Burger Court gave for the first time the Supreme Court's blessing to the practice of plea bargaining in the *Brady* trilogy and later upheld heavy-handed use of plea proposals,[122] and rejected a selective prosecution claim.[123] The Rehnquist Court also rejected selective prosecution claims and passed on opportunities to regulate plea bargaining.[124] It also declined to hold unconstitutional statutes that strengthened prosecutorial leverage in plea negotiations.[125] The Roberts Court has set some limits to guilty pleas and plea bargaining by strengthening the constitutional duties by defense counsel in this setting.[126] But these cases are not as much about limiting prosecutorial power or embracing a conception of prosecutors as neutral agents of the law as

---

[117] DAVID ALAN SKLANSKY, POLICE AND DEMOCRACY, *supra* note 19, AT 39–43.

[118] Sklansky, *Unpacking*, *supra* note 14.

[119] *See, e.g., Massiah v. United States*, 377 U.S. 201 (1964); *Kirby v. Illinois*, 406 U.S. 682 (1972).

[120] *See, e.g., Brady v. Maryland*, 373 U.S. 83 (1963); *United States v. Jackson*, 390 U.S. 570 (1968); *Griffin v. California*, 380 U.S. 609 (1965).

[121] *See, e.g., Gideon v. Wainwright*, 372 U.S. 335 (1963); *Duncan v. Louisiana*, 391 U.S. 145 (1968).

[122] *Brady v. United States*, 397 U.S. 742 (1970); *McMann v. Richardson*, 397 U.S. 759 (1970); *Parker v. North Carolina*, 397 U.S. 790 (1970); *Bordenkircher v. Hayes*, 434 U.S. 357 (1978). But see *Santobello v. New York*, 404 U.S. 257 (1971).

[123] *Wayte v. United States*, 470 U.S. 598 (1985).

[124] *McCleskey v. Kemp*, 481 U.S. 279 (1987); *United States v. Armstrong*, 517 U.S. 456 (1996); *United States v. Bass*, 536 U.S. 862 (2002); *United States v. Ruiz*, 536 U.S. 622 (2002).

[125] *Harmelin v. Michigan*, 501 U.S. 957 (1991). But see *Roper v. Simmons*, 543 U.S. 551 (2005), in the final term of the Rehnquist Court.

[126] *Padilla v. Kentucky*, 559 U.S. 356 (2010); *Lafler v. Cooper*, 132 S.Ct. 1376 (2012); *Missouri v. Frye*, 132 S.Ct. 1399 (2012).

about effective assistance of counsel and enabling better informed guilty pleas. In fact, in the context of failure to disclose exculpatory evidence, the Roberts Court passed on holding prosecutors accountable.[127] In addition, the limits the Roberts Court has set on excessive punishment and mass incarceration have focused on excluding some defendants from certain types of punishment and on limiting prison overcrowding, rather than on restricting the exercise of prosecutorial discretion that may be one of the sources of punishment levels and of overcrowding.[128]

In the case of limiting judges' sentencing discretion, Congress and state legislatures passed sentencing guidelines. At Congress, conservatives and liberals reached an agreement on the guidelines because while conservatives wanted "truth in sentencing" and higher punishments, liberals were concerned with racial sentencing disparities.[129] But in the political climate of the 1980s, 1990s, and early 2000s, there did not seem to be political room for legislatures restraining prosecutors' power without being perceived as soft on crime. If anything, legislatures had the incentives to set harsher criminal laws and then leave discretion to prosecutors to apply them, in fact increasing prosecutors' power while leaving their discretion intact.[130]

One way of understanding the absence of meaningful judicial supervision of prosecutors in the United States is that prosecutors are viewed as advocates rather than agents of the law; the Supreme Court has not seen fit to regulate prosecutors, because it does not expect any greater neutrality from them than from defense counsel. But as Jennifer Laurin points out, the judicial deference can also be understood as reflecting an understanding that prosecutors *are* more than "mere advocates" – that they are neutral and professional, and can be relied upon to ensure that justice is done.[131] In fact, the Supreme Court has described the United States Attorney – the key official overseeing federal prosecution – as a representative "not of an ordinary party to a controversy, but of a sovereignty whose obligation to govern impartially is as compelling as its obligation to govern at all, and whose interest, therefore, in a criminal prosecution is not that it shall win a case, but that justice shall be done. As such, he is in a peculiar and very definite sense the servant of the

---

[127]   *Connick v. Thompson*, 563 U.S. 51 (2011).
[128]   *See Graham v. Florida*, 560 U.S. 48 (2010); *Miller v. Alabama*, 132 S. Ct. 2455 (2012); *Brown v. Plata*, 131 S. Ct. 1910 (2011); JONATHAN SIMON, MASS INCARCERATION ON TRIAL: A REMARKABLE COURT DECISION AND THE FUTURE OF PRISONS IN AMERICA (2014).
[129]   *See, e.g.*, KATE STITH AND JOSÉ CABRANES, FEAR OF JUDGING. SENTENCING GUIDELINES IN THE FEDERAL COURTS (1998).
[130]   STUNTZ, COLLAPSE, *supra* note 7; Stuntz, *Pathological Politics, supra* note 7.
[131]   *See* Laurin, *supra* note 111.

law. .... "[132] Prosecutorial standards in the United States have referred to the prosecutor as not only a zealous advocate, but an "administrator of justice" and "an officer of the court" whose primary duty "is to seek justice within the bounds of the law, not merely to convict."[133] And the independent judgment of prosecutors – particularly but not exclusively at the federal level – is frequently touted as an important value; witness the tradition of relative independence of appointed United States Attorneys,[134] the self-removal by the politically appointed Attorney General of the United States from making decisions in some politically sensitive cases, and the appointment of special prosecutors to deal with politically sensitive cases at the federal and state levels.

As elsewhere, prosecutors in the United States are mediating figures that bridge key conceptual and organizational divides between adversarial and inquisitorial forms of procedure, between law and discretion and between the police and the courts.[135] As mediating figures, prosecutors work at the intersection of conflicting ideals about them, including the ideal of the prosecutor as an elected representative of the people versus prosecutor as an agent of the law. But there is no doubt that the ideal of the prosecutor as an agent of the law does not capture the normative ideals about prosecutors and the practice and self-perception of prosecutors in the United States to the same extent as in other places.[136]

Now that the punitive tide has been ebbing to a certain extent in the United States and that concerns about equality in the criminal justice system have come back with renewed force,[137] one of the questions is whether there is more

---

[132] *Berger v. United States*, 295 U.S. 78, 88 (1935).

[133] AMERICAN BAR ASSOCIATION CRIMINAL JUSTICE STANDARDS COMMITTEE, ABA STANDARDS FOR CRIMINAL JUSTICE: PROSECUTION FUNCTION AND DEFENSE FUNCTION, STANDARD 3-1.2(b) and (c) (4th ed. 2015).

[134] Daniel Richman, *Political Control, supra* note 105; Adrian Vermeule, *Conventions of Agency Independence*, 113 COLUM. L. REV. 1163, 1202–03 (2013).

[135] Sklansky, *Unpacking, supra* note 14. See also, David Alan Sklansky, *The Nature and Function of Prosecutorial Power*, 106 J. CRIM. L. & CRIMINOLOGY 473 (2017).

[136] *See, e.g.*, PROSECUTORS AND POLITICS: A COMPARATIVE PERSPECTIVE (Michael Tonry ed. 2012); THE PROSECUTOR IN TRANSNATIONAL PERSPECTIVE (Eric Luna & Marianne Wade eds. 2012).

[137] Recent empirical studies on prosecutorial decisions have found persistent disparities based on race. *See, e.g.*, Robert J. Smith & Justin D. Levinson, *The Impact of Implicit Racial Bias on the Exercise of Prosecutorial Discretion*, 35 SEATTLE U. L. REV. 795 (2012); Sonja Starr & Marit Rehavi, *Racial Disparity in Federal Criminal Sentences*, 122 J. POL. ECON. 1320 (2014); Sherod Thaxton, *Disciplining Death: Assessing and Ameliorating Arbitrariness in Capital Charging*, 48 ARIZONA STATE LAW JOURNAL (forthcoming 2017); *Prosecutor's Guide for Advancing Racial Equity*, VERA INST. OF JUST., www.vera.org/sites/default/files/resour ces/downloads/prosecutors-advancing-racial-equity.pdf (last visited September 16, 2016).

room for reforms or practices that advance the rule of law ideal of consistent, equal, unpoliticized application of the law by prosecutors. Even if contemporary prosecutors in the United States remained more sensitive to politics than to law,[138] there could be reforms that could advance this rule of law ideal in the United States.

III LIBERAL DEMOCRACY: PROSECUTORS AS DEFENDERS OF LIBERTY, DIGNITY, AND EQUALITY

Another perspective about the relationship between prosecutors and democracy, that several contributions to this volume assumed, but did not always make explicit, is that prosecutors, however they are selected and supervised and regardless of whether their legitimacy is more legal or political, should respect and advance "democratic values."[139] The content of these democratic values would depend on what conception of democracy one embraces.[140] In this regard, this book's chapters, consistently with a substantial part of public discourse in the United States and Western Europe, have embraced liberal democracy values that would include not only or even primarily the rule of law, but also, and more importantly, liberty, dignity, and equality.[141] From this perspective, what democracy requires of prosecutors is, first and foremost, that they treat suspects and defendants with dignity and respect, that they scrupulously comply with both the letter and the spirit of constitutional limitations on the penal power, that they work to ensure that no individuals or groups are beyond the reach of the law, and that everyone receives the equal protection of the law and equal access to justice and public office.

In the United States, constitutional law includes many of the rights of criminal suspects and criminal defendants also recognized in international human rights instruments and conventions. These constitutional rights set limits to the work done by criminal justice public officials, including prosecutors. When these rights are not respected, courts are supposed to enforce them. But there is no doubt that courts underenforce many substantive criminal law and criminal procedure rights, by design or necessity. In certain areas, there are separation of powers and epistemological considerations that prevent courts

---

[138] Simon, *Better Politics of Prosecution*, supra note 10.

[139] *See* Ingrid V. Eagly, *Prosecuting Immigrants in a Democracy*, in this volume [hereinafter *Prosecuting Immigrants*]; Daniel Richman, *Accounting for Prosecutors* in this volume [hereinafter *Accounting*]; Cohen, *supra* note 45.

[140] For a description of some of the main alternatives in this respect, see HELD, *supra* note 39.

[141] *See, e.g.*, Sharon Dolovich, *Legitimate Punishment in a Liberal Democracy*, 7 BUFF. CRIM. L. REV. 304, 313–14 (2004).

from second-guessing the prosecutor's and office of the prosecutor's decisions. The charging decision is an example; prosecutors have the constitutional power to execute the laws and have knowledge about the whole caseload that puts them in a better epistemological situation to make decisions on individual cases.[142] Another example is discovery, because while prosecutors know all the elements of proof available in their investigation, judges have more scattered knowledge about the case and the supporting evidence. Courts sometimes underenforce criminal law and procedure rights because they assume that prosecutors are subjected to professional discipline rules that are often not enforced.[143] In other settings, courts underenforce rights due to weaknesses in the U.S. adversary system in which, as a general rule, courts may decide upon a rights violation only if one of the parties raises it.[144] Partly because of the underfunding of indigent defense, defense attorneys often do not raise sound rights violations.

Judicial underenforcement has arguably become a more serious issue in the last few decades since prosecutors have increased their power in the criminal justice system due to, among other factors, an increase of sentences and of the number and types of criminal offenses. This increased power, combined with the practice of guilty pleas, plea agreements, and deferred prosecution agreements, have enabled prosecutors to be *de facto* adjudicators of a large portion of criminal cases in the United States either by prosecutors alone or in conjunction with the defense.[145]

In this context, some commentators have called for larger judicial enforcement of rights and other external limitations and constraints on prosecutors.[146] But other scholars have called on prosecutors and their offices to embrace their obligation to advance democratic values; these scholars have argued that prosecutors in the United States should collectively take responsibility for ensuring that constitutional values are protected even when – or especially when – effective judicial oversight is lacking.[147] How this requirement

---

[142] *See, e.g., United States v. Armstrong*, 517 U.S. 456 (1996).

[143] Sklansky, *Unpacking, supra* note 14. [144] Sklansky, *Anti-Inquisitorialism, supra* note 110.

[145] Langer, *Rethinking Plea Bargaining, supra* note 111; Gerard E. Lynch, *Our Administrative System of Criminal Justice*, 66 FORDHAM L. REV. 2117 (1998).

[146] *See, e.g.*, DAVIS, DISCRETIONARY JUSTICE, *supra* note 113; Abrams, *supra* note 108; William J. Stuntz, *Bordenkircher v. Hayes: Plea Bargaining and the Decline of the Rule of Law, in* CRIMINAL PROCEDURE STORIES 351 (Carol S. Steiker ed., 2006).

[147] *See* Richman, *Accounting, supra* note 139, at 9: "As the link between the police and the adjudicative process, prosecutors are responsible for ensuring that a defendant gets the legal process that the law has deemed his 'due' and that liberal democracies value at their core." *See also, e.g.*, Russell M. Gold, *Beyond the Judicial Fourth Amendment: The Prosecutor's Role*, 47 U.C. DAVIS L. REV. 1591 (2014); Eric S. Fish, *Prosecutorial Constitutionalism*, 90 S. CAL. L. REV. 237 (2017).

translates into an institutional context in which prosecutors have pressing needs, are typically elected, and act within an adversarial process has to be discussed in context-specific ways. But the articulation of the ideal may in itself open room for the discussion of these issues. In the context of the United States, this will require leadership from head prosecutors – district attorneys and United States Attorneys – but it may also require structural changes within prosecutors' offices.[148]

Jonathan Simon's call in this volume for a prosecutorial politics of dignity can be understood, in part, as a call for prosecutors, whether elected or appointed, to commit themselves to the advancement of liberal democracy – and, more particularly, to respect for and protection of the human dignity of criminal suspects and criminal defendants. That obligation can be rooted both in human rights and in the citizen's right to equal concern and respect.[149] Regarding human dignity, groups of people who have been dehumanized by criminal justice policies in the United States include those who commit certain criminal offenses, prisoners, and undocumented immigrants. The "tough on crime" Text has included abstractions such as the "sexual predator," the "violent gang member," and the "dangerous felon" that dehumanize people who commit and are imprisoned for the commission of crime. In this regard, one can contrast United States with Western Europe, where those who commit crimes and are incarcerated still tend to be considered members of society and the political community, at the very least after their release.[150] Regardless of how they are appointed and whether their legitimacy is more legal or political, there is a straightforward argument that democratic prosecutors should advance these ideals.[151]

Antony Duff argues in his chapter that democratic values include not only "equal concern and respect," but also the "eyeball test" as a test of civic recognition, under which " ... republican citizens must be willing, as well as able, to look at each other in the eye – to recognise each other as participants in the civic enterprise. That is one way in which we display equal concern and respect for each other: in our willingness to look each other in the eye, with a look not of threat or fear, but of recognition of fellowship."[152] Duff maintains that prosecutors are also citizens, subject to the same demands and

---

[148] *See, e.g.*, Rachel E. Barkow, *Institutional Design and the Policing of Prosecutors: Lessons from Administrative Law*, 61 STAN. L. REV. 869 (2009); Fish, *supra* note 147; Langer, *Rethinking Plea Bargaining, supra* note 111.

[149] Duff, *supra* note 38, at 5 "Respect concerns such values as dignity, autonomy, privacy."

[150] On this contrast, see JAMES Q. WHITMAN, HARSH JUSTICE (2003).

[151] Simon, *Better Politics of Prosecution, supra* note 10.   [152] Duff, *supra* note 38, at 12.

duties of democratic citizenship as all their fellows, and consequently have to treat defendants as fellow citizens.[153]

Duff argues that criminal law in a democracy is the law of the citizens of that polity; it is part of the duties that citizens have to each other. What, then, about a prosecutor's treatment of non-citizens – people who are sometimes thought to be formally outside or on the periphery of the political community? Duff answers that "... a decent republic will be welcoming to would-be citizens rather than treating them with exclusionary distrust; and non-citizens within a polity's jurisdiction should be treated as guests, a distinctive normative position that requires concern, respect and recognition – and equal treatment by the criminal justice system."[154] In her chapter, Ingrid Eagly gives a different answer, arguing that the core democratic values that guide criminal law – such as individual liberty, dignity, and bodily integrity, and respect for human rights – must apply equally to the citizens and noncitizens that are subject to its power.[155] In fact, the enjoyment of substantive criminal law and criminal procedure rights in the United States has traditionally not been subjected to citizenship requirements. In other words, non-U.S.-citizen defendants have enjoyed the same substantive criminal law and criminal procedure rights as citizen defendants. However, as Eagly points out, changes in the last few years in immigration policy and its enforcement have blurred the line between criminal justice and the immigration system and made non-citizen defendants more vulnerable to criminal prosecutions and convictions in the United States.[156]

More broadly, prosecutors can advance democratic values not just by *restraint* – by respecting the *limits* placed on their authority by concerns for liberty, dignity, and equality – but also in more affirmative ways, through the criminal charges that they bring and take to trial. Democratic values may require from prosecutors not only to not prosecute defendants on impermissible or arbitrary grounds, but also the duty to prosecute those who commit serious offenses to enforce equality and protect individuals and groups. Under the Equal Protection Clause of the U.S. Constitution, defendants have a right not to be prosecuted on the basis of impermissible criteria such as ethnicity, gender, and race.[157] Antony Duff points out that if "we ask what could justify a policy of focusing prosecutorial resources on crimes of racial hatred, or on domestic violence, or on police conduct towards members of particular racial groups, the most plausible answer is that such policies can serve the rule of law principle of equality before the law by focusing on kinds of crime that have too

---

[153]   *Id.*   [154]   *Id.* at 12.   [155]   Eagly, *Prosecuting Immigrants, supra* note 139.   [156]   *Id.*
[157]   *Yick Wo v. Hopkins,* 118 U.S. 356 (1886); *Wayte v. United States,* 470 U.S. 598 (1985); *United States v. Armstrong,* 517 U.S. 456 (1996); *United States v. Bass,* 536 U.S. 862 (2002).

often been ignored, and that are typically committed by the more powerful against members of civically vulnerable groups."[158] Equality before the law would then mean, among other things, that there are no people who are above the law and may commit crimes with impunity. Prosecuting crime is thus a way to enforce equality as a value.

Relatedly, international human rights law recognizes, among others, a right to judicial and State protection.[159] For instance, Article 1.1 of the American Convention on Human Rights establishes that the States Parties to the Convention "... undertake to respect the rights and freedoms recognized herein and to ensure to all persons subject to their jurisdiction the free and full exercise of those rights and freedoms, without any discrimination for reasons of race, color, sex, language, religion, political or other opinion, national or social origin, economic status, birth, or any other social condition." The Inter-American Court of Human Rights has held that this article imposes to public authorities a duty to investigate and punish human rights violations and that this is an obligation of means, not of results.[160] The European Court of Human Rights has also held that States Parties of the European Convention have to enact criminal-law provisions to punish serious human rights violations through adequate penalties and to establish criminal-law machinery and enforce criminal-law provisions as well as to prosecute where the outcome of the investigation warrants it.[161]

There is important variation among countries on the extent to which they accept and fulfill this duty to prosecute. In Germany, critics have argued that prosecutors underenforce criminal law and have not prosecuted enough

---

[158] Duff, *supra* note 38, at 29.

[159] See, e.g., American Convention on Human Rights, Articles 1, 8 and 25; European Convention on Human Rights, Articles 2, 3, 4, 5 §1 and 8.

[160] See, e.g., Inter-American Court of Human Rights (IACtHR), Case of *Velásquez Rodríguez v. Honduras*, Judgment of July 29 of 1988; IACtHR, Case of *Garibaldi v. Brazil*, Judgment of September 23 of 2009; IACtHR, Case of *Anzualdo Castro v. Peru*, Judgment of September 22 of 2009; IACtHR, Case *Pueblo Bello Massacre v. Colombia*, Judgment of January 31 of 2006.

[161] See, e.g., Judge Ksenija Turković, *International and National Courts Confronting Large-scale Violations of Human Rights*, in OPENING OF THE JUDICIAL YEAR – SEMINAR 1, 2 (January 29, 2016)(citing *Osman v. the United Kingdom*, October 28, 1998, § 115, *Reports of Judgments and Decisions* 1998-VIIII; *Mastromatteo v. Italy* [GC], no. 37703/97, §§ 67 and 89, ECHR 2002-VIIII; and *Menson v. the United Kingdom* (dec.), no. 47916/99, ECHR 2003-V; *Hugh Jordan v. the United Kingdom*, no 24746/94, §§ 105–09, May 4, 2001; *Douglas-Williams v. the United Kingdom* (dec.), no. 56413/00, January 8, 2002; *Esmukhambetov and Others v. Russia*, no. 23445/03, §§ 115–18, March 29, 2011; and *Umarova and Others v. Russia*, no. 25654/08, §§ 84–88, July 31, 2012; mutatis mutandis, *Öneryıldız v. Turkey* [GC], no. 48939/99, § 96, ECHR 2004-XII; *Okkalı v. Turkey*, no. 52067/99, § 65, ECHR 2006-XII (extracts); and *Türkmen v. Turkey*, no. 43124/98, § 51, December 19, 2006), available at www.echr.coe.int/Documents/Speech_20160129_Turkovic_JY_ENG.pdf.

Holocaust perpetrators, hate crimes, crimes against women, and corporate crime.[162] In the United States, neither the law nor the courts have established a prosecutor's duty to prosecute. Courts have not interpreted the U.S. or State Constitutions as requiring such a duty either under equal protection before the law or the right to judicial or state protection.[163] In fact, if anything, one of the distinctive features of U.S. law is that prosecutors have almost unlimited discretion not to prosecute. However, the moral intuitions and political claims that underlie this international human rights duty to prosecute serious crimes have been present in the United States. This may be the case behind many of the complaints for the non-prosecution by district attorneys or federal prosecutors of cases as different as the use of waterboarding and other techniques to interrogate suspects of terrorism, police officers who unnecessarily kill black men and women, corruption among public officials, Wall Street traders' victimization of unsophisticated or vulnerable clients, and domestic violence, to mention just a few possible examples. This is echoed by Daniel Richman, who notes in his contribution to this volume the many ways in which prosecutors hold private citizens as well as the police accountable for their actions. In this context, it is also worth emphasizing that the issue of whether a jurisdiction formally acknowledges a duty to prosecute serious crimes is different from the issue of whether and to what degree it actually prosecutes these crimes. The latter is an issue that comparative law and other comparative literatures have explored inadequately, and it would be crucial in determining to what extent prosecution in a given jurisdiction is democratic in the sense explored in this section.[164]

Democratic values may have implications not just for the cases that prosecutors bring and for how they bring those cases, but also for the composition of prosecutors' offices. This isn't just because the demographics of prosecutorial personnel – how diverse they are, and how representative of the polities they serve – can have implications for how evenhandedly they administer justice. One of the values of democracy since ancient Greece is the right to participate

---

[162] See, e.g., BOYNE, THE GERMAN PROSECUTION SERVICE, *supra* note 55, at 119–145; Boyne, *German Prosecutors*, *supra* note 52.

[163] On how the original understanding of the Equal Protection Clause in the United States included protection by authorities through criminal prosecutions and on how it was later abandoned, see STUNTZ, COLLAPSE, *supra* note 7, AT 99–122.

[164] For comparative studies of prosecutions against powerful defendants, see e.g., Langer, *The Diplomacy*, *infra* note 179; van Aaken et al, *supra* note 41. Federalism and the possibility that the same conduct is prosecuted by federal and state prosecutors may be important to explain how this issue actually works in the United States. *See, e.g.*, Edward L. Glaeser et al., *What Do Prosecutors Maximize? An Analysis of the Federalization of Drug Crimes*, 2 AM. L. & ECON. REV. 259 (2000).

in public office. Every citizen, as a member of the polis, should then have an equal opportunity to get a position as a prosecutor as long as she is qualified for the job. Diversity in public office may not only advance this right, but also communicate to the people that this right is actually effective in a given political community.

Relatedly, in her chapter, Mathilde Cohen argues that "representative democracy should be extended to include the demographic representation of citizens in key public offices" and defends the notion of "representative bureaucracy" that "suggests that a public workforce representative of the people in terms of race, ethnicity, gender, and sexual orientation, but also socio-economic status, regional origin, abilities and disabilities, helps ensure that the interests of all groups are considered in decision-making processes."[165]

As with the previous ideals, this one exists also in the United States and is reflected in recent prosecutorial standards: "In selecting personnel, the prosecutor's office should also consider the diverse interests and makeup of the community it serves, and seek to recruit, hire, promote and retain a diverse group of prosecutors and staff that reflect that community."[166] French judges and prosecutors have also acknowledged the issue in relation to gender, geographic, and socio-economic inequality, but not regarding racial and ethnic diversity.[167]

However, as essays in this volume have shown, offices of the prosecutor in France and the United States are short of this ideal; minorities are underrepresented in these offices.[168] In the case of France, advancing this value may be particularly challenging given the French "universalist" tradition that denies the reality of race and ethnicity and generally prohibits, even on constitutional grounds, to collect statistics on these categories.[169] In order to live up to these democratic values, offices of the prosecutor around the world should keep statistics on this issue, make them available, and implement policies when they find themselves short of this ideal. Single-jurisdiction and comparative law studies should also explore further how offices of the prosecutors are composed in different jurisdictions and identify offices that could serve as models in the embracing and implementation of this ideal.

---

[165] Cohen, *supra* note 45, at 124.

[166] AMERICAN BAR ASSOCIATION CRIMINAL JUSTICE STANDARDS COMMITTEE, ABA STANDARDS FOR CRIMINAL JUSTICE: PROSECUTION FUNCTION AND DEFENSE FUNCTION, STANDARD 3-2.2(A) (4th ed. 2015).

[167] Cohen, *supra* note 45.

[168] *Id.*; Sklansky, *Unpacking, supra* note 14 (citing statistics on underrepresentation of Latinos in California and of African-American and Latinos at the federal level).

[169] Cohen, *supra* note 45.

IV PARTICIPATORY DEMOCRACY: THE ROLE OF THE CITIZEN IN PROSECUTION

The "community prosecution" movement, which we discussed earlier, can be understood as not just a way to strengthen *representative democracy* in prosecutor's offices, but also a way to strengthen *participatory democracy*, by making community members active partners in prosecutors' work. At least as a thought experiment, though, it is worth contemplating the argument for going further: for allowing victims and other private individuals to bring criminal cases. This book's chapters did not explore this possible relationship between prosecutors and democracy. However, if democracy entails self-rule by the people and prosecution of offenses is a key component of ruling a society, why shouldn't any citizen be able to prosecute crime? In Ancient Athens, while the victim (or his family) could bring suit in "private cases," any adult male citizen could initiate action in "public cases."[170] In the eighteenth century, Montesquieu considered that prosecution by any citizen was one of the features that characterized republics.[171] And private prosecution used to be a familiar feature of criminal justice in the United Kingdom – and also, albeit subject to greater limitations, in the United States.[172]

We do not live in an era of direct democracies and well-functioning states around the world have a developed system of public prosecution. However, many states still do allow for the participation of private individuals and private entities in the prosecution of crime. This participation comes in many forms. Some states allow any citizen or legal entity to prosecute crime in conjunction with or instead of public prosecutors.[173] Other states allow for non-governmental organizations to be a party in criminal

---

[170] *See, e.g.,* ADRIAAN LANNI, *LAW AND ORDER IN ANCIENT ATHENS* 10, 49–55 (2016) (explaining that in "private cases," the victim (or his family in the case of murder) brought suit, while in "public cases," any adult male citizen was permitted to initiate an action).

[171] MONTESQUIEU, *THE SPIRIT OF THE LAWS* 81 (Anne M. Cohler, Basia Carolyn Miller, & Harold Samuel Stone trans. and ed., 1989): "In Rome ... (a)nd in many other cities ... citizens were permitted to accuse one another. This was established in the spirit of the republic, where each citizen should have boundless zeal for the public good, and where it is assumed that each citizen has all the rights of the homeland in his hands."

[172] *See, e.g.,* LAWRENCE M. FRIEDMAN, *CRIME AND PUNISHMENT IN AMERICAN HISTORY* 29–30 (1993).

[173] *See, e.g.,* CONSTITUCIÓN ESPAÑOLA [C.E.] Article 125 (regulating the right of any citizen to prosecute crime as a people's prosecutor and the right to participate in the administration of justice through jury service, subjected to the requirements established by law); LEY DE ENJUICIAMIENTO CRIMINAL [L.E. CRIM.] [CODE OF CRIMINAL PROCEDURE] Articles 101, 270 (Spain) (any citizen may be a people's prosecutor); S.T.C. No. 34/94, January 31, 1994; S. T.C. No 1047/2007, December 17, 2007; S.T.C. No. 54/2008, April 8, 2007 (Spain); Prosecution of Offences Act, 1985, c. 23, §6(1) (England) (any person may institute or conduct

proceedings regarding cases related to the goal or expertise of the organization.[174] Many states allow the victim of crime to be a party in the criminal
process as either a civil party or a private prosecutor.[175] The procedural
powers of these private participants in the criminal process vary, ranging
from being able to act with full or almost full prosecutorial powers during
pretrial, trial and appeal, to being a companion of the public prosecutor who
remains in control of the case – in other words, they range from different
degrees of private control of the prosecution to different degrees of private
participation in the prosecution.[176]

The historical origins of private prosecutors also vary. In some states, giving
prosecutorial powers to private individuals was a way to make up for weak
public prosecution systems.[177] In other places, giving prosecutorial powers to
private individuals and entities has been a mechanism to advance democratic
ideals in the criminal process.[178]

Regardless of their historical origins, giving private individuals and
entities prosecutorial powers can be interpreted as a way to implement
democratic ideals such as people's participation in the administration of
criminal justice and bringing accountability to the criminal justice system.

---

any criminal proceedings); *Jones v. Whalley*, [2006] UKHL 41; *R (on the application of Gujra)
v. Crown Prosecution Service* [2012] UKSC 52.

[174] *See, e.g.*, C. Pr. Pén. Articles 2–1 to 2–23 (France) (describing entities that may become civil
parties in criminal proceedings on specific crimes); Código Procesal Penal de la
República Dominicana, Article 85 (Dominican Republic).

[175] *See, e.g.*, C. Pr. Pén. Article 2 (France); Strafprozessordnung [StPO] [Code of
Criminal Procedure §395 and §403 (Germany); Código Nacional de
Procedimientos Penales Article 109. XV (Mexico). For descriptions of the rights of victims
to participate in criminal trials on certain criminal offenses in Japan, see, e.g., Toshihiro
Kawaide, *Victim's Participation in the Criminal Trial in Japan*, available at www.sota.j.u-tokyo
.ac.jp/info/Papers/kawaide.pdf (last visited on November 22, 2016); Setsuo Miyazawa, *Citizen
Participation in Criminal Trials in Japan: The Saiban-in System and Victim Participation in
Japan in International Perspectives*, 2014 International Journal of Law, Crime and
Justice 1, 4–5.

[176] *See, e.g.*, on this issue in Argentina, Del'Olio, CSJN (July 11, 2006); Juri, CSJN (December 27,
2006); Quiroga, CSJN (December 23, 2004); Sandoval, CSJN (August 31, 2010); and
Santillán, CSJN (August 13, 1998).

[177] *See, e.g.*, John H. Langbein, Prosecuting Crime in the Renaissance. England,
Germany, France (1974).

[178] *See, e.g.*, Astrid Liliana Sánchez-Mejía, (Un)protecting Crime and Human Rights
Victims: The Adversarial Criminal Procedure Reform in Colombia (forthcoming
2017) (on file with the authors) (describing the expansion of victims' rights in the criminal
process in Colombia, partly inspired by the new democratic Constitution of 1991 and
international human rights); Langer, *Revolution, supra* note 4 (describing the expansion of
victims' rights in criminal procedure reforms to democratize the administration of criminal
justice in Latin America).

In fact, in Latin America and elsewhere, the role of private prosecutors have been crucial in avoiding the dismissal of charges or leading to trial and conviction cases that advance democratic values, but that public prosecutors may be reluctant to prosecute, such as human rights crimes committed by the military and public officials, and shootings and extra judicial executions by the police.[179]

There are, of course, serious criticisms that can be and have been advanced against private criminal prosecutions. First, private prosecutions may contribute to excessive levels of punitiveness and, more broadly, may subvert the public interest that public prosecutors are supposed to pursue.[180] Private prosecutors may also undermine due process or equality of arms between prosecution and defense if the defendant has to confront two prosecutors instead of one.[181] Private prosecutions may also undermine equality before the law because, unless the state is capable and willing to provide for legal assistance to victims, only those who can afford an attorney may be able to become private prosecutors.

In contemporary United States, public prosecutors have had the prosecutorial monopoly on whether a case has to be prosecuted, whether it should be disposed by a plea agreement or a trial, on the presentation of the inculpatory case at trial, and on appeals against interlocutory decisions that favor the defendant.[182] The

---

[179] *See* DANIEL M. BRINKS, INEQUALITY AND THE RULE OF LAW: THE JUDICIAL RESPONSE TO POLICE VIOLENCE IN LATIN AMERICA (2008); Máximo Langer, *The Diplomacy of Universal Jurisdiction: The Political Branches and the Transnational Prosecution of International Crimes*, 105 AM. J. INT'L L. 1 (2011); Veronica Michel & Kathryn Sikkink, *Human Rights Prosecutions and the Participation Rights of Victims in Latin America*, 47 LAW & SOC. REV. 873 (2013).

[180] On the contribution and use of victims' rights discourse and movements for higher punitiveness levels, see, e.g., GARLAND, *supra* note 6; SIMON, *supra* note 6.

[181] *See, e.g.*, Colombian Constitutional Court, Judgment C-209 of 2007, Justice Manuel José Cepeda; Daniel R. Pastor, *Una Ponencia Garantista acerca de la Acusación Particular en los Delitos de Acción Pública*, in XXV CONGRESO NACIONAL DE DERECHO PROCESAL 959 (2009). For a critical analysis of the decision by the Colombian Constitutional Court, see SÁNCHEZ-MEJÍA, *supra* note 178.

[182] Some jurisdictions in the United States do allow private prosecutions, at least for certain offenses. *See, e.g.*, *Robertson v. U.S. Ex Rel. Watson*, 130 S.Ct. 2184 (2010) (dismissed without majority opinion) (discussing private prosecution of criminal contempt in Washington D.C.); *Young v. U.S. ex rel. Vuitton et Fils S.A.*, 481 U.S. 787 (1987) (federal courts possess inherent authority to appoint a private attorney to prosecute contempt). However, the law allowing for, and especially the practice of, private prosecutions are exceptional and marginal in the United States. *See, e.g.*, Roger A. Faifax, Jr., *Delegation of the Criminal Prosecution Function to Private Actors*, 43 U.C. DAVIS L. REV. 411, 423–24 (2009) (calling the idea of the privately-retained prosecutor largely a historical one, while explaining that a small number of jurisdictions still permit victims to press criminal proceedings); Michael Edmund O'Neill, *Private Vengeance and the Public Good*, 12 U. PA J. CONST. L. 659, 661, 683 (2010)(private prosecutions remain common in present-day England even as they have all but withered away in the United States where although several states continue to allow private

"community prosecution" movement has impacted United States prosecutors more at the level of symbolism than at the level of the day-to-day operation of prosecutors' offices. Laypeople do play a role in the prosecution of crime through the grand jury that has among its functions, in many states and in the federal system, screening the prosecutor's charges to decide whether an indictment should be issued against a defendant. The grand jury also has investigating powers. But the grand jury may not make the prosecutorial decision on whether the case should be decided through a plea agreement or a trial, litigate pretrial motions, present the case at trial, or appeal against the court's decisions.

In recent decades, there have been strong victims'-rights movements in the United States. These victims'-rights movements have been characterized as a central part of the "tough on crime" political climate that predominated in the United States until the late 2000s, since they included in their agenda calls for higher punitiveness levels.[183] These U.S. movements and their rhetoric influenced and provided a point of reference and support to "tough on crime" victims'-rights agendas in other parts of the world.[184] These U.S. victims'-rights movements have also included a call for larger participation of the victim of crime in the criminal process. These demands have translated in actual legislation that have given to victims of crime the right to be heard by the prosecutor of the case, at the plea hearing, and at sentencing, among other procedural rights.[185]

But these rights pale in comparison to private prosecutions in many other countries because they do not include the right to file charges, to argue in court about pretrial motions, to decide whether the case should go to trial, to present a full case at trial, and to appeal. In this sense, even if the victims'-rights movements

prosecutions, most jurisdictions have either disallowed privately managed prosecutions completely or severely limited the role a private prosecutor may play); Andrew Sidman, *The Outmoded Concept of Private Prosecution*, 25 Am. U. L. Rev. 754, 765–66 (1976)(stating that a majority of American states and two federal courts that considered the question ruled that privately employed prosecutors may assist the state prosecutor's in conducting criminal proceedings, but the lack of recent cases upholding the use of private prosecutors in several jurisdictions may be an indication that the practice, although technically valid, is no longer employed in those states).

[183] *See, e.g.,* Markus Dirk Dubber, Victims in the War on Crime (2002); Garland, *supra* note 6; Simon, *supra* note 6.

[184] *See, e.g.,* Sally Engle Merry, Gender Violence: A Cultural Perspective (2011); John Pratt, Penal Populism (2007); Kent Roach, Due Process and Victims' Rights: The New Law and Politics of Criminal Justice (1999).

[185] *See, e.g.,* 18 U.S.C. § 3771. *See also* American Bar Association Criminal Justice Standards Committee, ABA Standards for Criminal Justice: Prosecution Function and Defense Function Standard 3-3.4(1) (4th ed. 2015). For discussion of possible ways for criminal justice professionals to inform and to consult crime victims in the United States, see Stephanos Bibas, The Machinery of Justice 150–53 (2012).

in the United States have been so culturally powerful and influential, they have not translated in as strong participatory rights of the crime victim and other private actors in a prosecutorial role in the criminal process as in other jurisdictions.

This may be good news since broader participatory rights for victims in the criminal process of the United States may contribute to making the already most punitive criminal justice system in the world even more punitive. It could mean that more democracy, in this case in the form of participatory democracy, is not necessarily a positive development. Without leaving these concerns aside, comparative experience would suggest two possible lessons to keep in mind in case victims' participatory rights in the criminal process further expand in the United States.[186]

The first point is that though criminal justice in the United States is over-punitive across the board, it may have problematic pockets of impunity that undermine the democratic values that nobody is beyond the law and of equal judicial protection. Police shootings could be one of these pockets.[187] If these pockets exist, larger victim's participation in the criminal process in these cases may be a positive development. If this were the case, one of the challenges here would be whether there would be a way of allowing for victim's or NGOs' larger participation in this type of criminal cases, while avoiding a slippery slope of victims' or NGOs' participatory procedural rights moving to cases in which there is no impunity and there is too much punishment.

The second point is that victims' participation in the criminal process can be conceived of in non-punitive terms. In fact, one of the main victims'-rights agendas behind recent reforms around the world have aimed at giving a non-punitive response to criminal cases through mediation, alternative dispute mechanisms, etc.[188] If this set of ideas could become a stronger or larger part of

---

[186] Recent amendments on the prosecution of sex-related offenses in the military justice system in the United States might be characterized as further expanding victim's participatory rights. *See, e.g.,* 10 U.S.C. § 806b; 10 U.S.C. § 1044e (special victims' counsel for victims of sex-related offenses); *LRM v. Kastenberg*, 72 M.J. 364 (2013); Major John C. Olson Jr., *Discovery for Three at a Table Set for Two: An Alteration of Rule for Courts-Martial 701 to Accommodate the Practical and Philosophical Realities of the Victim as a Limited Third Party*, 2015-NOV Army Law. 30; Walter B. Huffman and Richard D. Rosen, *Military Law: Criminal Justice & Administrative Process* §7:56 (March 2016 update). However, these reforms can also be characterized as mainly implementing in the military justice system reforms that had already been adopted in the federal criminal justice system. *See EV v. United States*, 75 M.J. 331 (2016); Major Troy K. Stabenow, *Throwing the Baby out with the Bathwater: Congressional Efforts to Empower Victims Threaten the Integrity of the Military Justice System*, 27 Federal Sentencing Reporter, 2015 WL 1417307 (2015).

[187] For a brief proposal in this direction, see Federico S. Efron, *The Role of the Complainant Victim in the Criminal Procedure* (2015) (on file with the authors).

[188] *See, e.g.,* Braithwaite, Restorative Justice and Responsive Regulation (2002).

victim's rights movements in the United States, or included as part of the reform program of "smart on crime" or similar reform labels, larger participation by crime victims in the criminal process might reduce punitiveness levels, rather than increase them.

V CONCLUSION

Representative democracy, legal democracy, liberal democracy, and participatory democracy – as we have employed those terms in this Epilogue – are not rival "theories" of democracy. Nor do we mean to suggest that these are layers or facets of democracy, each of which is essential to "true" democracy. Instead, what we have tried to suggest is that there are at least four separate clusters of ideas associated with the concept of democracy, and that each of those clusters of ideas has implications for prosecutors working in a democratic society. Further, we have tried to suggest that those implications are sufficiently strong and sufficiently rich that pursuing them is a useful – indeed, essential – exercise for anyone interested in coming to grips with the organization and exercise of prosecutorial power in modern criminal justice systems.

What we have tried to show in this Epilogue, thus, is part of what we hope and believe this entire book has demonstrated. The relationship between prosecutors and democracy, in the United States and elsewhere around the globe, is complex and important. It is worth trying to disentangle and to understand; indeed, that is or should be a critical part of any serious effort to reform prosecutors' offices. Moreover, despite the wide variations in the ways that different nations organize, supervise, and regulate prosecutors, and the equally wide variations in the legal and political cultures in which those prosecutors operate, there are benefits to carrying out this inquiry cross-nationally – or at least keeping a comparative perspective when studying or discussing the prosecutors in any particular country. The United States is far from being the only country grappling with the growing power and importance of prosecutors. Prosecutors increasingly seem to be the key players in criminal justice systems elsewhere as well, including Europe and Latin America. The contributions to this volume have not suggested that any country has hit upon a solution to all the problems presented by prosecutorial power, let alone a solution that could be readily exported. But we think this book does vindicate the claims we made in the introduction: that the relationship between prosecutors and democracy is complex and important, and that a comparative perspective can be helpful in making greater and more productive sense of that relationship.

Index